INSTRUMENTS OF DARKNESS

Crime in Seventeenth-century England: A County Study

Crime in Early Modern England, 1550–1750

"William Holcroft his Booke": Local Office-holding in Late Stuart Essex

Crime and the Law in English Satirical Prints, 1600–1832

Early Modern England: A Social History, 1550–1760

Judicial Punishment in England

Instruments of Darkness

Witchcraft in Early Modern England

JAMES SHARPE

PENN

UNIVERSITY OF PENNSYLVANIA PRESS

Philadelphia

Originally published by Hamish Hamilton Ltd
Copyright © 1996 by James Sharpe
First paperback printing 1997
All rights reserved
Printed in England on acid-free paper

10 9 8 7 6 5 4 3 2 1

Published by
University of Pennsylvania Press
Philadelphia, Pennsylvania 19104-4011

Library of Congress Cataloging-in-Publication Data
Sharpe, J. A.
    Instruments of darkness: Witchcraft in early modern England /
James Sharpe
        p. cm.
    Originally published: London : Hamish Hamilton. 1996
    Includes bibliographical references and index.
    ISBN 0-8122-1633-4 (pbk.)
    1. Witchcraft—England—History—17th century. 2. Witchcraft
—England—History—18th century. 3. England—Social life and
customs—17th century. 4. England—Social life and customs—18th
century.   I. Title.
BF1581.S52 1997
133. 4 '3' 094209032—dc21   97-11779
                                                              CIP

To Krista

And oftentimes, to win us to our harm,
The instruments of darkness tell us truths . . .

Macbeth, Act I, scene iii, lines 123–4

INSTRUMENTS OF DARKNESS

Crime in Seventeenth-century England: A County Study

Crime in Early Modern England, 1550–1750

"William Holcroft his Booke": Local Office-holding in Late Stuart Essex

Crime and the Law in English Satirical Prints, 1600–1832

Early Modern England: A Social History, 1550–1760

Judicial Punishment in England

Instruments of Darkness

Witchcraft in Early Modern England

———————

JAMES SHARPE

———————

PENN

UNIVERSITY OF PENNSYLVANIA PRESS

Philadelphia

Originally published by Hamish Hamilton Ltd
Copyright © 1996 by James Sharpe
First paperback printing 1997
All rights reserved
Printed in England on acid-free paper

10 9 8 7 6 5 4 3 2 1

Published by
University of Pennsylvania Press
Philadelphia, Pennsylvania 19104-4011

Library of Congress Cataloging-in-Publication Data
Sharpe, J. A.
   Instruments of darkness: Witchcraft in early modern England /
  James Sharpe
     p. cm.
   Originally published: London : Hamish Hamilton. 1996
   Includes bibliographical references and index.
   ISBN 0–8122–1633–4 (pbk.)
   1. Witchcraft—England—History—17th century. 2. Witchcraft
—England—History—18th century. 3. England—Social life and
customs—17th century. 4. England—Social life and customs—18th
century.   I. Title.
BF1581.S52 1997
133. 4 '3' 094209032—dc21   97-11779
                                           CIP

To Krista

And oftentimes, to win us to our harm,
The instruments of darkness tell us truths . . .

Macbeth, Act I, scene iii, lines 123–4

Contents

Acknowledgements

It is axiomatic that completing a major piece of historical research invariably involves the accretion of a number of debts by the researcher. For me these include, to begin with institutions, debts to the Bodleian Library, the Borthwick Institute of Historical Research, the British Library, Cambridge University Library, the Codrington Library, the Institute of Historical Research, Lambeth Palace Library, the J. B. Morrell Library of the University of York, the Public Record Office, York Minster Library, and the County Record Offices of Cheshire, Devon, Essex, Lancashire, Norfolk, Oxfordshire and Suffolk, while I was also allowed to use the Hartlib Collection at the University of Sheffield. I am grateful to the expertise and efficiency of the staff of all of these institutions. I was granted three terms of study leave by the History Department of the University of York in the period during which I was carrying out my research. One of these terms was spent as a Visiting Fellow at All Souls College, Oxford, and I am grateful to the Warden and Fellows of All Souls not only for their kindness and hospitality but also for providing me with an opportunity for a term working in the Bodleian. The British Academy awarded me a Small Personal Research Grant which allowed me to visit a number of local Record Offices, and also to work extensively on manuscript and printed sources in the British Library.

An earlier version of my thoughts on the Matthew Hopkins trials appears in Jonathan Barry, Marianne Hester and Gareth Roberts (eds.), *Witchcraft in Early Modern Europe: Studies in Culture and Belief* (Cambridge, 1996), while some of my thoughts on women and witchcraft first appeared in *Continuity and Change*, 6 (1991), and in Jenny Kermode and Garthine Walker (eds.), *Women, Crime and the*

Courts in Early Modern England (London, 1994). I was also able to develop my ideas on witchcraft before constructively critical audiences in research seminars at the universities of Cambridge, Durham, Leeds, Liverpool, London, Manchester and York, at the Maison des Sciences de l'Homme in Paris, and, perhaps most memorably, at conferences in Exeter in September 1991 and in Salem, Massachusetts, in June 1992.

I have acknowledged those who have passed references about witchcraft to me at the appropriate points. I have benefited more generally from discussions about witchcraft with Ian Bostridge, Robin Briggs, Miranda Chaytor, Simon Ditchfield, Peter Elmer, Michael Hunter, Mark Jenner and Lyndal Roper, and I am especially grateful to Dr Ditchfield and Professor Hunter for having read and commented on early drafts of sections of the typescript. On a less theoretical level, the York History Department's secretaries proved unfailingly helpful when coping with my panic-stricken queries on how to work our newly installed word processors. I am also happy to acknowledge a longer-term debt. It was while working under Sir Keith Thomas's supervision on my doctorate at the time when his *Religion and the Decline of Magic* (London, 1971) was being written that I first became aware of the existence of witchcraft as a serious topic for historical study, and also experienced the excitement of doing historical research with the guidance and example of first-rate historical intellect. The experience was a formative one.

Lastly, I am profoundly grateful for the support and interest my wife has shown me while I was writing this book, not least because the period in question was one when she had more than enough preoccupations of her own. It was, indeed, her remarkable ability to quote from English literature which suggested the book's title.

York, August 1995

Abbreviations and Conventions

APC	*Acts of the Privy Council*
CSPD	*Calendar of State Papers, Domestic*
DNB	*Dictionary of National Biography*
Ewen, *Witch Hunting and Witch Trials*	C. L'Estrange Ewen, *Witch Hunting and Witch Trials: The Indictments for Witchcraft from the Records of 1373 Assizes held for the Home Circuit A.D. 1559–1736* (London, 1929; reprinted 1971)
Ewen, *Witchcraft and Demonianism*	C. L'Estrange Ewen, *Witchcraft and Demonianism: A Concise Account Derived from Sworn Depositions and Confessions Obtained in the Courts of England and Wales* (London, 1933; reprinted 1972)
HMC	*Historical Manuscripts Commission, Reports*
Kittredge, *Witchcraft in Old and New England*	G. L. Kittredge, *Witchcraft in Old and New England* (Cambridge, Mass., 1929; reprinted New York, 1956)
Macfarlane, *A Regional and Comparative Study*	Alan Macfarlane, *Witchcraft in Tudor and Stuart England: A Regional and Comparative Study* (London, 1970)

Notestein, *A History of Witchcraft*

Wallace Notestein, *A History of Witchcraft in England from 1558 to 1718* (Washington, DC, 1911; reprinted New York, 1965)

PRO

Public Record Office

Thomas, *Religion and the Decline of Magic*

Keith Thomas, *Religion and the Decline of Magic: Studies in Popular Beliefs in Sixteenth- and Seventeenth-century England* (London, 1971)

Introduction

Thomas Colley was hanged on Saturday 24 August 1751. A butcher by trade, he had been found guilty of murder and sentenced to death at the Hertford assizes on 30 July. But it was decided to execute him not, as would have been the normal practice, at the assize town but rather at Marlston Green in Tring, the place where he had committed the murder, and afterwards to hang his body in chains there. An example was to be made of Colley, since the murder he had committed was an unusual one. It was not one of those incidents of domestic violence that went too far, or one of those alehouse brawls that ended in a fatality, which formed the staple of eighteenth-century homicide. Thomas Colley was the ringleader of a mob which had maltreated an elderly couple, John and Ruth Osborne, the woman having died as a result. And the reason mob violence had broken out against the Osbornes was that local opinion held them to be witches.

The grounds for this opinion can be reconstructed from the various accounts of the incident. Ruth Osborne was thought to have committed a number of acts of *maleficium*, that doing of harm through occult means which lay at the core of popular fears of witchcraft. Her husband was reputed to be a wizard, and despite his being 'a very stout able man of his age' (he was fifty-six, fourteen years younger than his wife), none of the local farmers would employ him, with the result that the couple were dependent on poor relief. In particular, they were thought to have exercised their malice against a farmer, subsequently turned innkeeper, named John Butterfield. Butterfield, so he and his neighbours claimed, had been forced to give up farming after his cattle were killed by the Osbornes' witchcraft, while he had himself been bewitched, going into convulsions and making animal noises. Butterfield seems to have been the organizer of the events which led to Ruth Osborne's death, and Colley later claimed it was the drink which Butterfield was freely supplying on the day of those events that caused him to play a leading part in them. The violence against the couple was evidently well planned. It was announced in a number of neighbouring towns – Winslow, Leighton Buzzard and Hemel Hempstead – that they were to be ducked. At Colley's trial, William Dell, town crier of Hemel Hempstead, recounted how he was given a paper to be read at the market there which announced: 'This is to give notice, that on Monday next, a man and a woman are to be publickly duck't at Tring, in this county, for their wicked crimes.'

Matthew Barton, the Overseer of the Poor at Tring, got wind of the planned action and placed the Osbornes, whom he considered to be 'very honest people', in the town's workhouse for their protection. By the time the trouble began, they had already been moved from there by Jonathan Tomkins, the master of the workhouse, who directed them to be lodged in the vestry room attached to Tring Church, hoping that 'the sanctity of the place would have some awe of the mob, if they came'. The mob, some 5,000 strong, did come and, thinking that the Osbornes were still there, began to demolish the workhouse and threatened to burn it down. Faced with this, Tomkins revealed the couple's whereabouts. Contrary to his hopes, they were pulled out of the vestry room and carried to a pond, where Ruth Osborne was thrown into the water, supported by a rope under her armpits, each end being held by a man. John Humphries, a witness at the trial, told how Colley ill-treated her, and how he

went into the pond again; and took hold of the cloth or sheet with which she was wrapt in, and pull'd her up and down the pond till the same came from off her, and then she appeared naked; and then the prisoner pushed her on the breast with his stick, which she endeavoured with her left hand to catch hold of, but he pull'd it out, and that was the last time he perceived any life in her.

After that, Humphries continued, Colley went round the assembly of spectators 'and collected money of them as a reward for the great pains he had taken in showing them sport in ducking the old witch, as he called the deceased'. A surgeon from Tring, who had been called to inspect Ruth Osborne's body by the Overseer of the Poor, confirmed in court that she had died from drowning.

Colley's story that he had, in fact, been trying to help the persecuted couple did not convince the court and he was found guilty. He was due to be executed on 16 August, but the decision to hang and gibbet him at Tring meant that a few extra days had to be taken for the necessary preparations. This gave him time to reflect on what he had done and to make arrangements for his family. He wrote letters to his wife and children (he advised one of his sons to 'have a care of his education'), and also wrote to a Mr Holmes, obviously a man of some influence locally, in the hope that he would encourage Colley's neighbours to help his family after his death: 'don't send my poor wife to the work house to break her heart; and if you can prevent my dear boys from any misfortunes, and be a friend to them, do for God's sake'. Shortly after he wrote these letters, a gentleman (unfortunately we do not know his name) visited Colley, 'in order to reason with him, and to convince him of his erroneous opinion, in believing that there was any such thing as witchcraft'. Colley told the gentleman about the damage which the Osbornes were reputed to have inflicted by their *maleficium*, and also recounted how, sixteen or seventeen years earlier, he had seen another old woman 'that was reputed a witch' swum (i.e. thrown into the water on the assumption that if she floated she would be proved to be a witch) at Stoke, near Leighton Buzzard in Bedfordshire. Death had occurred on this occasion, too, but because no action had been taken against any of the participants, Colley thought 'he might lawfully serve these two people in the same manner'. The gentleman eventually convinced him that 'witches had no manner of existence but in the minds of poor infatuated people, in which they had been confirm'd by the tradition of their ancestors, as foolish and crazy as themselves'.

On the day before the execution, Colley was taken to church, where an appropriate sermon was preached and an appropriate psalm (the fifty-first) sung. The service over, he was put with the executioner into a 'one horse chaise' and sent to St Albans, where he spent his last night in the town gaol. His wife and daughter visited him there, and 'seem'd to justify the action for which he was to suffer, and to assure him that he died in a good cause', although subsequently 'his more serious reflections and further conversation with some worthy gentlemen' got him back into the required way of thinking. The authorities were obviously fearful of the possibility of further rioting in support of Colley, and the next morning the chaise was escorted to the place of execution by 108 men 'draughted out of the Regiment of Horse Guards Blue, with their officers and their trumpets'. The soldiers were evidently jumpy and were put into 'some disorder' when one of their number accidentally discharged a pistol, thinking that they were being fired upon from a window.

Colley repeated at the gallows that he and the others at the centre of the riot had been encouraged by Butterfield, who had given them 'gin and ale, till they were quite intoxicated'. But he behaved well, making that 'good end' which eighteenth-century England required of the condemned at the scaffold. He made a speech warning those present of the danger of belief in witchcraft, prayed and then 'quietly submitted to his fate': the cart on which he stood was driven from under him and he was launched into eternity. Local opinion was unconvinced. Only a few hundred people stood near the gallows – the military presence had deterred a larger crowd – but thousands of others stood at a distance, and it was noted that 'so great was the infatuation of the people in general' that they insisted that 'it was a very hard case, that a man should be hang'd for destroying an old wicked woman, who had done so much mischief by her abominable charms and witchcraft'.[1]

つ A tale of obscure people, long dead, their world so removed from ours: mob violence, the belief in witchcraft, the drunken butcher pushing the old woman into the pond, the theatre of suffering of the eighteenth-century public execution, the body left to rot in chains after that execution. How tempting it is to write all of this off as evidence of the credulity and barbarity of a past age, and to turn to those themes of mid-eighteenth-century English history with which the textbooks have familiarized us. The political system, although oligarchic, was stable and certainly no worse than those operating in other European monarchies. Economically, England was becoming recognized as the most advanced state in Europe. Her ships carried trade across the world, bringing steady profits to the merchants of London, Bristol and a number of lesser ports. She possessed the burgeoning colonies on the eastern coast of North America, while in 1751 Clive's military career, which was to do so much to bring the Indian subcontinent under British rule, was already in progress. At home, the agricultural base was sound, and although a bad harvest might bring hunger to many, it was unlikely to bring mass starvation. The Midlands and parts of the North were beginning to experience the early stirrings of that process which was to bring what historians have traditionally regarded as one of the major breaks in English (and indeed British) history, the Industrial Revolution. It is all too easy to regard the central decades of eighteenth-century England with much the same complacency as stares back at us from the gentry family portraits of the period, and to push the tale of the old woman murdered at Tring in 1751 and the gibbeted body of her murderer subsequently rotting there to the margins of historical consciousness.

Yet Thomas Colley, Ruth and John Osborne, the gentleman who tried to persuade Colley of the non-existence of witchcraft, the clergymen who tried to prepare Colley spiritually for death, Colley's wife and daughter reaffirming popular attitudes when they visited him in prison, the nervous troops who surrounded the scaffold that August Saturday, the Hertfordshire countryfolk who held that the execution of a witch-killer was unjust: all of them were late participants in one of the most remarkable episodes in European history. The label to be put on that episode is uncertain. The term 'European witch craze', popularized a generation ago, is now rejected as hyperbolic. Even 'the witch-hunt in early modern Europe' is something of an overstatement. The more accurate 'period of witch persecution in Europe' is maybe a little clumsy. Yet whatever we are to call it, the interest of subsequent generations has constantly returned to those three centuries, between about 1450 and about 1750, when large numbers of Europeans of all social classes believed in the existence of witches and witchcraft, many of their Church leaders supported and helped foster such beliefs, and their law codes defined witchcraft as a crime and envisaged the prosecution and execution of persons thought to be witches.

As I have hinted, the European witch-hunts have attracted, and continue to attract, considerable attention.[2] Most people are aware of the witch persecutions in a general sort of way, although few have any detailed knowledge of them. The period of persecution is normally thought of as 'medieval', although in fact most trials took place after the mid-sixteenth century. The persecution is usually written off as evidence of ignorance and superstition, although some of the best brains in Europe advocated witch-hunting and wrote books providing ideological underpinning for it. The term 'witch-hunt' is in everyday use, although most people who were persecuted as witches suffered because of the fears of their neighbours rather than on account of politically directed 'hunts'. It is widely held that 9 million people were executed for witchcraft, although the real total for the whole of Europe during the three centuries in question was probably less than 50,000, about half the number as the deaths caused by the Civil Wars that racked Britain from 1642 and maybe less, on some of the lower estimates, than the total number of deaths caused by the Great Plague of London in 1665. The inroads that the execution of witches made in Europe's population were obviously minor compared to the mortality which war or disease could bring. Yet the fascination of witch-hunting as an historical phenomenon defies diminution by downward adjustment in the statistics of suffering. Ever since they ended, the witch persecutions have been one of those pieces of history which Europeans and North Americans (for the persecution spread to England's American colonies in the seventeenth century) have included in their cultural baggage, to be taken out and reinterpreted, like so many of the best bits of history, at regular intervals.

So remarkable was the episode, indeed, that even before the last legal witch-burning (so far as is known, in Switzerland in 1782) took place, people were trying to explain why the persecution had happened. By the mid-eighteenth century, Enlightenment thinkers were already establishing an interpretation to which we have already referred: the witch craze was the product of the ignorance and superstition of past ages, encouraged by that religious bigotry which the *philosophes* identified as one of their major targets. The opinions of that leading Enlightenment figure Voltaire were typical. For him, witch trials were aspects of those 'judicial murders which tyranny, fanaticism, or even error or weakness, have committed with the sword of justice . . . legal murders committed by indolence, stupidity, and superstition'. Intellectual weakness encouraged the 'belief in fascination and witchcrafts', and this belief was even made a part of religion, 'and nothing was to be seen but priests drawing out devils from those who were said to be possessed'. Magistrates, 'who should have been more understanding than the vulgar', tried and condemned witches, and this was a period when 'it was a sacred duty to put girls to the torture in order to make them confess that they had lain with Satan, and that they had fallen in love with him in the form of a goat . . . They were burned at last, whether they confessed or denied; and France was one vast theatre of judicial carnage.' And for France, as Voltaire would have accepted if pressed, it would have been appropriate to read Europe.[3]

Such sentiments encourage consideration of two lines of interpretation which ought to be dismissed immediately. The first, embedded in our thinking since Voltaire's time, is the tendency simply to write off witch persecution as a symbol of the barbarity, ignorance or superstition of past ages. Indeed, it is the seemingly alien nature of the phenomenon which helps explain its ability to maintain our interest. But to dismiss the belief in witchcraft, and the hunting of witches, in such terms is simply not good enough. First, writing as I do towards the end of a century which has witnessed Auschwitz and Katyn, Passchendaele and Hiroshima, the horrors unleashed by the Khmer Rouge, the obscenity of 'ethnic cleansing' in the former Yugoslavia, and the massacres in Rwanda which occurred between the writing of the first and second drafts of this book, I am a little less inclined than would have been my counterparts writing 100 years ago about the certainty of an uninterrupted onward march of human progress. Second, I became attracted at an early stage of my education as a historian to eschew what Edward Thompson described as 'the massive condescension of posterity': that is, the common habit of writing off the mental worlds of those of our ancestors who, we think, took a wrong turn while that march of progress was going on or who, more broadly, demonstrated that irritating habit of not sharing the values which we have come to think of as important. And third (and very much connected to this last) is the point that the belief in witches was shared by many people who were (in the context of their own times) as intelligent as we are and as capable of pursuing a career or doing a job, making money, running a household and raising a family. The issue is not to show that people who believed in witchcraft were unintelligent; it is rather to explain how a wide variety of people, ranging from the very intelligent to the fairly stupid, were able to hold that belief.

The other interpretation which I, and I suspect most of my readers, find untenable is that there is such a thing as malefic witchcraft, possibly involving the literal combination of human beings with the devil, and that witches can harm people or their goods through occult, invisible means. People who do hold such beliefs would find writing a book like this one easy, and it is ironic that a major figure in witchcraft research early in the twentieth century was, indeed, convinced of the reality of witchcraft. This was Montague Summers. Summers was a prolific writer, and performed an invaluable service for later scholars in producing editions of a number of early modern tracts on witchcraft, some of which he had himself translated. Unfortunately, this scholarly ability was linked to a religious fanaticism. He was a Roman Catholic of a type more commonly found in the fifteenth than the twentieth century, obsessed by thoughts of the devil and convinced that the devil's agents were at large in the world. These views coloured his two major works, *The History of Witchcraft and Demonology*, published in 1926, and *The Geography of Witchcraft*, which appeared a year later, both of them being subsequently much reprinted. Summers (whose books were published at about the same time as Aleister Crowley's works were attracting attention, and Dennis Wheatley's novels were becoming popular) played an important part in distorting the general public's view of witchcraft as an historical phenomenon, especially by spreading the view that an organized, Satan-worshipping sect of witches had existed.[4]

Yet Summers was neither the first nor the only writer to suggest that witches had been an organized body. The notion was probably first popularized in the modern era by the French writer Jules Michelet in his *La Sorcière* of 1862.[5] In this work Michelet imagined witchcraft as a protest movement of medieval serfs. The sabbat, to him, was a secret nocturnal meeting in which the peasantry came together to feast, perform pagan dances and act out folk dramas satirizing lord and priest alike. At the centre of proceedings sat (or, at certain points, lay) the witch of the book's title, in fact a priestess presiding over an ancient fertility cult. The crucial juncture in her ministrations came when she mated with a giant wooden figure, endowed with a massive penis, which represented Satan. None of this, alas, bears any resemblance to what can be reconstructed of the historical reality of witchcraft. Michelet, then aged sixty-four, wrote *La Sorcière* in two months, and it is little more than the product of the romantic imagination of an ageing radical. Yet despite the lack of any factual basis, the notions that witchcraft was some sort of subversive movement of the poor and that there was a connection between witchcraft and fertility cults, or, more generally, sexuality, persisted.

Indeed, the notion of witchcraft as a subversive movement, and as such something to be repressed by the Church, received a powerful boost early in the twentieth century from the writings of Margaret Murray. Murray, born in 1863 (she lived to be 100), originally envisaged a career in nursing, but had to seek an alternative when she was rejected as being too short for professional training. She turned to Egyptology, which she began to study at University College, London, in 1894, eventually becoming a lecturer and the author of extensive (and accomplished) publications. She is currently better remembered, however, for her *The Witch-Cult in Western Europe*, first published in 1921, a work which proved profoundly influential. Her main contention was that those prosecuted as witches in the sixteenth and seventeenth centuries were in fact members of a pre-Christian religion who attempted to maintain their beliefs in the face of persecution by the Christian Church. The 'devil' with whom the Church thought witches associated was in fact that religion's ancient horned god recast by Christian theology, or, in the case of the devils allegedly present at witches' meetings, a priest costumed to represent that god. Murray worked through a body of material (mainly derived from English and Scottish sources) to support this interpretation, and the widely held view that witchcraft was, and possibly is, an alternative religion to Christianity derives in large measure from her work. Unfortunately, her views are now widely discredited among serious scholars, mainly because of her distortion of evidence. The historian Norman Cohn has performed an exceptionally effective demolition job on her theories, and has demonstrated that as soon as the normal methods of historical criticism are applied to her writings, they appear about as substantial as the fictions which Michelet had produced sixty years before her.[6]

But the idea of witches as persecuted representatives of an ancient religion dies hard and in the 1970s it was revived powerfully when writers from within the women's movement turned their thoughts to witchcraft. The starting point was an incontrovertible one which had, in all fairness, previously been given

8

insufficient emphasis: in most parts of Europe during the persecutions, the majority of those accused and executed for witchcraft were women. As early as 1893 the United States suffragist and feminist Matilda Joslyn Gage had sign-posted the approach to be followed eighty years later in her *Women, Church, and State*, a book, incidentally, thought to be the first to popularize the myth that 9 million supposed witches were burnt. Later feminist writers, working out from Gage, have developed a number of ideas about women and witchcraft. The first is that in medieval society women had a monopoly on medical knowledge, and that these female folk-healers were executed in large numbers when a male-dominated medical profession arose and demanded that these rival practitioners be eradicated. Others, in the spirit of Michelet, saw witches as women peasant revolutionaries fighting a guerrilla campaign against a patriarchal state and a misogynistic Church. Yet others saw witches as proto-feminists, strong women who dared speak out for themselves and cause trouble, and who were sub-sequently burnt for their pains. Interesting though these interpretations were, they were usually developed with scant regard for historical evidence and with little idea of the broader historical context. The early modern witch makes a slightly unlikely role model for modern feminists.[7]

To some extent, elements of these feminist interpretations connected with another line of approach, linking the witch-hunts with what might be described as scapegoating theory. As I have noted, the term 'witch-hunt' figures promin-ently in current political discourse, and it is tempting to see in the early modern witchcraft persecutions something akin to such modern horrors as the Nazi ex-termination of the Jews or such lesser, if distasteful, episodes as the Mc-Carthyite persecution of the left in the United States of the 1950s.[8] Obviously the type of comparative perspective opened up by such an approach can be ex-citing and instructive, yet certain problems remain. The first arises from speci-ficity, from the constraints of historical context: it is all too easy to equate one episode of inhumanity with another, and hence to miss what is distinctive and peculiar in each. And, despite some parallels during some of the heavier periods of witch persecution, the degree of scapegoating to which witches were sub-jected never reached that levelled against (for example) Jews in Europe between 1941 and 1945, or, indeed, Jews in some parts of Europe in the Middle Ages. For whatever reason, the witch image never acquired the status of a universal symbol of evil, despite the best efforts of some demonological writers. And the propaganda and communication resources of the persecuting authorities (who, on close investigation, frequently lacked any hegemonic hostility to witchcraft anyway) were greatly inferior to those found in a modern state. The diffusion of the image of demonic witchcraft, and of the need to extirpate it, had to be a piecemeal and imperfect process given the reality of communications in late medieval and early modern Europe.

Other modern theory has been used by those attempting to interpret the witch-hunts. As might be expected, Freud spared the subject a few thoughts, and later commentators have sometimes employed a Freudian perspective when studying aspects of witchcraft in the past, notably (and not inappropriately) demonic possession. Freud thought that 'demons' were a manifestation of instinctive impulses that had been repressed, and the idea that many of those who thought themselves to be possessed by witchcraft or demonic influences were frustrated or repressed may have some substance to it. Thus in 1950 the American writer Marion Starkey followed an avowedly Freudian approach in her analysis of the New England adolescent girls whose accusations lay at the heart of the Salem witch panic of 1692. Sceptical early modern observers, moreover, were prone to attributing some witchcraft accusations and most witchcraft confessions to 'melancholy', a complex mental state which seems in some ways to have corresponded to what these days would be called depression. There are, however, problems with this approach. The first is the danger, yet again, of falling into simplistic reductionism, and simply writing off all witch beliefs and accusations as signs of madness or lesser forms of mental instability. The second lies in the applicability of modern psychoanalytic concepts, and modern terminology, when trying to explain the behaviour of people living three or four centuries ago. Their mental make-up and the anxieties they suffered may well have been analogous to those found in the modern industrial world, but it is unwise to take this for granted. Yet, at the very least, Freud's views on the link between hysteria and possession cases remind us of the medical dimension to many of the issues associated with the witch craze.[9]

Mental unbalance is not just caused naturally; it can also be induced by chemical and other means. As this insight became more commonly held with the advance of the drug culture in North America and Europe during the 1970s, parallels were drawn between aspects of the behaviour of people under the influence of hallucinogenics and some of the behaviour manifested in witchcraft cases. Again, there are justifications for this interpretation. Some early modern writers, puzzling over how witches could attend the sabbat while their bodies stayed in bed beside their innocent spouses, suggested that the witches' memories of their meetings were illusory, the product of rubbing their bodies with unguents. It has, moreover, been suggested that some large-scale outbreaks of witch-hunting (for example, at Salem) were initiated by accidental consumption of ergot, a fungus hosted by cereals, especially rye, which acts as a milder version of LSD. Peasants forced by a bad harvest to eat mouldy bread might, therefore, develop strange symptoms, among them a convulsive ergotism which would be interpreted as demonic possession. Once more, however, we are left with the feeling that interpretations of witchcraft provide us with evidence of the imaginativeness of the interpreter rather than anything which can be supported by strong historical evidence. While it would be foolhardy to argue that nobody involved in a witchcraft accusation had ever, voluntarily or otherwise, taken a drug of any sort, it is unlikely that such cases would form more than a minority. And nobody, so far, has proved chemically the hallucinatory potential of bat's blood and soot, the basic ingredients of fifteenth-century flying unguents.[10]

Rather more profit might be thought to exist in applying the concepts of modern social anthropology to late medieval and early modern witchcraft. The argument in favour of such a course is straightforward. There have been, and indeed still are, many cultures in the twentieth century where witchcraft was thought of as a living reality, a part of everyday life, and a fair number of these cultures have been studied by European or North American anthropologists. Witchcraft is, conversely, a phenomenon which is relatively distant from the firsthand experience of most modern historians and the societies in which they live. It would therefore seem to be potentially useful to apply the research done by anthropologists on cultures where such firsthand knowledge does exist to historical materials. The key breakthrough here was made by two British scholars, Alan Macfarlane and Keith Thomas.[11] Thomas had for some time been advocating a closer dialogue between historians and anthropologists, and Macfarlane's book, which originated as an Oxford doctoral thesis under Thomas's supervision, was a major demonstration of the value that might be derived from such a dialogue when witchcraft was being studied. But, as ever, there are problems. Perhaps the most important is the applicability of evidence from cultures far removed chronologically and geographically from those studied by historians. Thus despite a shared relatively low level of technology, it seems unlikely that the Azande of early-twentieth-century Africa had a great deal in common with the inhabitants of Tudor and Stuart Essex studied by Macfarlane. Yet the anthropological approach does make it more difficult to dismiss the beliefs about witchcraft held by these Essex villagers and their Continental contemporaries as mere peasant credulity. What Thomas, in his magisterial book *Religion and the Decline of Magic*, and Macfarlane demonstrated was that witchcraft beliefs, however distant they may seem to the modern observer, had a meaning, even a function, in earlier societies. People believed in witchcraft because it gave them a means of explaining the inexplicable, and also an approach to understanding human relations. Macfarlane's work, in fact, took this point a stage further by relating it to socioeconomic change in sixteenth- and seventeenth-century England.

Although research into the history of English witchcraft more or less stagnated after the publication of Macfarlane's and Thomas's books, work on other geographical areas continued apace. Most of this work, although deepening our factual knowledge, did little to inform our overall conceptions of what early modern witchcraft might have been about, but in 1981 there came an exception with a publication on the witch-hunt in Scotland, Christina Larner's *Enemies of God*.[12] It had long been acknowledged that Scotland, with its separate legal code, different social structure and more aggressively Protestant Church, had experienced a different level of intensity of witchcraft prosecutions from that obtaining south of the border, and Larner's work was an excellent comprehensive if succinct study of the subject. More importantly for our immediate purposes, the book reopened the possibility, seriously challenged by the approach Thomas and Macfarlane took, of studying witchcraft from 'above' rather than 'below'. Larner offered a more subtle version of the view that witchcraft was a product of the concerns of lawyers and clergy. She linked the rise of witchcraft accusations in Scotland to the presence on the throne of that well-known advocate of divine-right monarchy James VI (from 1603 James I of England) and, perhaps more significantly, to the pressures generated by the Calvinistic Kirk. To Larner, the new hard line of Christianity propagated by the Kirk represented an ideological force which aimed at reinforcing conformity. And, if conformity is reinforced by ideological means, quite often the process involves the creation of deviants, or at least the reinforcement of belief in a certain type of deviance. Larner, while sensitive to the world of peasant beliefs and local accusations, reopened the problem of how witchcraft beliefs were being affected by what was going on outside the narrow world of the village. Her book, in fact, gave considerable weight to the suspicion that the most fruitful way to approach the history of witchcraft could be by imagining how the phenomenon might appear both in the mental world of Voltaire and in the rather different mental world of his less celebrated contemporary Thomas Colley.

❥ Thus the student of witchcraft as an historical phenomenon suffers from no shortage of possible interpretations of the subject. But to those who, from the fifteenth century onwards, wrote the tracts that identified witchcraft as a menace, and to those who staffed the courts and the torture chambers whither witches were taken by legal process, this plethora of explanations would have seemed otiose. For them, witchcraft existed as a result of a combination of humankind's innate sinfulness and the malevolent influence of the devil. And the peculiar significance of the input of Christian theology was one of the distinctive features of the witch-hunt in Europe. Nearly all known societies have accepted the existence of witchcraft or of phenomena very similar to it. What was different in Europe between the fifteenth and the eighteenth centuries was that witches were seen not just as individual workers of evil; they operated as such, certainly, but they were also thought to be members of an organized heretical sect opposed to, and indeed constituting an inversion of, Christian society. And membership of this sect, and the possession of the power to do harm by witchcraft, was increasingly held to be a consequence of the individual witch's having made a pact with the devil. The processes by which this belief was created and gained wide acceptance were lengthy and complex. To make our story comprehensible, we must, however, consider them briefly.

First, though, it is necessary to turn to some problems of definition. I have so far used the terms 'witch' and 'witchcraft' as if they were self-evident and unproblematic. Obviously they do have widely accepted meanings, but it would be useful to ponder those meanings here, and to consider how they contrast to the meaning of that other very relevant term 'magic'.

Definitions of witchcraft, in the sense of what witches are supposed to *do*, as the anthropologists remind us, vary considerably. At their base, however, rests the notion of the occult power of the individual, most frequently the power to do harm. How this power is meant to be acquired also varies. To Christian intellectuals of the period of the witch-hunts, it derived from the pact with the devil; more popularly it was thought that witchcraft was variously a quality which could be inherited or a skill which could be learned. But once acquired it could be used directly, usually without recourse to other means. The classic formulation was made by the anthropologist E. E. Evans-Pritchard in his celebrated study of the Azande. The Azande believed that some people were witches and could injure others by virtue of an inherent quality: 'a witch performs no rite, utters no spell, and possesses no medicines. An act of witchcraft is a psychic act.' [13] Many of those thought to be witches in early modern England were supposed to have this sort of power, while the notion of the satanic pact made it possible to see the witch as the vehicle for powers far greater than herself, perhaps even as the unwilling agent of those forces.

With magic or sorcery, we encounter, in theory at least, a rather more complex set of issues. Whereas the witch is able to do occult harm through innate powers, the magician can produce good or bad effects through powers dependent on his knowledge or skill. To return to the Azande, Evans-Pritchard told how members of that tribe believed in sorcerers who could do them ill, either by performing magic rites or by using appropriate medicines,[14] while most of the inhabitants of Tudor and Stuart England believed in the power of local folk magicians to do good through spells, charms and their knowledge of the occult. This belief in sorcery and magic causes massive complications in the history of witchcraft. Knowledge of, and willingness to indulge in, magic and sorcery were not restricted to village practitioners. They involved, or were thought to involve, educated and highly placed people. Most royal houses (that of England included) thought themselves threatened by magic at certain points during the late Middle Ages, as did the papacy. What is most frequently referred to as 'ritual' or 'natural' magic was a recurring phenomenon throughout the Middle Ages and well into the seventeenth century. And this 'magic' was, throughout much of that period, very difficult to distinguish from what (to introduce another terminological problem) might be described as 'science'. Many contemporaries, indeed, would have seen natural magic as a branch of what modern terminology would call science, although those taking a theological hard line were never altogether happy with this. At the very least, an interest in magic and the occult among the educated élite caused considerable confusion for theologians and law enforcers in the past, and continues to do so for modern historians of witchcraft.

As might be imagined, maintaining a sharp distinction between witchcraft on the one hand and magic and sorcery on the other proves impossible; certainly, medieval and early modern commentators tended to jumble the terms together happily enough. The power to bewitch might be seen primarily as an innate quality, but witches were frequently described as using charms, images or spells as they exercised their *maleficium*. And the populace at large frequently resorted to counter-magic, again in the form of charms, rituals or spells, when they attempted to block the effects of malefic witchcraft, while on occasion they might turn and take mob action against practitioners of 'learned' and hence legitimate magic whom they thought to be dabbling in diabolical witchcraft. Thus there was a continuum from the learned and upper-class magician to the peasant witch, and it is sometimes difficult to see where the demarcation line between the activities of the two lay. What is certain is that by the sixteenth century what contemporaries described as witchcraft tended to encompass mainly the activities of peasants rather than scholars or courtiers. The occult activities of the latter tended to be described as magic, necromancy or sorcery. Generally speaking, the odd spectacular exception apart, élite practitioners escaped censure. Peasant witches, on the other hand, were burnt in their thousands. We shall spend the next few pages exploring how this situation came about.[15]

Our starting point must be that witchcraft, magic and the occult were deeply embedded in European culture, both popular and élite. Such matters had obviously been familiar in the classical world. Apuleius, in *The Golden Ass*, to take a much-quoted example, included tales of shape-changing, a description of Pamphile, a powerful sorceress who could even change the shape of the planets and annoy the gods, and other supernatural elements. Similarly, Ovid's *Amores* includes a description of Dipsas, an old hag of a witch (it has, in fact, been suggested that one of the distinctive contributions of classical literature to developing ideas on witchcraft was the stereotype of the female magician and witch), while the same author's *Metamorphoses* was widely quoted in later discussions of shape-changing. Such references were still of vital importance to writers on witchcraft between the fifteenth and seventeenth centuries. Most educated men and women were steeped in classical literature, and most of the writers of demonological tracts used references from that literature in their descriptions of what witches did.

With the fall of Rome, this literary tradition passed into temporary abeyance, but by the seventh century AD barbarian law codes were demonstrating that witchcraft was still a reality among the population of Europe, although the attitude of the law givers to the phenomenon was clearly somewhat ambivalent. The matter is in need of more systematic research, but for the present it seems safe to claim that the Germanic tribes of the seventh and eighth centuries clearly believed in witches, most frequently in the form of a night-flying cannibalistic female witch known as a *stria* or *striga*. Yet the law codes and moral tracts of the period were anxious to correct such beliefs rather than persecute witches, and to dissuade people from defaming each other with allegations of witchcraft. In the eighth century, indeed, we find St Boniface declaring that belief in witches was unchristian and Charlemagne ordering the death penalty for those who burnt witches in his Saxon territories, which had just been converted to Christianity. The ninth century saw some Christian authorities repudiating belief in night-flying, metamorphosis and the witch's ability to raise bad weather.[16] This doctrine was incorporated into the *Canon Episcopi*, a theological statement which was to remain a key text for sceptics.

The relatively relaxed official attitude to witchcraft which seems to have characterized the Dark Ages and the early medieval period changed in the wake of a harder line against deviants that set in during the twelfth century, a development which has led to claims for the emergence of a 'persecuting society' during the period.[17] This harder line was prompted by the arrival of popular heresy, which was swiftly followed by the formation of the Inquisition. The Inquisition's investigations, coupled with works of clerical propaganda, created an image of heretics as a secret sect which was aiming to overthrow Christian society, and whose mores represented an inversion of Christian values. The expropriation and mass murder of Jews came next, along with legends that the Jews trafficked with the devil and kidnapped and ritually murdered Christian children. Lepers and male homosexuals, 'sodomites' in contemporary terminology, were also identified as deviant groups by 1250 or so. The mass persecution of witches was only two centuries away.

The notion of a medieval 'persecuting society' is, perhaps, a little too schematic, while the notion of one set of scapegoats being simply replaced by another is a little oversimplified. Yet some significant cultural processes were clearly at work. There were signs, even before the arrival of the fully developed witch myth, that ideas about what witches did were becoming more complex. A key element was the notion, deeply embedded in peasant folklore, of witches as a sect who flew to their nocturnal meetings. The concept of night-flying witches is, indeed, very widespread, found not only in Roman literature and medieval Western Europe but also in many of the tribal societies studied by twentieth-century anthropologists. Moreover, opinion, and especially learned opinion, became increasingly concerned about what witches got up to when they arrived at their meetings. The fruits of this concern developed through the sixteenth century, as ideas about the sabbat became more elaborate, but from a comparatively early stage witches were thought to meet for nocturnal cannibalistic orgies, during which in particular the bodies of young or newborn children were thought to be cooked and eaten. This fantasy was one which had been applied to early deviant groups: heretics, before them Jews and, first of all perhaps, Christians in the Roman Empire in the second century. All of these were thought to have done such things and always, in all probability, on an equally slim factual basis. The origins of the ideas of what happened at the witches' sabbat lay in deep-seated paranoia about some of the worst, most inhuman, things human beings could do.

Yet at roughly the same time as the 'persecuting society' was developing, magical learning among the educated élite was becoming more widespread and more complex.[18] There were a number of influences at work. One was the massive expansion in learning which took place over the twelfth century as Arab texts, among them those containing the works of Aristotle and other Greek writers which had long been lost in the West, became available to Christian scholars. The impact of this accretion of new knowledge (over 100 works were translated from Arabic into Latin during the twelfth century) was immense. And, given that information on medical, scientific and magical matters was heavily intermixed, it became inevitable that those reading them in pursuit of what we would call medical or scientific knowledge acquired deeper insights into the magical and the occult. Astrology was one of the key areas of intellectual endeavour encouraged by this acquisition of knowledge via Arab culture, this being in turn reinforced, as cultural contacts continued to be made, by the mysteries of the Jewish cabbala. A second major influence was courtly magic. By the thirteenth century dabbling in magic was apparently common among courtiers, and a number of European courts, notably that of Pope John XXII (1316–34), were riven by scandals arising from the alleged use of magic in pursuit of love or political assassination. Such incidents probably explain why, in a number of territories, both the ecclesiastical and the secular authorities were becoming increasingly concerned over witchcraft. And in such spectacular cases involving the political élite as that of the Knights Templars in France in 1317 and Lady Alice Kyteler in Ireland in 1324–5 it is possible to trace a growing elaboration of ideas about demonic magic and its connections with upper-class sorcery. Thus in the Kyteler case we find an important addition to demonological lore when Lady Alice was alleged to have copulated with her personal demon. It is instructive that the conclusive evidence on this point came from one of the gentlewoman's servants, who had been persistently beaten on the orders of the investigating bishop.[19]

The sense of urgency engendered as revelations from such trials spread interacted with a strand of accepted Christian thinking which accepted the reality of demons and, if only by extension, witchcraft. If classical literature could be drawn upon to support arguments about witchcraft, so could the writings of the Church Fathers, not least the two most influential writers in Western Christendom, St Augustine and St Thomas Aquinas. Augustine (354–450) was one of the founding fathers of Christian thought, and his *De Civitate Dei* (*The City of God*) was a weighty vindication of both Christianity and the Christian God. Augustine was still a much-quoted authority in the sixteenth and seventeenth centuries (indeed, the predestinarian speculations in *The City of God* were of great interest to Protestants) and his work was fundamental in spreading ideas about demons. He identified them as fallen angels, intelligent and immortal incorporeal beings who inhabited the sublunary sphere. He attributed to them the ability to perform wonders which could be mistaken for miracles and envisaged, if only in a metaphorical or symbolic form, something like the pact between human being and demon which was to become fundamental to later demonology. Augustine had little to say on the type of malefic witchcraft which was to be so heavily persecuted in later centuries, but some of his writings seemed to accept something very much like it. Later demonological writers were to suppress the subtle and speculative way in which Augustine discussed such matters and eagerly mined his works for references which seemed to support the model of demonic witchcraft they were constructing.[20]

They did a similar disservice to a more recent writer, Thomas Aquinas (c. 1227–74). Aquinas was another influential theologian: the longevity of the respect he gained can be gauged from a papal encyclical of August 1879 which instructed Catholic priests to regard his teachings as the basis of their theology. He was, quite simply, the most significant thinker of the Middle Ages, and was to play a vital role in creating that blend of Christian belief and ancient, and especially Aristotelian, philosophy known as scholasticism which constituted the intellectual mainstream until well into the seventeenth century. Like Augustine, Aquinas had an essentially limited view of what demons could do and no great interest in *maleficium*. But, again, his speculations seemed to lend support to later writers for some of the main elements in early modern demonology. He accepted that demons were incorporeal and that they could not perform true miracles. He speculated, however, about the possibility of demons having sexual intercourse with women and fathering children on them. It was Aquinas who first propounded the possibility that a demon as a succubus could capture semen from a man and as an incubus subsequently use it to impregnate a woman, thus circumventing the impossibility of an incorporeal demon siring a child on a human woman. He also refined the notion of the pact, arguing that all those deviating from Christianity into superstition made a pact with demons, but that the varying degrees of deliberateness with which this was done could make the pact implicit or explicit. For Aquinas, the pact was still in large measure symbolic; later writers were to use his speculations, however, in support of the notion of a literal demonic pact.[21]

Further shifts in official attitudes were needed before spectacular cases among the élite and scholarly adjustment of theories about demons could be transformed into witch-hunting proper. On a theoretical level, changing notions of the devil were important. The process was a complex one, but it seems that in the centuries which followed the early Christian era the concept of the devil and of diabolical powers slowly changed. By the early fourteenth century, at about the same time as the suppression of the Knights Templars and the Alice

Kyteler case, the devil, with his battalions of lesser demon assistants, was becoming clearly identified as a threat to Christendom. The ritual magic cases which scandalized royal and papal courts began regularly to include allegations that demons were invoked, and by 1390–91 in two trials held in Paris we find the secular (not the ecclesiastical) authorities trying two poor women (not the highborn practitioners of ritual magic) for similar practices. In these two cases, however, it seems that such activities were still regarded as individual acts of heresy. The move towards official belief in a sect of witches was signalled in a number of cases in Switzerland between 1397 and 1406. Here the issue was malefic witchcraft: the inducing of miscarriages among women and infertility among cattle, the killing of children and the raising of hailstorms. But the accused, under torture, also revealed that they were a group of devil-worshipping witches.[22]

Pope John XXII, in a bull of 1326, had authorized the use of full inquisitorial procedures against suspected witches, and as the fifteenth century progressed they were used with increasing frequency. Gradually, the focal point of the Inquisition's war on religious deviants shifted from the suppression of heretics to the extirpation of witches. Reconstructing the exact process is difficult: it has been obscured by loss of records and, in any case, it was a piecemeal and very localized development, perhaps most marked initially in those areas which had experienced a severe persecution of Albigensian heretics. The end product, however, was a gradual and partial spread of the idea that witches existed in an organized, heretical and satanic sect.[23] The work of the inquisitors was aided by the dissemination of demonological texts. In the mid-1430s John Nider, an inquisitor, wrote the *Formicarius*, based mainly on the confessions of people tried for witchcraft in the Swiss territories. In 1450 Jean Vineti, Dominican Inquisitor of Carcassone, wrote what was probably the first tract (printed in 1480 as *Tractatus contra Daemonum Invocatores*) to formally identify witchcraft as a new heresy. The fables of nocturnal gatherings, of sexual deviance, of cannibalism, of offering a threat to Christian society, were now being transferred to witches. A new set of deviants was being created.

How far there was any witchcraft in reality remains problematic. The fundamental point is that, in so far as they can be reconstructed, the peasant belief systems of the period incorporated numerous 'magical' elements which were clearly held to be reprehensible by hard-line theologians. Indeed, it is evident that in the late Middle Ages what we would categorize as magic was a normal part of life for the population of Europe. People went to healers and diviners who used charms and sorcery. Midwives used charms, prayers, blessings and invocations as they officiated. Extensive use was made of protective amulets and talismans, and some insights into the connections between magic and the popular Christianity of the period can be gained from the practice of using fragments of both saints' relics and the eucharist in magical amulets. You could use magical means to attract a partner, while, conversely, one of the things which witches were meant to do was cause impotence among men. And (again here the border between magic and religion is blurred) there was widespread belief in the power of cursing and in the use of charms to do harm.

To some extent the development of the official fear of witches throughout the fifteenth century can be interpreted as a coming together of the demono-logical models which were beginning to obsess theologians and popular magic of this type. At least some clerical intellectuals became convinced that they were confronted by a heretical sect of witches, the devil's assistants in his struggle against Christianity. The reality of those dragged in before the inquisitors was very different. There were doubtless a few individuals who thought that they had occult powers, and certainly a fair number of people were willing to accuse their neighbours of such. But the existence of an organized sect of witches ex-isted much more clearly in the imaginations of inquisitors and the clerical writers of demonic tracts than in reality, and was essentially a product of the collision between the pure religion of the educated clergy and the folk religion of the peasantry. Most late medieval peasants would have seen themselves as Christian, and would have been familiar with at least the basics of Christian belief and Christian ritual. But this popular Christianity could coexist happily with traditional superstitions which could easily embrace magical elements. The learned inquisitors, increasingly trained to take a severe theological line on what constituted acceptable practices among Christians, and increasingly alert to the need to root out heterodox beliefs, could all too easily reinterpret these more-or-less harmless peasant superstitions as evidence of witchcraft.

Turning from the fifteenth century to a later period, an illustration of how this process might have worked comes from the Friuli, a region to the north-west of Venice.[24] There, from about 1575, the Inquisition uncovered puzzling evidence of what appears to have been a fertility cult. Local beliefs held that during the night the souls of members of this cult (the Benandanti) left their sleeping bodies and went off to do battle with the witches in the hope of de-fending the fertility of the crops. A handful of cases involving such beliefs were investigated over the years, and it is possible to trace how the Inquisition, whose reaction was initially one of bemused incredulity, redefined belief in the Benan-danti as witchcraft. By the 1640s this interpretation was shared by the local peasant population and, indeed, people who thought themselves to be Benandanti and had been subjected to inquisitorial interrogations. In the course of these investigations we see very clearly how the categories of folklore had been altered so that they could be fitted into the new conceptual framework of the Catholicism of the Counter-Reformation. Fortunately, the Roman Inquisition, which was the ecclesiastical authority in the Friuli, had always taken a fairly low-key approach to suspected witchcraft, and by the time the process of redefinition of Benandante into witch had been completed, it had moved more or less to a sceptical position. One feels that if these beliefs had been investigated by some of the inquisitors at work in the later fifteenth century, the outcome would have been considerably less happy.

Indeed, in the late fifteenth century the witch trials and demonological speculation had borne fruit in one of the key tracts in the witch-hunting canon, the *Malleus Maleficarum*. The *Malleus* was the work of two Dominican monks, Jacob Sprenger and Heinrich Kramer (also referred to as Institoris). Both of them were experienced inquisitors and established theological writers, while Sprenger in particular was to achieve high office in the Dominican Order. Their co-authored work was a lengthy, rambling and at times ill-disciplined and contradictory book, a masterpiece of late medieval Aristotelian scholarship. Its significance in the history of witchcraft is threefold. Perhaps most importantly, it acted as a summary of both theological theorizing about witchcraft and the knowledge that had been gathered on the subject at the time of its publication in 1487. Second, as feminist writers have emphasized, the *Malleus* was a key text in linking witchcraft with women: some passages at least are marked by a prurient misogyny. And third, the *Malleus* was important in encouraging the secular authorities to accept that they, and not just the ecclesiastical powers, had a duty to extirpate witchcraft. To that end, about a third of the book was devoted to informing judges how to try and punish witches.

The *Malleus* has been afforded considerable importance by twentieth-century writers, not least because since 1928 it has been fairly continuously available in an English translation. Certainly, the book was frequently reprinted in earlier periods; some extent of its availability can be gauged from a sale of antique works on witchcraft at Leipzig in 1912 which included twenty-nine editions of the *Malleus*. Yet there are clues that the work should not be regarded simply as a symbol of a triumphant and hegemonic ideological view of witchcraft. Kramer had been involved in trials at Innsbruck in 1485 at which his conduct outraged some of his fellow inquisitors and prompted the local bishop, under whose authority the trials were being held, to introduce a defence lawyer for the accused.

Arguably, the *Malleus* was defending a disputed position rather than representing a triumphant viewpoint. This suspicion is reinforced by the papal bull of 1484, *Summis Desiderantes Affectibus*, which is usually linked with the publication of the *Malleus*. Reading between the lines of this bull, the main purpose of which was to encourage witch-hunting, it was evidently prompted by a lack of enthusiasm among the secular authorities in a number of German territories to cooperate with the Dominicans in their crusade against witchcraft. Further ambivalence about the *Malleus* is suggested by the Spanish Inquisition's advice to its inquisitors, circulated in 1538, that they should not believe everything they read between the book's covers, even passages apparently written on the strength of firsthand evidence. Detailed work on the background to the writing of the *Malleus Maleficarum* and its reception might, one suspects, reveal that witchcraft was still very much an intellectually contested area at the end of the fifteenth century.[25]

In any case, the length of the *Malleus* and its frequent reprintings did not preclude the publication of a number of later works which elaborated the concept of witchcraft, often in the light of continued trials. Several of these deserve mention here. The *Malleus* had made little reference to the sabbat, and this deficiency was met by Paulus Grillandus's much-read *Tractatus de Hereticis et Sortilegis* of 1524, which became the standard reference work on the subject. There was then something of a lull in major publications, and possibly a lull in trials: the Reformation gave both theologians and lay and ecclesiastical courts alike a new set of priorities. But by 1580 demonological works were appearing on the presses again. In that year one of the most important intellectuals to write on witchcraft, Jean Bodin, published his *De la Demonomanie des Sorciers*, a work which was to prove very influential, especially among English writers. In 1595 Nicholas Remy, a judge in the Duchy of Lorraine who claimed to have presided over the trial of 800 witches, published his *Demonolatreiae*, another encyclopedic work, as was the *Disquisitionum Magicarum Libri Sex*, the work of the Low Countries Jesuit Martin Del Rio, which appeared in 1599. A number of other large works on witchcraft could be consulted by 1600, among them a major sceptical tract, the much-attacked *De Praestigiis Daemonum* of Johann Weyer, court physician to the Duke of Cleves, first published in 1563. Despite Weyer, the weight of learned authority at the beginning of the seventeenth century was heavily behind the linked propositions that witches existed and that they ought to be extirpated.

And extirpated many of them, or at least people thought to be witches, were. There was no uniform European experience: witchcraft trials remained, from first to last, phenomena which were local in their focus and sporadic in their incidence. In the fragmented political world of the Holy Roman Empire, to take the extreme example, it was possible to walk in a day from a territory where witchcraft was heavily prosecuted to another where it rarely figured in the business of the ruler's courts. But the decades around 1600, in some areas at least, saw a notable upsurge in prosecutions. In 1591 Scotland witnessed its first mass witch trials. From roughly that point, witch persecution was endemic in Lorraine, a French-speaking territory in the Holy Roman Empire. Trials in Bavaria increased rapidly at about the same time. And, to stay with Germany, the early seventeenth century was to see heavy persecution in a number of areas, notably in the Catholic ecclesiastical territories of Ellwangen, Mergenthem, Trier, Würzburg and Bamberg. At Ellwangen, a small Catholic territory independent of external control, there were nearly 300 executions for witchcraft between 1611 and 1618. At Würzburg, where Bishop Adolf von Ehrenberg unleashed a witch craze as part of his Catholicization campaign, 160 people were executed as witches between 1627 and 1629.[26] European peasant women were fortunate that this level of intensity of witch-burnings was very unusual.

❍ The Templars in France, Alice Kyteler in Ireland, trials in Switzerland and the Friuli, demonological tracts written by German Dominicans, French judges and a Low Countries Jesuit, mass trials in the Calvinist Lowlands of Scotland and Roman Catholic areas of Germany: the reader will have noted that in this account of the formation and coming to fruition of both witch persecution and demonological theory, England has so far figured very little. It is to this kingdom, poised on the very edge of Europe, that we must now turn.[27]

All sources suggest that from the Saxon period onwards, at about the same time as relevant evidence begins to survive for Continental Europe, the English held roughly the same sorts of beliefs about magic, sorcery and witchcraft as did the rest of Europe's population, and by the high Middle Ages a wide range of sources demonstrate that such beliefs were firmly embedded at all social levels. By the fourteenth century, chronicles and theological texts regularly referred to sorcery and related practices, although it is clear that, as on the Continent, the stereotype of the malefic, devil-worshipping witch had yet to be fully constructed.[28] Moreover, by the late fourteenth century, perhaps two generations after such matters had emerged as objects of serious concern in the more advanced parts of Europe, hostile plots involving magic and witchcraft became a regular problem for the English monarchy.[29] The key case here was that of Alice Perrers, the mistress of Edward III, accused in the last year of that

monarch's reign, 1376, of gaining his affections, procuring his madness and ener-
vating his bodily strength by magical arts. This set the style for the fifteenth century, when political tensions were frequently accompanied by allegations that
magic and necromancy were being used against the monarch or the royal family.

Perhaps the most celebrated case involving the late medieval political élite
occurred in 1441, when Eleanour Cobham, the second wife of Henry V's
brother, Duke Humphrey of Gloucester, was tried for sorcery. She had been
the duke's mistress during his first marriage and had allegedly used magic to
make him fall in love with her, annul that union and subsequently marry her. A
number of other people were involved in the plot and although Eleanour escaped with the lesser penalty of doing penance, one of her associates, Margery
Jourdemayne, was burnt as a witch and another, Roger Bolingbroke, a man with
a reputation as an astrologer, was hanged, drawn and quartered for treason.
Cobham and her associates were popularly held to have raised bad weather
when the young Henry VI had visited London in July, and a contemporary
chronicle attested to a widespread fear and knowledge of witches.

And so it was spoken amongst the people that there were some wicked fiends and spirits areared out of hell by conjuration for to noy the people in the realm and put them to
trouble, dissension, and unrest. And then it was known that certain clerks and women
that are called witches had made their operation and their craft to destroy men and
women, or whom they list, unto death by their false craft and working.[30]

If the fears of witchcraft circulating among the political élite were very similar to those found at that social level in parts of Continental Europe, it is evident that by the middle of the fifteenth century there was also a widespread
popular fear of witchcraft and a developing lore about 'women that are called
witches'.

This lore can be traced in the scattered references that have so far been un-
earthed in cases tried in medieval courts, both lay and secular. Although the
penalty seems to have been very infrequently inflicted, thirteenth-century English law codes accepted that convicted witches could be burnt, and a well-
documented instance of this practice survives from Northumberland in 1279.
However, cases tried in the courts from about this date onwards seem more
commonly to have involved magic or sorcery rather than malefic witchcraft. In
1302 a married couple and another woman were accused as witches and en-
chanters at the Exeter borough sessions. In 1324 John de Nottingham, a
necromancer with twenty-seven known clients, was charged, *inter alia*, with
trying to kill King Edward II and the Prior of Coventry with image magic. In

1426 the House of Commons appointed a commission to investigate widespread witchcraft allegations in Somerset, Dorset and Cornwall, and in 1438 a woman named Agnes Hancocke of Montacute in Somerset was accused and convicted of fortune-telling and incantation, and of being a healer or wise woman.[31] The scattered nature of these and similar references defies systematic analysis. What they do illustrate is that, although there was as yet no clear notion of a demonic sect of witches in England, witchcraft, sorcery and illicit magic were all phenomena with which both officialdom and the public at large were familiar.

Popular witchcraft beliefs are perhaps most frequently noted in the archives of the ecclesiastical courts. Fifteenth- and early-sixteenth-century records demonstrate that the concern here was with those magical practitioners who are most frequently referred to as cunning men or women in later centuries. In 1446 two Durham women were presented as witches, and more particularly for telling single women who wished to be married how they could get the men they desired. In 1435 Margaret Lindsay of Edlingham, Northumberland, defended herself successfully against three men who claimed that she and another woman were rendering men impotent through magic. In London in 1480 John Stokes was presented for curing fevers by magic spells. In 1513 a woman from Padiham in Lancashire was presented for having a reputation for practising fortune-telling and witchcraft. At Maidstone in Kent in 1557 a man called Cowdale, 'being of the age of a hundred yeares', was examined for using incantations and witchcraft, and on examination told how he healed people by prayers, saying 'v Pater Noster v Ave and a Cred'. Some accusations, it must be admitted, involved more menacing practices. In 1519 Elizabeth Robynson, a widow from Bowland in Lancashire, was presented before the local ecclesiastical authorities for intending to keep a fast called the black fast, and for praying for vengeance on Edmund Palmer.[32]

Witchcraft was, therefore, a widely known phenomenon, and such practices and beliefs as Elizabeth Robynson's black fast were exactly the sorts of folkloric sorcery which were being redefined as malefic witchcraft in parts of Continental Europe in the fifteenth century. Yet no such process appears to have taken place in England in that period, a fact all the more surprising because England did experience a local heretic problem in the shape of the Lollards, the followers of John Wyclif (c. 1330–86). Wyclif was an Oxford theologian who developed a number of lines of thought critical of the established Church, and also wrote extensively in English as well as Latin, the approved language of theological speculation. His writings were not identified by the authorities as dangerous until the Peasants' Revolt of 1381, in the aftermath of which any heterodox ideas were regarded as suspect. Further fuel for such suspicion was given by Lollard involvement in Oldcastle's Revolt of 1414, while in 1401 an act had tightened up the law against heretics, but Lollards survived in isolated groups and suffered periodic persecution through the fifteenth and early sixteenth centuries. The opening decades of the sixteenth century saw five burnings of Lollards in Kent in 1511, seven in Coventry in 1520 (there had been numerous trials there in 1511–12, with one burning and about forty-five abjurations) and heavy trials with about fifty abjurations and four burnings in the Chilterns in 1521–2.[33]

The history of the Lollards has been written largely in celebratory terms, with them being cast as the heroic forebears of the Reformation. Not very much has been written about the propaganda mobilized against them and until research into this topic has been undertaken, it is impossible to be certain if this propaganda included accusations of cosmic subversion of the type made against some Continental heretics. The impression, however, is that the ecclesiastical courts treated the Lollards comparatively mildly, preferring them to abjure and rejoin the Catholic faith rather than having to burn them, and there is little suggestion that anybody was attempting to recast them as witches. Indeed, Wyclif's views on magic and sorcery were entirely conventional. He regarded the use of charms, witchcraft, enchantments and divinations as vain, superstitious and potentially idolatrous. Yet there are clues that the heterodox opinions held by some of the fifteenth-century Lollards ran close to sorcery. The problem, as so often, is that the authorities tended to lump together a number of odd views under a heading with which they were familiar. Thus we find the Church courts investigating a man who held a number of Lollard tenets, but who also thought, like so many necromancers, that the paternoster should be said backwards, and another man who was charged both for holding Lollard views and for curing sick children by charms. We catch here a glimpse of the materials which the authorities could have used in a process of redefining heretical Lollards as witches.[34] But, as far as is known, nobody in the late medieval English Church was anxious to initiate such a process.

It was, perhaps, the coming of the Reformation which sharpened concern among the upper reaches of the clerical establishment. An interesting piece of evidence on this point comes from the writing of John Bale (1495–1563). Bale, despite his early education in a monastery, was to become a convinced Protestant, and his style of controversial writing in defence of the new faith was to earn him the sobriquet 'Bilious Bale' among his contemporaries. Whatever the tone of his other writings, though, Bale hit upon the notion of popularizing

Reformation theology by writing verse plays in which the fundamentals of religion were rammed home. After he was appointed Bishop of Ossory in February 1553, indeed, he had young people perform his plays at the market cross of Kilkenny, although the accession of Mary Tudor to the throne later that year cut short this promising experiment in spreading Protestantism among the Irish. One of Bale's plays, his *Comedy concerninge thre Lawes, of Nature, Moses & Christ* of 1538, portrayed Idolatry as an old witch, whose supposed activities give us a useful impression of how far the witch stereotype had spread in English reformed circles. This witch could tell fortunes and could also cure the ague, toothache and the pox by saying the Ave Maria and 'by other charmes of sorcerye'. She could recover lost property, raise the devil from hell, stop corn and cattle from thriving, prevent brewing and kill poultry. She was also a skilled midwife and could charm children against spirits. She was, in short, a combination of the good and bad witches of popular belief. But there were two wider dimensions of Bale's stereotype. The first, as we have seen, was that she could raise the devil. For the reformer, the diabolical element, although not central, was present. And second, it should be remembered that Bale's main project was an anti-Catholic one. Idolatry (in the character in the play as well as in Protestant theology) included not only witchcraft but also telling the rosary, going to Mass and saint worship.[35]

Whether due to the influence of reformed thinking or not, there is scattered but suggestive evidence that concern over witchcraft and sorcery was increasing throughout the middle decades of the sixteenth century. The visitation articles and similar local ecclesiastical policy statements of the period demonstrate this. In 1538, the year in which Bale characterized Idolatry as an old witch, Bishop Shaxton's injunctions to the Salisbury diocese instructed that every parish priest 'not only in his preachings, but also at all other times necessary, do persuade, exhort and warn the people' that they should 'beware and abstain from cursing or banning, chiding, scolding, backbiting, slandering, lying; and from adultery, fornication, drunkenness, sorcery, witchcrafts'. Persons 'notoriously faulty in any of these' were to be reported to the ecclesiastical courts, where they were to be corrected 'in example of other'. The royal articles of Edward VI demonstrated a more defined awareness of witchcraft, requiring local clergy to report 'whether you know any that use charms, sorcery, and enchantments, witchcraft, soothsaying, or any other wicked craft invented by the devil'. The same tone was retained in Mary Tudor's reign, when the religious pendulum swung back to Roman Catholicism. Bishop Bonner's visitation articles for the London diocese of 1554 asked each parish priest 'whether there be any that do use charms, witchcraft, sorcery, inchantments, false sooth-sayings or any such like thing, invented by the craft of the devil'. These articles, directed against what was evidently a strongly established area of popular superstition, also ordered that midwives 'shall not use or exercise any witchcraft, charms, sorcery, invocations or prayers, other than such as may be allowable and may stand with the laws and ordinances of the Catholic Church'.[36]

Hence although England was still far from the mass persecutions familiar in parts of Continental Europe from a century earlier, it is obvious that by the middle decades of the sixteenth century witchcraft was being seen, certainly among senior clergy and theologians, as one of a number of problems demanding serious attention. These years were also to see the fruits of concern by secular government in the matter with the first statute passed in England against witchcraft in 1542. As we have noted, there was considerable concern over treasonous plots involving witchcraft and magic in fifteenth-century England, and the issue never quite went away in the reigns of the first two Tudors. Henry VII confronted one such plot, connected with attempts to get the Pretender Perkin Warbeck on the throne in 1496, while allegations of witchcraft were among the many accusations levelled against Anne Boleyn at her trial in 1536. In general, however, it seems to have been prophecy rather than witchcraft or magic which worried Henry VIII. The fall and execution of the Duke of Buckingham in 1521, the execution of Lord Hungerford for treason in 1540, for example, and the charges against a number of other high-born traitors were accompanied by charges of having taken too much interest in prophecies about the length of the monarch's reign or the royal succession.[37]

Indeed, intensive research might well reveal that there was an intensification of interest in magic and related matters among educated circles in the middle of the sixteenth century. A tract that appeared in 1561, but providing evidence on the slightly earlier period, is relevant here. It was written by Francis Coxe, an obscure figure who apparently practised as a physician. He had been in trouble with officialdom over suspicions of necromancy and his pamphlet was a declaration of 'the detestable wickednesse of magicall Sciences, as Necromancie, Conjurations of Spirites, curiouse Astrologie and suche lyke'. He admitted that he had himself been 'an offender in these most detestable sciences' and wrote that necromancers were 'rebellious traitours' against God. But the tract revealed that its author had had contact with a wide range of magical lore and was aware, for example, of the 'blinde, enigmaticall and devilish prophesies of that heaven gaser Nostradamus'. Writings like Coxe's, along with a sense that allegations of magic in élite circles were increasing during the reign of Henry VIII and the presence of scattered magical manuscripts from the late fifteenth and early six-teenth centuries, are all suggestive of a widespread learned magical culture in early Tudor England.[38]

But this, together with the concern it might provoke among the secular and ecclesiastical authorities, was hardly enough to prompt the 1542 statute against witchcraft. As with so much Tudor legislation, the background of the 1542 act remains obscure. There may have been some worries left over from the Boleyn trial, and some of the other political trials of Henry VIII's reign, and about the discovery of an image of the young Prince Edward with pins stuck in it, while it has been suggested that the ecclesiastical courts were thought to be incapable of dealing with what was perceived as a growing witchcraft problem. The pre-amble to the act also identified the use of magic and the assistance of witches in finding buried treasure as a special problem, and here the legislators may have had some recent cases, details of which are now lost, in mind. The tone of such incidents had been set in 1510, when an investigation by the Archbishop of York revealed nine persons, among them several clergymen, using magical circles and invocations, as well as trying to raise demons, in hopes of finding a chest of gold.[39]

People encouraged by these matters to consider witchcraft a growing prob-lem meriting serious punishment would have been well satisfied by the 1542 statute.[40] This, the earliest English witchcraft act, was also the harshest. The stat-ute, as we have noted, identified the use of invocations and conjurations of spir-its as undesirable practices, and went on to refer to malefic witchcraft – that is, the use of 'witchcrafts, enchantments, and sorceries to the destruction of their neighbours' persons and goods'. It continued by referring to a wide variety of magical practices, including image magic and finding lost and stolen goods by magic, extending to the pulling down of crosses, which was obviously a cause for official concern at the time. Together, these practices were described as being 'to the great offence of God's law, hurt and damage of the king's sub-jects, and the loss of the souls of such offenders, to the great dishonour of God, infamy and disquietness of the realm'. The act made no mention of the demonic pact, or the sabbat, or of night-flying; these beliefs had, apparently, not penetrated the consciousness of legislators. It did, conversely, make all the practices which it identified felony without benefit of clergy punishable by death.

Relevant court archives are largely missing from the 1540s, and it remains un-clear how rigorously this statute was enforced. The general conclusion is that it was not much used, and it was, in any case, repealed along with much other

Henrician legislation in 1547, when the new regime of Henry's son, Edward VI, envisaged a new legislative programme. Edward's early death precluded putting this programme into practice, while the crowded reign of Mary Tudor (1553–8) left little time for the creation of a new witchcraft statute. From 1547 until the Elizabethan statute of 1563, therefore, witchcraft was not a secular crime in England. Yet a trickle of references in ecclesiastical court records demonstrates that concern about witchcraft was still current among the populace, and that this concern was now beginning to focus on malefic witchcraft. Wider beliefs were, of course, present. Thus in 1555 a woman from Taunton in Somerset, examined by the local Church court, named a number of her neighbours as witches and said that the fairies had revealed the identity of witches to her. More typical, perhaps, was a Devon case from 1558 in which Margaret Foxe, under investigation for witchcraft at the Church courts, claimed that her enemies defamed her for witchcraft and in particular had accused her of killing cattle by *maleficium*. A further note on this case revealed that Foxe had frequently changed her habitation because the slander of witchcraft had followed her 'in every place where she came'.[41] The witch was clearly a familiar figure in English society by that date.

Yet it is equally clear that England was one of those parts of Europe which had, up to the 1550s, escaped both mass witch-hunts and any serious writing on demonology. This escape, we must remind ourselves, was not because of a total absence of witch beliefs; indeed, many of those phenomena which contributed to the growing acceptance of the model of demonological witchcraft in Continental Europe were present in England. But despite the presence of the necessary ingredients, the mass persecution of witches never became a concern in late medieval England.

The precise reasons for this remain unclear, and we can only offer some suggestions. Much of the explanation must rest in the peculiar nature of England's political and legal systems, and in the relationship between Church and state. England was a large and, by contemporary standards, administratively unified kingdom, where the Church was, for most working purposes, willing to submit to secular control. This rendered England unlike most areas of Western Europe, where political authority was fragmented and the influence of the Church, sometimes in the very concrete form of a ruling prince-bishop, could be massive. There were, simply, too many checks and balances in the English system to allow a witch craze to develop, too many people who needed convincing before heavy persecution could begin. Even the persecution of Lollards took place on a piecemeal basis, so that there was no tradition of heretic-hunting for potential witch-hunters to build upon. If a particular monarch, or if a particular bishop or regional magnate, had developed a desire to persecute witches, then a hunt might have developed; but no such lead was ever given, and the widespread superstitions about witchcraft and magic were never focused on the malefic or demonological witch through mass trials. This was probably as much an outcome of England's position, intellectually as well as geographically, on the periphery of Europe as due to any uniquely idyllic English condition. Contacts between English ecclesiastical and, by the early sixteenth century, secular intellectuals with their opposite numbers on the Continent were good. But the intellectual centres and contacts which so many Continental scholars enjoyed remained relatively distant, and so, evidently, did the most advanced ideas on demonology.

How far this situation would have altered had Mary Tudor lived longer is a matter for speculation. Most recent interpretations seem to suggest that hers was an older style of Catholicism, with different concerns from those of the Counter-Reformed faith which was to help produce witch persecutions as a side effect of re-Catholicization in a number of European territories, and it is therefore possible that, for a generation or two after 1553 at least, witch-hunting in England would have remained low-key and spasmodic. But the queen died late in 1558, to be followed by another, the young Elizabeth I. Elizabeth was, by the end of her reign, to be transformed into a Protestant propaganda icon, while throughout Mary's reign the Protestant interest had regarded the accession of Elizabeth as their main hope for the future. There were at least some English Protestants who hoped that Elizabeth's reign would herald the arrival of that godly commonwealth which they so ardently desired. And in such a godly commonwealth there was no room for the servants of Satan.

❯ As I have suggested in this short review of the evidence, witchcraft was a widespread and widely recognized phenomenon in late medieval England; writing its history in a systematic way becomes considerably easier after the accession of the Virgin Queen.

With this book I am essentially attempting a task which has not been tackled since the days of those heroic pioneers of English witchcraft studies, Notestein, Kittredge and Ewen: to write a scholarly history of the subject in the period running from the mid-sixteenth to the mid-eighteenth centuries, the years when witchcraft could be punished as a crime at the secular courts, when witchcraft was a subject of serious intellectual debate and when the reality of witchcraft was accepted at all levels in English society. Much of this book will be taken up with studying belief systems, an area of historical investigation in which tracing change is notoriously difficult; yet I shall be attempting to construct a history of witchcraft which respects that most basic objective of historical writing, the delineation and explanation of change over time. I hope also to study witchcraft at a variety of social levels. The path-breaking work of Macfarlane and Thomas at the beginning of the 1970s changed our perception of Tudor and Stuart witchcraft by emphasizing the importance of witchcraft beliefs among the lower orders, but, while we must never lose sight of the importance of this, the time is now ripe to reopen the investigation of witch beliefs at higher social levels. Hence another major theme of this book will be the interplay between witchcraft beliefs at different points in the social hierarchy. And although this issue only rarely becomes overt, I feel that my approach to the subject has been heavily informed by my reading of work on witchcraft in the period with which I am concerned in other European and North American contexts. It is now, I would contend, impossible to sustain the idea that there was a separate 'English' witchcraft to be set against a monolithic 'Continental' witchcraft: the English experience of the phenomenon was a variation on a European theme.

I should also stress that my subject is English, and not British, witchcraft. Scotland enjoyed a separate experience of witchcraft, and, for the moment, I would direct anyone interested in the history of witchcraft north of the border to the works of Christina Larner; doubtless in a few years her interpretations will be challenged by a work of revision on Scottish witchcraft, but I will leave that to somebody with a better grasp of Scottish history and Scottish sources than I possess. In Ireland, there is little doubt that the indigenous Catholic Irish population held witchcraft beliefs, but the only detailed evidence available arises from a handful of accusations among English and Scottish settlers. Little evidence survives from Wales for the period under consideration, although when evidence does come through from the eighteenth century onwards, it suggests that witchcraft and magical beliefs were as firmly established there as they were anywhere else in rural Europe. Turning to the smaller component parts of the British Isles reveals interesting variations. In the Channel Islands, Guernsey witchcraft accusations reveal that a combination of a Roman law system and close cultural ties with France produced witchcraft beliefs very similar to those found in Continental demonological works, with the sabbat and the demonic pact. Research in progress into Manx records, conversely, reveals a very individualistic interpretation of witchcraft which was firmly embedded in local folklore. Evidently, anybody genuinely interested in early modern witchcraft as a

British problem would find themselves embarking on a formidable exercise in comparative history.[42]

It is, then, with England that we will be concerned, and it will become clear that the studying of witchcraft even in that single realm is a complicated enough matter. To try to alleviate this complexity, the book has been divided into three main sections. As already noted, evidence about witchcraft, from a variety of directions, seems to intensify during Elizabeth's reign, and accordingly the first section is concerned with witch beliefs in what was arguably a formative era of English witchcraft, the Elizabethan and early Stuart periods. There then follows a longer section, in which some of the major themes in English witchcraft are examined, many of them already evident in the sixteenth century, but persisting and becoming more firmly established in the seventeenth. And finally, before a concluding chapter, a section addressing that most intractable of issues, the reasons belief in witchcraft declined in the later seventeenth and earlier eighteenth centuries.

Throughout the writing of this book, I have been aware, sometimes acutely, of that fundamental tension in historical research which exists between the writer's consciousness of the sheer complexity of some of the matters under consideration and the need to discipline material so that something comprehensible can be written. Obviously, some of the themes or episodes to which I have devoted a paragraph or two are worthy of a major study in themselves. What I hope I have done is to provide the reader with a basic chart of the relevant issues, and some idea of what the route through them might be. As a first step in this exercise, let us turn to an examination of how witchcraft fitted into the mental world of our Elizabethan and early Stuart ancestors.

PART ONE

WITCHCRAFT IN ELIZABETHAN AND EARLY STUART ENGLAND

CHAPTER I

Witchcraft and
Élite Mentalities

As has been argued when reviewing the origins and development of
the 'European witch craze', belief in witchcraft was, for educated
and uneducated people alike, only one aspect of a broader intellectual system that incorporated other elements which the modern observer
would regard as 'irrational' or 'superstitious'. Moving beyond the temptation
simply to dismiss these elements in such terms is crucial in our attempts to
understand the phenomenon of witchcraft in Elizabethan and early Stuart
England. These 'irrational' or 'superstitious' beliefs, if we limit our discussion
to those current among the learned, were based on a formidable and complex body of knowledge which some of the better-equipped scholars of the
period were capable of familiarizing themselves with and deploying in argument. These were people who could read three or four languages other than
their own, who had the intellectual grasp to make connections between different bodies of information and who had a mastery of a massive range of
printed works. Also, the knowledge in question was, in modern terminology,
interdisciplinary. Currently, for whatever reason (a more institutionalized
education system, perhaps, allied to the sheer bulk of knowledge available
in the modern world), few of us, even the most intellectually gifted, can operate at a high level simultaneously in the varied fields of, say, physics, anthropology, medicine, philosophy and mathematics. Many thinkers in the early
modern period could do just that. The intellectual then was essentially a
polymath, while even the averagely educated man or woman had a working
knowledge of a number of intellectual fields. The idealized intellectual of
the sixteenth century was the Renaissance magus, a man of deep intellectual

and spiritual qualities, in possession of polymathic, and frequently occult, knowledge.

Both the notion of the Renaissance magus and the acceptance of a polymathic approach to knowledge were given an enormous boost, in England as elsewhere in Europe, by the spread of what are usually described as Neoplatonic ideas. Neoplatonism, like so many of the intellectual tendencies studied by historians, was a body of varied and in some ways contradictory elements, an intellectual position perhaps best described as a way of thinking rather than as a rigidly defined belief system. Its origins lay in the spread of hitherto unknown writings in Western Europe after the fall of Constantinople to the Turks in 1453, perhaps the most influential of them being those ascribed to an apocryphal ancient Egyptian, Hermes Trismegistus. These writings embodied an essentially mystical view of the world, which was conceived of as a place full of magical powers and hidden meanings, part of a universe whose secrets could be unlocked by only a chosen few. Following Platonic methods of thinking, the physical, material world was seen as 'unreal', because it was mutable and corrupt, the last and lowest sphere of existence. True perfection, and hence an ultimate 'reality', lay in the spiritual world. Matter was a link between the physical and the spiritual worlds, and the physical world was thought to reflect, however imperfectly, the higher spiritual realities. Neoplatonism tended to stress the notion of correspondences, with features of sets of phenomena on one plane mirroring features of phenomena on another: hence the earth was thought to be a microcosm of the spiritual world. The true role of the intellectual in this belief system was to contemplate and attempt to understand the mysteries of the universe. Thus even an activity like the study of mathematics could involve the mystical contemplation of ciphers as much as empirical calculations.

Neoplatonic ideas, of course, were never totally ascendant in England, and most educated people still viewed the world in terms of the existing Aristotelian system. But the influence of Neoplatonism (and I stress again that this is a label which historians have placed upon a broad and open-ended system of ideas and intellectual speculation) encouraged certain strands of thought in the Elizabethan period. Frances Yates, for example, has argued that Neoplatonic and related strands of thinking helped inform the celebration of the imperial theme in the reign of Elizabeth, and that the imagery mobilized to bolster the queen's image in royal portraiture demonstrates this. Neoplatonism – optimistic, immensely learned, dealing with the quest for ultimate realities and universal knowledge – did not in itself reinforce witch-hunting. But its presence as an intellectual tendency did help encourage an interest in magic and the occult, or at the very least helped foster the acceptance of the reality of the world of spirits. And in so doing it gave less magically minded persons in positions of authority stronger grounds for suspecting practitioners of natural magic of dabbling in undesirable activities, including witchcraft.[1]

This area of Elizabethan intellectual life is perhaps best illustrated by recourse to its most representative figure, John Dee (1527–1608). Born in London of Welsh descent, Dee went to Cambridge, where he proved an eager scholar, apparently studying for eighteen hours a day and allowing himself two for eating and recreation and four for sleep. In 1547 he went to the Low Countries to make broader intellectual contacts, and in 1548 began to study in Louvain, subsequently going on to Paris. By that time he had absorbed a considerable amount of astrological knowledge, and had also become a skilled mathematician, so much so, in fact, that he was offered the post of professor of mathematics at the University of Paris. He rejected the offer, but on his return to England in 1551 he found himself renowned as a man of learning, and on the accession of Elizabeth I seven years later he entered royal service, his astrological expertise being recognized by an official request that he cast a horoscope to determine the most favourable date for the new queen's coronation. For the remainder of the reign he acted as a sort of astrologer royal for Elizabeth, and was also consulted about medical treatment for her. From about 1584, however, he was increasingly involved in alchemic experiments and in attempting to raise angels, being aided in this latter enterprise by an Irishman named Edward Kelly. He also continued to travel on the Continent, and in the 1580s journeyed as far as Prague, then a great centre of European learning, whence his fame spread as far as Russia.

Dee's career epitomizes the way in which the sixteenth century failed to maintain a distinction between what the modern mind would consider worthwhile and worthless scientific endeavour: the criteria then existing were simply not the same as ours. Thus we find Dee called in to help cure the queen when she was ill in 1571, assisting in providing a geographical description of the lands to which she had the right to be sovereign in 1580 and advising the government over calendar reform in 1584–5. All of these activities would seem eminently reasonable to the modern observer. But, quite apart from the alchemy and the spirit-raising, Dee was called to court in 1577 to help inform speculations over the significance of the appearance of a new comet, and at about the same time he was asked to advise the queen on how best to cope with what was conceived of as an attempt to assassinate her through magic. And, of course, this side of Dee's activities left him very vulnerable to accusations of sorcery. As early as 1553 his connection with the then Princess Elizabeth led to his being investigated by the Star Chamber for trying to kill Queen Mary by poison or magic. In the 1580s his house at Mortlake was sacked by a mob when rumours spread that he was dabbling in witchcraft, while in 1604 we find him petitioning James I, asking that he might be cleared of accusations of being a 'conjurer, or caller, or invocator of devils'. In Dee, therefore, we find a number of strands of occult thought and practice coming together.[2]

Thus the belief system of the period meant that there were a number of areas of learned activity which were so heavily imbricated with magical elements as to skirt the edge of witchcraft. The now discredited sciences of astrology and alchemy, perhaps, come most readily to mind in this respect,[3] but the premise was equally true of a number of activities which modern thinking would regard as legitimate. One such was medicine, a contention illustrated by a leading medical practitioner in Elizabethan London, Simon Forman (1552–1611). Forman was a self-taught doctor who was never to gain a licence from the Royal College of Surgeons, with whom he was frequently in trouble, but who continually practised in Lambeth, outside the college's jurisdiction. Despite his problems with the medical authorities, Forman was clearly a dedicated physician, attracted to some of the more advanced medical thinking of his day, and was certainly no less effective in treating his patients than were officially sanctioned doctors. He also, like most medical practitioners of his time, cast horoscopes to assist him when treating his patients. And, from the late 1580s, he dabbled in necromancy and tried to get in touch with the spirit world by raising angels, while by 1595 he was engaged in the alchemic quest for the philosopher's stone. From about that time Forman's case books show men and women of all social groups coming to him for medical and, in increasing numbers, astrological advice. In a neat demonstration of how the world of practical men of business met that of what the modern mind would call superstition, his clients included merchants who wanted astrological information on the viability of projected trading voyages.[4]

Another medical practitioner whose case books were preserved in large numbers was Richard Napier, an 'astrological physician' described by the scholar who has completed a brilliant study of his activities as the last Renaissance magus.[5] Born a generation later than Forman, Napier is a good example of a figure standing at the turning point between two eras of intellectual discourse, the old one of natural magic and occult influences, and the new one of natural philosophy and what modern terminology would call scientific knowledge. Educated at Oxford, Napier remained a Fellow of Exeter College until

1590, and then became rector of the Buckinghamshire village of Great Linford until his death in 1634. For most of that period he entrusted the care of his parishioners' souls to a curate and devoted himself to the study of theology, alchemy and astrological medicine. He treated tens of thousands of people for a wide variety of maladies and, despite charging many of them low fees or refusing to ask some of them anything for his services, made a fortune. His religious views, outward at least, were perfectly orthodox, being moderately Calvinist in tone, and deeply held. He managed to combine his religious beliefs with a full acceptance of the validity of astrology and was also happy to provide his patients with such theologically suspect devices as amulets to protect them against evil spirits, a practice also resorted to by unlearned practitioners of folk medicine. Despite Puritan censures, many clergymen and physicians of this period regarded astrology as a science and found it particularly useful in the treatment of mysterious maladies, a handy tool but not the foundation of their practice. And for practitioners like Napier, the supernatural world was made all the more close by the common contemporary belief that mental disorder in particular might be attributable to supernatural as well as natural causes; those coming to Napier for the treatment of mental illness included many who thought they were being troubled by the devil or by witches.

Thus even a brief review of the scientific and medical world of the Elizabethan and Jacobean periods demonstrates the frequency with which magic and witchcraft intruded into everyday activities. For further evidence on this point, let us turn to another rich seam of material: the drama of the period.[6] Readers of Shakespeare will, of course, be familiar with the weird sisters in *Macbeth*, but it is salutary to remember just how often, leaving this obvious and very pertinent example aside, magic, the supernatural and witchcraft appeared in Shakespeare's plays: Prospero, the Renaissance magus of *The Tempest*, living on an enchanted isle whose inhabitants included Caliban, the offspring of a human being and a witch; the depiction of the fairy world in *A Midsummer Night's Dream*; the portrayal of Joan of Arc as a witch, complete with familiars, in *Henry VI Part One*. If we turn to other writers we find another Renaissance magus, in this case gone to the bad, in Marlowe's *Doctor Faustus*, and a satire of an area of occult pursuits in Ben Jonson's *The Alchemist*, a satire which is made all the more effective because of its author's manifest familiarity with alchemic terminology. Jonson also demonstrated how learned views on witches might enliven court drama in his *Masque of Queens* of 1608, while a neo-documentary approach to witchcraft was followed by the consortium of writers who in 1621 dramatized a recent prosecution in *The Witch of Edmonton*. Between these extremes came such works as Marston's *Sophonisba* and Middleton's *The Witch*, while even in plays where witchcraft and magic were not central themes, the language of the occult, of astrology, even of alchemy is frequently to be found.

This is not to say that playwrights or their audiences were obsessed with magic, witchcraft, the occult or the supernatural; indeed, the impact of references to such matters on the stage and the intentions of authors when including them in their works remain problematic. What is obvious, however, is that these writers assumed that their audience would be familiar with such issues and at least some of the discourse surrounding them. And, of course, the playwrights of the period were for the most part professionals, aiming to meet current tastes and reflect rather than lead opinion. It is, moreover, evident that the taste and opinion in question were those of the educated – people who knew about the classical models of witchcraft, who understood something of the terminology of astrology or Neoplatonism. Conversely, when Fabian advises Malvolio to take a sample of his urine to a wise woman in *Twelfth Night*, or when Falstaff disguises himself as a wise woman in *The Merry Wives of Windsor*, we enter (perhaps significantly through the medium of comic characters) into the world of contemporary popular beliefs. If few Elizabethan or Jacobean plays were primarily about witchcraft or magic, a surprisingly large number of them contained allusions to these or related matters. And for such allusions to have had any impact, they must have been recognizable by the contemporary learned culture.

❯ Thus the mental world of the educated Elizabethan or Jacobean was open to incorporating magic, astronomy, alchemy or that emphasis on the importance of the spirit world which was central to the currently fashionable Neoplatonism. Witchcraft may not have been central to this mental world, but it is easy to see how it might be accepted there, and it is to the issue of élite belief in witchcraft that we must now turn. There are two points which render such an investigation especially necessary. The first derives from the fact that, in England as in most of Europe, the late Middle Ages witnessed sporadic outbreaks of witchcraft accusations among persons high in the social hierarchy, sometimes indeed involving allegations of treasonable attempts on the lives of members of the royal family itself. It seems important to establish at what point witchcraft ceased to be a live issue at this social level. And second, the work of Keith Thomas and Alan Macfarlane has emphasized the importance of popular beliefs, and of interpersonal tensions among the lower social strata as the terrain from which witchcraft accusations were launched. The value of this approach cannot be denied, yet it does tend to obscure the extent to which witchcraft was a live issue for at least some members of England's political and social élite until well into the seventeenth century.

This point can be illustrated by a number of suits which entered the Star Chamber in 1622–3 and owed their origins to the amatory and marital problems of Robert Radcliffe, fifth Earl of Sussex.[7] Sorting out the true story from the welter of accusations and counter-accusations is difficult. Following one of the main lines of pleading, however, it appears that the earl's marriage to Bridget, the daughter of Sir Charles Morison, was not a happy one. After some initial problems, a reconciliation was effected in 1596, but after Bridget had lands worth £3,500 a year settled on her she apparently turned to open adultery and attempted to kill her husband 'by the continuall practices bothe of open violence and by sondrie secrett practices of poison'. The couple separated in 1612, and the earl turned for solace to a widow named Frances Shute, a woman, it seems, with a bad reputation. Allegations were levelled against her to the effect that she had tried to injure three of the earl's kinsfolk by magic, and that she had used witchcraft to turn the earl against his wife and make him alienate £1,500 worth of land to her. A known magician named Matthew Evans, it was alleged, had been involved in her attempts to do away with the earl's relatives in order to secure the future position of her children. Evans, although denying these charges, confessed under examination that he had cast a horoscope for one of Shute's daughters, had helped the widow further with astrology and physic, and had also been approached by her in the hope that he might render magical assistance to further her plans for gaining the affections of the royal favourite the Duke of Buckingham.

Buckingham, indeed, apart from the monarch probably the most powerful man in England during the 1620s, figured in a rather better-known incident, the death of Dr John Lambe. Lambe had begun life as a tutor to gentlemen's sons, then studied medicine and subsequently turned to fortune-telling and sorcery. He was indicted twice for witchcraft in 1608, but despite being found guilty on both occasions escaped execution and was imprisoned in the King's Bench gaol. He apparently conducted a successful practice from the prison, and it was probably at this stage that he first became a magical, medical and astrological adviser to Buckingham. It was, at any rate, commonly held that the duke was responsible for saving Lambe when he was convicted of the statutory rape of an eleven-year-old girl in 1623. By the summer of 1628, however, Buckingham's popularity was at rock bottom and on 15 June that year the London mob decided to take out their hostility to the nobleman by attacking Lambe, whom they thought of as 'the duke's devil', as he walked home from the theatre. Lambe died the following day from the beating he received.

The fall of the previous royal favourite, Robert Carr, Earl of Somerset, also involved witchcraft. His wife, Frances Howard, had formerly been married to the Earl of Essex, but the marriage had been ended on grounds of non-consummation in 1613, amid claims that Essex's impotency had been caused by sorcery. In 1617 the fortunes of Frances and her second husband crashed during investigation of the murder of Sir Thomas Overbury. It was revealed that she and a confidante, a widow named Anne Turner, had furthered their amatory and political plans with the occult assistance of Simon Forman. During Turner's trial, the court was regaled with a display of confiscated magical paraphernalia, including metal models of copulating couples which had, it was claimed, been used in love magic. Although by the early seventeenth century this type of magical dimension to aristocratic infighting was rare, the fact that such allegations were made in the course of litigation and criminal charges by people of this social level is instructive.[8] It is also noteworthy that by the 1630s the willingness to make such charges seems to have died out among the nation's élite.

Another case involving the aristocracy, in this instance linking that social level with the world of village witchcraft, broke in 1619, when two women were executed at Lincoln (another had already died in custody) for killing Henry Lord Roos and troubling other children of Francis Manners, the Earl of Rutland.[9] The accusations centred on Joan Flower and her daughters Margaret and Philippa, all of whom were employed as charwomen in the earl's household. All three had a bad reputation locally, and relationships between them and their employer had deteriorated steadily, a process which was accelerated when one of the daughters was dismissed for pilfering. The aristocratic family was smitten by mysterious illness: Henry Lord Roos, Rutland's eldest son, died, his brother followed a few years later, and his sister Katherine sickened. Suspicions focused on the Flowers women, and late in 1618 they were taken to Lincoln gaol and examined by justices of the peace. Joan, the mother, died in gaol after the initial examination, and her two daughters were tried and executed early in the following year. The examinations revealed a wider circle of suspected witches, and a number of other women were questioned, their evidence and that of the witnesses against them providing fascinating evidence of local beliefs. There was a general agreement that the Flowers had no power to harm the earl himself, so attacked his children. Henry, for example, in an interesting demonstration of contemporary views on sympathetic magic, had died because a glove of his had been buried, and his liver had rotted in his body as the glove had rotted in the ground. The pamphlet account of the incident suggests that the earl and those around him had no difficulty in believing in witchcraft.

Even the monarch was not yet free from threats of harm by witchcraft. The Elizabethan regime was briefly shaken in the summer of 1578 by what was taken to be evidence of a plot to kill the queen and two of her advisers by image magic. It seems that three wax figures were found hidden in a dunghill, one of them marked with the name 'Elizabeth'. The Privy Council ordered an investigation by the Lord Mayor and Bishop of London and other officials in the capital, and the incident seems to have caused considerable consternation. It was mentioned by Jean Bodin in his *Demonomanie*, and was also referred to by the sceptical writer Reginald Scot, who attributed the whole business to love magic wrought by a cheat on a credulous young gentleman. The affair's impact can be gauged from the fact that Ben Jonson the playwright was to remember the stir it caused many years later, while the Spanish ambassador, the soldier turned diplomat Bernardino de Mendoza, saw fit to mention it in his dispatches home. 'The central figure had the word "Elizabeth" written on the forehead,' he reported, 'and the side figures were dressed like her councillors, and were covered with a great variety of different signs, the left side of the images being transfixed with a large quantity of pig's bristles as if it were some kind of witchcraft.' Despite the stir which the discovery caused, it does not seem that any suspects were brought in for questioning.[10]

Although such direct threats against the monarch may have been rare, it is noteworthy that England's central governing body, the Privy Council, was constantly alert to threats or rumoured threats against the regime by witchcraft and related phenomena. As might be expected, one of the most persistent themes was concern over prophesying against the monarch, or attempting to predict by astrological or other means the date of the monarch's death. The shaky nature of Protector Northumberland's regime during the latter part of the reign of Edward VI is illustrated by the frequency with which reports of such matters surfaced at the centre. On 27 May 1551 the Privy Council heard how a certain William Tassell had been placed in custody for casting figures and prophesying. In April 1552 a former servant of the Duke of Norfolk (who was at that point in prison for treason) was reported to the Council for prophesying 'touching the king's majestie and dyvers noble men of his Councell'. On searching his rooms, 'certaine carracters and bookes of nigromancie and conjuration' were discovered. On 27 September 1552 the wife of an associate of this suspect was ordered to be set at liberty, along with the Countess of Suffolk, but they were both to be given 'a lesson to beware of sorseries &c' on their release. Earlier in the year, on 7 June, it had been reported that a man called Rogers was to be set in the pillory for seditiously repeating 'lewde propheties', and on 31 October an order was sent out to search the house of a man named Lytser, living in York, for books of prophecy. A trickle of similar cases continued to concern the Council up to Edward VI's death in July 1553.[11]

The frequency of such cases declined, yet they were to continue to surface occasionally throughout the reign of Elizabeth. In November 1583, for example, the regime became aware of a Catholic conspiracy against the monarch when one of the plotters, Francis Throckmorton, was arrested and interrogated under torture. Another key conspirator, Thomas, third Baron Paget, fled to Paris and died in exile a few years later. As was usual when Tudor conspiracies were uncovered by the authorities, further investigations broadened the range of people under suspicion, and evidence of the variety of those involved in this instance is provided by a document preserved in the state papers, probably dating from early 1584. This gave 'the names of the confederates gainst her majesty who have diverse and sundry times conspired gainst her life and do daily confederate against her'. It listed Paget, Sir George Hastings and Sir Thomas Hanmer, but then went on to include 'Ould Birtles the great devel, Darnally the sorcerer, Maude Twogoode, enchantresse, the oulde witche of Ramsbury', various other 'oulde witches', and 'Gregson the north tale teller, who was one of them 3 that stole the Earl of Northumberlandes heade from one of the turrettes in York'. Northumberland was one of the Catholic earls executed after the Northern Rising of 1569: his head would have been a potent totem for later rebels.[12] And, of course, official concerns about curiosity over predictions of the date of the monarch's demise continued. As late as 1594, a letter from Richard Young to the queen could refer to the examination of Mrs Jane Shelley, held in the Fleet Prison, 'who hath gone about to sorcerers, witches and charmers, to know the time of your majesty's death, and what shall become of the state'.[13]

More frequently, perhaps, the Elizabethan Privy Council found itself involved in witchcraft prosecutions as part of its more general function of occasional arbiter in difficult criminal cases. Sometimes, of course, it is possible to link the Council's interest in such matters with wider concerns with political stability, as in 1579, when it ordered the interrogation of a group of witches from Windsor who had allegedly used image magic, this a year after the supposed attempt on Elizabeth's life through the use of a bewitched puppet.[14] Frequently, however, the witchcraft investigated did not immediately threaten the regime. Thus on 25

March 1580 the Council wrote to a number of Buckinghamshire justices of the peace ordering them to investigate accusations from Edward Turner that a Jane Coleman was 'privie to certaine witchcraftes'. There was doubt about the validity of the jury's verdict (the case against Coleman had, in effect, been thrown out of court) and the justices of the peace were to reopen the case and take matters further. A subsequent letter revealed that the Council was taking this course 'for the furtherance of justice', in the light of what they obviously considered to be an incorrect verdict brought in the face of 'proofes and witnesses openlie heard at the last assizes' in the county.[15] A year later, evidence about witchcraft in the West Country came to the members of the Council when the Earl of Bedford wrote to them about the apprehension in Dorset of a notorious pirate named John Piers. Piers, a Cornishman, had an old mother, reputed to be a witch, living in Padstow, to whom, so report had it, the pirate 'conveyed all suche goodes and spoiles as he hath wyckedlie gotten at the seas'. The Council ordered the Mayor of Padstow to examine the old woman, 'whether she be a wytche indeede, and what spoiles and goodes she hath receyved from her sonne'.[16]

Such cases, although interesting, particularly in a period when other documentation on local witchcraft beliefs is relatively scarce, were not numerous, and it is obvious that for most of the time witchcraft was little more than a matter of sporadic and peripheral concern to the Privy Council. Equally, however, it should be stressed that when these matters did arise, not least in those instances when the safety of the monarch was felt to be at risk, they were taken very seriously. The situation was not unlike that which we have found in the drama of the period: witchcraft was rarely a central theme, but it was an occasional one which kept on appearing, sometimes in unexpected contexts. At the very least, it is obvious that well into Elizabeth's reign, witchcraft, prophecies and the casting of figures were seen as matters of concern to the central authorities. And Privy Councillors were important men, leading administrators, powerful aristocrats, high churchmen. If they were taking serious notice of witchcraft, on however occasional a basis, as part of the business of central government, our contention that the issue was still a live one among the political and social élite receives further reinforcement.

To the north of Elizabethan England, of course, there lay the kingdom of Scotland. In 1603, on the death of Queen Elizabeth, the Scottish monarch, James VI, became king of England as James I. And this new monarch was the author of a tract against witches, the *Daemonologie*. Traditionally, the accession of James was thought to have opened a more severe persecution of witches in

England, a tradition given strength by the passing of a stricter law against witchcraft in 1604, and by an increase in cultural references to the subject, of which the weird sisters in *Macbeth*, first performed in 1605 or 1606, are the most obvious example. James I has not received a good press from earlier generations of historians, and it was once traditional to lump his supposed interest in witch-hunting together with his other alleged deficiencies. Mrs E. Linton, in a collection of witch stories published in 1861, described James as 'treacherous, cruel, narrow-minded and cowardly, beyond anything that has ever disgraced the English throne before or since', his general bad qualities being rounded off by a 'lust for witch blood'. Robert Steele, writing some thirty years later, claimed that 70,000 people were executed in the wake of the 1604 act. In 1904 G. M. Trevelyan wrote of James that 'though he rejected the best part of the spirit of Knox, [he] was crazed beyond his English subjects with the witch mania of Scotland and the Continent'. By the beginning of the twentieth century, therefore, James had acquired a formidable reputation for witch-hunting.[17]

The *Daemonologie* was first published in Edinburgh in 1597, its writing prompted by James's recent experience of a treasonable plot against him by alleged witches which had resulted in mass trials and numerous executions in 1590–91. Two English editions followed in 1603, and the work was subsequently translated into Latin, French and Dutch.[18] It was short (about eighty quarto pages in its original form), very conventional and written, so its author informed the reader, in the face of 'the fearefull abounding . . . of these detestable slaves of the Divel, the witches or enchaunters' who had threatened him in Scotland, and also to 'resolve the doubting hearts of many' who found it impossible to believe in witchcraft.[19] The book, like so many didactic tracts of the time, took the form of a dialogue between two characters, Philomathus and Epistemon, in which most of the main issues about witchcraft were debated. The *Daemonologie* was, however, as much concerned with establishing the unlawfulness of certain forms of natural magic as it was with malefic witchcraft, yet another demonstration of how discussion of witchcraft on this intellectual level usually took place in the context of a wider intellectual discourse. But James subjected malefic witchcraft to its fair share of censure, and argued strongly that those convicted of witchcraft should be put to death, according to the method of the jurisdiction in which they found themselves, regardless of age, sex or social position.

The problem with his legendary status as a witch-hunter, as has long been known, is that despite his involvement in the trials of 1590–91 and his tract of 1597, James, at least as monarch of England, seems to have been more likely to intervene to save witches than to secure their convictions. The key incident is generally thought to have occurred in 1616. In that year nine persons were hanged for witchcraft at Leicester, mainly on the evidence of a boy aged twelve or thirteen. A month later, James arrived at Leicester on a royal progress. The boy was still suffering from what were thought to be witchcraft-induced fits, and a further nine suspects were in the county gaol awaiting trial. The king interrogated the boy and sent him to Lambeth Palace to be examined further by George Abbott, the Archbishop of Canterbury. Under examination, the boy's evidence was found to be fraudulent, the case collapsed and five of the suspects were released (the others, unfortunately, had died in gaol). Despite the status given to this dramatic incident, there is strong evidence from virtually the beginning of his reign that James adopted a sceptical stance over witchcraft accusations. He took an interest in the case of 'two maids suspected to be bewitched' at Cambridge in 1605, in the case of another possessed girl, Anne Gunter, in 1606 and in the supposed bewitching of six young girls in Caernarvon in 1611. In all of these instances he seems to have been interested in fair and careful investigation rather than in avid persecution. Thus it is no surprise that John Gee, a clergyman preaching one of the influential Paul's Cross sermons in 1624, when discussing the current case of a woman in London who thought herself to be possessed by the devil, should end by leaving 'the examination of this to him that sits on our throne, his maiestie, who hath a happy gift of discovery of such impostures'. A few years later Richard Bernard, the author of a demonological tract, could comment with approval on how James, now deceased, 'by his wisdome, learning and experience' had discovered 'divers counterfeits' when investigating witchcraft cases.[20]

The image of James as a man with a 'lust for witch blood' would thus seem largely unfounded. Yet there is a complication. In 1620, in an annoyingly badly documented incident, a schoolmaster named Peacock was arrested for plotting to influence James by witchcraft. Faced with a direct threat to his person, James's 'wisdome, learning and experience' led him to revive the attitudes which had characterized the North Berwick trials of 1590–91: Peacock was incarcerated in the Tower of London and interrogated under torture. And, if James demonstrated scepticism early in his reign, he took a hard line in January 1605 while at Huntingdon, investigating prophecies that there would be 'fire and sword throughout the land' over religious controversies. One of those questioned, a man called Butler, who had a local reputation 'as a witch and for supposed miraculous cures', and was also described as 'a poor creature who was whipped in the Queen's time for like prophecies', was sent for further interrogation before the Lord Chief Justice.[21] As these incidents suggest, perhaps the most accurate interpretation of James's opinions on witchcraft would be to regard them as part of his wider views on kingship. He was a keen advocate of divine-right monarchy and his ideas on witchcraft were very much formed by his experience in 1590–91 of what was conceived as a plot by witches to kill him. 'Rebellion,' so the biblical text ran, 'is as the sin of witchcraft', and for the divine-right monarch the witch, as the devil's handmaiden, was an obvious opponent of the Lord's Anointed. James was also a convinced Protestant, and, moreover, that rarest of beings, a British monarch with intellectual pretensions. His decision to write a witchcraft tract was thus partly fuelled by his desire to school his subjects on the danger of witchcraft to both the Stuart regime and the Protestant faith. Maintaining these concerns on a general level was not inconsistent, in the mind-set of the time, with being sceptical about particular witchcraft cases, like that of the allegedly possessed boy in Leicester.

❐ However, as James was well aware, the basis for a more thoroughgoing scepticism had already been laid. In the introduction to his *Daemonologie* the king, as we have noted, stated that one of his purposes in writing was to convince those who doubted the existence of witchcraft. He singled out two writers who were especially culpable in supporting this erroneous position. One was Johann Weyer, whose *De Praestigiis Daemonum* of 1563 was recognized, and vilified, throughout Europe as a key sceptical tract. The other came from nearer home, and his work added a major complication to the history of English witchcraft. Witchcraft may have been a widely recognized cultural phenomenon, but until the final third of Elizabeth's reign there were no English equivalents of those large-scale demonological tracts which were helping to form opinion about witchcraft in much of Continental Europe. Indeed, it is one of the great peculiarities of the history of witchcraft in England that the first major theoretical work on the subject published by an English writer, Reginald Scot's *Discoverie of Witchcraft* of 1584, was unrelentingly sceptical.

Scot was an obscure enough figure.[22] He was born into locally influential gentry stock in Kent, probably in 1538, and then went to Hart Hall in Oxford at the age of seventeen, although he did not take a degree. In fact, he returned to Kent, eventually held a number of local administrative posts there and, according to a later account of his life, 'gave himself up to solid reading, to the perusing of obscure authors that had by the generality of scholars been neglected; and at times of leisure to husbandry and gardening'. It was, in fact, these leisure-time activities which formed the background of the first book he published, the only other attributed to him apart from the *Discoverie*. This was his *Perfect Plat-forme of a Hoppe-Garden*, first published in 1574 and so popular that it was re-printed in 1576 and 1578.

Hop cultivation, however appropriate a theme for a Kentish author, was, as might be imagined, not one of the focal points of Elizabethan intellectual con-troversy, and it is uncertain why Scot decided to turn from that to the more con-tentious subject of witchcraft. For his *Discoverie* was a major achievement. This obscure Kentish squire pursued a coherent and reasoned argument over several hundred pages, and in the process referred to over 200 foreign and thirty-eight English works. Even if a proportion of these were being quoted at second-hand, Scot could not be accused of failing to complete a thorough exploration of the background literature to his subject. Thus when discussing what witches were meant to be capable of doing, he was able to cite (with many other author-ities) Ovid and Virgil from among the ancients, the *Malleus Maleficarum* and the English translation of Lambert Daneau's *Les Sorciers* from among more recent demonological works and such English tracts as those dealing with the Wind-sor trials of 1579 and a minor witch panic in Essex in 1582. What led him to mobilize this display of knowledge was, apparently, an out-and-out scepticism which, to the modern reader, seems surprisingly (and perhaps misleadingly) like a common-sense view of witches: they don't exist because what they are meant to do is patently absurd.

Witchcraft was, to Scot, 'a cousening art, wherein the name of God is abused, prophaned, and blasphemed, and his power attributed to a vile crea-ture'.[23] This notion of witchcraft as a 'cousening art' was central for Scot. If witches manage to perform any of the feats attributed to them, it is because they are able to fool the credulous by trickery and sleight of hand rather than as a result of any diabolically inspired power. To the common people, it was true, witchcraft was 'a supernaturall worke', but such an interpretation was 'in-comprehensible to the wise, learned, or faithfull', being 'a probable matter to children, fooles, melancholike persons and papists'.[24] That witchcraft was so widely believed in was largely because people had been misled by the writers of demonological tracts. Jean Bodin was subjected to constant mocking criticism, as were Kramer and Sprenger, the authors of the *Malleus Maleficarum*. 'These two doctors,' he wrote of them, 'to mainteine their credit, and to cover their injuries, have published those same monsterous lies, which have abused all Christendom . . . God knoweth that their whole booke conteineth nothing but stinking lies and poperie.'[25] The *Malleus*, full of papist errors, attracted Scot's particular odium, but English Protestant tracts fared little better: the account of the 1582

Essex trials, for example, was dismissed as 'a foolish pamphlet dedicated to the Lord Darcy'.[26]

Scot turned to the standard descriptions of what witches do and dismissed all of them as nonsense. The demonic pact was not only without scriptural basis but clearly absurd: 'what firme bargaine,' asked Scot, 'can be made betwixt a carnall bodie and a spirituall? Let any wise or honest man tell me, that either hath beene a partie, or a witnesse, and I will beleeve him.'[27] In his discussion of shape-changing he rejected Bodin's dependence on 'the greatest absurdities and impossibilities' contained in Ovid's *Metamorphoses*. He similarly rejected Bodin's depiction of the sabbat ('And here some of monsieur Bodin's lies may be inserted . . .'), arguing that the account he and others gave of how a witch attending the sabbat might leave a 'similitude' of his or her body in the marital bed shows that 'their incredulitie is incredible'.[28] Scot also attacked the notion that human witches mated with demonic incubi and succubi. Indeed, this aspect of the witch's activities caused considerable difficulties for many demonological writers, especially when they had to confront the technical problems of how human semen could be kept hot while hosted by an incorporeal body. Scot, predictably, had a lot of fun with this area of learned debate and maintained a complete scepticism about the whole process.[29] He also attacked prophesying, astrology, oracles, divination and alchemy.

Although Scot's major objective was to refute the arguments of the learned demonologists, he was also aware that witchcraft was a matter of concern among the populace of his native Kent. The book contains a number of illustrative stories drawn from his locality, and it is probable that a major impetus moving him to write the *Discoverie* was the disgust he experienced while attending a witchcraft trial at Rochester in 1581. Accordingly, the book contains criticisms of popular beliefs as well as of demonological writers. Scot noted that accused witches were usually elderly women, 'old, lame, bleare eied, pale, fowle, and full of wrinkles: poore, sullen, superstitious, and papists . . . what mischiefe, mischance, calamitie or slaughter is brought to passe, they are easilie persuaded the same is doone by themselves'. Such 'wretches' were 'so odious unto all their neighbours, and so feared, as few dare offend theme, or denie them anie thing they aske'.[30] Scot gave a description of how a witchcraft accusation might occur which many recent historians would regard as archetypal. These elderly women, he wrote, 'go from house to house, and from doore to doore for a pot full of milke, yest, drinke, pottage, or some such releefe; without which they could hardlie live'. If the desired 'releefe' was not forthcoming, the old woman 'sometimes she cursseth one, and sometimes another; and that from the master of the house, his wife, children, cattell, &c, to the little pig that lieth in the stie'. If misfortune then occurred in the household, an accusation of witchcraft followed: 'they, upon whom such adversities fall, weighing the fame that goeth upon this woman (hir words, displeasure, and cursses meeting, so justlie with their misfortune) doo not onelie conceive, but also are resolved, that all their mishaps are brought to passe by hir onelie meanes'.[31] Scot's acquaintance with witchcraft beliefs was clearly not limited to the contents of the books he had perused in his study.

But to portray Scot simply as a modern sceptical rationalist living before his time would not be wholly accurate. As well as demonstrating the absurdity of witchcraft accusations, he was also following a clear and logical theological line, one which was to provide sceptics with ammunition throughout the period of the witch persecutions. Scot's position essentially was that to ascribe to witches the powers they were meant to possess was to blaspheme by attributing to them powers which were limited to God. He noted that the feats ascribed to witches 'exceed in quantitie, qualitie, and number, all the miracles that Christ wrought here upon earth . . . and when Christ himselfe saith: "The works that I doe, no man else may accomplish": whie should we think that a foolish old woman can doo them all, and manie more?"[32] He noted elsewhere, using the terminology frequently deployed when this issue was under discussion, that 'all Christians see that to confesse witches can doo as they saie, were to attribute to a creature the power of the creator'. He also, following another standard sceptical line, attacked the supposed scriptural basis for belief in witchcraft: 'the whole course of the scripture,' he argued, 'is utterlie repugnant to these impossible opinions, saving a few sentences, which nevertheless rightlie understood, releeve them nothing at all'.[33] He set out to demonstrate that the argument that there was a biblical basis for believing in and attempting to extirpate witches rested on the mistranslation of a number of Hebrew terms, and claimed that in any case the magical practitioners described in Scripture had little in common with the old women being tried for witchcraft all over the Europe of his day.

But as for our old women that are said to hurt children with their eies, or lambs with their lookes, or that pull downe the moone out of heaven, or make so foolish a bargaine, or doo such homage to the divell; you shall not read in the bible of any such witches, or of any such actions imputed to them.[34]

As some of the quotations from Scot already cited suggest, another key element in his thinking was a rabid anti-Catholicism. At many points he simply equates (reflecting here an extreme form of a theme frequently appearing in

English Protestant works on witchcraft) what he considers to be the superstitious elements of Roman Catholicism with witchcraft: pilgrimages, veneration of saints, the Catholic view of transubstantiation, exorcism, the acceptance of papal authority – all of them attracted his harsh censure. In his discussion of the tricks played by conjurors, he wrote: 'I see no difference betweene these and popish conjurations: for they agree in order, words, and matter, differing in no circumstance, but that the papists do it without shame openlie, the other doe it in hugger mugger secretlie.'[35] Scot's views on popery place him firmly in his cultural context and create enormous problems for any attempt to portray him simply as an 'enlightened' or 'tolerant' thinker.

The austerity of Scot's theological position (one shared by many other Protestants) is displayed in his criticism of what he saw as a general tendency to blame misfortune on witches. Scot was, in 1584, apparently turning away from an earlier belief in extreme Protestantism (his book's publication should, perhaps, be placed in the context of the religious situation in Kent at that point) and, as well as his overt attack on Catholicism, he may have been attempting to distance himself implicitly from hell-fire Puritanism. Scot was convinced of the reality of divine providence: whatever happened to a human being was part of God's masterplan. This conviction left little room for disasters caused by witchcraft, and, according to Scot, to ascribe misfortune to witchcraft was a sign of imperfect faith. 'None can (nowadaies) with patience indure the hand and correction of God,' he declared, 'for if any adversitie, greefe, sicknesse, losse of children, corne, cattell, or libertie happen unto them; by & by they exclaime uppon witches.' God, argued Scot, punishes 'both just and unjust with greefs, plagues, and afflictions in manner and form as he thinketh good', and only 'faithless people' would believe that their afflictions came from the witch rather than God. 'I am also well assured,' Scot continued, 'that if all the old women of the world were witches, and all the prestes conjurers: we should not have a drop of raine, nor a blast of wind the more or lesse for them.'[36] The good Christian, as many sceptical writers after Scot were to agree, should suffer afflictions with equanimity, on the grounds that they came from the Almighty; they should read the Book of Job and eschew explanations involving witchcraft.

Unfortunately, and again like many later sceptics, in his determination to pare away 'superstition' from a core of right religion, Scot laid himself open to accusations that he was denying spiritual agency altogether. In the final section of the *Discoverie*, a 'Discourse upon divels and Spirits', Scot adopts a metaphorical and psychological interpretation which cuts the scope of spiritual agency in the affairs of the physical world to a minimum. Thus to say that somebody was possessed was simply to say that he was mad. On Scot's interpretation, the term 'spirit' 'dooth signifie a secret force and power, wherewith our minds are mooved and directed; if unto holie things, then it is the motion of the holie spirit, of the Spirit of Christ and of God; if unto evil things, then it is the suggestion of the wicked spirit of the divell, and of Satan'.[37] In effect (and despite his disavowals), the logic of Scot's arguments led to a denial of the reality of the spirit world as surely as it did to a denial of the reality of witchcraft. Thus, despite his reliance on Scripture, his denial of Sadduceeism and his patent enthusiasm for the Holy Spirit, what Scot was saying was very difficult to reconcile with the mainstream of late-sixteenth-century Christianity. Scot, as a recent commentator has put it, was 'a learned, independent-minded country gentleman, used to making decisions on his own initiative, and evaluating what he read against what he observed'.[38] But his independence of mind led him to positions which, however laudable they may seem to modern opinion, were, on the strength of other published works of the period, very isolated.

As might be imagined, Scot's *Discoverie* received a very hostile reaction from other writers on witchcraft. He himself was aware that he was writing against the weight of contemporary opinion, against 'the very doctors of the church to the schoolmen, protestants and papists, learned and unlearned, poets and historiographers, Jewes, Christians, or gentiles', and regretted that 'these writers, out of whom I gather most absurdities, are of the best credit and authoritie of all writers in this matter'.[39] Later writers of yet more works which Scot would have considered absurd were unimpressed by his arguments. James VI, as we have noted, claimed to be writing his *Daemonologie* partly in the hope of refuting the opinions of Scot. Henry Holland, author of a major witchcraft tract published in 1590, presumably had Scot in mind when he referred to those '(as they say) of learning and reputation' who affirmed that witchcraft 'containeth nothing but cousenage and secret practices of wicked men, and foolish women which are full of restless melancholick imagination'. William Perkins noted Scot as a sceptic in his work on witchcraft published in 1608. The exorcist John Darrell wrote in 1602, 'as for Mr Skot, there is none of any sound understanding, but he allows his judgement better in a hopground, than in a case of divinatie', while Richard Bernard, author of another major book on witchcraft first published in 1627, noted Scot's 'erroneous opinions'.[40] The tradition that James VI, on his accession to the English throne in 1603, ordered that surviving copies of the *Discoverie* should be burnt by the public hangman may lack the support of contemporary evidence but would seem to sum up the common attitude among contemporary witchcraft writers to the Kentish squire's work.[41]

The problem remains, of course, of how widely Scot's views were shared among those who were not writing tracts about witchcraft. If a country squire could reach the conclusions about witchcraft that Scot came to, it is possible that many other people may have done so. Perhaps the most accurate conclusion which can be reached is that a fair number of members of local élites entertained attitudes about the subject which, if not as well informed as, or leading to such a total rejection as did, Scot's, at least allowed room for a high degree of caution when dealing with witchcraft. Let us illustrate the point by staying in Scot's country but moving forward a generation after his death to 1641. In that year another Kentish squire, Henry Oxinden, wrote to his brother-in-law, a justice of the peace, on behalf of Goodwife Gilmot, 'maliciously or ignorantly, or both maliciously and ignorantly, accused to bee a witch'. In his letter Oxinden recounted and discounted various allegations of *maleficium* against the woman, and the 'evidence' that she had the witch's mark. He then turned to some more general musings about witchcraft which read very like Scot. When accident or loss came, wrote Oxinden, people blamed witches 'as if there were no God in Israell that ordereth all things according to his good pleasure, punishing both just and unjust with losses and afflictions according as hee thinketh good'. He continued, 'Moreover, I cannot see how any rationall man can persuade himselfe that a simple woman can doe such things as these . . . what power hath a witch or a woman to doe such things as in nature are impossible for her to doe and in sense and reason incredible.' But, Oxinden remarked perceptively, it was no wonder that the common people felt hostile to witches 'when almost all divines, physitians and lawyers, who should know most, herein satisfying themselves with old excuses, have given much credit to these fables'.[42]

The common people we will consider in the next chapter. What needs stating now is that, despite Oxinden's pessimism, educated people in Elizabethan and early Stuart England were able to hold a number of intellectual positions on witchcraft. Classical culture, at least some elements of Protestant thinking, the law, the demonological tracts from the Continent they might read, the folklore of their native culture and the growing body of pamphlets dealing with English witch trials, all of these might encourage the educated to believe in the reality of witchcraft and the threat that witches offered to Christian society. Conversely, other tendencies in Protestant theology, a rough practical scepticism, the ability to accept witchcraft in the abstract while rejecting the possibility that the particular old women suspected in particular cases were witches, any of these, alone or in combination, might temper the desire to extirpate witches. Thus some people in Elizabethan and early Stuart England, as Richard Napier's case books show, were worried about witchcraft to the point of obsession and mental unbalance. Others, as Scot demonstrates, were able to reject belief in the power of witchcraft altogether. Most people, one suspects, were somewhere in between: willing to accept witchcraft as a possibility, able to recognize or suspect it when they thought it was harming them or people they knew, yet seeing it only as one of the many hazards that life might throw at them, loath to believe in the cosmic danger posed by a sect of satanic witches, and unlikely to respond to a suspicion of witchcraft in an unthinking or hasty fashion. As studying Scot and the reactions to him suggests, there was no single hegemonic attitude to witchcraft among educated men and women in England but rather a plurality of possible positions. Understanding these positions and charting how they shifted are crucial to any attempt to delineate the history of the phenomenon.

CHAPTER 2

Witchcraft in
Popular Culture

Although the concepts of witchcraft held by educated, élite people were crucial to both the development of ideas about the subject of witchcraft and the definition of witchcraft as a form of deviance, the broad acceptance of witchcraft as a cultural phenomenon rested on the widespread belief in it among the population as a whole. Witchcraft was, quite simply, part of the everyday popular culture of the period. But in attempting to reconstruct and analyse this aspect of past popular culture we encounter two serious problems. The first is evidence. Reconstructing the mental world of illiterate people who lived three or four centuries ago is, clearly, no easy matter. Most of what we know of the beliefs of ordinary people in the Tudor and Stuart periods comes to us through sources which have been mediated by interested parties. Very few non-élite people from this period, at least before that flurry of pamphleteering which accompanied the Civil Wars, have left us with much by way of direct evidence of their beliefs. Thus practically all of our information on thinking about witchcraft among the population at large comes from two potentially biased bodies of source material: the records of courts and the opinions of educated observers, most prominently the clerical writers of demonological tracts. Not until the second half of the seventeenth century, when antiquaries like John Aubrey (1626–97) set about describing popular mentalities and customs, do we get much by way of a sympathetic account of popular culture.[1]

The second, equally serious problem is, to reiterate, the constant need to wrest ourselves from our own cultural assumptions, from our own sense of cultural superiority, and to eschew 'the enormous condescension of posterity' decried so powerfully by Edward Thompson. We must resist that temptation to be condescending to people in the past when studying topics like witch-craft, to resort to dismissive adjectives like 'superstitious', 'ignorant' or 'illiterate' and to return to those subjects which the established historical canon and the examination syllabuses have convinced us are the 'important' themes of Tudor and Stuart history: crown and commons, Elizabethan foreign policy, the gradual accumulation of wealth by London merchants and so on.

The people who believed in witchcraft and who found themselves involved in witchcraft accusations were, in most respects, not conspicuously stupid. They were petty gentry, some of them learned by the standards of their time, many of them capable of holding local government office. They were the hard-headed and increasingly market-oriented yeomen farmers whose economic skills were laying the basis for England's agricultural prosperity. They were husbandmen, the middling farmers immersed in the practicalities of peasant agriculture. They were labourers, men who, despite their lowly social status, were capable of turning their hands to a score of jobs around the farm and the workshop. And they were the womenfolk of these men, involved in the con-crete realities of raising children, running households and, frequently, working with their husbands in agricultural or industrial production. These people were able to live meaningful, even fulfilling lives under material conditions which most inhabitants of the modern West would find unbearably harsh. To dismiss them as 'ignorant' or 'superstitious' would seem to be not only disobliging to them but also unhelpful to us as we attempt to reconstruct their mental world.

For it is clear that these people had a mental world.[2] It was not (how could it and why should it be?) the mental world of an educated man or woman at the turn of the twentieth and twenty-first centuries. Religion featured prominently in this mental world, although (as clerical writers before the Reformation and for two centuries after it were wont to complain) it was not the religion of the learned. As far as we can reconstruct it, Christianity on a popular level served to reinforce notions of community, to reinforce ideas of right and wrong in everyday interpersonal dealings, to add meaning to the rites of passage of birth, marriage and death, to help give some sense of meaning to a difficult and at times harsh world. For most people (again to the despair of theologians), Christian belief of this type was perfectly compatible with a greater or lesser acceptance of other areas of belief which both we and their educated con-temporaries would describe as superstitious. There is ample evidence that people accepted the reality of ghosts, fairies, poltergeists, the power of proph-ecy and spirits of all sorts. In such a mental world, the presence of witches is hardly surprising.

The reading material which was available to those of the lower orders who were literate was more likely to reinforce than to challenge this mental world. The popular literature of early modern England, despite the efforts of a number of scholars, is still one of the great underused historical sources. Yet from the early Elizabethan period onwards the London presses were pouring forth accounts of wonders of all sorts: monstrous births, storms, earthquakes and shipwrecks, cities destroyed by fire or flood, the exotic, and usually fictionalized, animals and peoples discovered in the New World, the sinners who came to appropriate but unpleasant ends. Such accounts invariably had a heavy moral undertone which was very much in line with popular religious attitudes: the hand of God was present everywhere, and He was all too willing to unleash correction and punishment on to a sinful mankind. Thus a witchcraft pamphlet of 1613 could group together 'treasons, murthers, witchcrafts, fires, flouds' as evidence that the Day of Judgement was at hand.[3] Such notions were current in Elizabethan and Stuart England, and there is every indication that they coloured conversation when wonders and extraordinary events were discussed in the alehouse, in the village street, in the yeoman or gentleman's parlour, or in the churchyard after divine service on a Sunday. For people in this period inhabited a culture which was hungry for news, where gossip was an integral part of life; this was in many respects a story-telling culture. When witchcraft occurred or was suspected in early modern England, it was talked about; it was something which people knew about, something they had opinions about.

❥ As might be imagined, there was a wide range of ideas about witchcraft, running as it did into so many other aspects of popular belief. At the centre, however, lay the notion that witches were able to do harm – in contemporary technical terminology *maleficium* – to their fellow human beings. In the early 1970s, intensive research on Essex sources by Alan Macfarlane, and the wider trawl of materials completed by Keith Thomas, demonstrated that whereas the central concern of learned demonological writers was the witch's pact with the devil, the main concern of the population at large was the witch's capacity to do harm by occult means.[4] Again, as so often, we must pause to consider our evidence. Much of what we know about popular concerns regarding witchcraft comes from criminal court records, and it is perhaps unsurprising that these records should contain considerable information about the type of witchcraft upon which a criminal charge might be based. Yet, even making due allowance for this, the centrality of *maleficium* remains striking. And, as the work of Macfarlane and Thomas demonstrated, attitudes to *maleficium* were structured and patterned, and tell us much about the cultural significance of witchcraft accusations and their function in early modern English society.

Let us consider a typical accusation. On 31 December 1646 Henry Cockcrofte, a member of a locally important yeoman family living at Heptonstall in the West Riding of Yorkshire, gave evidence to two justices of the peace about the activities of Elizabeth Crossley. Crossley, a woman 'in an evill report for witchinge', came 'begginge an almes' at his door. Cockcrofte's wife gave Crossley something, but she went away displeased with what she had been given. That night Cockcrofte's son William, aged a year and three-quarters, 'beinge att that tyme in very good health', fell sick with mysterious fits, underwent a partial recovery only to sicken again and then died a little later. During his son's illness Cockcrofte confronted and beat another local woman suspected of witchcraft, Mary Midgely. She confessed to being a witch, but denied that she was involved in harming Cockcrofte's son, putting the blame squarely on Elizabeth Crossley, her daughter Sarah and another woman called Mary Kitchinge. But Cockcrofte's decision to take the affair to officialdom encouraged his neighbours to make formal accusations against Midgely. One of them, Richard Wood, told how Midgely had come begging for wool at his door, presumably in the hope of being able to sell it for a few pence after processing it for weaving. Wood's wife (again it was the woman of the house who found herself in the front line) refused her, telling Midgely that 'she hadd given her a good almes of wooll three weeks before, & would give her no more . . . but did give her an almes of milke, w[i]th which shee d[e]parted very angry'. In this instance it was cattle, 'milch kyne', rather than a child, which sickened mysteriously after the altercation between the householder's wife and the woman who came begging at her door.[1]

Analysis of this Yorkshire case reveals a number of themes which recur constantly in the period's narratives of village witchcraft suspicions. The first of these is the local reputation that certain people, normally women, would have for being witches: Crossley was in 'evill report' for being a witch, while Cockcrofte knew that when his child fell ill as a result of what looked like witchcraft, Midgely was a person to go and interrogate. The second is the connection that was made between illness (in one case of a child, in another of cattle) and witchcraft. Witchcraft, under appropriate circumstances, might be invoked as the cause of an otherwise inexplicable disease or other misfortune. Third, what frequently helped determine that the circumstances were appropriate to suspect witchcraft was an altercation, or 'falling out' as it was most often termed, between somebody in the household who was to experience misfortune and the woman with a reputation for being a witch. And fourth, at least in the case of

Cockcrofte's wife and Elizabeth Crossley, the altercation was between a representative of one of the most powerful families in the village and a woman who
had to beg to get by; admittedly within the narrow world of the early modern
village community, we are encountering considerations of social power and
social hierarchy.

The final incident before the unleashing of *maleficium* varied considerably and
could be very trivial. For example,.Thomas Darling, a godly youth from Derbyshire, was thought to have been thrown into torments by a witch whom he
offended when he accidentally broke wind in her presence.[6] But however trivial
the final altercation, it is evident that in many communities certain people were
feared as possessing the occult power to do harm, while in some cases it is
possible to see the witchcraft accusations as a final severing of relationships,
either between two individuals or between a local community (or at least a
section of such a community) and an individual within it who had gradually
come to be defined as a deviant.

Macfarlane, in his work on Essex, was able to take this recurring paradigm of
altercations and deteriorating relations further and place it within a broad
framework of socioeconomic change. He noted that accusations were typically
launched by richer villagers against poorer ones, and that the type of altercation
when alms or favours were refused by a richer villager to a poorer one to which
we have alluded was common. Essex in this period was an economically
advanced county whose agriculture had become increasingly capitalist and
oriented towards the London market, while here as elsewhere population
growth, given the relatively inelastic capacity for economic expansion, was creating a widening gap between rich and poor. There was also, Macfarlane claimed,
something of a hiatus in attitudes about how the poor should be treated. Before
the population increase set in around the mid-sixteenth century, the poor could
be dealt with (both practically and morally) by the traditional institutions of
Church and manor, while in the second half of the seventeenth century an
institutionalized poor law, dependent on local ratepayers, provided both a basic
safety net and a culturally recognized remedy for poverty. In the intervening 100
years richer villagers were less certain about how to deal with the poor, who were
becoming more numerous and who must have been seen as an increasing
nuisance by substantial householders. Under such circumstances, the witchcraft
accusation became a means of transferring guilt: the transgressor of community norms (which were in flux anyway) was not the householder who refused alms, but rather the malevolent beggar whose mumbled threats preceded
the sickness or death of a child or cattle. It is unfortunate that records for other

counties do not permit more than partial comparisons with these findings for Essex, although such work as can be done suggests that this type of socio-economic model is not universally applicable (it is also uncertain why Kent, Hertfordshire, Middlesex and Surrey, counties undergoing the same type of socioeconomic change as Essex, had far lower levels of witchcraft prosecution). But it remains clear that, typically though not invariably, the witch was drawn from the poorer end of village society.

Also, equally typically, the witch was a woman. The quality of records does not allow us to be precise in these matters, but it is possible to build up something of an impression of the type of woman who was likely to be a witch. She was economically marginalized by being poor, and possibly (although we are unable to be certain on this point) she was more likely than the female population at large to be widowed and hence more likely not only to be poor but also to be outside husbandly control. Macfarlane's work on Essex also suggests that witches tended to be elderly, perhaps typically aged between fifty and seventy. Sceptical writers from the late Elizabethan period onwards were able to lampoon the popular stereotype of the witch as a bent, aged, poor and isolated woman.

These women also had a reputation for doing ill. The better-documented cases demonstrate that people might have established a reputation for witch-craft twenty years before an accusation entered the official record. Certainly, it was not unusual for people giving evidence in such cases to remember and report incidents which had occurred many years previously. The suspected witch also usually had a reputation for being a nuisance on a wider scale. Reconstructing detailed case histories is difficult, but there is enough evidence to suggest that the witch, identified as she was as a member of the undeserving parish poor, was frequently seen as a representative of that section of local society which would be given to irregular church attendance, petty theft, drunkenness, sexual immorality and scolding, abusing and troubling their neighbours. Typical were three women from North Moreton in Berkshire who were suspected of malefic witchcraft early in the reign of James I. Two of them, Agnes and Mary Pepwell, were generally considered to be 'p[er]sons of lyttle creddytt' by their neighbours, one of whom deposed that Agnes was given to wandering up and down the countryside, and in her wanderings had become pregnant with Mary after a liaison with a lame beggar. The third, Elizabeth Gregory, 'was & is taken amongst all or most of her neighbours to bee a most notorious scolde and a maker of great debate & fallinge owt' and 'a very unquyett woman & one that . . . doth use to curse & threaten her neighbours & is a comon disturber of

them'.[7] The early modern village was not the closed, static community of
sociological myth; but it was a place where reputation and 'credit' in its symbolic
rather than its financial sense mattered and were evaluated, a place where gossip
and story-telling were important aspects of sociability. In such an environment,
it is easy to see how a burgeoning reputation for deviance might help feed that
process which Keith Thomas has described as 'the making of the witch'.

Another measure of their reputation was the extent and the variety of
mayhem which might be attributed to individual witches. In 1601–2 a number
of depositions were made against Alice and Michael Trevisard and their son
Peter of Dartmouth in Devon. Between them, this trio were thought to have
killed two children, the husband and a servant of Alice Butler; driven mad the
husband and injured a child of Joan Baddaford; sunk ships in which a sailor
named William Thompson sailed on two successive voyages, resulting on each
occasion in his suffering a year's imprisonment, first with the Portuguese, then
with the Spaniards; injured the child and husband of Joan Davye; caused the
illness of a stepchild of William Cozen, whose wife, on her deathbed, demanded of him that if Alice Trevisard came to her grave he should drive her
away; caused the loss of a boat and the sickness of a child of Walter Tooker;
prevented the setting up of a timber fold of a Mr Martyn; caused the destruction of a barrel of ale after being denied a halfpenny worth of ale by Joan
Laishe; caused the illness of the children of John Venman; and caused the
illness of the wife of John Galsworthie – the woman was first lamed so that she
had to go on crutches and then died (she had attempted to recover a loan from
Alice Trevisard) – and also caused the unborn pigs in a pregnant sow of his to
rot in the animal's belly. The Trevisards, like so many witches, were clearly
thought of as powerful people. A servant of John Venman, whose children
allegedly suffered as a consequence of witchcraft, was so fearful of Alice Trevisard 'because she said she heard she was a witch' that she even refused to
accept a letter from her.[8]

That such a wide range of misfortunes could be attributed to a single family
of witches should not lead us to underestimate the sophistication of our ancestors. It was, rather, a reflection of the fact that theirs was an insecure world in
which diseases or accidents that today would be diagnosed or accounted for in
other terms, or misfortunes that might simply be attributed to bad luck, were
explained by witchcraft. Certainly, learned writers were prone to decry the ease
with which the populace attributed problems to witchcraft. 'Fear and imagination make many witches among countrey people,' wrote Richard Bernard in
1627, adding that 'it is the generall madnesse of people to ascribe unto witch-

craft, whatever falleth out unknowne, or strange to vulgar sence'. George Gifford, an Elizabethan clergyman whose works on witchcraft provide numerous
insights into popular beliefs, perhaps more shrewdly, noted late in Elizabeth's
reign how 'conceit doth much, even where there is an apparent disease. A man
feareth hee is bewitched, it troubleth all the powers of his mind, and that
distempereth his bodie, maketh great alterations in it, and bringeth sundrie
griefs.'[9] Obviously, with some people fear of witchcraft, or fear of a particular
person thought of as a witch, would surface very rapidly, yet for most witchcraft
was merely one of a range of possible explanations for misfortunes. Pamphlet
accounts of witchcraft cases in particular frequently describe illness or misfortune being ascribed to witchcraft only after a range of other possible explanations had been considered and rejected. Mulling over such explanations would,
of course, be a shorter process if the supposed victim of witchcraft already
thought that he or she had offended somebody thought to be a witch. And
when considering the possible origins of misfortune, it was always more com-
forting to ascribe it to the agency of a deviant human being than to divine
displeasure. We return to the premise, so often stated in the period, that to too
readily ascribe the problems of the world to witches downgraded the importance of God.[10]

It is striking, however, that the misfortunes attributed to English witches
were normally personal and local. In parts of Continental Europe and, in the
1590s at least, Scotland, witches were thought willing and able to wreak more
cosmic havoc: to raise storms or spread the plague. Although there are odd
mentions of these wider powers in English evidence, on the level of popular
belief the evil done by witches was almost invariably interpreted in interpersonal terms. Even this personal evil inflicted by witches was more restricted
than can be found in some Continental contexts. English witches, for example,
were rarely held to have interfered with sex and procreation as witches in some
other lands were supposed to have done, by causing impotence in men or
stillbirths or miscarriages in women.

Thus at the core of English ideas about witchcraft we find a set of concerns
which, given the initial premises of the contemporary belief system, make
witchcraft a more understandable, even rational, phenomenon. On this reading,
the witchcraft accusation had an important function in severing social relations,
particularly when there was a need to confirm the rupture of the link between
a richer and poorer villager. Witchcraft also served a useful function as an explanation for misfortune. And if nothing else, the witchcraft accusation was
something which existed firmly within the wider context of relationships and

interpersonal interaction within the local community. This functional approach to witchcraft with the emphasis on acts of *maleficium* is not the whole story, but it does offer an important route into understanding popular attitudes to witchcraft.

If concern over *maleficium*, the doing of harm, is one of the major recurring themes of early modern English witch beliefs, the other is, conversely, that many members of the population at large believed in the existence of 'good' witches, magical practitioners whose powers produced beneficial results. Such good witches were known by a number of titles ('blesser', for example, seems to have been the preferred usage in the North-West) but they were referred to most frequently as 'cunning' (that is, skilful or knowledgeable) men or women.

The works of English demonologists and sceptical writers alike were full of denunciations of these cunning folk and, tellingly, their popularity with the general populace. 'Most men are wont to seeke after these wise men, and cunning women, such as they call witches, in sicknesse, in losses, and in all extremeties,' wrote the cleric Henry Holland in 1590. Just as the ministers of God helped their flocks, declared the theologian William Perkins a few years later, so 'the ministers of Satan, under the name of wise-men and wise-women, are at hand, by appointment, to resolve, direct, and helpe ignorant and unsetled persons, in cases of distraction, losse, or other outward calamities'. The supposedly good witch, according to Perkins, was so popular among the people that 'they hold themselves and their countrey blessed to have him among them, they flee unto him in neccessitie, they depend upon him as their God, and by this meanes thousands are carried away to their final confusion'.[11]

Convincing 'ignorant and unsetled persons' of the ungodliness of going to cunning folk was an uphill task for the godly. George Gifford had one of his characters declare that a certain cunning woman 'doth more good in one yeere than all these scripture men will doe so long as they live . . . it is a gift which God hath given her. I think the Holy Spirit of God doth teach her.' Richard Bernard, another of the 'scripture men' who wrote a tract about witchcraft, listed the popular justifications for resorting to cunning men and women: the widespread feeling that they did good, and hence must derive their powers from God; they could cure illness; they were the only form of help available for some problems; where other sources of help, notably doctors, were available, the services of the cunning folk were cheaper and just as effective; and they 'speake against bad wytches, and often discover them, and therefore cannot they themselves be bad'.[12]

As is attested by their popularity, the troubles that cunning folk were felt able to assist with were very varied, but four main areas recur. The first was help in finding lost or stolen goods, and in the latter case of helping identify those who had taken them. The second was offering remedies for a wide range of illnesses, among both humans and farm animals. The third was the general area of fortune-telling, taking in such matters as predicting the sex of unborn babies or (a major concern among serving maids) providing the identity of future husbands. The fourth, as Richard Bernard noted, was help in identifying witches and then in dealing with witchcraft. Such was the expertise of some cunning folk in this field that it is not unusual to find provincial doctors confronted by cases of suspected witchcraft recommending a cunning person of good reputation to the witch's supposed victim.

The techniques employed by cunning folk varied enormously. Many of them used charms and spells, and most of them used some sort of doggerel based on the Bible or well-established prayers. Typical in this respect was Henry Baggilie, examined by the justices of the peace in Lancashire in 1634. He claimed that about twenty years previously his father had been taught 'by a Dutchman certaine Englishe wordes and praiers to repeate, whereby to blesse or helpe anie sicke person or cattell'. His father had passed the prayer on to him, and it ran, 'Tell thee thou forspoken toothe and tongue, hearte and hearte ... the three things thee boote most: the father, sonne and holighoste', which was to be used with the Lord's Prayer and 'the beleeve' three times over. Baggalie continued (taking us further into the realms of popular belief) that when he effected cures by use of this prayer he had 'alwaies beene suddenlie taken with sicknes or lamenesse and that alwaies in the same manner that the man or beaste that hee blessed was trobled withal'.[13] Although this last detail is rarely found elsewhere, both the comments of hostile writers and detailed statements by or about alleged cunning folk indicate that the use of prayers and verbal charms was widespread among these 'good' witches.

Another common technique was the use of the sieve and shears in various forms of divination. The basic method was set out in a sixteenth-century manuscript, where it was described as 'another waye to finde out a theefe'. A pair of shears was to be set in the 'rinde' of a sieve, and two persons were each to put the tops of both of their forefingers to the upper part of the shears, making an invocation to St Peter and St Paul as they did so. 'At the nomination of the guilty p[er]son,' the formula continues, 'the syve will turne rounde.' Alice Scholfield, examined by the Lancashire justices in 1641 for her 'devillish practiseing' with a sieve and a pair of shears, used exactly this technique, including calling on the two saints, when trying to identify suspected thieves, and for attempting to ascertain if two women were pregnant. A few years later, an Exeter woman named Anne King apparently performed the same ritual in the hope of finding who had stolen a purse full of money. The sieve turned when the name of the woman she suspected was called out, and the suspected thief was charged and committed to prison. Further scope for this form of divination was suggested by the Essex woman presented before the Archdeacon of Colchester in 1589 for using the sieve and shears to locate lost goods and to determine the sex of unborn babies. Such scattered references suggest that this was an extremely widespread form of popular magic.[14]

The more sophisticated cunning man or woman might make use of something very like the crystal ball of the modern fortune-teller. Again, much of our evidence comes from cases where attempting to identify thieves was the main objective. Thus Thomas Ady, a physician writing in 1656, noted that 'cunning men, or good witches . . . will undertake to shew the face of the thief in the glass, or of any other that hath done his neighbour wrong privily'. As might be imagined, this technique, like the sieve turning when the name of a suspected thief was mentioned, tended to be most effective when the client of the cunning man or woman already had a shrewd suspicion of the identity of the thief. A good example of what must have been a common practice comes from Essex in 1578. One of a number of former clients coming to a cunning man, Miles Blomfield of Chelmsford, in this instance in the hope of recovering stolen linen, described how, a few days after an initial consultation, Blomfield invited him to look into a magic glass, and 'as farr as he could gesse, he shulde see the face of him that had the said lynnen'. The client asked the cunning man for confirmation that the face he saw was indeed that of the thief, but Blomfield declined to do this. He had provided his client with the mechanisms for making a choice, but was unwilling to make it for him. In this, as in other cases, the face seen in the magician's glass was that which the client already had in mind.[15]

Most cunning folk were simple local practitioners, depending on rudimentary spells, a knowledge of herbal remedies and the resources of local knowledge and local gossip to help them identify suspected thieves and supposed witches. Some, however, were people of at least a little learning whose techniques shaded off into those of the educated medical practitioner or astrologer. Such people inhabited an intellectual frontier zone between popular and élite magical beliefs. Among them was Anthony Ledgard of Heckmondwike in Yorkshire, consulted by Thomas Armitage in 1649 about the theft of wool from a relative of his. Armitage went to Ledgard because he was 'a man comonly reputed and taken to be one who can tell where goods lost or stolne may be founde', yet more evidence of how a cunning man or woman would enjoy a local reputation for their skills. On Armitage's arrival, Ledgard commanded 'a little wench in the howse' to bring him 'an almanacke as he called it', and also consulted another book. He then told Armitage that 'he found by the plannetts that it was of the ayre of water and saide I find that lighes between 10 or 11 o clocke . . . in a taverne or tarnpitt covered with much wood', and continued to give further information in that vein. Ledgard was evidently a superior quality of cunning man, literate and using astrological jargon to lend authenticity to his prognoses.[16] Other evidence suggests that he was not a unique figure, while local sources also demonstrate that, perhaps less commonly as the seventeenth century progressed, educated people were willing to dabble in this type of magic. Thus visitations in Elizabethan Yorkshire revealed, disturbingly for the authorities, a number of clergymen who practised sorcery, while in 1585 the parishioners of Great Bardfield in Essex presented their schoolmaster before the local archdeacon's court as one who took it upon himself to tell fortunes and provide charms for agues. We must remind ourselves that concern with magic and witchcraft was not limited to the ignorant or illiterate.[17]

The rewards of being a cunning person are difficult to assess, but those at the upper end of the trade could probably make a comfortable living. In one extreme case Richard Bernard recorded having a conversation with a Cambridgeshire cunning man who reckoned he could earn £200 a year, a good income at a time when a skilled craftsman would be unlikely to earn more than a shilling a day. Others seem to have taken much less, apparently undermining the contemporary assertion that they were 'all meerely coseners and deceivers . . . to deceive you of your money'. Anne Urmestone, a Lancashire cunning woman examined in 1630, claimed that she never took any money from her clients, 'but what they would give her of good will'. Henry Baggilie, who, as we have seen, cured men and animals with a prayer he had learned from his father, denied taking silver or any reward other than 'meale, or cheese, or commodities of the like nature'. A similar disregard for material rewards was demonstrated by a supposedly deaf and dumb cunning man who arrived in the house of Lancelot Milner at Nesfield in Yorkshire in 1651. The man, whose name was unknown to Milner, was sought after by 'wenches' desiring to know 'what husbandes they should have, whence they should come: whether they should be widdowes', and by men inquiring after stolen horses. The man (who, according to a passing soldier, came from the London area) answered these inquiries 'by signes in chalke, and poynting with his hand', and, according to Milner, many of those so advised declared that 'the sayd dumbe man did directe them very truly'. Yet he took only a penny, two pence, a can of ale or in some cases nothing for his advice, one local woman claiming that he 'to her knowledge demanded nothing of any either by signes or otherwise'.[18]

Thus cunning folk provided useful services, were seen as beneficial by the local populace and, despite the fulminations of theologians and the efforts of the local courts, proved impossible to eradicate. Their significance in the history of English witchcraft is considerable. The investigation of their activities by local authorities, and the descriptions of those activities given by hostile writers, furnish considerable evidence on popular ideas about magic and witchcraft and how these ideas interacted with everyday concerns: human sickness, livestock disease, stolen goods, the identity of a future husband, the sex of an unborn child. Some of them at least provide us with evidence of what was happening in the frontier zone between what we are pleased to divide into popular and learned beliefs. And, perhaps most importantly, they demonstrate the problems many contemporaries had in differentiating between 'religion' and 'magic', or, as contemporary theologians might have put it, between right religion and devilish superstition. Cunning folk used occult knowledge or supposedly inbred magical powers, but both they and their clients saw their activities as being compatible with good Christian beliefs: after all, the cunning man and woman used prayers as they worked and, if we are to trust the learned writers, most people thought that they derived their powers from God. That the services of such people were to be sought well into the nineteenth century is proof of the enduring conviction that they offered something of value.

Ɔ Our initial exploration of popular witch beliefs as they existed between about 1550 and 1650 would appear to demonstrate a simple dichotomy between the opinions of learned writers and those of the populace at large. The former were concerned with the theoretical problem of witchcraft and were convinced that malefic witches and cunning folk alike derived their powers from the devil. The common people were less interested in theory and less concerned with diabolic input, especially where the cunning man or woman was concerned. They seem to have been more worried about concrete issues – the tangible harm that a bad witch might do and the tangible good that might result from consulting cunning folk. Yet this polarized view of beliefs, and the related notion that English witch beliefs were non-diabolic, are over-simplifications.

The gulf between learned theory and popular practice was, in fact, filled with a shifting and developing body of ideas of considerable richness.

Perhaps the best documented of these beliefs, and certainly one of the most instructive, is the notion of the witch's familiar spirit. The origins of the concern over familiars, it seems likely, lay in the activities of élite magicians and sorcerers in the Middle Ages. They were frequently alleged to operate with the assistance of a demonic spirit, while other magicians, until well into the seventeenth century, regularly attempted to raise spirits. Although the presence of familiars may never have been a necessary element in an English witchcraft trial, the idea that a witch was usually assisted by a familiar in the shape of an animal constantly recurred in pamphlet accounts; indeed, it was present in two of the first surviving pamphlets concerned with witchcraft, both published in 1566, one describing the trial of malefic witches in Essex, the other the investigation of a learned Dorset cunning man called John Walsh.[19] However learned the origins of the notion of the familiar, it was evidently one which had entered the popular consciousness: by the mid-seventeenth century witnesses describing the activities of witches in Devon regularly deposed that they used toad familiars.[20] The precise reason for the prominence enjoyed by familiars in accounts of English witchcraft remains elusive. Certainly, the employment of the familiar by the witch was not a major theme during the development of demonological theory on the Continent during the fifteenth and sixteenth centuries, and an examination of secondary literature suggests that the Basque country was the only zone other than England where witches were commonly held to use such spirits.[21]

Yet they were present in accounts of English trials from 1566, and the descriptions of them create problems for the allegedly non-diabolic nature of English witch beliefs. In the very first pamphlet account of an English trial we have, which deals with three witches in Essex, we find that one of the accused, Elizabeth Francis, apparently confessed to having been given a familiar at the age of twelve by her grandmother. The familiar was in the form of a cat which she called Satan (or 'Sathan' in the contemporary spelling). The cat spoke to her, early in its career brought her eighteen sheep (the limit, apparently, of her perception of what wealth might be) and attempted to gain the love of Andrew Byles for her. She began to employ the familiar for malefic purposes when Byles refused to marry her, even after having had sexual relations with her. The cat first wasted his goods, then killed him. And, so the pamphlet runs, every time Sathan did something for her, he took a drop of her blood, which she gave him after pricking herself, sometimes in one place, sometimes another. The status of such pamphlets as a 'popular' art form, certainly in the early Elizabethan period, is uncertain, and we have no way of knowing how widely diffused the ideas about familiars contained in them were. Yet they clearly offer something very near to the satanic pact and, at the very least, demonstrate a potential perspective on English witchcraft beliefs other than that offered by village tensions and concern over *maleficium*.[22]

Later pamphlet accounts demonstrate the growing lore about familiars. In another pamphlet describing witchcraft in Essex, this time published in 1582, we find familiars portrayed more as domestic pets than as demonic spirits. These familiars had names, although 'Sathan' had been replaced by Jack, Robin and Tyffin, and they were kept in the houses of the supposed witches in a modicum of comfort: one eight-year-old girl described how her stepmother kept her familiars in 'a little lowe earthern pot' lined with wool, and fed them on milk out of a black dish. Witnesses in this case described hearing witches talking to their familiars as if they were children. Something of the flavour is conveyed by one of the confessing witches, who told how her four imps came to her 'a little before Michaelmas last', saying to her, 'I pray you dame give us leave to go unto Little Clapton to Celles, saying, they woulde burne barnes, and kill cattell'. In 1589 in another Essex case a witch, the octogenarian widow Joan Cunny, was said to have taken her newly acquired familiars 'home in her lap'; she then 'put them in a box and gave them white bread and milk'. Lest this last example should convey too cosy a view of the nature of familiars, it should be noted that the pamphlet described how they were acquired after Cunny had performed an invocation she had been taught by 'one mother Humpfraye of Maplestead' which included a prayer to 'Sathan the cheefe of the devills'.[23]

As the 1566 Essex case and the examination of John Walsh in that year both revealed, an integral part of the relation between witch and familiar was that the latter should be allowed to suck blood from the former. It seems that the earliest example of this practice occurred in Yorkshire in 1510. In the course of an investigation by the archbishop of the use of divination to find stolen treasure, a witness told how John Steward, a schoolmaster at Knaresborough, kept three spirits in the shape of humble bees, 'and gave each of them a drop of blood of his finger'. By 1566 this notion of the familiar sucking blood was clearly also current in the South-West and the South-East, and later accounts of trials mention it regularly. False allegations of witchcraft surfacing in London in 1574 included a claim that the witch's familiars took drops of blood from the forefinger of her left hand. In 1579 one of a number of witches accused at Windsor admitted to feeding her familiars with a drop of blood when she sent them to do harm. In 1589 a familiar in the shape of a ferret, again named Sathan, was supposed to have taken blood from the forefinger of a witch named Joan Upney, while in 1593 Mother Samuel, at the centre of allegations of witchcraft at Warboys in Huntingdonshire, included in her eventual confession the admission that her familiars sucked blood from her chin.[24]

It was obviously not a very large step to equate the witch's mark, already an established part of beliefs about witches, with the place from which the familiar sucked blood. In Continental demonological tracts the marks were often thought to be exotic in their shape, imprinted in the impression of the devil's claws or teeth, or taking the form of toad or spider. Such marks were thought to be insensible, and it was one of the indications that a suspect was a witch if a pin could be thrust into such a mark without causing pain or any bleeding. In England, the notion of the mark's insensitivity, although not entirely absent, was infrequently referred to, while the mark itself was frequently much more nondescript; indeed, the Cambridgeshire justice of the peace Michael Dalton suggested it could resemble a flea bite.[25] And by the time the first edition of Dalton's handbook for justices of the peace was published in 1618, it was firmly established in English witch beliefs that the mark was produced by the familiar taking blood from the witch. This notion was, if we are to trust the 1566 Essex pamphlet, already present in the early years of Elizabeth's reign. During the trial of Agnes Waterhouse, the Queen's Attorney asked her if her familiar sucked her blood. On her denying this, he instructed the gaoler to lift the kerchief covering her head, revealing marks on her face and nose. Questioned again, she confessed that her familiar had sucked her blood, although not for a fortnight.[26]

In the early pamphlet accounts the place where the witch was sucked varied: face, nose, chin and forefinger, but also thigh, shoulder and wrist. By the end of James I's reign, however, the mark was most often thought to be located on the genitalia or near the rectum of the witch. Elizabeth Sawyer, a Middlesex woman executed for witchcraft in 1621, confessed that the place where 'the divell suckt my bloud was a little above my fundament, and that place chosen by himselfe; and in that place by continuall drawing, there is a thing in the form of a teate'. The doctor John Cotta included a cautious discussion of the mark in his witchcraft tract of 1625, and noted that 'they are most commonly found in the privie parts'. By the time of the mass East Anglian trials of 1645–7 this notion was obviously widely accepted and most of the witches examined then were thought to have marks in what contemporary usage described as their 'fundament'. It is not, perhaps, over-fanciful to see in this belief an echo of that sexual prurience which was so manifest in some Continental accounts of the witch's relations with the devil. The notion that the witch had sexual intercourse with the devil came late to England and was never established very firmly. But the motif of the familiar sucking blood from or near the female witch's pudenda was a very close parallel; it is noteworthy that those trying Elizabeth Sawyer thought it worthwhile to ask her if she lifted her skirts while her familiar sucked blood from her.[27]

By the end of Elizabeth's reign, the devil was beginning to join his animal-shaped subordinates in the popular conception of witchcraft. There was, as might be expected, a certain conflation in the confessions of witches between the devil proper and the familiar spirit (the devil's custom of appearing in animal shapes helped confuse matters here). In the 1574 London case we have already alluded to, one of the girls making the false accusations claimed that her mother instructed her to pretend to see the devil 'as sometimes a man with a gray beard, sometimes lyke five cattes, sometimes to ravens and crowes, &c'.[28] The notion of connections between the devil and the witch was clearly present at the time of the Warboys case in 1593. At one point Mother Samuel confessed that she had 'forsaken my maker, and given my soule to the divell' ('these were her verie wordes', the account of the case assures us). She was perhaps taking her cue from one of the children she had allegedly afflicted, who told her 'thou hast foresaken thy God, and given thy selfe to the devill', evidence that such notions were common among the children of the provincial gentry. And when she claimed to be pregnant in court after sentence of death, the jury of women appointed to examine her (she being aged about eighty) found her not to be pregnant, 'unlesse (as some saide) it was with the divell'.[29] Sexual intercourse between the devil and the witch was rarely a salient feature in accounts of English witchcraft, but it was clearly not a totally alien concept.

The related notion of witches giving their souls to the devil was spreading by the early seventeenth century. When Agnes Pepwell, a Berkshire witch of that period, was questioned, it was assumed that the devil had tempted her to become a witch, and she had no problems in telling her questioners how he had done it. In 1608 a Church court defamation case from Bury in Lancashire turned on the comment, concerning some local women, that 'they are all witches, they have given theire selves to the devill'.[30] By about this time, indeed, the devil had begun to make appearances to witches in the shape of a man. In 1612 Ann Whittle or Chattox, aged about eighty and one of the central figures in the Lancashire trial of that year, confessed that some fourteen years previously she had decided to become a witch on the persuasion of another woman.

The devil appeared to her in the shape of a man, sucked blood from her side and gave her a familiar in the shape of a spotted bitch. In 1616 Mary Smith, accused of witchcraft at King's Lynn in Norfolk, was approached by the devil in the shape of a black man; he spoke to her in a 'low murmuring, and hissing voice' and offered her revenge on some of her neighbours whose superior skill in selling cheese had aroused her envy. Margaret Johnson, confessing during the Lancashire investigations of 1633–4, said that she met the devil in the shape of a man clad in black with silk points (i.e. the laces to attach sleeves to a man's doublet).[31]

Perhaps the key to popular conceptions of the connection between the witch and the devil lay not so much in popular views of witchcraft as in the popular image of the devil. The work of the nineteenth-century investigators discovered that the devil, albeit a very different being from the devil as conceived by early modern theologians, was a key figure in folklore, and there is no reason to suspect that the same was not true in the sixteenth and seventeenth centuries. A suggestion of one aspect of this is provided by Alexander Nyndge, who, when suffering fits as a result of diabolical possession in 1573, was described as 'monstrously transformed as it was before, much lyke the picture of the devil in a playe, with a horrible roring voice, sounding helbownd'.[32] People were convinced of the devil's existence, and of his capacity to appear on earth, something which made the meetings with the devil occasionally found in witches' confessions all the more plausible. Thus the papers of the clerical astrologer-psychiatrist Richard Napier include a number of references to people who thought they were afflicted by the devil or had met him. One such case from 1603 involved the miller of Foxley in Norfolk who, going from his water mill to his windmill, 'sawe as it were a man in blacke going before him'. The miller called to this stranger, 'desiring him to stay that he might have his company to the mill', upon which the man in black turned into a black dog, 'And when the miller came to the mill he sawe him agayne like a man. And as soone as he spoke to him he was turned into a blacke beare and so vanished away.'[33] The devil was evidently firmly established in the popular consciousness.

If the connection between the witch and the devil was slowly developing on a popular level, so too was the notion of the sabbat. In general, historians have been loath to accept that the idea of the sabbat took much of a hold in England. Ewen, in his pioneering book of 1933, thought that in English accounts of witchcraft 'little or nothing of the black mass is to be traced, and there is remarkably limited enterprise in the way of *al fresco* conventions', while more recently G. R. Quaife has declared that 'in England, witchcraft was neither a religion nor an organization. Witches in England showed no signs of co-operation with each other, no continuing or common aspect in ritual.'[34] Such statements are broadly correct. Contrary to some twentieth-century theories, we must reiterate, there is absolutely no evidence that early modern English witches were either organized devil-worshippers or the persecuted members of some pre-Christian religion. There is little trace in English trial records or in witches' confessions of the orgiastic or blasphemous sabbat which was to be found in Continental European trial records. Even English demonologists had little to say about the sabbat, probably regarding the writings of their Continental counterparts on such matters as the sorts of prurient fantasies which the popish imagination might engender. This lack of official or theological concern makes such traces of popular conceptions of the sabbat as do survive all the more intriguing.

On a very basic level, we should not be surprised that villagers suffering from witchcraft should think that their tormentors might act together; indeed, despite the notion that the English witch was essentially an individualistic agent of evil, early pamphlet accounts often describe three or so witches cooperating in working evil, while it is not uncommon for indictments reaching the criminal courts in the Elizabethan period to accuse two or three women from the same parish. What should be stressed is that in these early accounts there was little more than suspicions of ad hoc cooperation between witches and certainly little by way of organized rituals or the worship of a devil who was present in person. The pamphlet describing the Windsor witches of 1579 had about six of them coming together to plot *maleficium*, their meetings being presided over by a cunning man named Father Rosimond. Similarly, in the Berkshire case investigated in 1606, one of the suspected witches, Agnes Pepwell, told how she, Elizabeth Gregory '& some other wyches' met at 'a place called the fower ashes' to summon their familiars.[35]

The first approximation to a sabbat in England came with the Lancashire trials of 1612 and even here what appeared to have happened is far removed from the fantasies of Continental demonologists. This was a meeting of 'all the most dangerous, wicked and damnable witches in the country farre and neere', among them children and friends of witches under suspicion, held on Good Friday 1612. If the meeting took place, its purpose was almost certainly to allow those who were already suspected as witches to discuss the best defensive tactics as official accusations loomed. Yet the language used in the tract describing the case is suggestive. The coming together of the alleged witches was described as 'a speciall meeting', where the participants 'according to solemne appointment, solemnized this great festivall day according to their former order, with great cheare, merry company, and much conference'. Whatever really occurred, in his account of the incident Thomas Potts was obviously imagining something fairly organized. Indeed, a more developed notion of the sabbat was given by the central participant in the 'other' Lancashire trial of 1612, that of the witches of Samlesbury. Three women from that parish were accused of being witches by a fourteen-year-old girl called Grace Sowerbutts who, among other details, gave an account of being carried to a witches' meeting where the body of a recently deceased child was exhumed, cooked and eaten. The three accused were acquitted and it was noted, in an interesting indication of where 'Continental' demonological ideas might come from, that Grace had been schooled in notions of witchcraft by a Catholic seminary priest.[36] Even without such influences, ideas of the sabbat continued to crop up. Less than a decade after the Lancashire trials, over the border in Yorkshire, the teenage daughter of a family belonging to the gentry was able to imagine a witches' meeting. Helen Fairfax, supposedly possessed as a result of witchcraft, told how early in 1622 she came upon a meeting of witches near her home, dining off roast meat at midnight, with one of the suspected witches presiding and acting as cook. And there was another participant at the feast: at the upper end of the table sat the devil.[37]

By the end of the next decade another young girl, in this case a domestic servant, was clearly conversant with some folklorized version of the sabbat. In 1638 a number of witnesses gave evidence to the Devon quarter sessions concerning speculative gossip about witchcraft which centred on Jane Maxie. Maxie's version of the sabbat was again very different from that of the learned demonologists. According to her, every Midsummer Eve 'those that would be witches must meet the divell upon a hill and that then the divell would licke them and that place was black'. This process would be repeated on the following Midsummer Eve, when 'the divell would meet them againe, and licke them as before'. It is intriguing and instructive that a country girl in the South-West, apparently without recourse to the opinions of learned demonologists, was able to construct a notion of the sabbat. We are left to wonder how many other people similarly formulated individualistic, and folklorically based, conceptualizations of the sabbat when they discussed witchcraft.[38]

But five years before Maxie's opinions attracted the attention of the Devon justices of the peace, a much fuller view of the sabbat had been articulated, once more in Lancashire. In what could have developed into a witch scare of major proportions, a boy named Edmund Robinson claimed to have met with witches and been transported to the sabbat by them. Central government stepped in and prevented mass trials, but not before a few suspected witches had been examined. One of them, Margaret Johnson, told of meeting the devil, of entering into a pact with him, of having a familiar and of having sexual intercourse with it. She also told of being at a meeting with thirty or forty other witches, the objective of this meeting being 'to consult for ye killinge and hurtinge of men & beastes'. The witches had their familiars there, and there was also present 'one greate or grand devill or spirit more eminent than the rest'. Johnson had also, probably as a result of memories of the 1612 trials, picked up the notion that Good Friday was 'one constant day for a yearly gen[er]all meetinge of witches'. What happened at the sabbat was described by the young Robinson. Meat and bread were freely available 'upon a trencher', and there was 'drinke in a glasse', both of which he refused. The witches, in groups of six, pulled on ropes which were fastened to the top of a house, and at their pulling roast meat, butter and milk came into sight, all of it falling into basins placed under the ropes. Robinson was later to retract his accusations, but, as with Jane Maxie, we are left to speculate on how the notions that formed his and Margaret Johnson's imagined sabbat came together. What is clear is that popular views about witches were able to develop and become more elaborate while having only very uncertain contact with the concepts of the learned.[39]

In this survey of beliefs current about witchcraft in Elizabethan and early Stuart England we have come a long way from the two best-documented themes, the accusation of malefic witchcraft following a neighbourly altercation and the activities of the cunning man and woman. These two areas were of central importance to popular witchcraft beliefs, but such beliefs also comprehended a much wider body of notions about what witches did and how they fitted into the broader pattern of popular cosmology. Often we have been forced to argue from isolated scraps of evidence, but the reconstruction of most aspects of the mental world of our unlearned forebears has to be based on scanty and imperfect materials. Even this initial survey has demonstrated the diversity of beliefs, and also the apparent capacity of these beliefs to change over time. It has also posed the question of the relationship (to return to that tiresome but necessary dichotomy) between élite and popular culture. What is obvious is that any idea of a straightforward model of witchcraft beliefs being imposed on the populace from above is vastly over-simplified. As can be seen with familiars, the demonic pact and the sabbat, what might have originated as an élite concept could be incorporated into popular thinking about witches, but was frequently changed in the process. And we should never forget that notions about witchcraft were part of a much wider set of beliefs, incorporating both 'superstition' and popular religion. Unravelling these beliefs and tracing the connections between them are tasks which historians have only just begun to undertake.

CHAPTER 3

The Theological and Legal
Bases for Witch-hunting

● As we have seen, for Reginald Scot scepticism about witchcraft was compatible with being a good Protestant to the extent that for him witchcraft was something most easily believed in by Roman Catholics, or by those who had not emerged from the superstition and ignorance which he held to have flourished under popery. He would have been surprised by the way in which a number of twentieth-century historians have connected the prosecution of witches in England with the arrival of a harder-line Protestantism, by the way witch-hunting in Lowland Scotland after 1590 was encouraged by a Calvinistic Kirk and indeed by the tendency for the authorities in a number of Catholic territories, notably Spain, Venice and the Papal States, to take a comparatively relaxed attitude to witchcraft. Despite differences in emphasis, Catholic and Protestant demonologists shared much theological common ground in their discussions of witchcraft. After about 1560 the rulers of both Protestant and Catholic states were concerned with similar campaigns for ideological conformity and political obedience, and the position of witchcraft on their respective agendas had no obvious connection with the side of the religious divide on which they stood. In England, as elsewhere, it is possible to trace the growth of both a theological rationale for attacking witches and legal sanctions against them. But, again as elsewhere, the growth of these ideological foundations of witch-hunting has to be treated as something more complex than the simple outcome of monolithic élite fears.

There existed, however, a consistent strand of theological thinking about witchcraft which, while never becoming ideologically hegemonic, did colour many educated people's thinking about the subject, or at least gave them a set of points of reference to which they could turn if ever they needed to know more about witchcraft. This strand of thinking will form our main concern in this chapter, and our main source, initially, will be a body of demonological works produced by English writers between 1590 and 1627, the English contribution to a much broader and more substantial corpus of works on demonology produced in Europe during the period of witch persecution. It is in these works that the modern reader will find collected the clearest and most elaborate discussions about witchcraft, and this, if nothing else, justifies the analysis of such books. But before starting, two points need to be made. First, ideas on witchcraft and demonology can be found scattered in the theological writings of the period (texts dealing with idolatry, notably those found in commentaries on the Decalogue, would, for example, seem to be especially promising in this respect), and a full discussion of learned theological views on witchcraft would have to be based on a more comprehensive reading of the religious works of the period than I have attempted here. And second, it is somewhat artificial to label the writers of demonological tracts as 'demonologists'. If the English experience is typical, most of the writers of such tracts produced not only books about witchcraft but also a wide-ranging oeuvre of theological and pastoral works, and there is sometimes a distinct impression that our understanding of their thoughts on demonology would benefit from their being placed in the context of this wider writing. Indeed, it would seem that the authors of the big English works of demonology were writing from the perspective of a broader set of Protestant concerns about the nature of sin, the nature of true godliness and the need to attack what they described as 'superstition'.

Of the English writers of demonological tracts, by far the most distinguished was William Perkins (1558–1602). The leading English Protestant thinker of his day, Perkins was a theologian of international repute whose works were translated into every European tongue from Irish Gaelic to Czech. Noted in his student days for recklessness, profanity and drunkenness, he went through a typical Puritan conversion process, triggered, tradition has it, when a woman who saw him in the street tried to frighten her child with the sight of 'drunken Perkins'. The reformed young man took his M.A. at Cambridge in 1584, became a fellow of Christ's College and subsequently enjoyed a remarkable career as a preacher, a theological writer and a university teacher. His *Discourse of the damned Art of Witchcraft* was published posthumously in 1608, apparently having originally appeared in the form of a series of sermons. The book did not enjoy the international currency of some of his more mainstream writings, but English adherents of witch prosecution were, for a century to come, to take comfort in the fact that so eminent a person had written in support of their position.[1]

Although Perkins's book is unusual in its complexity, solid scriptural basis and the reputation of its author, a number of other English writers put their thoughts on witchcraft into print. Even before Perkins's tract was published, another clergyman with a Cambridge background, Henry Holland, published *A Treatise against Witchcraft* in 1590. In 1616 John Cotta, a Cambridge trained physician, published his *Tryall of Witch-Craft*. Cotta's book is interesting in that it provides a medical perspective on the subject and, although Cotta was a believer in witchcraft, he was sceptical about most popular beliefs surrounding it. In the same year Alexander Roberts, an obscure clergyman living at King's Lynn in Norfolk, published *A Treatise of Witchcraft*, a brief tract in which theoretical points were discussed before turning to an account of the prosecution at King's Lynn of a witch called Mary Smith. A more substantial work came in 1617 with Thomas Cooper's *The Mystery of Witch-Craft*. Cooper was another orthodox Protestant clergyman, vicar of a Coventry parish when the book was published and author of a number of other tracts, including one celebrating England's deliverance from the Gunpowder Plot. Perhaps the most important of these works, however, was Richard Bernard's *A Guide to Grand Iury Men with respect to Witches*, published in 1627 and reprinted in 1629. Bernard (1568–1641), another product of Christ's College, Cambridge, was a well-connected Puritan divine who combined being a religious controversist with a long record of effective ministry in the Somerset parish of Batcombe. His *Guide* was an influential book which, as I shall argue at a later point, serves as an exemplar of a distinctively English demonological style.[2]

Whatever the allegedly distinctive features of Protestant, Calvinist and Puritan writings on demonology, the basic premise of all the English demonologists was the one that had been developed in the formative period of demonological theory in the fifteenth century: for witchcraft to operate the three elements that needed to be present were divine permission, satanic power and human agency in the form of the witch.

The emphasis on divine permission leads us back to one of the major concerns of Christianity: how to account for the presence of evil in the world. In particular, to allow the devil complete free agency to wreak evil would be to attribute to him powers equal to those of God; to adopt this dualist position would be to fall into the temptations of Manichaeanism, that recurrent heresy which had first been outlawed by Christian theologians in the third century. Thus all demonologists had to face the problem of warning their readers of the power of the devil, while also delimiting that power sufficiently to preclude any break with theological orthodoxy.

The early sections of Perkins's *Discourse of the damned Art* demonstrate the difficulties. The devil was setting up on earth 'a spirituall regiment of sinne, as a meane to encounter the kingdome of grace, and, if it were possible, to bring the same to ruine'. Yet despite these ambitions, as Perkins told his readers, witch-craft, 'a wicked arte, serving for the working of wonders', was assisted by the devil only 'so farre as God shall in iustice permit'. Or, as Alexander Roberts put it, 'if God did not suffer it, neither the divell, nor the witch, could prevaile to do any thing, no not so much as hurt one bristle of a swine'.[3] The reason God permitted the devil and his witches to do such harm as they did was, all writers agreed, to chasten sinful humankind: to punish sin directly; to punish human-kind's ingratitude in not accepting revealed truth; to shake up the godly who were lapsing into sinfulness; to test Christians to see if, under adversity, they would cleave to God or desert Him for the devil. For Thomas Cooper, Satan could be 'God's instrument to execute his iudgements in the world', or 'the instrument of divine justice upon the children of disobedience'.[4] It is instruct-ive that the Book of Job should figure so prominently in the English witchcraft writers' repertoire of scriptural texts.

Thus the devil, although a real force on earth and an essential element in witchcraft, did not have universal power. The point was well explained by John Cotta:

Though the divel indeed, as a spirit, may doe, and doth many things above and beyond the course of some particular natures; yet doth hee not, nor is able to rule or com-maund over generall nature, or infringe or alter inviolable decrees in the perpetuall and never-interrupted order of all generations, neither is he generally master of universall nature, but nature master and commander of him. For nature is nothing els but the ordinary power of God in all things created, among which the divell being a creature, is constrained, and therefore subject to that universal power.[5]

If the devil could do more than human beings, it was because he had a greater knowledge of nature than they had: the devil, as Perkins explained, was a spirit 'of great understanding, knowledge and capacity in all naturall things' who had the additional advantage of having been around for 6,000 years.[6] And as the theologians were keen to emphasize, the works of the devil were *mira* rather than *miracula*: that is, 'wonders' rather than those true miracles which could be performed only by God (or, in the case of those attributed to Old Testament prophets, through God's power) and whose age was, in any case, past. So for

Henry Holland 'sathan's woonders are produced of natural causes, & not supernatural, as Christ's were'.[7]

The wonders which the devil was able to perform, the demonologists were agreed, could be either illusory or real, but a desire not to risk overstating the devil's powers meant that demonological writers tended to categorize most of the wonders which the devil's agents, witches, performed as illusions. Thus for Perkins the shape-changing which figured so prominently in witchcraft lore was illusory, 'for it is a worke surmounting the devill's power, to change the substance of any one creature into the substance of another'. This point caused tremendous problems for all writers on the subject and their arguments around it sound very unconvincing to the modern reader. To continue with Perkins, the devil could not create a body or put a soul into a body,

> yet by his dexteritie and skill in naturall causes he can worke wonderfully. For he is able, having gathered together fit matter, to ioyne member to member, and to make a true bodie either after the likenesse of a man, or some other creature: and having so done, to enter into it, to moove and stirre it up and downe, and therein visibly and sensibly to appeare unto man.

The exact nature of the devil's powers, and the question of under what circumstances puzzling phenomena should be interpreted as of diabolical origin, were to remain problematic throughout the seventeenth century. All theologians agreed, however, as Cooper expressed it comfortingly, that although the devil's 'malice be infinite, yet his power is limited'.[8]

Theologians were also agreed that whatever the devil's other talents might be, he was extremely good at working on human frailty. The post-Reformation stress on humankind's innate sinfulness helped explain why individuals should want to become witches. Sinful humanity was only too prone to encourage, or at least not resist, the devil's advances: 'if the devill were not stirred up, and provoked by the witch,' wrote Perkins, 'he would never do so much hurt as he does'. Cooper voiced conventional Puritan wisdom when he declared that because of 'our owne cursed nature . . . we are sathan's slaves naturally', or referred to 'that corruption wherewith we are infected even from the mother's womb'. Against this general background, two more specific symptoms of depravity were thought to encourage men and women to enter into league with the devil and become witches. The first was that, as Perkins put it, 'the nature of man is exceeding impatient in crosses, and outward afflictions are so tedious unto mortall minds, and presse them with such a measure of grief . . . they care not what meanes they use, what conditions they undertake to ease and helpe themselves'. Thus people who were suffering unusual afflictions, or who wished revenge upon the world in general or on individual neighbours, or who wanted to improve their material lot, were all felt to be especially susceptible to the devil's wiles. And, conversely, there were those persons who were over-curious about nature or over-ambitious to know its secrets (the Faustus legend again), people engaged in what Cooper described as the 'search after knowledge and hidden mysteries', or who were 'young scollers puffed up with knowledge' and were thus attracted to magic.[9] Throughout, indeed, there was a feeling that the sin of pride put the individual at risk of falling into witchcraft. Overall, however, there was a feeling that people who ended as witches had to want, or at least behave as if they wanted, to be tempted, and that the devil was quite capable of matching the temptations he offered to what he perceived to be the weak points of the individual potential witch.

To the English demonologists, the fundamental step in becoming a witch was making a pact with the devil. 'The ground of all the practices of witchcraft,' wrote Perkins, 'is a league or covenant made betweene the witch and the devill; wherein they doe mutually bind themselves to each other.' There was, unfortunately, a major stumbling block here: as Perkins admitted, there was little by way of scriptural reference to the pact, although it was frequently referred to 'in the writings of learned men, which have recorded the confession of witches'. Puritan logic helped underpin this firsthand evidence: the pact with the devil was the natural inversion of the covenant between the Almighty and the Christian, for, as Cooper declared, 'as God has his covenant with man: so will Satan have a special covenant also with his servants'. The conclusion to be drawn from this was that the witch was a traitor to his or her creator and had broken the covenant with God to make a pact with the devil. Cotta could refer to witchcraft as 'this high treason against God, and adherence unto his enemie the divell', and commentators on this point could always cite the biblical text equating rebellion with the sin of witchcraft.[10]

A wide range of beliefs more or less associated with witchcraft also attracted hostile comment. Astrology was singled out for special notice. As Perkins informed his readers, 'All the rules and precepts of astrology . . . are nothing els but meer dotages and fictions of the braine of man', while Holland attacked 'judicial astrologers, and devilish mathematicians, which under colour of false artes worke many evils by meanes of satan, that instructeth and prompteth them'.[11] Divination by other means, by charms or dreams for example, was equally reprehensible, as was attempting to raise spirits. What is striking, however, is the frequency with which Roman Catholic practices were directly attacked or popular superstitions abutting on witchcraft were equated with them. Perkins picked out making the sign of the cross, 'wherein the crosse carrieth the very nature of a charme, and the use of it in this manner, a practise of inchantment'. More generally, Cooper thought witchcraft was most likely to exist 'where grosse ignorance and popery most aboundeth, or where the truth of God is with-held, and prophaned, by unrighteousnesse and hypocrisie'. He noted that the 1612 Lancashire trials occurred in a region of 'grosse ignorance and popery', while Richard Bernard was just one writer to comment on how witches tended to use 'popish lip-prayers, ave maries, beads and pater-nosters by set numbers' as their charms.[12]

The disapproval of 'superstitious' beliefs and practices, whether tainted with popery or not, extended to those forms of counter-magic which were so important an element in popular reactions to witchcraft. Exorcism was clearly impermissible. 'The gift and power of casting out devills and Curing witch craft,' wrote Perkins, 'be ordinarily ceased since the apostles' times, it beeing a gift peculiar to the primitive church, and given to it onely during the infancie of the Gospel.' As Bernard put it succinctly, 'divels are to be cast out onely by the finger of God'.[13] Given this general position, specific popular remedies against witchcraft were equally reprehensible. Perkins attacked the scratching of witches, the burning of animals supposedly bewitched, the burning of the thatch of suspected witches' houses and the swimming test, declaring, 'God hath imputed no such virtue in their natures to these purposes, or added the same unto them by speciall and extraordinarie assignment.' But it was the scratching of witches to draw blood from them which seems to have aroused his special disapproval. A person scratching a witch, according to Perkins, 'may be healed, but the truth is, he sinneth and breaketh God's commandment. For the using of these meanes is plaine witchcraft.' Scratching was 'a means which hath no warrant or power thereunto, either by the word of God, or from nature, but onely from the devill'.[14]

Even greater odium was reserved for cunning men and women. The general line of thought was that these supposedly good witches, like bad ones, derived their powers from the devil, and the fact that they used these powers under pretence of doing good made them doubly worthy of censure. All writers attested to the popularity of the cunning folk. Perkins wrote how people resorting to them claimed

they for their part meane no hurt, they know no evill by the man whome they seeke to, they onely send to him, and he does them good, how and in what manner they regard not . . . may they not in extremitie repaire to the inchanter, and see what he can doe for them, rather than their goods and cattell should be lost and spoyled?

'Such miserable people,' declared Henry Holland, 'commit a most horrible & dreadful sinne, that they are iustly brought into sathan's snares, for the contempts of God and his word, that they seeke helpe of the same serpent that stung them.' The cunning folk themselves, 'blessers and good witches, as we call them,' wrote Thomas Cooper, were 'commonly ignorant, prophane and superstitious', and were 'verie dangerous instruments, for the restoring and encrease of the kingdome of Antichrist'. The powers attributed to them, all writers agreed, could not come from God, and must therefore have come from the devil. 'Death, therefore,' concluded Perkins, 'is the iust and deserved portion of the good witch.'[15]

In the face of witchcraft, English writers agreed, all that the afflicted could do was pray and throw themselves upon the mercy of God in the hope of divine assistance. Rather than turn to counter-magic or cunning folk, argued Perkins, 'it behooveth us rather to get unto ourselves the precious gifts of faith, repentance, and the feare of God, yea to goe before others in a godly life and upright conversation, then to excell in effecting of strange workes'. Victims of witchcraft should 'enter into a serious examination of themselves', turn to prayer and fasting, and remind themselves that their affliction was God's will. Cooper urged that such people should 'search out the true cause of this affliction, namely their sinnes'. Obviously, to these clerical writers here as elsewhere the presence of an effective ministry was of vital importance in leading the individual believer along the right path. Holland emphasized the role of the pastor in generally keeping up high standards of godliness when trying to advise his flock in matters of witchcraft, while Cooper thought that 'the planting and the continuancy of a settled and powerful ministry' was of key importance. Sure of their faith and assisted by godly ministers, good Christians could stand against witchcraft: 'if any keepe the commandements of God, and constantly, by a lively faith, cleave fast unto Christ,' Alexander Roberts reassured his readers, 'he shall overcome'.[16]

In general, then, the English Protestant demonologists' treatment of witchcraft fitted into the broader programme of establishing right religion: 'where the light of the Gospell hath once taken footing . . . so satan falls downe like lightning,' wrote Thomas Cooper, while 'at the preaching of the gospel . . . the grosenesse of witchcraft is well cleared, and banished'.[17] These writers did not involve themselves in those more extreme fantasies which mark the pages of so many Continental tracts: the orgiastic sabbat, infanticidal midwives, unbridled copulation between witches and demons and so on. Their concern was almost as much with what they saw as the ungodly superstitions surrounding cunning folk and counter-magic as with the demonic witch. Indeed, English demonological writers often placed themselves in the somewhat paradoxical position of decrying popular beliefs about witchcraft as avidly as they attacked witchcraft itself, which frequently results in what seems to the modern reader to be a somewhat muted tone to their works. Yet even if the prurience and near hysteria of the *Malleus Maleficarum* were absent, these English writers left their readers in little doubt as to where witchcraft fitted into the cosmic order of things. Witches, according to Perkins, were to be extirpated not because they killed or harmed people but because they were in league with the devil, because they were traitors who had renounced God and formed a pact with the devil. And the devil, as all good English Protestants knew, was locked into a permanent struggle against God and his people. 'There are two spiritual kingdomes in this world,' wrote Henry Holland, 'which have continual hatred & bloody wars, without hope of truce for ever. The lord and king of the one, is our lord Jesus, the tyrannical usurper of the other, is sathan.' And, as Holland continued, 'albeit sathan have many champions, and many artes . . . there is no arte more effectuall and dreadfull in my judgement, then those his wicked faculties in witchcrafte'.[18] To combat this damned art, however, more was needed than sound religion and a godly ministry; these were of fundamental importance, but they had to be reinforced by secular authority, with wholesome laws added to the word of God.

 ● Thus by the 1620s there was a substantial body of demonological works in print in England. Yet it is one of the peculiarities of English witchcraft that this demonology completed its evolution more than fifty years after the introduction of the main legislation against witchcraft. The repeal of the 1542 act in 1547 left England without statutory provisions against witchcraft, and during the brief and troubled reigns of Edward VI and Mary Tudor the presence of more urgent matters on the political agenda rendered the enactment of any new law unlikely. But the death of Mary and the accession of the Protestant Elizabeth paved the way for renewed legislation. To the extreme Protestants who returned from exile abroad or emerged from imprisonment or hiding in England, the way now seemed clear for the building of the godly commonwealth. And such a commonwealth needed, among many other things, sound laws against witchcraft. One of the returned Marian exiles was John Jewel, shortly to be Bishop of Salisbury and one of the first apologists for the Elizabethan Church. At some point in the winter of 1559–60 Jewel, who had already written to the Continental reformer Peter Martyr about the prevalence of witchcraft in western England, found himself preaching before Elizabeth. Among other things, he warned her:

it may please your grace to understand that this kind of people (I mean witches and sorcerers) within these few last years are marvellously increased within this your grace's realm. These eyes have seen most evident and manifest marks of their wickedness. Your grace's subjects pine away even unto the death, their colour fadeth, their flesh rotteth, their senses are bereft.

Jewel's remedy for this situation was that effective laws should be put into practice against witches.[19] Just over a year later another influential figure in the Elizabethan Church, Edmund Grindal, then Bishop of London, wrote to the Queen's Secretary, William Cecil, urging the Privy Council to take action against a priest who had added 'magic and conjuration' to his attachment to popery and noting that consultation with the Lord Chief Justice had revealed major gaps in the secular law against such offences.[20]

It is, however, easier to assert a general link between a resurgent Protestantism and the passing of laws against witchcraft than it is to demonstrate direct connections. As so often with Tudor legislation, the exact background to the eventual Elizabethan statute passed in 1563 remains difficult to reconstruct. It seems that in 1559 a bill was introduced in the Commons attempting to revive the repealed Henrician legislation against conjuration and witchcraft, prophecies and buggery (that is, male homosexuality and bestiality). The bill received its second reading in the Lords, but progressed no further. It was revived in February 1563, with the next sitting of Parliament, and another repealed Henrician act, that protecting masters from robbery by their servants, was added to the proposed legislation. On reaching the Lords, the bill (presumably under official influence) was split into four separate acts. Thus although the exact circumstances of the origins and progress of the 1563 act remain elusive, there can be little doubt that it was seen, both in the Commons and in governmental circles, as part of a wider legislative programme aimed at ensuring the security of the Elizabethan regime. There is no method of reconstructing the contribution of bishops to debates in the House of Lords, but it is probably worth noting that that Congregation was sitting and discussing godly reforms at the same time as the statute was being debated.[21]

The limitations of godly influence were, perhaps, demonstrated by the way in which the statute defined witchcraft in terms of *maleficium* rather than an alliance between human beings and Satan. The preamble of the act, in what was the entirely conventional rhetoric of such documents, noted that since the repeal of the Henrician legislation the secular law had provided no punishment for witchcraft. As a result, 'many fantastical and devilish persons' had

devised and practised invocations and conjurations of evil and wicked spirits, and have used and practised witchcrafts, enchantments, charms and sorceries, to the destruction of the persons and goods of their neighbours and other subjects of this realm, and further lewd intents and purposes contrary to the laws of almighty God, to the peril of their own souls, and to the great infamy and disquietness of this realm.

Witchcraft had, therefore, been identified as a problem by this legislation. Yet it was essentially harming by witchcraft, rather than the diabolic pact or connected beliefs, that was seen as the major issue.

The penalties to be inflicted for witchcraft under the 1563 act were firmly within the existing legal framework for dealing with felony. Killing persons by witchcraft was punishable by death without benefit of clergy. Witchcraft by which any person 'shall happen to be wasted, consumed or lamed in his or her body or member or whereby goods or chattels of any such person shall be destroyed, wasted or impaired' was to be punished on the first offence by a year's imprisonment, with exposure in the pillory in a market town four times within that year, and on the second offence by death. Using witchcraft or sorcery to find hidden treasure, or finding things lost or stolen, or with intent to provoke any person to 'unlawful love' or with the intent of hurting or destroying persons or their goods was punishable by a year's imprisonment and four sessions in the pillory for a first offence. On the second, offenders were to suffer forfeiture of all their goods to the crown and life imprisonment. Under this legislation killing or destroying persons was the only offence which, in the first instance, was punishable by death. And, it should be noted, death was inflicted by the standard method in English felony cases, hanging. With very rare exceptions, notably when a woman was convicted of killing her husband by witchcraft, and was hence guilty of petty treason rather than felony, witches in England, unlike their counterparts in many European states, were not burnt but hanged.

This legislation was extended by another statute, this being passed in 1604. Again, the exact background to the act is uncertain, although it was clearly connected to the accession to the English throne in 1603 of James VI of Scotland, a monarch with a known interest in witchcraft. The initial bill was examined by a fairly high-powered committee which consisted of six earls and twelve bishops, aided by a number of legal experts, among them Sir Edward Coke and Sir Edmund Anderson, the latter Lord Chief Justice of the Common Pleas and one of the few English judges known to have expressed a strong hostility to suspected witches. The outcome was a harsher act than the Elizabethan one. It retained the death penalty for causing the death of humans by witchcraft, and extended it to wasting, consuming or laming persons and wasting, destroying or impairing their goods on a first offence, and all forms of witchcraft on a second. The act also made it a capital offence to 'consult, covenant with, employ, feed or reward any evil and wicked spirit to or for any intent or purpose', and also 'to take up any dead man, woman or child out of his, her or their grave, or any other place where the dead body resteth, or the skin, bone or any other part of any dead person' with the intent of using them for any form of witchcraft, sorcery or enchantment. Clearly, the 1604 statute saw a shift from *maleficium* as the main matter of witchcraft legislation. Indeed, Wallace Notestein went so far as to suggest that 'one of the things which the framers of the statute were attempting to accomplish . . . was to make the fact of witchcraft as a felony depend chiefly upon a single form of evidence, the testimony to the use of evil spirits'.[22] At any rate, after this statute death could be, and was, inflicted for acts of witchcraft other than causing the death of humans.

The statutes of 1563 and 1604 constituted the main legislation against witchcraft, although it was also referred to (albeit in a tangential form) in a number of statutes concerned with the security of the realm. As we have seen, certain forms of prophesying had long been regarded as seditious, and the law against them was clarified by an act of 1581 (23 Eliz I, cap. 2) 'against seditious words and rumours uttered against the queen's most excellent majesty'. This act, as its title suggests, was mainly concerned with tightening up the law against seditious words, but as a by-product made legal provision for the possibility that the life and reputation of the monarch, along with the security of the realm, might be threatened by occult practices. In particular, those attempting to foretell the length of the queen's reign 'by setting or erecting of any figure or figures, or by casting of nativities, or by calculation, or by any prophesying, witchcraft, conjuration, or other like unlawful means whatsoever' were brought under the compass of the act, which prescribed death for those convicted. It is difficult not to concur with Professor Elton's conclusion that though half of Elizabeth's reign had passed before this act came into being, it does point to a growing fear of witchcraft.[23] We might add, however, that this growing fear focused on magic against the monarch rather than village *maleficium*. Once again we are reminded that witchcraft was more than just a matter of interpersonal tensions among peasants.

The laws against witches, once on the statute books, were enforced through a variety of courts. England, like most early modern states, enjoyed a complex court system and references to witchcraft cases can be found scattered in the archives of a number of types of tribunal. By the late Elizabethan period, however, prosecutions for malefic witchcraft were most likely to be tried at the assizes. The English assize system, originally set up in the late twelfth century, was a remarkably effective method of bringing centrally directed justice into the localities. Persons suspected of felony, usually after examination by a local justice of the peace, were held in the county gaol (typically housed in a more-or-less disused castle) until the arrival of the assize judges from Westminster. These came into the counties twice a year, normally in January or February and around Midsummer, two of them being allotted to each of the six 'circuits', or groupings of counties, into which England was divided for the purpose. Thus persons accused of witchcraft under the statutes of 1563 and 1604 were most frequently tried by professional judges (often men on their way to high legal office) who were agents of central government, who were trained in the law and sensitive to contemporary notions of standards of proof in criminal cases and who normally had little knowledge of and little interest in the local pressures which so often underlaid a witchcraft accusation. This situation can be contrasted with, for example, Scotland, where witches were frequently tried by commissions which, although granted by the central authorities at Edinburgh, usually consisted of local landholders and clergymen, with maybe a lawyer or two added. English witches coming to the assizes were at least being tried by professional judges unaffected by local animus against them.

But not all felonies were tried at the assizes. Some still went to county quarter sessions, although there is every indication that normally the county gentlemen who served as justices of the peace, while willing enough to examine suspected witches and commit them to gaol, were as unwilling to judge on witchcraft as on other capital offences at their sessions. Hence although Alan Macfarlane noted over sixty references to witchcraft in the records of the Essex quarter sessions between 1565 and 1664, few were formal indictments for malefic witchcraft; these were outnumbered by stray references to witchcraft, or cases involving a cunning man or woman.[24] Many boroughs possessed the right of gaol delivery and among the records of their courts it is possible to find scattered references to witchcraft prosecutions. Thus in December 1588 a woman named Thomasina Harris was indicted twice for witchcraft at the Norwich City sessions, and executed and gibbeted on one count, that of killing the daughter of John Lee. Between April 1589 and April 1591 another woman, Joan Balls, was indicted four times for killing children by witchcraft at the same court, in each case being acquitted.[25] Many similar cases may lie undiscovered in borough court records; the possible importance of such sources is indicated by evidence from Harwich, where five witches were executed in a local panic in 1601.[26] As well as such indictments for *maleficium*, the tendency to counter informal accusations of witchcraft with defamation suits meant that scattered references to witchcraft can be found in all manner of courts, from those of the local borough or manor to the Star Chamber at Westminster.

More importantly, minor forms of witchcraft and sorcery were presented at the ecclesiastical courts. Although the intent and result of the statutes of 1542, 1563 and 1604 were to place the prosecution of malefic witchcraft under the secular law, cunning folk, sorcerers and those charged with defaming people as witches might all come before the Church courts. We have already encountered Edmund Grindal as Bishop of London complaining about the lack of effective secular laws against witches early in Elizabeth's reign. He later became Archbishop of Canterbury, and his visitation articles of 1576 instructed clergy and churchwardens to inquire 'whether there be any among you that use sorcery or witchcraft, or that be suspected of the same, and whether any use any charmes or unlawful prayers, or invocations in Latin, or otherwise . . . and whether any do resort to any such for help or counsel, and what be there names'.[27] As a result of these and similar articles, references to witchcraft and sorcery are scattered among the records of bishops' and archbishops' visitations, and in the various ecclesiastical courts, notably those of archdeacons. Such references help add to our knowledge of those practices involving sorcery, charming, fortune-telling and conjuration which were unlikely to form the grounds for an assize indictment. Moreover, the Church courts constituted a handy forum where people might litigate against any of their neighbours slandering them as witches, and hence ecclesiastical court defamation suits contain many references to witchcraft.

As we have noted, the 1563 statute defined the legal offence of witchcraft fairly narrowly, and even that of 1604 extended that definition only in certain directions. Yet it is evident that all those processing witchcraft prosecutions as they went through the legal system, whether as accusers, witnesses, examining justices, jurors or assize judges, were having to come to grips with a wider range of ideas of what witchcraft was about and how it might be legally proved. The point is well made in a much-reprinted handbook for justices of the peace, Michael Dalton's *The Countrey Justice*, first published in 1618. In a slightly later edition, we find justices being guided through that thorniest of problems, how to establish legal proof in witchcraft cases: 'the justices of peace may not alwayes expect direct evidence, seeing all their [i.e. witches'] workes are the workes of darkness, and no witnesses present to accuse them'. So the investigating justice had to depend on other forms of proof. The two most important of these, according to Dalton, were the presence of a familiar, 'as in the shape of a man, woman, boy, dogge, cat, foale, fowle, hare, rat, toad, &c', and the presence of the witch's mark, 'some big or little teat upon their body, and be oftenest in their secretest parts'. For Dalton, 'These first two are maine points to discover and convict these witches; for they prove fully that those witches have a familiar, and made a league with the devil.'

He also listed a further thirteen points which indicated witchcraft: the existence of 'pictures of clay or wax' used in image magic; the personality of the witch; his or her 'implicit confession'; the suspect's taking too close an interest in the condition of the afflicted party, his or her appearance to afflicted parties in their fits, or the sick party calling out on them; 'the common report of their neighbours, especially if the party suspected be of kinne, or servant to, or familiar with' a convicted witch; the testimony of other witches; the bleeding of the corpse of a person supposedly killed by witchcraft if the suspected witch touched it; 'the testimony of the person hurt upon his death'; the examination of the children (if 'able and fit to answer') and servants of a witch; the witch's voluntary confession, 'which exceeds all other evidence'; and the finding of suspect materials in the witch's house. Thus by the 1630s justices consulting Dalton's handbook would come away with a wide range of notions about witchcraft. And it is noteworthy that in this handbook for working justices, Dalton acknowledges two main sources for his section on investigating witchcraft: Richard Bernard's *Guide to Grand Iury Men* and the 'booke of the discoverie of witches' written about the Lancashire trials of 1612.[28] His acknowledgement of these sources leads us to another avenue of approach in our attempts to understand the development of ideas about witchcraft in early modern England.

⊃ Our examination of ideas about witchcraft in Elizabethan and early Stuart England has revealed two gaps. The first is chronological: the major statute against witchcraft in this period was passed in 1563, yet fully articulated theoretical grounds for witch-hunting, at least as enshrined in the demonological tract, did not really develop until the early seventeenth century. The second is conceptual: there was, apparently, a massive gap between the central concern of the 1563 statute, harm done by *maleficium*, and the central concern of most demonological writers, the satanic pact and the witch's role as an agent of the devil. Arguably, what filled these gaps, for both contemporaries and later historians, was the growing body of tracts and pamphlets dealing with witchcraft trials published from the early Elizabethan period onwards.

Between the 1560s and the repeal of the witchcraft statutes in 1736 more than 100 tracts were published on witchcraft cases.[29] These varied enormously in length and complexity. Despite the modern tendency to think of such literature as a 'popular' form, some of these tracts were long (over 100 pages in some cases) and, as we shall see, sometimes examined the theological background to witch prosecution in some detail. Interpreting these texts is difficult: such matters as the objectives of their authors, the exact nature of the audience they were intended for and that audience's reactions to what it read all remain problematic. Yet they provide evidence of the complexity of beliefs about witchcraft and how these beliefs developed over time. These printed sources, which have not been analysed systematically for many years, provide an alternative view of witchcraft which falls, as it were, between the theological abstractions of William Perkins and the all too concrete concerns of a villager worrying about the bewitchment of his cattle. More relevantly to our immediate purposes, those published between the 1560s and the 1620s provide important evidence on the problem of the development of ideas about witchcraft.

The first English trial pamphlet was published in 1566. It appeared in three parts in the August of that year, and it dealt with the indictment of three women at the assizes at Essex (the relevant indictments survive in the assize files). The details of witchcraft given in it, allegedly based on the confessions of the three witches, confirm that, even at that date, people knew about familiars, the witch's mark and the notion of the witch making a pact, if not with the devil, then at least with a familiar, a pact that was sealed with the witch's blood. The anonymous author of this pamphlet was clearly presenting its readers with a more complex view of witchcraft than that of simple *maleficium*. The pamphlet was also introduced by a prose epistle and a verse preface which set witchcraft firmly, albeit in popular language, in the context of the struggle between God and the devil, between good and evil, between salvation and damnation. Whatever the veracity of the confessions attributed to the three women (Agnes Waterhouse, her daughter Joan and Elizabeth Francis), it remains clear that the author of this pamphlet and his readers were already seeing witchcraft as part of a wider intellectual and theological discourse. In this tract we can see an interplay between the 'learned' ideas of the author and (if we may trust the account of the confessions) of the ecclesiastical court judge and the assize judge who directed the interrogations of the witches, and the witchcraft of village tensions and personal animosities. Interestingly, the pamphlet also had an anti-Catholic slant: Agnes Waterhouse allegedly confessed on the gallows that although she went to church, she said her prayers in Latin because her familiar, named Sathan, would not let her say them in English.[30]

This first pamphlet was followed by a steady trickle of others which demonstrate the range of beliefs about witchcraft present in the Elizabethan period. One described a case involving witches at Windsor, with image magic, blood-sucking familiars, witches being able to tell what was happening at a distance, witches combining to perform evil and the causing of several deaths by witchcraft, including that of a former mayor of the town. This case led to four executions in 1579.[31] Another Essex incident, involving village *maleficium* and familiars, was described in a pamphlet of 1579.[32] Other pamphlets, some now lost, described a series of trials, mainly in the South-East: in London in 1574, Essex in 1579, Suffolk in 1581, two from Middlesex in 1585, Essex again in 1582 and 1589, Middlesex again in 1593.[33] A number of these tracts dealt with what was clearly one of the emerging themes in English witchcraft narratives, that of children or adolescents suffering from witchcraft-induced diseases or from possession as a result of being bewitched. Proof of the growth in the geographical spread of such cases came in 1597, when a pamphlet was published describing the sufferings of a youth named Thomas Darling, a thirteen-year-old from Stapenhill in Derbyshire, who allegedly suffered at the hands of a witch named Alice Gooderidge.[34]

Details of Thomas Darling's afflictions in fact emerged in print a few years after what was probably the most celebrated case of possession in Elizabethan England, that occurring at Warboys in Huntingdonshire. This episode, which provided the subject matter of a tract of over 100 pages and was apparently further publicized in a ballad, involved the bewitching of five daughters and a number of female domestic servants in the house of a gentleman named Sir Robert Throckmorton. Sir Robert and his wife, initially attributing the afflictions of the first child to suffer to a natural illness, called in a Cambridge physician, Dr Barrow, who, on being unable to effect a cure, asked if there were any suspicions of witchcraft. The Throckmortons' scepticism about such matters was eroded as others of their children fell ill in turn, and suspicions began to focus on a local woman with a bad reputation, Alice Samuel. A relative, Gilbert Pickering, took a hand in bringing the suspect to the Throckmorton household, whereupon the children fell into further fits and another relative, Lady Cromwell, fell ill and eventually died after an interview with the old woman. Yet another relative, Henry Pickering, some of his fellow Cambridge scholars and a number of clergymen were involved in investigating the case and giving succour to the afflicted. Suspicions spread to include Mother Samuel's husband and her daughter. The three were examined by the Bishop of Lincoln – Mother Samuel was by now so worn down that she was confessing to witchcraft – and were subsequently tried and executed at the Huntingdonshire assizes in 1593. The narrative of this case, in which the sufferings of the girls and their confrontations with the suspected witches were described in detail, set a pattern for its type.[55] The Warboys tract also demonstrates clearly how even very substantial families among the gentry could think their members afflicted by witchcraft: possession in such families presented a model for witchcraft which was, in both its form and its location in the social hierarchy, an alternative to that founded on fears of *maleficium* in the village community.

The widespread nature of concern over possession and dispossession, and the growing official interest in such matters, were emphasized later in the 1590s by the career of John Darrell. Darrell, a young and apparently undistinguished Protestant divine, achieved a certain degree of fame in the Midlands and north of England for his ability to help possessed persons. In 1586, aged not more than twenty, he exorcized a teenage girl called Katherine Wright at Mansfield, although consequent charges of witchcraft against a local woman named Margaret Roper were dropped. Darrell played a crucial role in the case of Thomas Darling, to which we have referred, shortly after which he was involved in the dispossession of seven persons (mostly children and young domestic servants) in the household of a Lancashire gentleman called Nicholas Starkie. The next case in which he was involved, which got him into considerable trouble with the ecclesiastical authorities, was at Nottingham, where a young apprentice musician called William Somers was suffering from strange afflictions. Under Darrell's direction, Somers declared that his afflictions were caused by witchcraft and named thirteen women as witches. In fact, all but two of these women were quickly released and, separated from Darrell by a sceptical group among the townspeople, Somers confessed that his afflictions had largely been simulated according to instructions from Darrell. The Archdeacon of Derby had alerted the Church authorities to what was happening and the

Archbishop of York appointed a commission to investigate the affair. Meanwhile, one of the accused witches stood trial at the assizes and the judge (Chief Justice Anderson, who in this instance was evidently in a sceptical frame of mind) dismissed the case and contacted the Archbishop of Canterbury, Whitgift, about it. As a result, Darrell and others involved in the affair were hauled before the High Commission in 1599, where it was judged that Darrell and his associate George More were impostors. This decision, coming after a lengthy controversy, combined with propaganda against Roman Catholic claims to be able to exorcize, served to discredit exorcism in the Church of England.[36]

If the pamphlets demonstrate a growing sophistication in theological debates about witchcraft, they also point to a firming up of legal proceedings against it. Perhaps the most interesting evidence on this point came in 1582 with the publication of a tract describing the prosecution of a number of witches living in and around St Osyth in Essex.[37] The author of this tract (again, a substantial work of around 100 pages) was almost certainly the examining justice Brian Darcy. This narrative is noteworthy for the depth of evidence it gives about the tensions which might underlie a local panic of this type, while it also demonstrates how the lore concerning familiars was developing. But it is mainly remarkable for showing what a justice of the peace, working within the English legal system, could do by way of orchestrating a set of witchcraft accusations. Darcy was apparently familiar with some Continental witchcraft treatises, which may have sharpened his hostility to witches; there were also rumours that his father had been killed through witchcraft, and the fact that the first suspicions arose among his tenants might have given a further edge to his interest. At the very least, his account of the interrogation of the suspects demonstrates how pressure and leading questions might bear fruit in detailed confessions. Thus Ursula Kemp, the first suspect, admitted to no more than having consulted a cunning woman in her first confession on 20 February, but by the time of her third on 24 February was confessing to owning a familiar (named Tyffin) and was accusing other women of keeping familiars and committing *maleficium*. More than ten women from St Osyth and adjacent parishes were indicted at the Hilary 1582 assizes, although it seems that only two were hanged. Darcy's handling of the case attracted heavy criticism in Scot's *Discoverie of Witchcraft*, and the published account of the trial was a factor in deciding Scot to write his sceptical work.

This description of a local witch panic leads us to what has become probably the most famous episode in English witchcraft history, the trial of the Pendle witches at Lancaster in 1612. Pre-trial examinations, depositions and confessions, along with summaries of the actual trials, were gathered and published by the clerk of the court trying the witches, Thomas Potts.[38] The content of this documentation still revolved mainly around *maleficium*, although there were some new emphases. Familiars were by now being conflated with the devil and were appearing before witches, tempting them with promises of vengeance or material reward and making pacts with them. There was a heavy stress on image magic. And, as we have already noted, in a reported meeting of 'all the most dangerous, wicked and damnable witches in the country farre and neere' at the 'Malking Tower' on Good Friday 1612, there was one of the first approximations to the sabbat to be found in an English source. Moreover, although his direct influence is less easy to trace than was Darcy's in the 1582 Essex case, it is evident that a local justice of the peace, in this instance Roger Nowell, played an active part in collecting evidence against the witches and was probably instrumental in coordinating their trials. These also depended heavily upon the evidence of a child, Jennet Device, daughter of one of the alleged witches. Although there is little evidence of theoretical demonological ideas affecting the examination of the witches or their trials, it is noteworthy that at various points Potts alludes approvingly to King James's *Daemonologie*, and it is possible that others involved, notably Roger Nowell, may have been influenced by it. Certainly, the evidence published by Potts demonstrates how witchcraft beliefs were growing more elaborate. Ten of these Lancashire witches were executed, as was one of their associates in Yorkshire, one suffered the lesser punishment of prison and the pillory, and five were acquitted.

Potts's very full account of the 1612 Lancashire trials was followed by a number of shorter pamphlets dealing with lesser incidents. Another account of 1612 mentions the trial and execution of five witches in Northampton (a contemporary manuscript account mentions five more). This episode is remarkable for being the first in England known to involve the practice of swimming witches, and also refers to the devil's ability to assume a bodily shape.[39] A year later a more elaborate account of the swimming test was contained in a pamphlet account of a Bedfordshire case. This involved the bewitching of a son and some of the servants of a gentleman named Enger by two women, who also destroyed one of his carts with the assistance of a familiar in the form of a black sow. Both were hanged.[40] Another case was described in a pamphlet of 1619, this time involving two women who were thought to have bewitched the children of the Earl of Rutland. This work, to which we have already referred, was remarkable for demonstrating how the aristocracy could still see themselves as victims of *maleficium*, while its introduction alluded to publications on witch-craft by King James, John Cotta, Alexander Roberts and George Gifford, men-tioned the Bedfordshire case of 1613 and also made reference to 'infinite other relations concerning the general conviction of witches, and their practices'.[41] Further credibility was added to witchcraft by an account published in 1621 by Henry Goodcole of the trial and execution of a witch named Elizabeth Sawyer from Edmonton in Middlesex. Goodcole, a respected minister in London, was the author of a number of tracts concerning the trial and execution of crim-inals, and his account of the Sawyer case, written in a factual style by a godly author, offered the reading public yet more detail on village *maleficium* and counter-magic, the ever-developing lore of familiars and courtroom practices.[42] As such, it serves as a suitable point to end our chronological survey of early English witchcraft trial pamphlets.

That this literature was incredibly rich in its description of witch lore, appar-ent even from the brief review offered here, will become clearer as we move on to examine some of the various themes in English witchcraft. What must be stressed is that these pamphlets did not merely describe witch beliefs and witch trials; they also located them in a moral framework. And this moral framework was one in which the devil featured prominently, and in which the witch was clearly seen as the devil's agent. The epistle to that first trial pamphlet, pub-lished in 1566, brought out the opposition of heaven and hell, and expressed the hope that 'by the admonition of this littel boke' its readers would learn 'to keepe our soules, by fixed and assured faith in Christ, from the sinking puddle of filthy pollution, then shal we escape from that horrible place prepared for the ungodly and wycked livers'.[43] The verse preface to this tract was written as 'an exhortation to all faithfull men; willing them to set God's feare before their eyes, and sathan's practices utterly to despise'.[44] The later pamphlets rarely lost sight of the didactic function explicit here: their readers had to be warned against witchcraft, but the warning was normally couched in terms of the war between God and the devil. And there can be little doubt that the tract writers were fully aware of a broader mission. Thomas Potts, in his account of the Lancashire trials of 1612, argued that such tracts as his were justified because 'it is necessary for men to know and understande the meanes whereby they [i.e. witches] work their mischiefe, the hidden misteries of their divelish and wicked enchantmentes, charmes, and sorceries, the better to prevent and avoyde the danger that may ensue'.[45]

What use such tracts as Potts's might be put to is demonstrated by a work referred to earlier, Richard Bernard's *Guide to Grand Iury Men* of 1627. Bernard, let us remind ourselves, was a well-known controversist, a clergyman of great learning and some reputation. It is therefore instructive to look into the origins of some of his ideas about witchcraft. Interestingly, although a number of others are mentioned, only two Continental demonologists, Del Rio and Bodin, figured prominently in his work. He also cited a number of English writers, notably Gifford and Roberts and (mainly in refutation) Scot. Equally numerous, however, were the occasions on which he referred to a wide range of the English incidents which we have encountered in our survey of pamphlet literature: the Warboys case, the 1612 Lancashire case, the cases from Bedfordshire and Northamptonshire, and the bewitching of the Earl of Rutland's children we have already encountered. Thus for this learned Protestant writer, putting together what was to be an influential tract (remember how Michael Dalton depended upon it), the printed accounts of English witchcraft cases which had appeared over the previous thirty years were as useful in constructing and illustrating his own views on witchcraft as were the works of the great demonologists. Indeed, at certain points the sources he used to illustrate his argument showed a cheerful willingness to draw equally upon English trial pamphlets and Continental demonological tracts – a nice indication perhaps that English beliefs were not as hermetically sealed from the wider European context as some historians have implied.

Bernard's book, first published two years after the death of James I, is a perfect point at which to end this examination of how ideas about witches were developing in the Elizabethan and early Stuart periods. As we have seen in this chapter, there was a demonological position on witchcraft and a rather different legal one. There was also, on the evidence of the witchcraft tracts, a third position, resting between the 'learned' view of witchcraft and the 'popular' one, drawing on and connecting with both of them. We do not know how widely these tracts and pamphlets were read, although some intriguing clues on this point occasionally surface. We do know that they give a view of witchcraft as part of what might be described as a practical demonology. This did not lay too great an emphasis on the devil, yet it saw witches as his agents and placed them in the context of that great struggle between good and evil, between God and Satan, which was central to the learned demonologists. It did not accept the absurdities of the sabbat or of copulation between witches and demons, yet it portrayed witches as something more complex than the mere launchers of *maleficium*. They were people who had entered into some sort of compact with evil and occult forces and were dangerous; people who had lost their own souls to the devil and were all too ready to harm those who had not. The pamphlet literature, combined with the more substantial demonological works and the practices of the courts, had created by the end of the reign of James I a rich and well-documented foundation for contemporary witch beliefs. It is a great irony that by that date the rhythm of witch prosecutions in the courts seems to have been slackening.

PART TWO

FIVE THEMES

Patterns of Prosecut*i*
and Punishment

A number of sources, of which the pamphlet literature dealing with witch trials is perhaps the richest, allow us to trace a developing set of beliefs about witchcraft and also confirm the impression that witchcraft trials could be noteworthy, indeed sensational, occurrences. But what these sources cannot do is show the relative frequency with which witchcraft came before the courts, the nature of the witchcraft which was prosecuted there or what punishments were inflicted on convicted witches. These problems can be examined only through the systematic analysis of court archives. Important pioneering work was carried out in this area during the 1920s by C. L'Estrange Ewen, and all subsequent researchers have been vastly in his debt. More recently, however, a number of other scholars have turned their attention to the investigation of early modern court records.[1] As a result of their labours, our knowledge of how courts functioned in this period, and how crime, including witchcraft, was dealt with by them, is now far deeper than that available to even so gifted an early researcher as Ewen.

One of the most important findings to emerge from this more recent work is that formal court prosecutions, for witchcraft as for other more mundane offences like theft, were often something only resorted to when other more informal means of settlement were exhausted. There existed, we must remember, a wide range of methods by which the threat of witchcraft could be combated or its effects alleviated other than taking the suspected witch to court. These alternative strategies were probably made all the more attractive by the knowledge that formal prosecution could be a troublesome and costly business. It involved the prosecutor in paying fees to the clerical staff of the court in question for

.g up the necessary documentation. It also involved the time, trouble and
ense needed to go from one's home to the town where the court was held,
_me which might entail loss of earnings. These considerations became even
more serious if the expenses of witnesses had to be met. Some accusations
were, of course, malicious; but in most cases taking a suspected witch to court
was not something to be embarked upon lightly. Where supporting evidence is
available, it is clear that the act of witchcraft recorded in a formal court document
as providing the basis for prosecution was often only the tip of a much larger and
more varied iceberg of deviant behaviour. Any attempt to understand witchcraft
in this period on the basis of criminal court archives has to accept that what
appears in the record is a selected sample of a much wider range of conduct.

This is merely to say that statistics of witchcraft prosecutions, like any criminal statistics (not least those dealing with crimes which occurred three or four
centuries ago), have to be treated with caution, and we need to be very careful in
what we allow ourselves to deduce from them. Even so, the counting of witchcraft cases is an important step towards our understanding of witchcraft as an
historical phenomenon. It shows us what aspects of witchcraft people felt were
worthy of prosecution. It shows us how the authorities, in the shape of the
judiciary, reacted to witchcraft accusations. And it affords us, through the
chance informal note on a court document or what we can deduce from formal
documentation, wider insights into contemporary ideas about what witches did
and what ought to be done about them. As we shall see, systematic analysis of
court records produces some unexpected results.

The initial step must be to consider the quantity and quality of such court records as have come down to us. As we have noted, a number of different courts
were empowered to deal with witchcraft. The Church courts, the county quarter
sessions and the courts of those boroughs enjoying a right of gaol delivery all
heard witchcraft cases. But by far the most important courts for dealing with
witchcraft as defined by the statutes were the assizes. As we have already seen,
twice a year, normally commencing in January and around Midsummer, two
judges were assigned to each of England's six assize circuits, riding off to carry
out a number of judicial tasks, which included the trial of criminals held in the
county gaols. It was they who, from the late sixteenth century onwards, most
frequently tried serious crime in the localities: homicide, grand larceny, burglary,
highway robbery, rape and witchcraft.

So the records of the assize courts are of vital importance to the historian of
witchcraft. Yet on turning to these records, we encounter one of the major frustrations which await the historian of witchcraft in England, and indeed of crime

in general in the early modern period. In theory, the courts of assize generated a mass of material relevant to the history of witchcraft.[2] Depositions, the pre-trial accounts of witchcraft suspicions taken by local justices of the peace, should have been sent to the assizes, as should recognizances, again taken by a justice, binding over prosecutors and witnesses to appear in court. Gaol delivery rolls and gaol books, giving skeletal but often vital details about offences and punishments, should have been drawn up by the clerical staff of the assizes. So too should the most important source for a statistical inquiry into witchcraft prosecutions, the indictment, which gave details of the alleged offence and, frequently, of the defendant's plea, the jury's verdict and any subsequent punishment meted out to the convicted witch. Doubtless, all of these documents were compiled; tragically, for reasons that are now largely obscure, the vast bulk of them have been lost. Before the middle of the seventeenth century, little survives apart from the indictments generated by the Home Circuit of the assizes covering the counties of Essex, Hertfordshire, Kent, Surrey and Sussex. Our immediate task will, accordingly, be to analyse this run of documents.

In studying the Home Circuit indictments we are fortunate in that a large amount of editorial work has already been completed on them. In early investigations into the sixteenth- and seventeenth-century court records, Ewen worked through them and produced a calendar of Home Circuit witchcraft accusations which is still an invaluable tool. This foundation was built on in 1970 by Alan Macfarlane, whose researches on the county which encountered the highest levels of witchcraft prosecution, Essex, added a number of new cases and gave more details on some which Ewen had already noted. Further light on this source (and details of a few more cases) came with J. S. Cockburn's calendar of Home Circuit indictments between 1559 and 1625. Combining the efforts of these scholars provides a firm basis for a statistical survey of witchcraft accusations in the South-East. Before we embark on this survey, however, we must consider two further problems.

The first, once again, is record survival. Although the survival rate of Home Circuit files improves markedly after about 1645, before that date something like a quarter of the files are missing. Thus any account of witchcraft drawn from these indictments is inevitably based on a sample of what was recorded in the Elizabethan and early Stuart periods, and we have no way of knowing how many witchcraft indictments have simply been lost from the series. The second, as was discovered when systematic work on early modern court records began in the late 1960s, is that the indictment is in many respects a very fragile historical source. Theoretically it should provide totally accurate information about a number of key aspects of a case, as factual inaccuracy on an indictment could, by law, have rendered a criminal charge invalid. In practice, however, the information given was frequently false; what was 'legally sufficient' for an Elizabethan assize clerk was not the type of accurate information which the modern historian, bent on quantifying, needs. Details of occupation or status were often inaccurate, a problem made doubly serious for historians of witchcraft by the practice of describing married women as spinsters, the notion being that this was legally more 'sufficient' than describing a woman as a man's wife. When other evidence, notably recognizances, can be used to check the information, it becomes apparent that the date of an offence as given on an indictment is frequently inaccurate, while depositions frequently show that the parish of residence of the offender given on the indictment was often simply the parish where the offence had taken place. These considerations place limits on the usefulness of much of the information contained in indictments.

Having noted these technical difficulties, let us now turn to tracing the main lines of the prosecution of witchcraft in south-eastern England between the accession of Elizabeth and the early eighteenth century. Leaving aside scattered references to suspected witches on gaol calendars or recognizances, there are 785 cases for which either an indictment for witchcraft or sufficient information to allow the reconstruction of the type of details which an indictment would provide survives.[3] These cases involved 474 alleged witches, 425 of whom (89.7 per cent) were women. As the figure shows, the pattern of prosecution is clear. There were few prosecutions in the immediate wake of the 1563 statute (although it should be noted that two indictments against a man for murder by witchcraft reached the assizes before that statute was passed[4]), but they then leapt to a total of 109 cases in the 1570s, 166 in the 1580s and 128 in the 1590s, these three decades accounting for just over half of the known prosecutions in the century and a half under consideration. Levels of prosecution then fell in the early seventeenth century, with only twenty cases in the 1620s and nineteen in the 1630s. The two middle decades of the seventeenth century, however, saw a revival in prosecutions, mainly due to a large outbreak in Essex in 1645, part of the wider East Anglian prosecutions associated with Matthew Hopkins, and a local panic in Kent in the 1650s. Thereafter, prosecutions declined rapidly in the South-East, tailing away markedly towards 1700.

Thus the evidence of the Home Circuit demonstrates two main features in the pattern of prosecution. The first is that prosecution was at its peak in the South-East during the reign of Elizabeth. Despite the 1604 statute and James I's earlier interest in witchcraft, the tradition that his accession to the throne led

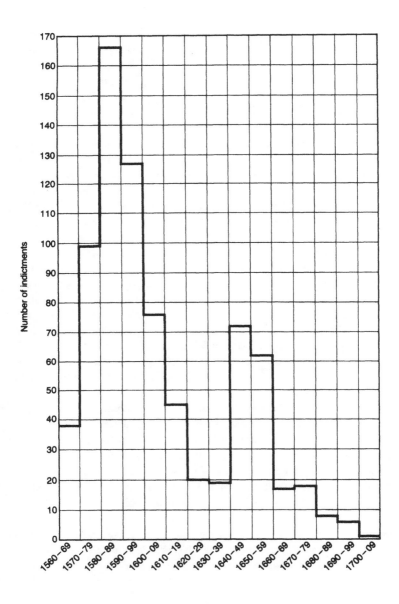

Indictments for Witchcraft, Home Circuit Assizes, 1560–1709 (by decade)

to an upsurge in witchcraft prosecutions is clearly groundless as far as this region is concerned. Assize files for the period 1600–1639 survive at roughly the same rate as they do for the Elizabethan period, so it is implausible that the fall in prosecutions is merely apparent, attributable to gaps in the records. Second, and following from this, it would seem that by the 1620s and 1630s the prosecution of witchcraft in south-eastern England was clearly tailing off. Too much should not be made of this limited sample of regional evidence, but it is intriguing to note that at about the same time witches were being hunted less avidly in a number of other parts of Western Europe. In France the high-class lawyers who staffed the Parlement of Paris were, by the 1630s, regularly rejecting the death penalty in witchcraft cases that came to them on appeal from provincial courts. In Germany, suffering from the impact of the Thirty Years War, the 1630s also witnessed a drop in trials, which in some German territories had been running at their highest in the two previous decades. There had already been little persecution of witches in the Dutch Republic since 1600, while in Spain, to take both the Dutch Republic and England's most deadly enemy, witchcraft accusations had fallen away after the Inquisition declared its scepticism about the value of witch-hunting in the face of mass prosecutions in the Basque country in 1612–13.[5] The falling off of trials in the South-East may, therefore, have been part of a more general Western European trend. In any case, it is tempting to argue that, but for the disruption of the Civil Wars and their aftermath, which led to a renewal of prosecutions in the 1640s and 1650s, witchcraft prosecutions on the Home Circuit might well have petered out around the middle of the seventeenth century.

The overall figures, however, disguise some major variations in the patterns and levels of prosecution experienced by different counties. Perhaps the most obvious of these, and one which still defies explanation, is the overwhelming contribution made by Essex prosecutions to the total. Four hundred and sixty-four indictments, naming 279 witches, come from Essex, in each case some 59 per cent of the total for the Home Circuit. The table below sets out the contribution of Essex and other counties to these totals.

As Table 1 (overleaf) makes clear, the contribution of the other counties on the Home Circuit was much smaller than Essex's. In Sussex, which in the years under consideration experienced only thirty-six indictments against sixteen witches, just one of whom was executed (in 1575), witchcraft was clearly, as far as the courts were concerned, a very peripheral problem. It was Essex which was responsible for the overall curve of Home Circuit indictments. Yet it should be pointed out that whereas Hertfordshire, Surrey and Sussex indictments showed,

Table 1: Witchcraft on the Home Circuit by County, 1560–1701

	Prosecutions		Witches	
	Total	Per cent	Total	Per cent
Essex	464	59	279	59
Hertfordshire	79	10	45	9.5
Kent	129	16.5	79	16.5
Surrey	77	10	55	11.5
Sussex	36	4.5	16	3.5

on a smaller scale, the same general patterns as Essex, Kent experienced a somewhat different flow of witchcraft accusations. There the peak of prosecutions
(thirty-three of 129) came in the 1650s. As we shall see, other counties experienced a peak in prosecutions mid-century, and it may well be that there was an
alternative pattern in prosecutions to the familiar Essex one.

Further complications arise when the punishment of witches is considered.
Surviving documentation shows that 209 of the 474 witches known to have
been indicted on the Home Circuit were found guilty. Of these, 104 (22 per cent
of the total indicted) were hanged and forty-seven (10 per cent) suffered the
lesser penalty of a year's imprisonment punctuated by four spells of standing in
the pillory. Of the remainder, seven were women who, after capital conviction,
convinced the court that they were pregnant. Under English law, a pregnant
woman could not be executed, and although these seven should have been
hanged after the delivery of their children, it is likely that a number of them, like
other women pleading pregnancy, would be reprieved. Indeed, some of the
pregnancies recorded by the courts under such circumstances were legal fictions
designed to allow the judge to extend clemency to female offenders. Eleven
convicted witches were subsequently reprieved, fourteen were pardoned and a
further fifteen were remanded, at the judge's discretion, before or after judgement; thus forty witches escaped the rigour of the law due to the clemency of
the judicial system. In a further nine cases we know from the indictment that
the accused was found guilty, although no details of punishment are given; one
convicted witch was punished by a spell in the stocks and a period of incarceration in the house of correction, and one, convicted for cozening by witchcraft,
suffered the cheat's punishment of being set in the pillory.

The chronological pattern of punishments is also clear. The period 1570–

1609 witnessed nearly two-thirds of the total of executions, sixty-four, of which fifty-three involved witches convicted in Essex. The crazes in Essex in the 1640s and Kent in the 1650s were largely responsible for the upsurge in executions in those two decades. As with accusations, however, the statistics of punishment make it obvious that witchcraft was being regarded very sceptically at the assizes in the South-East in the 1620s and 1630s. What is even more intriguing is the slightly earlier decline in the use of the secondary punishment prescribed by the statutes, imprisonment for a year and the pillory. Surviving documentation suggests that only four witches convicted on the Home Circuit after 1600 underwent this punishment. This again would point to scepticism on the part of the courts about the reality of less serious forms of witchcraft, although it is equally possible that the redefinition of witchcraft by the 1604 statute, which extended the range of alleged witchcraft punishable by death, might also have contributed to the decline in the imprisonment of witches. Even before 1604, the secondary punishments prescribed by the 1563 statute, by placing convicted witches in the unhealthy atmosphere of the early modern gaol, had the effect of ensuring that a number of them died: twelve of the thirty-one Essex witches sentenced to imprisonment and the pillory are known to have died in gaol, most of them of disease. Of the fourteen witches who were pardoned, ten were Essex witches who escaped the rigours of the law in the 1640s, while six of the fifteen witches who were remanded had been indicted in the 1640s or 1650s.

It is thus evident that witchcraft was not an offence with a high conviction rate. The 22 per cent of accused witches executed on the Home Circuit is a very low proportion when set against the figures derived from some Continental European samples. Ninety per cent of witches whose fates can be ascertained were executed in the Pays de Vaud between 1537 and 1630, 69 per cent in Luxemburg between 1509 and 1687, and 63 per cent in Neuchâtel between 1568 and 1677. The only place currently known to have experienced a capital conviction rate similar to south-eastern England was Geneva, where 21 per cent of accused witches were executed between 1537 and 1662, although it is the Finnish province of Ostrobothnia, with 15 per cent of 132 accused witches being executed between 1665 and 1684, which experienced the lowest proportion of executions yet discovered by historians.[6] Figures for punishments, and especially for executions, would therefore seem to support the suspicion that witchcraft was something which English judges were likely to handle in a cautious manner and that the judicial machine in England was never so consistently severe in its treatment of accused witches as were many of its Continental equivalents. Yet an observation needs to be made. It will be remembered that Home Circuit records reveal that over the period 1570–1609 sixty-four of 263 accused witches, or 24 per cent, were executed. This may be a low level of executions when compared to some Continental samples, but the proportion of hangings for these witchcraft cases is very much the same as that obtaining for all types of felony tried before English courts in the same period. In other words, it may have been a broader peculiarity of the English criminal justice system, rather than some peculiar attitude to witchcraft accusations, which accounted for the level of executions for witchcraft. Indeed, the English assizes were courts which, to modern eyes, had very low conviction rates generally. As we have seen, around 32 per cent of witches accused on the Home Circuit are known to have suffered punishment of some sort. Taking the Essex assizes and quarter sessions between 1620 and 1680, we find that the same was true of 45 per cent of those accused of burglary and housebreaking, 40.5 per cent of those accused of theft, 29 per cent of those accused of homicide and 19.5 per cent of those accused of rape.[7] Considered in the light of other serious offences tried before the English courts, rather than in comparison with Continental examples, the conviction rate for English witches does not seem too anomalous.

So, to summarize our findings so far, witchcraft accusations on the Home Circuit were declining by the 1620s, while, on at least one reading of the low levels of execution of alleged witches, the judicial attitude towards charges of witchcraft does not seem to have been severe. A third overall point needs to be made. Witchcraft as tried on the Home Circuit (and, as far as we can tell, before other assize courts) was essentially about *maleficium*. English villagers prosecuted their neighbours as witches not on the grounds of night-flying, intercourse with demons or taking part in orgiastic rites at the sabbat; they did so because they thought the alleged witch had done harm to them, their children, their spouse or their farm animals. In this, it is likely that English villagers shared the concerns of their counterparts in the rest of Europe. How this concern might manifest itself varied from region to region, but for most areas from which relevant evidence survives it is clear that the basic peasant concern when bringing a witchcraft accusation was with *maleficium*; it was the input from judges obsessed by or educated into demonological knowledge which was usually responsible for the more exotic aspects of witchcraft which surfaced in so many Continental courts. Yet, we must remind ourselves, the assize indictment was the result of a number of filtering processes and as such should not be taken as too rigid a guide to the nature of English witch beliefs. The statutes had not encompassed the totality of these beliefs, but rather defined what types of witchcraft might be prosecuted at the assizes. Most prosecutors were sufficiently hard-headed to know that certain forms of witchcraft were easier to 'prove', and hence more likely to form the basis for a successful prosecution, than others. Where they exist, depositions and pamphlet accounts of trials demonstrate that the relatively concrete accusations made in witchcraft indictments might be surrounded by a much broader range of ideas about witchcraft, ideas that were unlikely to intrude into the terse Latin of an indictment.

⊃ The evidence about witchcraft given on indictments must, therefore, be regarded as only one facet of a much broader corpus of evidence. Yet for our immediate purpose, the types of *maleficium* indicted must be considered more fully. The 785 indictments record 794 specific acts of witchcraft, the slight discrepancy in the totals being accounted for by a few indictments which record a number of alleged offences. Of these 794, thirty-six involved dealing with or raising spirits, and a further ten (some of them describing behaviour very similar to that found in the first category) involved cozening through sorcery or related offences. Against these figures may be set 415 cases in which adult humans were killed or injured through witchcraft, 161 where the victims were children, 164 where livestock or poultry of one sort or another had allegedly been harmed through witchcraft and a further eight where other forms of goods or property were harmed. Overall, *maleficium* figures in 94 per cent of all indictments for witchcraft tried on the Home Circuit.

Here as elsewhere the malefic witch was predominantly female. Overall, as we have noted, women accounted for just under 90 per cent of accused witches on Home Circuit indictments. This figure seems to have been fairly consistent over the period dealt with here, although it is perhaps worth noting that the proportion rose to 95 per cent of the forty witches prosecuted after 1660. In only one decade, the 1570s, did anything like a significant proportion of male witches appear, fourteen out of seventy, even here forming only 20 per cent of the total. The problem of gender and witchcraft will be addressed in Chapter 7, but two preliminary points should be made at this stage. The first is that, although most male witches tried at the assizes were accused, like women witches, of malefic witchcraft, a substantial minority of them were accused of practices for which women were rarely indicted, like cozenage through witchcraft or the use of spirits to discover sums of money. Thus Robert Chambers was indicted at the Essex assizes in 1577 for invoking evil spirits for the purpose of obtaining money, Thomas Barker was tried in the same county a year later for the same offence, William Bennet and Edward Mason were indicted on a similar charge in Essex in 1588, while Thomas Heather was similarly indicted in Hertfordshire in 1573. In 1598 another Essex case involved Robert Browninge, accused of conjuring to find sums of money and of cozening people.[8] So, while fewer men than women might be indicted, they were accused of a wider variety of acts involving witchcraft; accusations against women were limited almost entirely to acts of *maleficium*, while that handful which were not usually involved keeping familiars, supposedly in hopes of committing such acts.

Questions of gender also figure prominently when we turn to the alleged victims of witchcraft. On the strength of the Home Circuit statistics it is evident that if an overwhelming majority of alleged witches were female, so were a small majority of their supposed victims. Witches were accused of killing 149 adult and seventy-two child or adolescent females, and with harming a further seventy-five women and sixteen child or adolescent females. Male victims included 131 men and sixty-one boys or youths killed by witchcraft, with a further sixty men and twelve child or adolescent males harmed. Thus of 576 human victims, 312, or 54.2 per cent, were female, and 264, or 45.8 per cent, male. Fear of witches and suspicions of being bewitched were evidently not limited to men.

The sparse nature of the details given on assize indictments precludes a comprehensive description of the types of harm allegedly inflicted on humans by witches, but the evidence of depositions and pamphlets provides enough graphic accounts to compensate for this defect. What is obvious, though, is that death through witchcraft was rarely instantaneous. Far more common was death through a wasting disease, which must have given victims and their associates ample time to reflect on the likely source of their misfortunes. The standard formula on the indictment would relate how the victim had been bewitched on a certain date and that he or she had then lingered (the most usual translation of the relevant Latin terminology is 'languished') until the date of death. Occasionally more details are given, as, for example, in a Surrey case of 1567 when Sarah Caldwell, aged two, fell from her mother's arms into a fire as a result of witchcraft on 30 April, eventually dying of the injuries thus sustained on 29 September.[9] Similarly, details of the illnesses caused in non-fatal instances of witchcraft are normally absent, although indictments include references to such misfortunes as lamed legs, a paralysis of the right side of the body which prevented a stone-hewer from following his trade and blinding. These rare examples give us only a very imperfect insight into the range and intensity of afflictions which could allegedly be caused by a witch's malice.

The damage allegedly inflicted on livestock by witches varied enormously.

Sometimes the harm done by the individual witch to a neighbourhood's flocks and herds could be considerable. Elizabeth Brooke of Great Leighs in Essex, hanged for killing a woman by witchcraft in 1584, was also convicted for killing six cows and horses and mares belonging to James Holmested, a cow, five heifers and four hogs (valued at £10) belonging to James Spylman, two cows and two horses (valued at £5) belonging to Thomas Cornyshe and a number of sows belonging to George Fytche. Another Essex woman, Joan Thatcher, was convicted in the same year for killing three cows, ten sheep and a pig belonging to John Dix, a bullock, a cow, fourteen sheep, a pig and a sow belonging to Christopher Hamsteede, and a horse, a cow and a pig belonging to Nicholas Frende.[10] Overall, it has been estimated that in Essex between 1560 and 1680, 110 cows and calves, sixty-three horses and colts, 124 pigs and piglets, 123 sheep and ewes, and eleven chickens and capons were recorded on assize indictments as having been bewitched.[11] The impact on individuals of such losses should not be underestimated, for the economic consequences could be severe. When Sarah Kempsley was indicted in 1649 at the Kent assizes for killing four horses and four cattle by witchcraft, the £31 they were valued at represented roughly twice the then average annual income of an agricultural labourer's family.[12] Interestingly, cases involving the alleged bewitching of animals gradually decreased as a proportion of total witchcraft indictments on the Home Circuit: they constituted 25.5 per cent of the total between 1560 and 1609, 13.5 per cent between 1610 and 1659, and a mere 4 per cent between 1660 and 1709. Throughout, however, the owners of the cattle and other animals in question were male. Of 164 cases, only one – in Essex in 1588, when a cow, steer and lamb belonging to a widow named Joan Denfall were bewitched – involved a female owner.[13]

To some extent this decrease in the proportion of cases involving the bewitching of animals was offset by an increase in the number of accusations in which children figured as victims. As we shall see, more qualitative evidence provides considerable information on the role of children and adolescents as victims and accusers of witchcraft. The Home Circuit indictments demonstrate that, despite the dramatic impact which the bewitching of a child might have, children were, statistically, less likely than adults to be involved as the victims of witchcraft. Here as elsewhere, the information given on indictments is not as extensive as might be wished, and it is possible that as the ages of victims were not invariably given, a number of adolescent victims have been included with the adults in our calculations. But as a minimum figure, the documentation suggests that of 576 human victims of witchcraft, 161 (28 per cent) were children or adolescents, as opposed to 415 (72 per cent) who were adults. The number of cases involving children, in fact, was slightly exceeded by those involving animals. Yet by the closing phases of prosecution the proportion of cases involving children as victims was increasing, from 19.5 per cent of all cases in 1560–1609, through 20 per cent in 1610–59, to 32 per cent in 1660–1709. Whatever the figures, the loss or affliction of a child through supposed witchcraft must have been a highly traumatic experience. Witches were sometimes found at the centre of a tangle of accusations in which they had allegedly inflicted death or wasting illnesses on a number of children either in a parish or drawn from one family.

The other forms of damage inflicted by witchcraft constitute a scatter of cases which frequently represent areas of witches' supposed activities which, although doubtlessly annoying to those supposedly suffering from them, were rarely felt to be serious enough to be worth taking to court. An Essex case of 1582 involved the bewitching of twenty brewings of beer. In another, tried in 1589, Joan Dering (also accused of causing illness in two people by witchcraft) was accused of bewitching a pail of milk belonging to Stephen Clerke so that his servants were unable to turn it into cheese. Two years later another Essex witch (indicted on four other counts and hanged) was accused of bewitching four gallons of cream and preventing them from turning into butter.[14] More serious were two cases of committing arson by witchcraft. In the first, tried in 1584, an Essex yeoman named Edward Mansell was accused of using magic and incantations to burn a barn, a stable, a cartload of hay, a cart and its fittings, a wagon and harness, and domestic goods belonging to Edward Burgesse, the total value coming to £49 10s. In the second, tried in Kent in 1657, a woman was convicted and hanged for burning a barn and corn.[15] Serious damage by arson was likely to prompt an indictment, but charges of preventing beer from brewing or stopping milk from turning into butter or cheese, despite the probability that suspicions that witches were doing such things were widespread, were likely to surface as assize indictments only if the supposed witch was also being prosecuted on more serious charges.

Awareness that all but a few assize indictments centred on *maleficium* has helped support the claim that English witchcraft was little concerned with diabolism and hence was somehow different from 'Continental' witchcraft. Yet even this type of document provides occasional insights into wider beliefs about witches. Certainly, the case of Margery Smith, tried before the Sussex assizes in 1566 for sending two toads to suck the udders of a cow, suggests that even at the beginning of English witch trials there was a fairly wide view of what witches did.[16] The first indictment for keeping familiars (in the shape of a dog, a cat and a mole, all of them with pet names) comes from Essex in 1584. The same county provided a unique case in 1616, when a woman named Susan Barker was indicted for taking a skull from Upminster churchyard in the hopes of using it to bewitch another woman (Barker was, in fact, hanged for bewitching two men). A woman called Margaret Lambe was indicted, and acquitted, at the same session for consulting and entertaining evil spirits with the intention of exercising witchcraft, charming and sorcery with their aid.[17] It was not, however, until the Essex trials of the 1640s and the Kent trials of the 1650s that such accusations figured with any frequency in indictments. The persistence of these beliefs is indicated by some of the last cases tried on the Home Circuit, brought in Kent in 1692, when a widow and two labourers' wives were accused of consulting and covenanting with evil spirits in the shape of mice.[18]

The systematic working through formal court accusations which forms the basis of this chapter, although an essential exercise, tends not to reveal the fears and passions that so often lay at the basis of a witchcraft accusation. The indictment, that most austere of documents, rarely gives us much insight into human emotion. Even so, it is sometimes possible to trace a little of the fear and hostility with which a witch might be regarded. Occasionally, these can be inferred when a group of indictments was brought against a witch, especially if incidents which had occurred several years previously were remembered and used as a basis for an indictment. When Elizabeth Johnson was indicted in Kent in 1582 for the murder by witchcraft of a young boy who had died a few months before the assizes met, she was also tried for bewitching women in 1566, 1569 and 1576.[19] Other evidence of the degree of tension a witch might create around herself is demonstrated in some of the later indictments where considerable numbers of witnesses (not all of them, perhaps, hostile) might be involved. The indictment of three witches tried in Surrey in 1664 for (among other things) bewitching Naomi Fisher involved fifteen witnesses, including a medical doctor. A case in the same county a year later involved twelve witnesses, while another Surrey case, tried in 1682, involved eighteen. When Katherine Barren or Barrett, a Woolwich widow, was tried at the Kent assizes in 1671 for consulting with, entertaining, employing, rewarding and feeding a familiar spirit in the likeness of a rat, sixteen witnesses were called. When a Kent labourer named Thomas Whiteing was accused in 1681 of bewitching Sara Curtiss, twenty witnesses, including three medical doctors, were involved.[20] Pamphlet accounts of trials from this later period, which often contain good accounts of witnesses' statements, demonstrate a tremendous range of tensions, emotions and, by the late seventeenth century, degrees of scepticism.

⊃ The Home Circuit assize indictments, whatever their defects, are clearly the most valuable source we possess upon which to base a discussion of patterns of witchcraft prosecution. A number of other court archives exist, however, which permit comparisons. One of the richest of these, and one very relevant to our discussion of witchcraft accusations on the Home Circuit, is the archive of the ecclesiastical courts of Essex. Witchcraft references in these records have been listed by Macfarlane and provide yet more evidence for the high levels of witchcraft accusations in the county, and for the peculiar chronological rhythm which such accusations followed. Macfarlane found 277 references to witchcraft in Essex ecclesiastical records, of which the bulk (247) appeared in the records of the courts of the archdeaconries of Essex and Colchester (court records for the archdeaconry of Middlesex, which had jurisdiction in the north-west of the county, do not survive). Most of these references are to less serious aspects of witchcraft accusations: sorcery, going to a cunning man or woman, slander cases prompted by accusations of witchcraft. Relevant records for the archdeaconry of Colchester do not survive before 1573, but those for the archdeaconry of Essex reveal nineteen presentments (formal charges) for witchcraft and related matters in the 1560s, and twenty-three in the 1570s. In the 1580s, the period of maximum prosecution at the Essex assizes, cases before the Church courts increased dramatically, with sixty-four presentments in the archdeaconry of Colchester (compared with eight in the period 1573–9) and twenty-nine in the archdeaconry of Essex. The two courts combined to hear sixty-seven presentments in the 1590s and twenty-three in the first decade of the seventeenth century. Thereafter cases were reduced to a trickle in the Archdeacon of Essex's courts, the last case in the archdeaconry of Colchester being presented in 1611. The pattern of ecclesiastical court presentments for witchcraft in Essex was, then, very like that experienced in the county's assizes: a massive rise of cases in the 1580s and a fairly rapid decrease in the early seventeenth century.[21]

Few other bodies of Church court materials have been systematically searched for witchcraft cases and the most that can be said at present is that such searches would probably reveal wide regional variations. Thus in Wiltshire study of Church court records has revealed few traces of witchcraft. In Yorkshire a steady trickle of presentments came to the attention of the ecclesiastical authorities, although fewer than might have been expected given the Calvinistic leanings of all the archbishops of York between 1570 and 1628. A total of 177 cases relating to witchcraft or similar matters was recorded in the archbishops' visitation records between 1567 and 1640. The nature of most of these was unspecified, sixty-two of them being listed simply as 'witchcraft' or 'charming'. Of the remainder, eighteen were concerned with the placing or lifting of spells on animals, and nineteen with the casting or lifting of spells on human beings. Only four or five of the cases involved cursing or malefic witchcraft. Twenty-four of the offenders were simply dismissed by the court, there is no evidence of an official decision being reached in twenty-one cases, while twenty-four offenders were ordered to do penance (thirteen of them while making a 'declaration') in their parish church. The low level of presentments for witchcraft and sorcery and the lenient treatment which alleged witches were afforded by the archbishops' officials suggest that, however much clergymen might deplore witches and their works in the abstract, they were unwilling to see that general sentiment translated into harsh measures against individual witches.[22]

Although, as we shall see, some records of the Northern and Oxford circuits of the assizes survive from the later seventeenth century, the only circuit other than the Home for which a good series of records survives, even for a limited period, is the Western, for which gaol books exist from 1670.[23] This was, of course, the period of the decline in witchcraft prosecutions, and the Western records are especially tantalizing as they show that levels of prosecution then were higher in the South-West than in the South-East, possibly pointing to a peak in indictments, now lost to the historical record, in the middle of the seventeenth century. The details of prosecutions given in these gaol books, essentially abstracts of the information given on indictments, are sparse and only skeletal information can be gleaned from them. Nevertheless, they permit the reconstruction of the basic details of seventy indictments. Half of these fell in the period 1670–79, twenty in 1680–89, eleven more in 1690–99 and four between 1700 and 1707, in which year the last witch prosecuted on the Western Circuit, Mary Stevens, was acquitted on a charge of bewitching another woman. Fifty-two witches are named in the gaol books. Forty-nine were women, so this admittedly small sample shows a higher proportion of female witches, 94 per cent, than that found on the Home Circuit.

The limited nature of the information given in the gaol books makes it impossible to provide even as much detail about the nature of prosecutions as that given in Home Circuit indictments, but a few points of comparison can be made. First, there is an impression that in the South-West harming people through witchcraft was more frequently prosecuted than killing them. The phraseology used in the later gaol books makes it impossible to follow this line of argument through, but in the 1670s, when the books allow analysis of this type, witches were accused of killing thirteen people and harming twenty-one. Here, as on the Home Circuit, by this date witches were hardly ever accused of bewitching animals: only one such case was recorded, when Elizabeth Peacocke was accused of killing eight geldings and seven mares in 1672. It was probably the high value of these animals, £150, that prompted her accuser, Henry Dennynge, to take her to court, while Peacocke, who had already been tried for witchcraft in 1670, was also being indicted for killing four women by witchcraft. Of the human victims a high proportion, forty-six out of sixty-eight, or 67.5 per cent, were female, although the nature of the records does not allow calculation of how many of them were children. Most of those accused, even for capital witchcraft, were acquitted. One woman was sent to the house of correction, one was bound over to be of good behaviour after acquittal, one was remanded after capital conviction and four were hanged. Three of these, Temperance Lloyd, Susanna Edwards and Mary Trembles, were sentenced at the summer 1682 assizes in Devon, and a contemporary pamphlet confirmed that they were indeed executed. The fourth, another Devon woman named Alice Molland, was sentenced in 1685. If this sentence was carried out, Molland has the distinction of being the last person known to have been executed for witchcraft in England.[24]

It is unfortunate that the only English county enjoying a similar (indeed superior) run of records to those surviving for the Home Circuit, Cheshire, experienced little by way of witchcraft accusations.[25] The records of the Palatinate Court of Great Sessions at Chester, the local equivalent of the assizes, survive in a virtually unbroken series over the period with which we are concerned, and form a major and as yet virtually unworked source for the historian of serious crime. Research carried out in the 1920s by Ewen, weaving together the evidence of indictments, crown books and crown plea rolls, reveals sixty-nine formal charges of witchcraft, all of them falling within the period 1589–1675. The pattern of prosecutions was very different in Cheshire from that obtaining on the Home Circuit. A trickle of cases passed through the Court of Great Sessions in the late sixteenth and early seventeenth centuries, but they were largely concerned with sorcery, prophesying and conjuring. A woman called Ann Acson was indicted for bewitching cattle in 1590, but the first indictment for malefic witchcraft against persons did not come until the September 1613 session, when two women had seven indictments lodged against them. Accusations continued throughout the 1620s and 1630s, but were still concerned with a wider range of problems than *maleficium*. A man called John Davies was accused of practising medicine through magical arts, another, John Hockenhall, was accused of buggery and sorcery and another was tried on suspicion of conjuring. It was, indeed, the involvement of the Court of Great Sessions in such cases that accounts for the high proportion of male witches in the total for Cheshire, thirteen from forty-seven, or 27.5 per cent.

Malefic witchcraft was prominent in the business of the Court of Great Sessions only in the 1650s, when it figured in nineteen of the twenty-two witchcraft cases tried, with, correspondingly, seventeen of the eighteen accused witches being female (the only male witch was accused of being a wise man and claiming to help people to find stolen goods). The records do not allow us to calculate how many of the witches' alleged victims were children, but the witches accused in the 1650s were charged with killing six females and four males by witchcraft, harming two females and four males and harming cattle on two other occasions. Witchcraft subsided in the court's concerns fairly rapidly after 1660, with five prosecutions in the 1660s and two in the 1670s, the last coming in 1675. Only eleven of the forty-seven witches are known to have been found guilty. Three suffered secondary punishments, one was pardoned after successfully pleading pregnancy and seven, all of them women, were sentenced to be hanged. The first of these died in 1631, five more in the 1650s (three of them in 1653 for bewitching the wife of a gentleman named Ralph Furnivall to death). The last, Mary Bagnley, was sentenced in 1675, although a gap in the crown plea rolls at that point prevents confirmation that the sentence was carried out. The occupations given for both the victims and the accused (or, to be more accurate, the husbands of accused women witches) show that in Cheshire, as in the South-East, witchcraft accusations were essentially the business of the middling and lower orders: labourers, husbandmen, artisans, tradesmen and women drawn from the same social strata.

Another run of figures can be drawn from the records of the Middlesex sessions. The legal status of this court was complex, but, briefly, it enjoyed a jurisdiction equivalent to that of the assizes. Its records exist from the mid-sixteenth century, but only in a very imperfect series; it is probable that something like a third of the Middlesex sessions' records for the sixteenth and seventeenth centuries have been lost. Such records as did survive were edited in the late nineteenth century by J. C. Jeaffreson, and his findings were subsequently reworked by Ewen. These findings have been challenged by a recent thesis completed by Barbara Singleton, which has uncovered more references to witchcraft in the Middlesex records, but until she is in a position to publish her findings we must continue to base our analysis on Ewen's calculations.[26] His and Jeaffreson's work demonstrates that as with the assizes and Chester Court of Great Sessions, the archives of the Middlesex sessions record references to witchcraft in a number of ways, but some sixty-three indictments survive from between 1574 and 1659 (the last reference given by Jeaffreson, the binding over of a woman to appear before the court to answer suspicions of witchcraft, comes from 1673). These indictments, which name forty witches, formed only a very small part of the total of indicted crime in the county. Middlesex, some parts of which, abutting London, were already built-up areas, suffered from a relatively high rate of serious crime, with property offences predominating, and witchcraft was, statistically, of very limited importance. We have evidence of 7,660 cases tried before the Middlesex sessions between 1550 and 1625, of which 7,158 were property offences, 400 homicide and infanticide, and a mere twenty-one witchcraft.[27]

The sixty-three cases of witchcraft tried in Middlesex between 1574 and 1659 constitute a small but typical sample. Thirty-four adults and twenty-two children and adolescents were allegedly killed or harmed by witchcraft, with harm to animals figuring in another seven cases (the last of these being tried in 1614). Three cases involved sorcery or invoking spirits, and a further two cozening by witchcraft. The periods of heaviest prosecution, on Ewen's evidence, came in 1610–19, with fifteen cases, and 1650–59, with nineteen (the recent research by Singleton has emphasised the peak in the 1610s, adding a few more indictments, and, interestingly, relating this fluctuation to a local witch scare). Of the forty indicted witches, thirty-five were women and five men. Six of the accused, all women, were hanged, the last of them, accused of bewitching five children, in 1653. Two other women (one of them named Dorothy Magicke) were sentenced to prison and pillory, a fate probably shared by two more women who were found guilty but for whom no details of punishment survive. Another of the accused, a Stepney spinster, was acquitted in 1657 but, obviously felt to be a bad character, she was sent to the house of correction, while an alleged witch named Josia Ryley apparently dropped dead in court ('*mortuus in facie curie*') while being tried in 1597. The totals of cases and witches are too small to make deep statistical analysis a meaningful exercise, but it is worth noting that 87.5 per cent of the accused witches were women, 25 per cent of witches were convicted and in Middlesex, as in Kent and Cheshire, the peak period for witchcraft prosecutions was the 1650s.

Evidence from only two further assize courts, the Northern and the Oxford, survive in anything like a useful quantity, and even here the records provide little assistance in charting the long-term flow of witchcraft prosecutions. Northern Circuit records include both indictments and depositions, but commence in anything like a series only in the 1640s. The indictments contain few witchcraft cases, and, in so far as anything of consequence can be said about them, they indicate a steady decline in accusations from the mid-seventeenth century, the last indictment coming in 1691, when a Yorkshire labourer's wife named Mary Hansom was accused of bewitching and wasting Richard Robert.[28] Only a few indictments survive for the Oxford Circuit, but these can be supplemented by a series of gaol books which commence in 1658. These reveal eight suspected witches in the last years of the 1650s, twenty-nine in the 1660s, one in the 1670s and four in the following decade, the last coming in 1689. Nine of these forty-two witches were men, although at least two of them were indicted as cunning men, charged with using sorcery to help people find stolen goods (ironically, one of these, Richard Butter, tried in 1659, was also indicted and hanged for burglary). Only one of the suspected witches, Mary Denton, indicted at the Stafford assizes in 1664, was found guilty, although it is unclear whether she was executed or suffered a lesser penalty. Thus on the Oxford Circuit as elsewhere, by the later seventeenth century witchcraft accusations were being brought to the courts in the face of an almost total unwillingness to find witches guilty.[29]

So we have examined a range of surviving court records with the objective of producing findings that may be used for comparisons with the patterns of the prosecution and punishment of witchcraft revealed by the analysis of Home Circuit records. The task has not been an easy one. Western, Oxford and Northern Circuit records contain only late indictments, although the evidence from all three regions suggests that levels of prosecution were falling away from a mid-century peak. The records of the Court of Great Sessions at Chester and of the Middlesex sessions, although covering a chronological span similar to that enjoyed by the Home Circuit indictments, recorded little by way of witchcraft prosecutions, although they do concur in showing that the most common period for such prosecutions in these counties was the 1650s. The records of all areas demonstrate that execution for witchcraft was a very rare phenomenon after that decade, although the Western Circuit gaol books show that witchcraft prosecutions were being brought with some regularity throughout the 1670s. Other common features included the high proportion of women among the accused and the rarity with which the bewitching of animals featured in these later trials, the concentration being almost exclusively on incidents where human beings were victims. The records of the ecclesiastical courts obviously need further attention, but it is likely that with them also, although different regions might well demonstrate different levels and chronological patterns of prosecution, the witchcraft coming before the courts – namely sorcery, the activities of cunning folk, the charming of cattle and slander cases arising from allegations of witchcraft – was probably broadly similar nationally.

⊃ The investigation of the prosecution of witchcraft in the English courts can, therefore, provide only incomplete and in some respects contradictory results. To some extent this is a consequence of the exigencies of record survival. In particular, given the high levels of witchcraft prosecution in Essex, the loss of the archives of the adjacent Norfolk Circuit of the assizes is particularly regrettable, as, given the nature of its records when they do commence, is the loss of Western Circuit records before 1670. Perhaps the most unwelcome consequence of this limited survival of court records is that it renders any attempt to calculate the numbers of persons tried and executed for witchcraft in England little more than an exercise in educated guesswork. Ewen, whose guesses in this respect must be regarded as more educated than most, thought that 1,000 executions was the upper limit for England and that the real total was probably considerably lower. More recently, Christina Larner, in a persuasive critique of Ewen, has suggested that the total was probably less than 500.[30] Research carried out for the present book does little to challenge these estimates, and it would seem that a total of somewhere less than 500 executions for witchcraft in England between the passing of the first statute in 1542 and the eventual repeal of all witchcraft statutes in 1736 would be correct. Once again, we are reminded that the interest and significance of witchcraft cannot be measured in terms of the frequency with which its alleged perpetrators were convicted at England's courts of law. And, once again, we must regret the massive gaps in the relevant court archives which will prevent us from ever possessing categorical evidence on this point.

Yet such documentation as does survive provides a solid basis from which a number of important matters can be investigated: the relative proportions of male and female witches; the frequency with which witches were convicted and punished; and the nature of the offences for which witches were indicted. From these investigations a number of conclusions can be drawn: witches were overwhelmingly female; levels of execution for witchcraft in England were lower than in most Continental areas for which we have evidence; the peak periods of prosecution were, according to region, the second half of Elizabeth's reign and the period 1640–59; and indictments brought at the assizes were usually concerned with *maleficium*, with doing harm by witchcraft to humans, animals and, more rarely, other property.

Consideration of the levels of witchcraft prosecution and the fate of accused witches leads us back to the theme, already touched on, of the degree of concern felt by the judicial and ecclesiastical authorities in England about witchcraft. As we have seen, laws were passed against witchcraft, theologians like William Perkins wrote tracts against witches and there is every reason to think that a large number of people believed to some degree in the reality of the witch's ability to do harm, a proportion of them on occasion considering themselves to be the victims of witchcraft. Yet if these varied concerns were not translated into a mass of witchcraft accusations before the courts, such records as do survive, from Cornwall to Northumberland, from Kent to Lancashire, suggest that, broadly, fears of what witches might do and notions of the types of neighbourly dispute lying behind a witchcraft accusation followed a national pattern. Everybody knew what witches did, everybody knew under what circumstances they might reasonably attribute a child's illness or a horse's death to witchcraft. These fears and this knowledge, for whatever reason, did not result in high levels of prosecution, but their sheer pervasiveness reinforces the impression that the cultural significance of witchcraft was wider and deeper than the statistics of formal prosecution would suggest. We must agree with Robin Briggs, who, after studying witchcraft in early modern Lorraine (an area experiencing levels of prosecution comparable to Elizabethan Essex), commented that one of the greatest problems arising from his studies was that of explaining why there were not considerably more prosecutions than were actually brought.[31]

Finally, although lack of information from other areas should make us cautious about postulating a national trend, it seems that both the desire to prosecute witches at the courts and the willingness to execute them were slackening among the nation's élite by the 1630s. Such a conclusion is borne out by statistics from the Home Circuit and from Middlesex (only one indictment for witchcraft survives from that decade) and by Macfarlane's work on Essex ecclesiastical courts. It is also borne out by the treatment of what could have been a serious outbreak of accusations in Lancashire in 1634. There had been four executions in the county in 1633 and more seemed likely when, in the wake of these, accusations were made by a ten- or eleven-year-old mason's son called Edmund Robinson, whom we have already encountered in our discussion of popular notions of the sabbat. Different sources give different numbers of accused witches, although it is probable that nineteen were condemned, and a letter from May 1634 mentions that another sixty people were under suspicion. It seems that the assize judge was unhappy with the verdicts, remanded the convicted persons and referred matters to higher authority. The Bishop of

Chester was directed to re-examine seven of the accused (four of them, he found, had already died in gaol). Robinson and his father were brought down to London on the orders of the Privy Council, which also organized the examination of a number of the witches in London by a medical team headed by William Harvey and two royal surgeons. Robinson retracted his stories and no executions followed, although a number of the reprieved witches died in gaol.[32]

Not only does this treatment of what could have been a mass of prosecutions contrast with the Lancashire trials of 1612, but there is a related indicator of cultural change. It is noteworthy that the incident provoked a distanced and semi-farcical treatment of witchcraft in Heywood and Broome's contemporary play *The Trial of the Late Lancashire Witches*. And although the issue demands further research, it would seem that during the early years of Charles I's reign, allegations of witchcraft and sorcery among the high aristocracy were less common than they had been in his father's day. Thus by the 1630s, at least in the metropolitan area and the Home Counties, witchcraft prosecutions were ebbing, and educated opinion was obviously becoming very sceptical about the usefulness of indicting suspected witches and hence, possibly, of the reality of malefic witchcraft. It was, therefore, ironic that the next decade should witness the outbreak of the most severe witchcraft prosecutions that England was ever to experience.

CHAPTER 5

England's Mass Witch-hunt:
East Anglia, 1645–7

The East Anglian witch trials of 1645–7 constitute one of the most remarkable episodes in the history of English, and indeed European, witchcraft. An extensive body of relevant contemporary material, both manuscript and printed, survives,[1] although there are enough gaps in the records to ensure that a comprehensive history of the episode will never be written. The main outlines, however, are clear enough. Over the winter of 1644–5 Matthew Hopkins, an obscure petty gentleman living at Manningtree in north-eastern Essex, became worried about the presence of witches in his neighbourhood. His worries initiated a series of investigations. The first suspect to be interrogated, an aged, one-legged widow called Elizabeth Clarke, confessed on 25 March to keeping familiars. Setting a pattern for what was to follow, her confession was encouraged by a process known as 'watching', in the course of which the suspect was kept awake, sometimes for two or three nights at a stretch, in the hopes that she would be betrayed by her familiars visiting her. The sleep deprivation that was the by-product of this process, along with general rough handling and psychological pressure, allied to leading questions, helps explain why witches were so prone to confess during the Hopkins trials. The confessions continued through the spring of 1645, more women were implicated and in due course thirty-six witches, of whom perhaps nineteen were subsequently executed, were tried at Chelmsford on 17 July.

By that time accusations had spread into Suffolk. The records do not allow us to trace the dynamics of this process with any precision, but the geographical location of Suffolk settlements from which suspected witches came suggests that accusations began in a number of villages just over the border from the affected parts of Essex (among them Shotley, Tattingstone, Bramford, Polstead and Shelley), and then spread more widely, from Sudbury at one corner of the county to Bungay at the other. We know of 117 witches who were examined or tried in Suffolk in this period. A stray reference[2] suggests that forty were tried, half of whom were executed, at the Norfolk assizes in 1645, while further trials took place in Huntingdonshire (where eight witches were tried and at least five executed in the summer of 1646), Cambridgeshire, Northamptonshire and Bedfordshire, totals for these last three counties probably not being very high. A number of independent borough jurisdictions were also busy trying witches in 1645-6; a mere one at Norwich, but six (of whom five were executed) at Great Yarmouth, seven executed at Aldeburgh, yet others (we do not know the number) at Stowmarket and King's Lynn,[3] while depositions in the assize records of the Isle of Ely reveal that a further seventeen suspected witches were examined there in 1646-7. Hopkins and his associate, another Manningtree resident named John Stearne, played an active, if sometimes indirect, role in most of these accusations. Altogether, we have references to nearly 250 witches who came before the authorities during the Hopkins trials, over 200 of them being tried, or at least investigated, between July and December 1645.

Calculating the number of witches executed is even more difficult than trying to arrive at a global total of those suspected. There were nineteen in Essex, perhaps as many in Norfolk and another twenty or so from Huntingdonshire, Great Yarmouth and Aldeburgh combined. Evidence of cases in other areas adds a few more scattered references to executions. Unfortunately, there is no certain total for Suffolk, the most affected county. Francis Hutchinson, who, as a clergyman in Suffolk after the Restoration, apparently spoke to many who had firsthand memories of the events of 1645, records a firm tradition that forty were executed there, with some of his informants suggesting that there might have been as many as sixty.[4] This latter figure may be what Samuel Butler had in mind when, in his satirical poem *Hudibras*, he referred to a witch-finder (obviously Hopkins) hanging three score witches 'in one shire'.[5] Taking these figures, it seems safe to suggest that a minimum of 100 people were hanged for witchcraft, and that the real total may have been comfortably over that figure. The best known contemporary suggestion for an overall total, John Stearne's assertion that 200 were hanged, would seem to be an over-estimate, although it is worth reflecting that Stearne was in a better position to be well informed than most.[6]

As these statistics suggest, the East Anglian trials of 1645-7 represent a major witch panic, comparable in its extent to a number of Continental outbreaks. Indeed, there were few Continental crazes which witnessed the prosecution (frequently followed by execution) of 200 witches in a six-month period. Some idea of the local impact of the craze can be gathered from Suffolk, where, at the height of accusations in August 1645, an order at the county quarter sessions admitted that the normal measures for feeding prisoners held in the county gaol were breaking down under the pressure of the number of witchcraft suspects and sought to meet the costs of supporting them by reallocating money from other areas of the county's finances and placing a rate on those parishes from which accused witches came.[7]

Yet the trials of 1645–7 have been regarded as unusual for reasons other than their sheer number. With the presence of Matthew Hopkins and his associate John Stearne, we have, unusually for England, if not 'professional' witch-hunters, at least two men who were interested in witch-hunting and who came to claim expertise in that activity. There was also, in the sleep deprivation and other forms of pressure used in the interrogation of suspects, something approximating to the torture and inquisitorial procedures so familiar in Continental trials. And lastly, witches in these trials were charged with and confessed to much more than *maleficium*, that doing harm by witchcraft which had long been the staple of English witchcraft accusations. Trial records show that many were condemned for consorting with familiar spirits, and what we can reconstruct of pre-trial depositions demonstrates that many of those suspected confessed to keeping familiars, allowing them to suck their blood, to making pacts with the devil and (less frequently) to having sexual intercourse with him.

It is this latter point which raises the greatest problems. The Matthew Hopkins trials offer a challenge to that standard interpretation of English witchcraft which stresses its roots in neighbourly tensions and village disputes and tends to downgrade the importance of the devil and all his works in the popular thinking on the subject of the period. The confessions and indictments of 1645–7 sit uncomfortably with this interpretation and, understandably, historians of English witchcraft have tended first to emphasize the peculiarities of these trials and then to attribute these peculiarities to the presence of Hopkins, who is normally portrayed as the agent through which 'Continental' ideas on witchcraft entered the minds of East Anglian witches and their accusers. In 1933 C. L'Estrange Ewen suggested that the demonic aspects of the Essex and Suffolk trials were connected with 'Master Hopkins' reading of some continental authority'. Later researchers have reached much the same conclusion. Alan Macfarlane, for example, likewise attributed the peculiarities of the 1645 Essex trials to 'the influence of continental ideas, perhaps mediated through Matthew Hopkins'.[8]

It is tempting, therefore, to write off the Hopkins trials as an aberration, in which 'continental ideas' temporarily sullied the English witch's normally peculiarly non-demonic nature; it is no accident that Keith Thomas described the Hopkins prosecutions as 'highly untypical'.[9]

Even while making allowances for any peculiarities in the Hopkins trials, and while accepting that the circumstances of the 1640s were exceptional, it would nevertheless seem that the prosecutions of 1645–7 are too important to be written off as an unEnglish aberration. The records relating to them, whatever their imperfections, do after all constitute the largest single body of evidence concerning English witchcraft we possess, and it would be unhelpful to dismiss their superficially unusual features as untypical and probably generated by Matthew Hopkins's alleged familiarity with Continental witch beliefs. If we turn to the records of these trials and examine who those accused of witchcraft in them were, what they were meant to have done and what wider beliefs about witchcraft were present, we will find not only that our understanding of the significance of the Hopkins episode is deepened, but also that we need to make modifications to our views on witchcraft beliefs in early modern England.

❯ Let us begin our discussion of the Hopkins trials by analysing who the suspected witches were and what they were supposed to have done. First, and importantly if we are considering the typicality of these trials, the traditional stereotype of the witch did not break down. Of the 184 witches tried during the Hopkins trials whose sex can be determined, 161, or 87.5 per cent, were women. Similarly, although detailed research on this point needs to be undertaken, most of those accused seem to have been drawn from the poorer elements of village and small-town society.[10] In general, there was none of the erosion of the social stereotype of the witch that occurred in some of the larger Continental crazes. There were, of course, a few exceptions. A contemporary newsletter mentioned 'a parson's wife' named Weight among the early Essex accused, although a later reference, referring to her as 'Wyat', suggested that the allegations against her were rapidly regarded as a 'palpable mistake', since she was known as 'a gentle-woman of a very godly and religious life'. John Stearne noted 'one Henry Carre of Ratlesden, in Suffolke, who I have heard was a scholler fit for Cambridge (if not a Cambridge scholler) and was well educated' who died in gaol before trial. Mother Lakeland, burned at Ipswich in 1645 for killing her husband by witchcraft, clearly had good social connections and had previously been thought of as a godly and respectable woman.[11] Perhaps the best documented of these socially exceptional witches was John Lowes, vicar of

Brandeston in Suffolk. Although the tradition that Lowes had popish leanings was probably unfounded, it is clear that he was, as a later note in Brandeston parish register put it, 'a contentious man' who had already been prosecuted for barratry and had been involved in witchcraft accusations thirty years previously. Lowes had been instituted to his living in 1596, and was an octogenarian when he was swum in the castle ditch at Framlingham, subsequently being subjected to sleep deprivation for several nights and being run around the room in which he was kept until he was breathless.[12]

Lowes was also unusual in the type of harm he was meant to have caused. Some of the witnesses against him testified that he had inflicted the normal damage attributed to witches: causing the death of a child after an altercation with its father and the killing of numerous cattle. Yet one witness, Daniel Rayner, also claimed that Lowes had confessed to employing a familiar to do all the harm he could between Great Yarmouth and Winterton, while Hopkins testified that Lowes had admitted to using a familiar to sink a ship off Landguard Fort, near Harwich. There are few other cases in which the accused were thought to have inflicted unusual harm: two women were held to have sunk boats through witchcraft, a Suffolk woman confessed that the devil told her to blast corn, one of the Isle of Ely accused was suspected of destroying corn in a field, while in another Ely case it was alleged that after an altercation with its owner a witch caused a mill to collapse.[13]

But for the most part the harm inflicted was similar to that which had formed the basis for English witchcraft prosecutions over the previous eighty years. Some witnesses, indeed, recalled very minor incidents: the bewitching of a cow so that it gave 'naughty milk of two of her teats and since hath dried upp', or the use of witchcraft to hinder beer from brewing.[14] In general, however, witches accused during the Hopkins period were meant to have caused the sickness or death of human beings or farm animals. The archival materials for 1645–7 allow us to reconstruct 110 narratives of witchcraft suspicions. These include thirty-six incidents where the targets of the alleged witch's wrath were adult humans, fifty-six involving children, fifty-three cattle and nine inanimate objects. These figures can be compared with those for the Home Circuit between 1610 and 1659, when of 192 indictments for witchcraft involving harm to persons or property, sixty-one involved adults, forty-four children, twenty-nine animals and two other forms of property. Thus the East Anglian craze of 1645–7 seems to have experienced an unusual emphasis on the killing of children and cattle. The youth of the witches' victims in the Hopkins period becomes more marked when it is realized that a large number of those classified here as adults were servants, so often in the front line of altercations with suspected witches, many of whom must have been in or barely out of their teens.

Many of the accusers and witnesses, again along very familiar lines, testified how witchcraft fears followed an altercation, or 'falling out' as they so frequently put it. Many of these altercations involved those tensions which followed a refusal to give or lend money or goods and which so often precipitated a witchcraft accusation. Numerous other occasions for altercations between the suspected witch and her neighbours were recorded, although these, as might be imagined, were very varied. Mary Sexton told how a dog came to her while she was ill and asked 'if she would revenge her selfe of the constables that had carried her to Ipswitch upon [a] misdemeanour'. Elizabeth Clarke, the first Essex witch to confess, was thought to have killed the couple in whose favour her landlord had turned her out of her tenancy. Elizabeth Chandler, one of the Huntingdonshire accused, claimed she desired revenge of Goodwife Darnell, 'having received some hard usage from the said goodwife Darnell, by causing her to be duckt'. Frances Moore told how William Foster, some sixteen years since, 'would have hanged two of her children, for offering to take a piece of bread', and how she had subsequently cursed him and caused his death. Two witches, one in Essex and one in the Isle of Ely, were thought to have used their powers against parish officers who tried to press their sons into the army.[15] Yet whatever the range of circumstances in specific instances, it is clear that in East Anglia in the 1640s, as more generally, members of the community with limited access to other forms of power were suspected of using witchcraft to revenge themselves on those who had offended them.

This being so, it is unsurprising that another familiar theme to surface in these narratives is the assertion that the accused had a long-established reputation for witchcraft. A witness deposed of a Suffolk witch that 'the parents of this woman and this woman have been formerly counted and commonly reputed for a witch'. John Abrahams claimed of Peter Burbush of Ely that 'he hath bin com[m]only reputed a witch & his mother before him'. In another Ely case, an alleged victim accused Joan Briggs of being a witch 'because they have had many fallens out & the s[ai]d Jone hath used many threatning speeches ag[ains]t this informant she having been a woman that hath a long tyme been suspected for a witch'. A fuller denunciation was made by one of the witnesses against Ellen Garryson of Upwell: 'she hath bin a long tyme accompted a witche and her mother before her, and that shee is a com[m]on curser, and that by reporte of her neighbours much harme and damage hath befallen such as had difference with her.' Voicing such suspicions too vociferously could, of course, bring trouble down upon the accuser. Remembering an incident which demonstrates anti-witch feeling at the grass roots, another of the Isle of Ely accused, Dorothy Ellis, confessed to laming John Gotobed by witchcraft 'because he cald this ex[aminate] old witch & flung stones att this ex[aminate]'.[16]

At one level, then, the witchcraft of the East Anglian outbreak of 1645–7 was hardly untypical: most of those accused of witchcraft were women from the lower orders; many of them had a long-standing reputation for practising witchcraft; their *maleficium* was usually restricted to harming children, adult humans and cattle; and this harm was normally inflicted after some sort of altercation between the witch and the victim or one of the victim's household. It was not these aspects of the Hopkins trials that made them remarkable, leading later historians to think of them as untypical. It was, rather, the high profile which dealings with the devil enjoyed in the witches' accounts of their activities; indeed, John Stearne, after recounting a number of such cases, declared, 'if I should goe to pen all of these sorts, then I should have no end, or at least too big a volume'.[17] Stearne's contention is confirmed when we find that of our sample of 110 narratives, sixty-three involve accounts of the witch's meeting with the devil in one form or another (as we shall see, the varied nature of these forms raises a number of interesting issues). This evidence obviously challenges the accepted view that English witchcraft, on a popular level, was non-diabolical and hence merits serious analysis.

In fact, these tales of dealing with the devil open up a rich seam of contemporary beliefs about him. We have, for example, accounts of a range of circumstances under which the witch met the devil for the first time. Susan Marchant, a Suffolk witch, told how the devil first came to her when she was 'milking off a cow and singing off a psalme, and asked her why she singe psalmes as she was a damned creature', from which time she received familiars. The devil came to Priscilla Collet and tempted her to do away with herself or her children, 'or else she sho'd always continue poore'; she did, in fact, subsequently try to kill one of her children, although it was rescued by another. Some first saw the devil, as demonologists warned that people would, when they were riven by despair or anger. The devil first came to Abigail Briggs a month after her husband died, and she told how he came to her shop 'and lay heavy upon her' and spoke to her 'in the voyce of her husband'. Similarly, the devil appeared to Mary Skipper shortly after her husband's death, and told her 'if she wold enter a covenant w[i]th him he wold pay her debts'. Mary Beckett recounted how the devil came to her and told her that 'her sins were so great there was no heaven for her'. The devil first came to Ann Moats 'after she had beene cursinge of her husband and her childering'. Margaret Wyard was offered material temptations when the devil told her that 'there weare some witches had gold ringes on theyre fingers'.[18]

At the first meeting, or shortly after it, the devil began to try to convince the witch to enter into a covenant with him. He usually offered revenge, or, as the confession of Margaret Wyard suggests, material wealth. Abigail Briggs, according to John Stearne, said the devil told her she would be revenged on her enemies in return for giving herself to him, but, as was so often the case, 'she s[ai]d she found Satan a liar'. Elizabeth Richmond told how the devil 'came to her & imbraced her and asked her to love him & trust in him & wold defend her & curse her enemies'. Elizabeth Hobard confessed that the devil had come to her thirty years previously, and 'at the same time she covenanted w[i]th him that he shod have her body and soule and would avenge her of those that angered her', adding that 'he would furnish her w[i]th money but never p[er]formed it'. Similarly, the devil promised Ann Usher that if she denied Christ she would get richer, but he brought her nothing. Elizabeth Currey, a widow of Riseley in Bedfordshire, confessed that the devil 'had the use of her body, and lay heavie upon her, and that through her wilfulnesse, and poverty, with desire of revenge, she denied God, and Christ, and sealed it with her blood'.[19]

The motif of the devil taking a few drops of blood to seal the covenant between him and the witch runs through these narratives. Even more unexpectedly there are fairly frequent references to sexual liaisons between the devil and the witch. In a practically unique case, Ellen Driver of Framlingham in Suffolk, aged sixty, confessed that many years previously

the devill appeared to her like a man & that she was married to him . . . and that he lived with her 3 years and that she had 2 children by him in that time which were changelinges . . . after she was married he had the use of her but was cold, and inioyned her before marriage to deny God and Christ.

Most of those who confessed to having intercourse with the devil found the experience an odd and not entirely pleasurable one. As we have seen, Elizabeth Currey felt the devil 'lay heavie upon her', while Ellen Driver found him physically cold. These notions, strikingly similar to those attributed by Continental demonologists to witches copulating with the devil, were echoed by other confessing witches in the Hopkins trials. The devil came two or three times a week to Widow Bush of Barton, 'but she said he was colder than a man, and heavier, and could not performe nature as a man'. The devil constantly had the use of

Mary Skipper's body after she made a covenant with him, 'but she felt him always cold'.[20]

Witches confessing to covenanting or having sexual intercourse with the devil were, apparently, undeterred by his habit of appearing in a variety of shapes. Frequently, of course, he was of human appearance: 'in the shadow of a man'; 'a handsome young gentleman with yellow hayre and black cloathes'; 'in the shape of a proper gentleman, with a laced band, having the whole proportion of a man'; 'in the likeness of a man called Daniel the Prophet'. Even with the devil in his human shape, however, there might be problems. Some of these East Anglian villagers knew that the devil was meant to have a cloven foot. Ellen Driver of Framlingham recounted that when she was in bed with the devil 'she felt his feet and they weare cloven'. Margaret Wyard, in the very act of making a pact with the devil, 'observed he had a cloven foot'. Even more alarming was the experience of the Huntingdonshire witch Jane Wallis, who noticed the ugly feet of a man she met, 'and then she was very fearfull of him for that he would seem sometimes to be tall, and sometimes lesse, and suddenly vanished away'. Others told how the devil might appear in animal form. As Joan Salter was going from her house, according to one of the witnesses giving evidence against her, 'a black horse came to her & crept betwixt her legges & carried hir over the green to hir own house, w[hi]ch this inform[an]t beleaveth to be the divell in the likeness of a horse'. Confessing witches claimed to have encountered the devil in the shape of 'a great mouse' or a crabfish, while one reported seeing the devil variously in the shape of a cat, a bear or a man.[21]

With such confessions we confront directly the interplay between educated (or, as several historians have put it, 'Continental') ideas on the devil's role in witchcraft and those of the populace. As we have seen, some of our sample of witches claimed to have encountered the devil of the learned demonologists: coming to them at moments of stress and despair, frequently appearing in human shape, offering wealth or the power to revenge, making a covenant, sealed with the witch's blood, in which God and Christ were renounced, and then indulging in sexual relations, often of an unsatisfactory nature. Such a pattern would have been recognizable to Continental writers of witchcraft tracts like Bodin or Remy, or to English ones like William Perkins, and there is every likelihood that its pervasiveness in the confessions of 1645–7 owed much to the investigative techniques of Matthew Hopkins and John Stearne. But what are we to make of accounts of seeing the devil in the shape of a 'great mouse', or a crabfish, or a black horse; or of Ann Usher, who told not of how she experienced the cold and unsatisfactory embraces of a humanoid devil, but rather how she felt the sensation of '2 things like butterflies in her secret p[ar]tes'?[22] Here we are encountering, surely, not the devil of the learned demonologists, but rather something very like those animal familiars which had long been a central feature of English witch beliefs. Whatever was untypical in the Hopkins trials, the familiar was not.

And, as we have argued, the widespread belief in the existence of familiars introduces something very like a diabolical element into early modern English witchcraft. So, while it is noteworthy that the records of 1645–7 furnish us with considerable evidence about popular beliefs concerning the devil, even more significant are the insights they provide into the folklore of familiars, or 'imps' as they were frequently referred to in the documentation in question. Seventy-eight of the 110 narratives involve familiars. They came in numerous animal guises: mice, dogs, chickens, rabbits, turkey cocks, a rat, a polecat. Like the familiars described in earlier depositions, they were given names. Many witches claimed that their familiars were passed on to them directly after the covenant was sealed, although others deposed that they had received them from their mother,[23] grandmother[24] or friends.[25] The witches in this sample occasionally used their familiars in unison to do harm, or shared or borrowed them, while Margery Sparham, a Suffolk witch, told how she sent two of her three imps 'after her husband beeinge a soldier to p[ro]tect him'.[26] Most female witches confessing in 1645–7 claimed that they allowed their familiars to suck blood through teats in their genitalia, and the Hopkins material contains rich details about the resultant witch's marks. Indeed, one of the most graphic images furnished by this documentation comes from Margaret Wyard, who confessed that she had seven imps, but only five teats, so that 'when they come to suck they fight like pigs with a sow'.[27] One suspects that Wyard did not owe this particular image to Continental notions foisted upon her by Matthew Hopkins.

❧ Thus it would seem that the ideas about witchcraft which surfaced during the Matthew Hopkins period reveal as much that was well established as was novel. The alleged witches, and the harm which they were meant to have done, were firmly in the English mainstream. The wealth of information about, for example, familiars is remarkable, but then we are dealing with a remarkably rich body of documentation. The presence of the devil is unusually marked, but even here English beliefs were, to a large extent, conflating the devil of the learned demonologists with the neo-diabolical familiars of the English witch-craft tradition, thus demonstrating a rather more complex situation than a straightforward imposition of learned beliefs on the populace. The evidence rather supports the suspicion that beliefs about witchcraft were in a constant state of development, and that the exact relationship between popular beliefs and the demonological input of Hopkins and Stearne remains problematic. Clearly there is enough conformity (the sealing of the covenant with a few drops of blood, the devil's limitations as a lover) in the confessions to suggest that much was owed to the leading questions of the interrogators. Yet it is also possible that a broad cultural vocabulary of demonological beliefs was being focused by the processes of interrogation, which would in turn suggest that the populace did possess a repertoire of beliefs about the devil, and that what appeared in the witches' confessions was not merely imposed from above.

The way in which one old woman's 'confession' was constructed was described by Francis Hutchinson:

Old women are apt to take such fancies of themselves, and when all the country was full of such stories, and she heard the witch-finders tell how familiar the devil had been with others, and what imps they had, she might begin to think that a beggar-boy had been a spirit, and mice upon her mother's bed had been her imps; and, as I have heard, that she was very harmless and innocent, and desirous to die, she told the story to any body that desired it; and besides, as she was poor, and mightily pitied, she had usually money given her when she told the story.[28]

Here we find a number of factors interacting in what was probably not an unusual combination: the objective circumstances of the individual old woman; the stories about witchcraft, doubtlessly based on popular beliefs, which were circulating in the heightened atmosphere of the craze; and the prompting of the witch-hunters. There is little indication that 'Continental' ideas were simply implanted into the mind of the confessing witch by the witch-hunters; their input was only one element in a rather more complex process.

Similarly, examination of the tracts published by Hopkins and Stearne makes it difficult to accept that they were responsible for the promotion of 'Continental' ideas about witchcraft. Hopkins's tract, apart from a reference to James I's views on the validity of the swimming test,[29] demonstrates little acquaintance with learned works on witchcraft. In fact, he explicitly denied that his skill in witch-hunting was founded on 'profound learning, or from much reading of learned authors concerning that subject', attributing it rather to 'experience, which though it be meanly esteemed of; yet is the surest and safest way to judge by'.[30] Stearne's rather longer publication presents more complexities. It is evident that he was familiar with the Warboys case, with the Lancashire trials of 1612 and bewitching of the Earl of Rutland's family in 1618–19, while he also alludes to Thomas Cooper's *Mystery of Witchcraft*, of 1617.[31] As G. L. Kittredge demonstrated in 1929, he also made heavy and unacknowledged use ('enormous plagiarism' is Kittredge's phrase) of Richard Bernard's *Guide to Grand Iury Men*, first published in 1627.[32] Bernard, whose witchcraft book we have already discussed, was familiar with the works of Bodin, Del Rio and other Continental authors, but he leant equally heavily on that selection of English trials which had attracted wide publicity. Thus what we can reconstruct of the intellectual background of the written works of Hopkins and Stearne suggests a dependence on mainstream English writings on witchcraft rather than on the works of Continental demonologists, while for both men the actual experience of witch-hunting seems to have assumed a greater importance in forming their ideas on witchcraft than did familiarity with demonological tracts.

Indeed, the confessions given by the witches examined by Hopkins and Stearne, and the leading questions which we must assume formed those confessions to at least some extent, point to the presence not of 'Continental' ideas but rather of that evolving nexus of English demonological ideas whose presence is one of the recurring themes of this book. It is altogether appropriate that Stearne should have leant so heavily on Richard Bernard's *Guide*, because it can be regarded as the summation of the formative period of educated ideas on witchcraft in England, bringing together as it did a basic theological position with what could be learned from the most important published accounts of the actual investigation of witchcraft. The one great puzzle is the frequency with which sexual relations with the devil, something hitherto largely absent from English trials and English demonological tracts, figured so prominently in 1645-7. But other elements, notably the way in which witches were expected to meet the devil while in a state of despair and the emphasis laid on the covenant with him, were gradually becoming established elements in English witchcraft beliefs before the Civil Wars. Their pervasiveness in the Hopkins trials doubtlessly owed much to the peculiar circumstances of East Anglia in the 1640s and to the input in the interrogation chamber of Hopkins and Stearne. Yet these ideas were hardly as new or as alien to earlier accounts of English witchcraft as some historians, attached to the 'non-demonic' interpretation of witchcraft in England, have suggested.

We must reiterate that the evidence of these trials suggests that the notion of a polarity between a 'learned', 'Continental' or 'demonological' set of beliefs and a 'popular' witchcraft centred on concern over *maleficium*, is a gross over-simplification. Obviously, at certain points in the Hopkins trials it is possible to see confessions coming through under pressure from Hopkins and Stearne, and some of the more stereotyped aspects of accounts of dealing or sexual inter-course with the devil may have owed much to the suspect's thoughts being moulded to accept the concepts of learned demonologists. Conversely, these confessions were not wholly stereotyped, and the impression is that any 'learn-ed' notions came into an agitated interaction with a jumble of popular beliefs via the conditions of a mass witch-hunt.[33] Close reading of the confessions, not least those which show the difficulty of distinguishing between the devil and the animal familiar, reveals a host of variations and the presence of elements which owed little to learned demonology. The sense is not of the imposition upon the populace of the devil's role in witchcraft but rather of a wide range of ideas interacting and being allowed to enter the historical record due to an unusual set of circumstances.

There can be little doubt that the Hopkins episode did owe much to the peculiar circumstances of 1645. By that year England had for three years been involved in an increasingly bitter Civil War which was, for many partici-pants and observers, being conceived of increasingly in ideological terms. East Anglia was not a front-line area, but the population of the region was nevertheless feeling strains and pressures. One element was the erosion of traditional structures of authority. Wallace Notestein, in his analysis of the Hopkins trials, thought that by 1645 England was in 'a state of judicial an-archy'.[34] This is clearly an exaggeration, not least for East Anglia, where something like effective governmental structures were in place. Yet it is un-deniable that the witch craze flourished there because some normal restraints, notably the presence of assize judges, were lacking in the key early stages. The Earl of Warwick and Sir Thomas Bowes, who presided over the first Essex investigations, were important figures on the national and local political stages, but for that very reason neither of them had much experience of the technicalities or pitfalls of questioning suspected witches. The commission sent by Parliament to try witches in Suffolk in the summer of 1645 consisted of two clergymen and a serjeant-at-law. The arrival of assize judges a few months later ensured the return of more normal methods of trial (Hopkins's tract was written in response to queries raised about his methods by the pre-siding judges at the Norfolk assizes), but by that time the witch craze was running free. Local justices, preoccupied with the problems of keeping the war effort going, had allowed local pressures for witch-hunting to get out of hand.

Curiously, this partial hiatus in local government was replicated, on a small scale, in the very parish where the hunt began. Manningtree had recently lost the services of its long-standing rector, Thomas Witham, apparently a man of mildly Puritan views, and it is unclear if a resident clergyman had replaced him by early 1645. Moreover, in 1638 the Lord of the Manor, Paul, Viscount Bayning, had died, leaving the manor to his two young daughters, Anne and Penelope. Thus at a vital point in Manningtree's history two of the natural opinion formers in the local community were lacking. It is interesting to speculate whether clear guidance from a sceptical Lord of the Manor or experienced parish priest, had it been available, might have operated to defuse the situation which led to the first accusations.[35] As the craze spread, it may well have flourished most strongly in townships where there was a similar absence of local authority. Francis Hutchinson claimed that 'it was very requisite, that these witchfinders should take care to go to no towns but where they might do what they would, without being controlled by sticklers', but added that they would have found few such towns 'if the times had not been as they were'.[36]

Doubtless the problems caused by the erosion of traditional authority were made heavier, in Puritan East Anglia, by the populace's previous exposure to sermons and other forms of religious consciousness-raising in which the devil and his works figured prominently. The statements of some of those participating in the Hopkins episode, whether as accused, accusers, witnesses or assistants to Hopkins and Stearne, demonstrate that at least some of the middling and lower sorts of Essex, Suffolk and the Isle of Ely had acquired a basic awareness of the threat offered to the godly commonwealth by the devil. Yet the direct influence of clergymen on the trials seems to have been mixed. A number of clergy were actively involved in the search for witches: three were present in the early Essex investigations,[37] while others were involved in Suffolk.[38] More remarkably, the Special Commission of Oyer and Terminer sent to try witches in Suffolk in 1645 included two divines, Samuel Fairclough and Edmund Calamy. Both of them had local connections, although it should be noted that the exact impact of these two worthies on the rhythm and content of accusations remains elusive.[39] Other clergy were overtly hostile to the witchfinders. Francis Hutchinson wrote that 'several clergymen preached, and spake against them, as far as those times would suffer', and mentioned one (unfortunately unnamed) cleric who was reprimanded by the County Committee (the organ which controlled the county on behalf of Parliament) after preaching against them.[40] A full-scale attack on their activities was launched in 1646 by John Gaule, vicar of Great Staughton in Huntingdonshire and a minor religious controversist. Gaule, while accepting that witches existed, attacked the practice of witch-hunting, the investigative techniques used by Hopkins and Stearne and the popular superstitions about witchcraft which he thought that their activities were encouraging.[41]

It was, perhaps, not the formal Protestantism of the educated clergy which helped fuel the East Anglian witch-hunt, but rather a popular Puritanism which was being reinforced by the war. It is difficult to assess such matters precisely, but it is hard not to believe that many of the justices, local clergy and parish notables of the region were affected by a parliamentary propaganda which was increasingly portraying royalists as agents of the devil, or by the tremendous fillip which the dramatic events of the war had given to the literature of apparitions and wonders. More concretely, Essex and Suffolk had, in 1643–4, experienced campaigns aimed at rooting out scandalous and malignant clergy. In these campaigns grass-roots Puritanism had flexed its muscles as villagers, often led by men from the social stratum from which Hopkins and Stearne came, had turned on clergymen felt to be ungodly or not active enough in providing ideological support for Parliament's cause.[42] And, in 1644, a Suffolk man of respectable yeoman stock, William Dowsing, had, under parliamentary authority, led a campaign of iconoclasm in which ornaments or decorations in churches in 150 locations in Suffolk were subjected to mutilation or destruction.[43] 'Religious belief,' as Wallace Notestein commented, 'grew terribly literal under the tensions of war.'[44]

In such a context, the eruption of a witch-hunt is hardly surprising. Yet it remains clear that Matthew Hopkins provided an essential catalyst. Hopkins, as I have suggested, is a very obscure figure. The best guess is that he was the son of a Suffolk clergyman named James Hopkins, that he was a young man in 1645 and that he died, probably of consumption, in 1647.[45] His motivation seems, initially at least, to have been a straightforward hostility to witchcraft. Certainly the tradition that he engaged in witch-hunting because of the profits which were thus to be made is overstated. Even when, in late 1645 and 1646, his expertise in finding witches was sought by local authorities, he seems to have been working for what these days would be described as expenses and a consultancy fee. It seems probable, on the strength of John Gaule's evidence, that he was gaining in self-importance by 1646, but the safest conclusion is that, throughout the period of the trials, both his and John Stearne's major concern was with the eradication of witches. That Hopkins and Stearne should come to such prominence in the 1640s is hardly surprising: at that time men from their social stratum were forming (and writing pamphlets explaining the ideas of) radical sects and the Leveller movement, were assuming command of companies and regiments in the New Model Army, were, like William Dowsing, implementing parliamentary ordinances and were even, in some areas, starting to make their way into the charmed circle of urban and county government. As those higher in the social hierarchy were becoming painfully aware, conditions in the second half of the 1640s were providing ample scope for people like Matthew Hopkins and John Stearne to deploy their talents in a wide variety of fields, witch-finding among them.

If the tradition that Hopkins was motivated by financial gain is not well founded, there is little doubt that his techniques of investigation and interrogation were extremely irregular. The standard procedure was to take suspects into a room and strip them naked so that they could be searched for the witch's mark. They would then be placed on a stool in the middle of the room, perched with their feet off the ground and watched for up to three days without food or sleep in the hope, as we have noted, that their familiars might come to them. In this process they would be subjected to considerable psychological pressure to match their physical discomfort. If Hopkins or Stearne were present, suspects might be subjected to leading questioning. And, as witnesses' depositions suggest, they would also be subjected to questioning from other interested parties in the room (we return to the essentially public nature of the examination of witches). Francis Hutchinson, writing many years after the events but on the basis of conversations with those who had witnessed witch-hunting in Suffolk in 1645, invited his readers to

imagine a poor old creature, under all the weakness and infirmities of old age, set like a fool in the middle of a room, with a rabble of the town round about her house: then her legs tied cross, that all the weight of her body might rest upon her seat. By that means, after some hours, that the circulation of her blood would be much stopped, her sitting would be as painful as the wooden horse [a form of military punishment]. Then she must continue her pain four and twenty hours, without any sleep or meat ... what wonder was it, if when they were weary of their lives, they confessed any tales that would please them [i.e. their interrogators], and many times knew what not.[46]

We are left to wonder how often these or similar techniques might have been used against witches in earlier episodes for which detailed evidence does not survive.

The documentation generated by the Hopkins trials also demonstrates that that great invasion of personal privacy, the search for the witch's mark, was also of vital significance. In parish after parish searchers came forward to aid the witch-hunters by searching the bodies of suspects for evidence that they had been sucked by familiars; possibly as a result of the wording of the 1604 statute, this 'proof' of witchcraft had obviously, by 1645, attained a central importance. The description of the trial of eighteen witches at Bury St Edmunds in August of that year commented on how the accused had 'teats or dugs that their impes used to suck so often as they came to them . . . under their armes, some under their tongue, some in the roofe of their mouth, some in their fundament, and divers other places'. John Stearne, in his tract, spent several pages describing the mark, discussing its significance and answering hypothetical queries about it. 'I am confident, and my conscience tells me,' he wrote, 'that those who shall be found with these marks, are expressly guilty of that diabolical art or practice of witchcraft, whether they have done witchcraft or not . . . they have renounced God and Christ, and betaken themselves to the devil.' Hopkins devoted some space in his own tract to the significance and nature of the mark, and commented (in a further demonstration of the extent of popular participation in the craze) that the marks found on individual witches were normally discussed with 'a dozen of the ablest men of the parish, or else where . . . and most commonly as many ancient skilfull matrons and midwives'.[47]

Indeed, the numerous accounts of watching and interrogation which have come to us from 1645–7 make it obvious that the East Anglian craze of those years cannot be attributed solely to the malign influence of Hopkins. It is evident that he received active cooperation and encouragement from a large section of the region's population. Hopkins and Stearne may have provided a catalyst for witch suspicions, but those suspicions, and the willingness to do something about them should the opportunity arise, were clearly present in strength. Only microscopic research on individual communities will illustrate the point clearly, but it is obvious from depositions that in most settlements the lead in reporting suspected witches, watching them and organizing the search for their marks was taken by a few interested individuals, normally with the support and cooperation of a large section of the local community. Work on the early Essex accusations has shown how they were generated in the context of a web of local tensions. Accordingly, Hopkins and Stearne were aided by three local clergymen; a prominent local gentleman named Richard Edwards figured at the centre of a number of accusations and here (as at other points throughout the seventeenth century) the searching for the witch's marks was made possible by the active participation of a group of women from the neighbourhood.[48]

As the craze spread, the reputation of the witch-hunters grew and the local populace became ever more willing to call on their services. John Stearne, admittedly arguing a case, defended Hopkins from allegations that he had used 'extremity' against witches by claiming that 'at first, before he or I ever went, many towns used extremity of themselves, which after was laid on us'. Hopkins himself asserted that he 'never went to any towne or place, but they rode, writ, or sent often for him, and were (for aught he knew) glad of him'. The image of the two witch-hunters imposing their views on a population indifferent to persecuting witches is a very unconvincing one. At the very least, it is obvious that the excitement generated by the craze spread among the local populace. 'The country people talk already,' noted a disgruntled John Gaule, 'and that more frequently, more affectedly, of the infallible and wonderfull power of the witch finders, then they doe of God, or Christ, or the Gospell preached.'[49]

Some idea of how local authorities might encourage the activities of Hopkins and Stearne can be gleaned from the records of Aldeburgh, a small and, by 1645, economically declining borough on the Suffolk coast. Between September 1645 and early 1647 the borough authorities spent nearly £20 in meeting the costs of a local witch-hunt in which seven witches were executed. Hopkins was called in twice, on each occasion receiving £2 for his expenses. Mary Phillips, a widow from Manningtree who had been involved in the first Essex trials and had established a broader reputation for her skill in finding the witch's mark, was brought in to give evidence against the witches, and paid £1 5s. expenses. A woman was paid £4 7s. 'for diet and wine' consumed while Hopkins was in Aldeburgh, and for 'charges for the witches'. Among other disbursements, John Paine was paid 11s. for hanging seven witches, William Daniell received £1 for erecting the gallows, 'Henry Lawrence the roper' received 8s. 'for 7 halters and making the noghts [knots]', and 6s. was paid for 'a post to sett by the grave of the dead bodies that were hanged and burying of them'. Whatever profits Hopkins may have been making, it is clear that the costs of witch-hunting for a local community could be substantial. That a town like Aldeburgh was willing to make such an outlay is an indication of how seriously witchcraft was regarded.[10]

The Hopkins episode, therefore, demonstrates what could happen when witchcraft suspicions were allowed to develop freely. Events in East Anglia in the spring and summer of 1645 show clearly that England had as great a potential for mounting large-scale crazes as any other European nation. The Hopkins trials were not imposed from above and were certainly not brought about purely by the influence of Matthew Hopkins and John Stearne. They were, as I have suggested, the product of unique circumstances in the eastern counties in the closing stages of the English Civil War, which allowed Hopkins and Stearne to act as a catalyst on witchcraft fears. That a witch craze of such intensity, so obviously fuelled by long-standing suspicions, should come after a steady decline of witchcraft prosecutions in the South-East is a chastening reminder of the gap which could exist between witchcraft suspicions and witchcraft beliefs in society at large and what was entering the historical record.

Yet it should be noted that even in the midst of the craze some sceptical voices were raised. John Gaule wrote his book in criticism of the witch-finders' techniques and other clergy were doubtful about what was happening. John Stearne recounted disgustedly how one of the early Essex accused was protected and saved from execution by a local faction.[51] The steward of the Earl of Warwick, Arthur Wilson, was present at the Chelmsford trials and was very sceptical about the whole business.[52] One of the few contemporary newsletters to mention the trials took an equivocal stance, noting that 'life is precious and there is need of great inquisition before it is taken away'.[53] Such scepticism and caution as we attempt a general assessment of the importance of the Hopkins trials lead us to a final irony: for the generation immediately following them, the greatest significance of the accusations of 1645–7 probably lay in how they provided post-Restoration sceptics with ammunition against over-active witch-hunting. Fairly or otherwise, witch-hunting became associated in many educated minds with extreme sectarian Protestantism, with the radicalism of the 1640s and 1650s, and the general instability of those decades which allowed petty gentry like Stearne and Hopkins to gain temporary prominence as witch-finders, or allowed yeomen like William Dowsing to gain temporary prominence by smashing church decorations. After 1660 a distaste for plebeian religious 'enthusiasm' among those social élites whose status had been restored as assuredly as had the Stuart monarchy became one of the major obstacles to a renewal of large-scale witch-hunting.

Even so, it is clear that the 1640s and 1650s were a period in which witchcraft was re-established as a matter of interest for both the criminal courts and intellectual speculation. As we have seen, there is every indication that by the 1630s, for reasons which are as yet unclear, England may well have been ready to join those other Western European countries where witchcraft was at best of little more than peripheral concern both to the learned élite and to the criminal justice system. Prosecution of witches at the assizes in the South-East was rare, central government played a vital role in dampening down the Lancashire scare of 1633–4, playwrights were not regarding witchcraft as a serious subject and, we might add, the 1630s were virtually free from the publication of either full-scale demonological tracts or those trial pamphlets which had proliferated during the reigns of Elizabeth I and James I. But if witchcraft was a dying subject in the 1630s, it was one which was revived massively in the aftermath of the Civil Wars. The Hopkins trials are well known, but, as we have seen, less familiar criminal court evidence from a number of areas other than East Anglia points to a rise in witchcraft prosecutions in the 1640s and 1650s. These two decades also saw the publication of a number of trial pamphlets, of larger works on witchcraft and a reprinting of Reginald Scot's *Discoverie*. It would be an exaggeration to suggest that witchcraft was a matter of central concern in these decades. But the context they created – notably through the erosion of established authority and the flurry of religious speculation they witnessed – created an atmosphere in which witchcraft accusations might be more readily countenanced at the courts, and in which witchcraft was again considered a matter which was both newsworthy and deserving serious intellectual consideration. It was to remain so, as we shall see when we turn to the problem of the decline of witchcraft beliefs, for many years after the Restoration of the Stuart monarchy in 1660.

CHAPTER 6

Accusations, Counter-measures and the Local Community

With the Matthew Hopkins trials, then, we are forced to confront a phenomenon which was in all conscience remarkable enough and which, indeed, was sufficiently remarkable for some historians of witchcraft to claim that it constituted an aberration from the normal pattern of English witchcraft. But this view is in some measure misleading, for even in the mass trials of 1645, a number of the 'normal' themes of English witchcraft were strongly present: the concern over *maleficium*, the witch stereotype of the poor elderly woman, the importance of that distinctive element in English witchcraft, the familiar spirit. We have already examined the basic elements of popular witchcraft beliefs and argued that they fitted into a wider belief system which, first, was too rich to be written off as 'superstition' and, second, changed and became more elaborate over time. The point has now come to return to this problem of popular belief and to consider a number of phenomena which, although they were doubtlessly long-established, became better documented as the seventeenth century progressed.

The fundamental problem is that of evidence, or, to be more precise, what we are to make of such evidence as we possess. This issue, in a sense, concerns a tension between the quantity of our evidence and its quality. Let us return to one of our major sources of information about witchcraft, the records of the criminal courts. Outside Essex in the second half of Elizabeth's reign, and Essex, Suffolk and Norfolk in 1645, witchcraft did not figure prominently among the statistics of serious crime. Normally the assizes were concerned with offences which modern thinking would recognize as 'real' crimes: homicide, theft and burglary. And yet, looking at other sources, there is a sense that witchcraft was much more important, or at least much more pervasive, than the statistical level at which it was prosecuted might, for most of the time, suggest. And examination of this wider evidence re-emphasizes the sheer complexity of witch beliefs, and the fact that they were widespread and culturally patterned rather than being the product of individual credulity.

Witchcraft, we must reiterate, is an historical topic which is amenable to being studied on a variety of levels. The objective here is to return to the level of interpersonal tensions, of local fears and local accusations against the witch, and to try to reconstruct what witchcraft meant to those involved in a witch-craft accusation, or those attempting to protect themselves from witchcraft. The nature of the evidence makes it impossible to conduct this exercise on anything other than an anecdotal basis; there are no prospects here of an analysis based on quantification. Yet adopting this line of approach leads us back to the very heart of witchcraft as a cultural phenomenon.

❥ Many modern interpretations have portrayed those prosecuted for witch-craft as the victims of various forces: thus, for followers of Margaret Murray's thesis, they could be regarded as adherents of a pre-Christian fertility cult who were victims of the intolerance of the Christian Church; for writers within the women's movement, they were the victims of patriarchy and misogyny; for Alan Macfarlane, they were the victims of the social consequences of economic and demographic pressures. Many inhabitants of early modern England, not least those who thought they or their families or cattle were being bewitched, would have seen things very differently. To them, the witch was frequently a frightening individual who could do harm with terrible speed and terrible ef-fectiveness. Elizabeth Stile, one of the Windsor witches tried in 1579, allegedly gave 'one Saddock a clap on the shoulder, for not keeping his promise for an old cloak to make her a safeguard [i.e. an outer garment], who presently went home and died'. Yorkshire assize depositions from the seventeenth century reveal a number of similar incidents. In 1649 Abraham Hobson of Idle at-tended a 'pig feast' where Jane Kighly was present. He had already suspected her of bewitching a pig of his, but she reassured him that 'shee loved him and all his house' and gave him 'a little clappe on his knee'. The next day the knee was 'like it had been nettled, & very angry', and eventually a general paralysis set in. Mary Allanson of Appleton Wiske fell sick an hour after Elizabeth Lively took her hand while thanking her for alms given at Allanson's door. In 1654 a Mr Francke of Rothwell fell ill when Katherine Earle, with whom he had been drinking in an alehouse, gave him a blow between the shoulders.[1]

Given such ability to do harm, it is little wonder that people were frightened of witches. We have already noted Reginald Scot's comment on how 'these miserable wretches are so odious unto all their neighbours, and so feared, as few dare offend them, or denie them anie thing they aske'. Other commentators confirm this impression. George Gifford, in his *Dialogue* of 1593, had one of his characters say of a woman in his parish, 'I have been as careful to please her as ever I was to please mine own mother, and to give her ever and anon one thing or other, and yet methinkes she frownes at me now and then.' Edward Fairfax noted that one of the supposed tormentors of his daughters so frightened her 'wealthiest neighbours' that 'none of them refused to do anything she required; yea, unbesought they provided her with fire, and meat from their own tables; and did what else they thought would please her'. Oliver Heywood, the Yorkshire Restoration Nonconformist minister, noted a general disinclination to come to his house 'for fear of witches' after his maidservant was 'distempered and strangely taken' as a result of a chance meeting with a suspected witch on her way home to the Heywood residence. The effect of the fear of the witch on the individual was, perhaps, best demonstrated in those cases where a person thought to be bewitched saw visions of his supposed tormentors. William Bastin, a Devon man supposedly bewitched by Katherine Bright and her son Edward in 1660, in his fits saw the two of them 'run to him with swordes & speares in their handes & stabb and pricke him in the breast & in severall other partes of his bodie to his great torment & payne'.[2]

The sudden harm which might be inflicted by witches and the fear they might engender lead us to a basic proposition which it is easy to lose sight of: on this level, witchcraft was about power. The word crops up fairly frequently in witchcraft cases. A woman came to Old Demdike, an alleged witch who was at the centre of the 1612 Lancashire trials, and asked her assistance in killing a man, saying 'her power was not strong ynough to doe it her selfe, being now lesse then before time it had beene'. A witness in a Yorkshire case of 1674 alleged that she heard one witch tell another that if she could induce Thomas Haigh 'to buy threepenny worth of indicoe and look him in the face, wee shall have power enough to take his life'. A cunning woman who was called to cure a sick child at Scarborough in the same county in 1651 told its mother that it was bewitched and that the suspected witch 'did gett power of the s[ai]d child in the father's arms as he was bringing itt from the fair'. Oliver Heywood, in the case of the bewitched maidservant referred to, thought that Jaggar's wife, the supposed witch, had 'got power' over the girl. In 1672 a Cumberland man claimed that Elizabeth How was bewitching him, and that he 'did . . . alwaies thinke and conceive in his mind that she had gotten some power of him'.[3] One of the areas of witchcraft history which awaits further research is what might be described as the psychodynamics of accusations, the personal and psychological tensions which so often affected the relationship between the witch and his or her accuser. And in such instances, as so often, we sense the need for detailed, contextualized case studies.

The people making statements of the type listed above, unfortunately for the modern historian, rarely gave their views on where this power came from. Contemporary theologians, of course, argued that it was derived from a pact with the devil, and it is probable that this explanation gained some ground among the population at large. More commonly, however, the power was seen as either an innate quality or one which had been inherited: pamphlet writers and witnesses giving depositions alike frequently noted that the mother of an alleged or convicted witch had also enjoyed a reputation for witchcraft. Otherwise, there was a feeling that witchcraft was a power which could be passed from one person to another, usually with a familiar thrown in to facilitate matters, and there are even some suggestions that the ability to perform witchcraft was thought to be learnable or acquirable. William Perkins opined that 'witches are wont to communicate their skill to others by tradition, to teach and instruct their children and posteritie, and to initiate them in the grounds and practices of their own trade'. Thomas Potts, in his description of the Lancashire trials of 1612, noted how Old Demdike 'brought up her owne children, instructed her grand-children, and tooke great care and paines to bring them to be witches. Shee was a generall agent for the devill in all these partes.' Such attempts to pass the ability to perform witchcraft across the generations were not always successful. Joan Upney of Dagenham, tried for witchcraft in 1589 and possessor of familiars in the shape of toads, told how her eldest daughter 'would never abide to meddle with her toad, but her youngest daughter would handle them [sic], and use them as well as her selfe'.[4]

Evidence of how an individual was thought to be able to become a witch in the absence of a mother like Upney is difficult to find, although there are traces. In 1647 William Shelley of St Mary's parish in Ely repeated Peter Burbish's instructions on 'how any man might come to be a witch':

W[he]n a man came to the sacram[en]t let him take the bread & keepe it in his hand & after yt he hath drunke the wine to goe out w[i]th the bread in his hand & pisse ag[ains]t the church wall, at which time he shall finde something like a toade or frogge gapeing to receive the s[ai]d bread. And after yt ye party should come to the knowledge how to be a witch.

This formula is echoed by a Devon girl named Jane Maxie in 1638. 'When anie that woulde be witches did receive the communion,' she allegedly declared, 'they shoulde drincke the wyne and keep the breade and take it to the next bodie they met with; and that sholde be a tode.' At the very least, these two pieces of evidence, widely dispersed geographically, demonstrate how, a century after the Reformation, magical properties were still attributed to communion bread in the popular consciousness.[5]

Once the power to perform malefic witchcraft had been acquired, the problem remained of how to put it to use. Certainly, contemporary opinion was familiar with the notion of the evil eye. William Perkins noted the popular belief that witches 'by malitious and wrie lookes in anger and displeasure, may and doe hurt those upon whome they looke, whether they be men or other creatures'. Thomas Cooper recorded that it was 'conceited' that the witch could do harm 'by her lookes'. How this might operate in practice was demonstrated by a Derbyshire case of 1650, in which a widow named Ann Wagg was supposed to have bewitched a maidservant called Elizabeth Parkson. As the girl went into church one Sunday, Wagg 'stood in the way & frowned upon the said maide but uttered noe words, & presently the mayd fell sick'. Something very like this incident probably formed the basis of a Yorkshire Church court defamation suit in 1632. A servant deposed how her mistress attributed a child's sickness to Margaret Awcocke, and repeated Mary Atkinson's opinion that 'Margaret Awcocke was the cause of it, and that she was a witch and had an evill eye'.[6]

Harm might also be inflicted if one were incautious enough to accept a gift, or food or drink, from a witch. One of the witches tried in Essex in 1579 bewitched a man by giving him a jug of drink; another bewitched a servant girl by giving her some apple cake. William Somers, accuser of a number of witches at Nottingham at the end of Elizabeth's reign, was bewitched after he accepted a piece of bread and butter from an old woman. Another servant girl, this time resident in Devon, recalled in 1658 how a widow named Margery Stulston came to her master's house and gave her bread and butter, after which her master's hitherto tractable cows went mad and attempted to kill her as she tried to milk them. Joan Booth of Warmfield in Yorkshire told in 1650 how Margaret Morton came to her house and gave a piece of bread to her son, he 'being about fower yeares old & then in good health & likeing'. The child fell ill and his body began to waste, and, although doctors diagnosed worms, the boy did not respond to treatment. Two years earlier another Yorkshire boy told his mother how he had met with a woman who followed him with an apple and a piece of bread, '& would not p[ar]te with him till she caused him to byte both of the apple and the bread'. Soon afterwards the boy began to spit blood, fell ill and died.[7]

Perhaps the magical technique most regularly used in English witchcraft cases was image magic. The witch would make an image in clay or wax of the person they wished to harm and, as William Perkins put it, then proceeded 'to burie the same in the ground, or to hide it in some secret place, or to burn it in the fire, thereby intending to hurt the partie resembled'. The use of this technique figured prominently in the accusation of witches at Windsor in 1579, and also in the Lancashire trials of 1612; Old Demdike, indeed, held that the quickest way to take a man's life through witchcraft was by using a 'picture of clay' which would be pricked with a thorn or pin. Similarly, it was thought that obtaining and damaging a possession, most frequently an item of clothing, of the person intended for bewitchment was a method of inflicting harm. And there was that bewitching of the son of the Earl of Rutland, reported in 1618, when 'there was a glove of the said Lord buried in the ground, and as that glove did rot and wast, so did the liver of the said lord rot and wast'. Other techniques, such as the 'framing of circles, using of amulets' noted by Thomas Cooper, were also allegedly employed by witches.[8]

Most frequently, however, the malevolent power of the witch was thought to operate on the victim primarily or solely through the power of the spoken word. The general issue of how the power of words and speech was regarded in early modern England awaits further investigation. Suits for slander, one of the major areas of litigation of the period, demonstrate a concern over verbal aggression, and it is interesting that ecclesiastical defamation suits were, like witchcraft cases, an area of litigation in which women figured prominently. Scolding, another predominantly female offence, also involved high levels of verbal aggression. Indeed, it seems possible that verbal aggression was thought to have been something peculiar to women, and the ballads and joke books of the period indicate a widespread cultural belief that physical violence was characteristically a male attribute, while verbal aggression was a female one.[9] And, lest we should be tempted to play down the importance afforded to verbal violence, we should note that one seventeenth-century scholar recorded how, within living memory, two women had literally scolded a third to death. Little wonder that William Perkins should feel it necessary to attempt to persuade his readers that the spoken word had no physical force and that 'the voice of man by nature, hath no power to worke any wonders'.[10]

Evidence that, despite Perkins, many people felt the spoken word did indeed have the power to work wonders comes from instances of formal cursing. Thomas Cooper portrayed the curser 'invocating, upon her bare knees (for so the manner is) the vengeance of God upon them. And if she can conveniently to their faces, breathing out these fearfull curses and direfull execrations against them.' This, to Cooper, 'apish and blasphemous imitation of the divine justice' seems to have occurred with some regularity. Thus in 1622 we find Helen Hiley, a widow from Wetherby in Yorkshire, going down on her knees before her neighbour John Wood and saying, 'a vengeance of God light upon the[e] Wood . . . and all thy children and I trulie pray this praier for so long as I live'. Much the same ritual was performed at Chester in 1593 by Mary Weston, who was seen to 'fall down upon her knees, openlie on the rowe, manie being lookers on', and proceed to curse a man 'in raylinge & cursinge manner in anger'. Such cursing was felt to be efficacious. Thomasina Bafford of Liverpool was sued for defamation at the Church courts in 1690 for claiming that Ann Bushell cursed a brother and sister of hers, with the result that 'her said curses were the cause of their death or being drowned'.[11]

It was a very short distance from this type of curse, with this type of outcome, to the imprecations hurled by witches at those who were to become their victims. Cooper thought 'the effect of cursing' sufficient grounds to investigate a suspected witch, 'for when a bad tongued woman shall curse a partie, and death shortly follow, this is a shrewd token that shee is a witch, because witches are accustomed to execute their mischevous practices by cursing and banning'. The everyday experience of witchcraft provided many examples to confirm this view. Ellen the wife of Robert Garryson, whom we have met as a suspect towards the end of the Matthew Hopkins trials in 1647, was 'a long tyme accompted a witche and her mother before her, and that shee is a com[m]on curser', and that according to her neighbours 'much harme and damage' had been inflicted on those she had fallen out with and cursed. Demonological tracts, trial pamphlets and the evidence of witnesses recorded in court archives all agreed that the typical witch, like Elizabeth Sawyer executed in 1621, was given to 'cursing, swearing, blaspheming, imprecating'.[12]

Yet on many occasions the words allegedly spoken by the witch before *maleficium* could be ambivalent, even friendly. A witch investigated in Colchester in 1599 came into the house of Parnell Abbott and complimented him on his pigs, saying 'these be goodly pyggs, God save them', one of the animals dying the following morning. In 1636, among other accusations against a Lancashire woman named Joan Elderson, it was noted how she met with a child of Thomas Baxter. When she had ascertained the identity of the child from the girl who was holding it, she 'said shee would kisse her cosen and did so'. The child fell into a trance that night and died subsequently. In 1658, Abraham Hartley, son of a West Riding labourer, was thought to be bewitched by Mary Armitage, alias Capp's wife. Asked about his relations with the woman, he stated that there had been no 'falling out' between them, but rather that she had 'stroked him over the heade & sayde he was a fine boy'. Even so, the lad had enough sense to fear a woman with a reputation for witchcraft; he said he had been frightened of her for half a year 'by reason of some speeches he had heard'.[13]

❥ So witches were dangerous people who could injure you, your family or your animals with a look, a curse or an ambivalent phrase, or who might have such a reputation for exercising their malefic power that local gossip, 'some speeches' such as a boy might hear, would lead you to fear them even if you could identify no particular grudge they might hold against you. What could be done to frustrate the powers of such people?

The most effective way of dealing with a witch, certainly in the opinions of contemporary officialdom, was to accuse him or her before a court of law. Thomas Cooper, repeating one of the standard premises of demonologists, stated that 'the power of all witches is restrained by the authoritie of the magistrate . . . if once the magistrate hath arrested them, Sathan's power ceaseth, in being not now able to hinder and defraud the justice of the Almighty'. This position seems to have been reinforced by a widespread belief that bringing a witch before the authorities led to an immediate curtailment of her powers. Elizabeth Mallory, the daughter of a family of the Yorkshire gentry who in 1656 suffered from fits supposedly induced by witchcraft, declared that if the married couple thought to be bewitching her were committed to prison, 'shee should have noe more such fitts'. A witness deposed that, indeed, after 'shee was assured certaynly that they weare both in holde she was freed from hir fits'. The daughter of another family of the Yorkshire gentry, the Corbetts of Burton Agnes, thought to be similarly afflicted a few years later, was equally insistent that her chances of recovery would be enhanced if the two women thought to be bewitching her were brought before the authorities. The statements of witches themselves might help confirm such beliefs. Elizabeth Sawyer, according to Henry Goodcole's account of her trial in 1621, claimed that 'the divell never came unto me since I was in prison, nor I thank God, I have no notion of him in my minde, since I came to prison, neither doe I now feare him at all'. Clearly, the fact of the witch's imprisonment could be a widespread source of relief.[14]

The other respectable means of combating witchcraft, for obvious reasons most strongly advised by theological writers, was prayer. There was, indeed, a widespread belief that the godly were, if not totally immune from witchcraft, at least less likely to be afflicted by it. The clerical writers of demonological tracts, eager to persuade their readers of the unlawfulness of going to cunning folk or resorting to counter-magic in the face of witchcraft, stressed the need to depend on God alone when suffering from such afflictions (the Book of Job was frequently cited at this point) and there is some evidence that this attitude was operating on a popular level. Some, like Alexander Roberts in 1616, claimed that a lively faith in Christ was sufficient defence against witchcraft, and there is evidence that this attitude was present among the population at large. When in the early 1650s a servant of the Huddersfield widow Hester Spring expressed fears that she had been bewitched, her mistress replied that 'she hoped she had better faith than to fear either witch or devill', a reminder that one position open to English Protestants was to maintain a deep scepticism over the whole issue of witchcraft. More conventionally, perhaps, another Yorkshirewoman, the mother of Margaret Wilson, confronted by her daughter's having been reduced to tears in the aftermath of an altercation with the suspected witch Ann Wilkinson, 'bad her put her trust in God, & she hoped she could doe her no harm'. In 1661 Robert Phillip, a Newcastle upon Tyne labourer, fell sick and, seeing the spectre of the woman who was thought to have bewitched him, told it 'he trusted in Christ, he was his rock in whom he trusted', upon which, so Phillip deposed, 'he heard a voice (from whence it came he knows not) saying whosoev[er] trusted in that rock Christ Jesus shall nev[er] perrish'. The voice commanded the witch and her associates to go, upon which they vanished.[15]

Few received the benefit of such immediate divine intervention as a reward for their godliness and, as might be expected, putting one's trust wholly in God seems to have been more common the higher the position of the supposed sufferer in the social hierarchy. Prayers and fastings were regularly sought as a means of relief when children of the gentry were possessed by witchcraft, and it is occasionally possible to find direct evidence that the sufferers or their parents sought divine aid. Thus Elizabeth Mallory, when asked at one stage in her sufferings who was afflicting her replied 'she knewe not but only trusted in God and desired them to pray w[i]th her', which, we are told by a witness, 'this informer and the rest of the company did accordingly'. Edward Fairfax, the

Yorkshire gentleman whose daughters supposedly suffered a long period of affliction at the hands of witches from the autumn of 1621, at first contemplated counter-magic in defence of the bewitched girls, but decided to leave 'charms, tongs and schratchings to such that put confidence in them'. He opted rather to adopt the theologically exemplary position of relying on 'the goodness of God, and invoked his help, without tempting him by prescribing the means'.[16]

Not everybody, however, was capable of following this austere line and, as Fairfax's comments suggest, the temptations to resort to counter-magic, even among the educated and godly, could be immense. Oliver Heywood was involved in a case which illustrates this point. He was called in to help Abraham Swift, a boy aged about twelve, who had 'lyen long under a strange and sad hand of God in his body'. A doctor had been consulted, but had declared that 'it is not a naturall distemper, that he is troubled with, but he hath some hurt by an evel tongue'. The doctor recommended that the parents of the boy should 'take his water [i.e. urine] and make a cake or loaf of it, with wheat meal and put in some of his haire into it, and horse-shooe stumps, and then put it in the fire'. This was, in fact, a recipe for one of the standard forms of counter-magic, the 'witch cake'. It was held that by using it the witch would suffer considerable pain as a result of not being able to urinate and would reveal herself to the afflicted as she appeared in search of the source of her discomfort. The boy's mother came to Heywood and a Mr Dawson in search of advice, fearing that 'it may be some kind of charm . . . being afraid to offend God in such a tryall'. Heywood consulted with Dawson, and 'we both concluded it not to be in any way of God, having no foundation either in nature or divine revelation in scripture', although Heywood was aware of the superstitious belief that 'the witch that had hurt him would come and discover all' if such a course of action were followed. In the end, Heywood noted, 'I utterly disliked it, soe did her husband and she – I told them the right way was to go to God by fasting and prayer, they consented, we appointed yesterday.'[17]

As this account suggests, those who thought themselves afflicted by witchcraft had a number of remedies at their disposal, and at least some of them were willing to consider a number of alternatives: doctors, godly ministers or counter-magic. It is striking that, in this case as so often, the range of possibilities was left open until a fairly late stage, and the afflicted had no problems with considering several sources of assistance. Heywood and Dawson might have led Swift's parents to a suitably godly course of action, but it should be noticed that recourse to doctors was also a respectable and, among social strata of at least modest means, frequent step to take when witchcraft was feared. This medical dimension of witchcraft is one which still awaits detailed research; what needs to be grasped immediately is that witchcraft was, until well into the seventeenth century, a valid explanation for illness, and that many doctors either realizing the limitations of their own skill or being unwilling to meddle in such a religiously, legally and medically uncertain area, seemed very willing to pass doubtful cases on to cunning men and women. Thus in 1652 Grace Matthew deposed to the Exeter authorities how, when her husband had fallen sick, supposedly of witchcraft, she had gone to a local doctor named Browne. The remedies prescribed by Browne had proved ineffective and on her return to him he said that 'hee could formerly doe something to cure people that had byn bewitched', recommending that she should go 'to a woman in Broadclift who was sometyme his servant for that purpose'. Matthew went there, and received both medicines and advice as to the identity of the witch.[18]

We have considered the role of cunning men in assisting people thought to be bewitched at an earlier point, and a detailed discussion of their activities in that respect is not needed here. What must be reiterated, however, is that cunning folk were often widely known. Widespread evidence shows how, when suspicions of witchcraft were being discussed or counter-measures against it formulated, local cunning men with a reputation for effectiveness came readily to mind. Edward Fairfax, although rejecting their services, noted how at one point in his daughters' afflictions his household spent an evening discussing the reputation of cunning men in his area of Yorkshire and the success which those resorting to them had enjoyed.[19] Similar widespread knowledge about cunning men was revealed at the beginning of the seventeenth century in another case concerning the daughter of a gentleman, in this instance Brian Gunter of North Moreton in Berkshire. Having received no effective assistance from physicians, Gunter turned to cunning men, and was particularly anxious to obtain the services of John Wendow of Newbury, 'being a p[er]son supposed to be cunning in matters conc[er]ning witchcrafte'. Gunter sent his servants to Wendow, who gave good advice but was away from home when the servants were sent again when the girl's fits recurred. Gunter was anxious to send them yet again, but one of them, unwilling to repeat what would probably be a fruitless journey, recommended to his master another cunning man, named Blackwall, who, he assured Gunter, was as competent as Wendow. We return to the conclusion that people knew where to find a cunning man or woman if they needed one.[20]

Apart from doctors, clergymen and cunning folk, there seem to have been odd individuals with a claim to expertise in witchcraft who were called in to assist in witchcraft cases. Edward Fairfax, although unwilling to go to cunning men, was happy to call on the advice of someone he felt to be a legitimate adviser, Robert Pannell, a 'mere stranger travelling towards York', who visited the Fairfax household when he heard of the girls' possession. He asked if he could experiment with them to see if they were bewitched, 'which,' wrote Fairfax, 'I did condescend to, the rather for the said Pannell used to serve upon juries at the assizes, being a freeholder of good estate'. Accounts of possession frequently refer to interested parties with some knowledge of witchcraft taking a hand, or to people claiming skill in such matters making their way to the house of the possessed. And every witchcraft case must have served a useful educative function. By the end of the Matthew Hopkins trials it is no surprise to find the identification of teats on suspects as proof of witchcraft by 'some that were there whoe p[re]tended to have some skill in the discovery of witches'.[21]

There were, of course, more direct means of taking action against suspected witches. Despite their reputation for being powerful people, many suffered violence at the hands of those who thought themselves to be bewitched. Oliver Heywood, indeed, noted in 1667 that three men had been hanged at the York assizes for the murder of a Wakefield woman suspected as a witch. Mary Midgely, another Yorkshire witch, was threatened and beaten by Henry Cockcrofte, who believed she was responsible for bewitching one of his children. One of the characters in George Gifford's *Dialogue*, first published in 1593, told how 'some wish me to beate and claw the witch, untill I fetch blood on her, and to threaten her that I will have her hanged'. He added, reflecting what must have been the real experience of many who thought themselves victims of witchcraft, 'if I knew which were the best, I would do it'.[22]

In fact, the practice to which Gifford referred, the drawing of blood from a witch in the hope of bringing relief to the bewitched person, was very widely resorted to. The logic of this course was summed up succinctly by Richard Browne, the victim of a Yorkshire witch named Elizabeth Lambe, in 1652. He claimed that 'he was cruelly handled at the heart with one Elizabeth Lambe, & that she drew his heart's blood from him . . . he desired to scratch her, saying that she had drawne blood of him, & if he could draw blood of her, he hoped he should amend'. This form of counter-magic was extremely well known. Depositions and pamphlets dealing with cases from all parts of England attest that it was widely used by the early seventeenth century, while it was one of the practices censured by demonological writers: William Perkins, for example, singled it out for special comment. Witches were frequently compelled to enter the houses of those whom they were thought to have afflicted, and forced to submit to being scratched, ideally on their forehead, until they bled. Thus in the Warboys case of 1593, the parents of the afflicted girls considered scratching the main suspect, Mother Samuel, but desisted after they had 'taken advise of good divines of the unlawfulnes thereof'. Their afflicted daughters had no such inhibitions, one of them, Elizabeth, scratching Agnes Samuel's hand 'and seemed to be marveilous ioyfull that she had gotten bloud'. Evidence of the effectiveness of the practice was provided after the suspects in this case were imprisoned. Contrary to the belief that incarceration destroyed the witch's power, they allegedly afflicted the gaoler's son. The gaoler brought Mother Samuel to his son's bedside, 'and there helde her, untill his sonne had scratched her, and so presently his sonne amended'.[23]

Even without scratching, one of the recurrent themes of accounts of witchcraft is that of the dramatic confrontation between the supposed victim and the alleged witch. This could include the deployment of very direct counter-magic against the witch. In 1626 Goodwife Wright was brought before the authorities in the Colony of Virginia as a suspected witch. During a discussion about witchcraft she had apparently shown a suspicious degree of knowledge about the subject: in particular, according to one witness, Wright recalled that when she was in service at Hull,

being one day chirninge of butter, there cam a woman to the howse who was accompted for a witch, whereuppon she by direction of her dame clapt the chirne staffe to the bottom of the chirne and clapt her hands across the top of it by w[hi]ch means the witch was not able to stire out of the place where she was for the space of six howres. After w[hi]ch time good wiefe Wright desired her dame to aske the woman why she did not gett her gone, whereuppo[n] the witche fell downe on her knees and asked forgivenes, and said her hand was in the chirne, and could not stire before her maide lifted up the staff of the chirne.

Another witness deposed how Wright also told how while she was at Hull her dame was sick and thought herself to be bewitched. She directed Wright that when the woman suspected of bewitching her came to the house, she was 'to take a horshwe [horseshoe] and flinge it into her dames urine, and so long as the horshwe was hott, the witch was sick at the harte'.[24]

The object of other confrontations or meetings between the witch and her supposed victims was either to establish proof or to attempt to effect a reconciliation. Thus late in Elizabeth's reign the grandmother and aunt of Thomas Darling, bewitched by Alice Gooderidge, 'making conscience to accuse her till it appeared upon sure proofe, sent for her unto the towne to talke with her privately'. Henry Bullock, one of the accusers in the Lancashire trials of 1612, engineered a meeting with Alice Devise, whom he thought to have killed one of his children by witchcraft, at which she fell to her knees and begged his forgiveness. Some years later a Yorkshire woman, Margaret Morton, was thought to have bewitched the child of John Booth of Warmfield. Booth brought her before the child and Morton asked its forgiveness three times. A further confrontation involved Mary Midgely, who, as we have seen, was subjected to a beating and threats by Henry Cockcrofte. Another of her supposed victims, the wife of Richard Wood, went to her in the hopes of negotiating after cattle fell ill. After some hesitation, Midgely accepted six pence from her, 'and wished her to go home for the kyne should mende and desired her to take for every cow a handful of salte and an old sickle and lay underneath them and if they amended not to come to her again'.[25] It is in such meetings that something of the drama of a witchcraft accusation, of the need to confront, negotiate with or browbeat people with occult power, can be most fully sensed.

There were, of course, other less personally confrontational methods of combating the occult power of the witch. There was a widespread belief that burning something belonging to the witch, most frequently the thatch from her roof, would either force the witch to reveal herself or alleviate the witchcraft. It was in such a hope that, during the possession of Brian Gunter's daughter, the thatch of one of the suspected witches, Elizabeth Gregory, was burnt, while in 1621 the clerical author of the pamphlet describing the trial and execution of Elizabeth Sawyer in Middlesex could refer to the practice of burning thatch as an 'old ridiculous custom'. It was not just the witch's thatch which was in danger. At one point in the Gunter case the supposed victims of Elizabeth Gregory wanted to burn some of her hair 'for their better satisfaccons & for their daughter's ease'. In the Warboys case it was suggested to Mistress Throckmorton that she should burn some of Mother Samuel's hair and her 'hairlace'. In a London case of 1599 the parents of a bewitched child were advised by a cunning woman that 'for the childe's recovery they should cut of a piece of the witche's coate with a payre of sheeres & burne it togeather with the child's under cloth: which they did, and the childe accordingly was healed'.[26] As so often, taking any course of action, either traditionally prescribed or recommended by cunning folk, must have constituted a significant psychological release from the sense of helplessness which being the victim of malefic witchcraft frequently engendered.

Another testimony to the efficacy of fire as a force to counter witchcraft was the practice of burning animals supposedly suffering from witchcraft. Edward Fairfax deplored the practice, common in his area, of following cunning folk's advice 'to burn young calves alive and the like' when cattle were thought to have been bewitched, but the usage seems to have been very common. At Warboys in 1593 Mother Samuel was thought to be killing the calves and pigs of Robert Throckmorton of Brampton, who had 'dealt verie roughly in speeches' with her. He was advised 'that whatsoever next died, to make a hole in the ground, and burne the same'. He did this with a cow that died a little later, 'and after that, his cattle did well'. Here the secret of success was not release from psychological pressure, but possibly something more concrete: such a move may have broken the chain of infection among naturally infected animals. Certainly such practices were not universally conducive to the peace of mind of the owner of the cattle. Anne, the wife of Thomas Harrison, gave evidence to the Lancashire justices in 1629 about the bewitching of her animals by Janet Wilkinson. She burnt one of her oxen, 'but in the night whylest the said oxe was in burneing', she was so troubled with thoughts of the supposed witch 'that shee could not rest in her bed, shee still thinkinge the said Jennet was at the bedd syde disquieting her, whereupon this inform[er] fell to her prayers'. Falling to his prayers might have saved a lot of trouble for John Crushe of Hawkwell in Essex, who in 1624 was presented to the archdeacon's court for burning a supposedly bewitched lamb alive during Sunday service and accidentally setting the common on fire, to the disruption of the parish's religious devotions.[27]

These are only the more consistently documented forms of counter-magic. Contemporary sources name a wide variety of methods by which persons supposing themselves to be bewitched could attempt either to identify their tormentor or to block the witch's power: hanging amulets around the neck, putting tongs in the fire to immobilize the witch, nailing a horseshoe to the door to prevent the witch's entry and so on.[28] Together these provided forms of relief which, despite the strictures of theologians, were clearly regarded as effective by the population at large. That evidence of such beliefs is so widespread supports the contention that fear of witchcraft was much more pervasive than the number of formal prosecutions surviving in court archives might suggest.

❑ It is evident that witchcraft beliefs and practices were deeply rooted in local society and, we must reiterate, such witchcraft accusations as came to court were more likely to be generated by local tensions within the community than to owe their origins to pressure 'from above'. It is also clear, despite some evidence of change, that the concerns at village level, the stereotype of the witch and the range of remedies available with which to combat witchcraft, remained relatively stable from the sixteenth to the eighteenth century. It is, of course, all too easy to regard popular beliefs about witchcraft, and popular culture in general, as unchanging and immobile. Popular notions did change, most frequently as a result of the influence of élite ideas. The odd popular voice claiming to prefer prayer to the services of the cunning man, or recognizing the importance of the diabolical pact, is evidence of this, although here, as ever, we are usually having to construct our knowledge of popular attitudes from scattered and imperfect materials. Yet the central concerns of village witchcraft, with *maleficium* performed typically by an elderly, poor woman and which could be combated by a variety of forms of counter-magic, were as clear around 1700 as they were in the early years of Elizabeth's reign. It is, therefore, all too easy to contrast a monolithic, unchanging set of popular attitudes with the changing perceptions of witchcraft which are all too well documented in the large body of printed works written by the learned.

However, before we accept this clear-cut dichotomy it is necessary to confront a few complications. Perhaps our logical starting point should be the proposition that the early modern English community, whether rural or urban, was a place where gossip thrived, where reputations were evaluated, where discussable news was a welcome entity. In such an environment there is little doubt that witchcraft suspicions were among the more avidly discussed of topics. When suspicions crystallized against the Bedfordshire witch Mary Sutton, who was thought in particular to have harmed the property and family of a gentleman named Enger, so a contemporary source tells us, 'the report of this was carried up and downe all Bedford-shire, and this Marie Sutton's wicked and lewde courses being rumoured as well abroad, as in Master Enger's house'. Cases of possession were especially prone to attract large numbers of interested spectators, and it was, indeed, thought appropriate that certain stages in the treatment of the possessed were best performed in front of an audience. Thus during the possession of the Starkie children in Lancashire in the 1590s, 'all this while the honest neighbours neare about, coming in, the roome filled apace, some holding and tending the sicke possessed, & some sitting by'. Mother Samuel, confessing after heavy pressure to witchcraft in 1593, was forced to confirm her words 'in the bodie of the church . . . before her neighbours'. Even witches imprisoned while awaiting trial were open to the attentions of the general public. Henry Dunnant, in Colchester in 1582 at assize time on other legal business, went 'with severall of his neighbours unto the castle, to see the witches that were committed thyther', and there questioned one of the witches, Ursula Kemp, about the death of his daughter.[29]

Given such interest, it is unsurprising that some evidence survives of discussion within the local community either about witchcraft as a general issue or about specific cases. More frequently, however, the presence of such discussion has to be inferred. When, for example, Jane Maxie in Devon was examined by the justices in 1638, and expressed her views on the sabbat and related matters, it is difficult to conceive how she could have uttered the statements attributed to her other than as part of a general airing of witch beliefs. Similarly, a number of references in Edward Fairfax's account of his daughters' bewitchment in 1621–2 suggest that the witchcraft was one of the things that the girls gossiped about with their neighbours. Perhaps the most forceful direct evidence, however, comes from the Lancashire witch scare of 1633–4. This, it will be remembered, originated in accusations made by a young boy named Edmund Robinson and contained accounts of shape-changing, of sexual intercourse between familiars and witches and of the sabbat. Robinson withdrew his charges when he and his father (who seems to have encouraged the boy's accusations), along with some of the witches, were taken down and examined in London. In his retraction, Robinson stated that 'the tale is false and feigned, and has no truth at all, but only as he has heard tales and reports made by women, so he framed the tale out of his own invention'. One can imagine all too readily the content of these 'tales and reports', framed as they were in an area which in 1612 had experienced one of the most celebrated trials in the history of English witchcraft. Memories of one of the key figures in that earlier episode were evidently still current in 1627, when one Lancashire woman was accused of defaming another as 'a witch and Demdyke', adding 'God blesse me from all witches'.[30]

This keen interest in and avid discussion of witchcraft might all too easily lead to widespread fears from which something like a local panic might emerge. 'The pulpits also rang of nothing but divels and witches,' wrote a sceptical observer of a witch scare in Nottingham in 1597, with the result that many inhabitants 'durst not stir in the night, nor so much as a servant almost go into his mayster's celler or about his businesse without company. Fewe grew to be sicke or evil at ease, but straight way they were deemed to be possessed.'[31] Such episodes, together with the many instances of apparent communal maltreatment of suspected witches, have lent further support to those who would portray popular attitudes to witches as monolithic and unquestioningly hostile. Thus Lawrence Stone, in his discussion of interpersonal relations in the early modern community, has argued that the village was 'a place filled with malice and hatred, its only unifying bond being the occasional episode of mass hysteria which bound together the majority in order to harry and persecute the local witch', while Keith Thomas has referred to a 'tyranny of local opinion' in witchcraft cases.[32]

There is, without doubt, evidence enough to support such views, but, conversely, other evidence suggests a more complex situation. First, that so many people felt able to launch defamation suits after one of their neighbours had described them as a witch is evidence of the possibility of a wider range of reactions to suspicions of witchcraft. In 1622 two women in Almondbury, Yorkshire, fell out and in the course of their altercation one, Anne Coke, accused the other, Jane Kay, of being a witch and of having killed a child by witchcraft. 'Upon speaking of these wordes', according to a witness, Sarah Williamson, Kay 'tooke witnesse' and asked Williamson and other people there present to act as witnesses on her behalf. Clearly, Kay was confident that local opinion was fairly flexible. And the notion of 'mass hysteria' against the witch does ignore the issue of popular scepticism. This is ill documented, but does crop up, sometimes in rather unexpected places. The author of the tract recording the afflictions of Thomas Darling in 1597 noted, with evident irritation, a passing stranger who called at the boy's residence, told him he was dissembling and declared that there were no witches. The tensions which preceded the Lancashire trials of 1612 provide another interesting example. John Nutter, one of the accusers at the trials, was cheerfully told by a relative to whom he confided his fears that he was bewitched that 'thou art a foolish ladde, it is not so, it is thy miscarriage [i.e. misfortune]'. In 1684 a Yorkshireman, involved in a discussion in a Leeds alehouse about the likelihood of two local people being witches, expressed the opinion that there were no such things. Too much should not be made of such sentiments, but neither should they be totally ignored.[33]

At the very least, the common people, like their educated betters, were capable of maintaining the distinction between the possibility of the existence of witchcraft and the probability that an individual suspect was a witch. Around 1591, at Headington near Oxford, in another incident which emerged as a Church court defamation case, William Wrigglesworth said to Emma Knott, 'thow art a witche, & iff there be anie witches in England thow art one'. Wrigglesworth was advised to quieten down by a number of his neighbours, among them John Dann, who testified that Knott had a good reputation and had never been 'touched or spotted w[i]th anye such faulte or cryme'. In 1661, again in a Church court case, a Cheshire servant girl called Lucy Williams was sued for defaming another girl as a witch. Witnesses testified to the alleged witch's good reputation, and a number of them agreed that her accuser was 'a very simple and ignorant woman' who had been reprimanded for reporting the defamed girl as a witch by others in the household. Edward Fairfax noted that the case against his daughters' supposed tormentors was undermined by a petition to the assize judges in support of the accused witches' good character. A similar petition, dating from 1651, survives in the Northern Circuit assize records. This, to which 200 signatures were appended, was in support of Mary Hickington, 'now a condemned prisoner in Yorke castle for witchcraft'. The petitioners declared that both she and her husband (who had previously served in the parliamentary army at Hull) were good and honest in their behaviour, and that Mary was never 'in the least wise suspected to be guilty of sorcery or witchcraft or any other misdemeano[ur] not becoming a Christian'. Witchcraft accusations were probably as likely to be contested within a community as to receive unanimous support.[34]

But it is only rarely that sufficient documentation survives to afford the modern observer deeper insights into both the full nature of a witchcraft accusation and the broader community context in which it took place. One such case surfaced at Rye in Sussex in 1609.[35] Something like 20,000 words of evidence about the case remain in the town's archives (Rye, as a Cinque Port, had its own criminal jurisdiction), while the general social and economic history of the town has been studied in depth. The case centred on accusations against Anne Bennett and her daughter, Anne Taylor, both of whom had reputations as cunning women. The two women were apparently approached by Susan Swapper, who was troubled by visions of fairies, and their attempts to help her by contacting her tormentors led to accusations of consorting with spirits (a capital offence under the 1604 statute), while Anne Taylor was accused of murdering a man by witchcraft. Reconstructing the background of these accusations sets them firmly in their context. Rye, a small coastal town, was suffering from economic decline and was disrupted by internal faction fighting between groupings centred on different trade interests, this conflict being further exacerbated by religious splits. This situation was also complicated by the eagerness with which some members of the town's governing élite joined in the witch-hunting, and the way in which all parties joined together when an outsider, Henry Howard, Earl of Northampton and Lord Warden of the Cinque Ports, attempted to limit the mayor and jurats' powers by denying their right to try witchcraft cases. As even this brief description of the incident demonstrates, witchcraft was not limited to rural villages; it could involve people of at least a local importance, and it might arise not so much from local 'mass hysteria' as from the fissures opened up by economic and religious factions.

For a final illustration of how witchcraft accusations might be contested locally, as well as evidence of their potency, let us turn to another Yorkshire case, this time dating from the mid-1670s. As a result of information given by a teenage girl called Mary Moor, suspicions of witchcraft fell on Ann Shillito, Susan Hinchcliffe and her husband, Joseph. This accusation prompted a petition in support of the alleged witches, signed by fifty members of the Hinchcliffes' home parish, Denbigh. The petition attested to the good character of Susan Hinchcliffe, noted that 'touching the said girl that now informs, some of us could say too much concerning her, of a quite different nature', and declared the accusation of witchcraft 'gros and groundless (if not malitious)'. The local justices, obviously worried by the case, seem initially to have planned not to transfer it to the assizes but to try it locally. Their efforts, and those of the petitioners, were in vain. Oliver Heywood recorded that,

One Joseph Hincline and his wife being accused of witchcraft, and upon deposition on oath being bound to the assizes, he could not bear it but fainted, went out one Thursday morning, Feb 4 1674–5 hanged himself in a wood near his house, was not found till the Lord's day, his wife dyed in her bed, spoke and acted as a Christian praying for her adversarys that falsely accused her, was buryed on Feb 4 – before he was found.

Arguably the impression created by such stories provides the surest guide to the social and cultural significance of witchcraft accusations in early modern England.[36]

With witchcraft, then, we are confronted with a complex set of beliefs and practices which, by their very nature, were fluid, ambivalent and sometimes ill defined. It is obvious that for most individuals most of the time witchcraft was not a central feature of life. In England, unlike some societies studied by anthropologists, it was not usual to attribute all misfortunes to witchcraft. Conversely, witchcraft was something which people knew about. It was lodged firmly in the general consciousness and related to those finely graded hierarchies of wealth, status, reputation and power which operated even in the most backward village community and whose existence, despite their elusiveness, historians ignore at their peril. When these hierarchies were challenged or had to contain or explain conflict, witchcraft was one of the phenomena which were thought relevant. Even if the model of transferring guilt when beggars were turned away from the door is not universally applicable, it is evident that most witchcraft accusations were related to competition and aggression. On a general level, witchcraft accusations usually involved overt hostility and a denial of those norms of neighbourliness and communal solidarity which the age held so dear.

But individual cases prompted gossip, and allowed many members of the local community to become spectators, even participants. Moreover, as far as we can surmise from scattered scraps of evidence, witchcraft was something which might be discussed in the abstract. This meant that people's response to witchcraft was patterned. They knew what to do when they thought they were bewitched, they often had all too clear a notion of who potential witches might be and, in general, they knew where the local cunning man was to be found. Yet, as the last few paragraphs have suggested, popular attitudes to witchcraft were not simply characterized by a monolithic and automatic credulity. The common people, within the perhaps narrow confines of their mental world, were generally able to assess information and reputations, and at times to form a sceptical opinion about the reality, if not of witchcraft as a whole, at least of the powers attributed to the individual accused of witchcraft. But whatever complications close reading of surviving evidence about popular witchcraft beliefs suggests, one recurring element in the patterned responses remains of fundamental importance: powers of malefic witchcraft were overwhelmingly ascribed to women.

CHAPTER 7

Women and Witchcraft

One of the greatest problems facing the historian of witchcraft is why so many of those thought to be witches were women. Taking Europe as a whole, something like 80 per cent of those accused of witchcraft at the courts were women, while in England a figure nearer 90 per cent was not uncommon in samples of cases tried at the assizes. Surprisingly, before the 1970s such statistics aroused comparatively little comment from historians, a result partly of the fact that most of them were male and partly of a general blindness to the importance of gender issues. But during that decade attention was focused on the problem by a number of authors writing from within the women's movement. Their interpretation of the connection between gender and witchcraft accusations was, however, all too predictable. For Barbara Ehrenreich and Deirdre English, authors of a widely read pamphlet on women healers, the witch craze was 'a ruling class campaign of terror directed against the female peasant population ... witches are accused of every conceivable sexual crime against men. Quite simply, they are "accused" of female sexuality.' For Mary Daly, author of a number of influential feminist works, the witch craze was a 'specifically Western and Christian manifestation of the androtic state of atrocity', a 'sado-ritual syndrome' which was 'closely intertwined with phallocentric obsessions with purity', while, in addition, 'it is well known that witches were accused of sexual impurity'. Perhaps the most recent restatement of this line of interpretation has come from Marianne Hester, who reiterated the notion that witchcraft accusations were one aspect of the male domination of women. Given the deep-rootedness of such ideas in some feminist circles, it is little wonder that the German writer Silvia Bovenschen should speculate on

169

the possibility that witches were for feminists what Spartacus, French revolutionaries and the Bolsheviks were for socialists.[1]

Although many may find the polemical tone not entirely to their taste, it remains clear that these and other writers have identified an important problem. Yet most historians would find their explanations over-simplistic, and would be appalled by their lack of acquaintance with a broad body of evidence, their limited grasp of historical context and their frequent factual errors: powerful historical myths usually make bad history. The problems are neatly illustrated by the use these writers made of that most celebrated of demonological texts, the *Malleus Maleficarum* of Heinrich Kramer and Jacob Sprenger. This work has provided writers with ideological positions as divergent as those of Hugh Trevor-Roper and Mary Daly with a handy lucky dip from which to draw materials to illustrate some of the more bizarre aspects of educated clerical beliefs about witchcraft.[2] The *Malleus* was marked by a deeply misogynistic streak, and it is no surprise that Daly should tell us that 'in order to grasp how thoroughly males justified their massacre it is necessary only to look through the *Malleus Maleficarum*'.[3]

Unfortunately, things are not quite as straightforward as that. Despite its frequent reprintings, there is some question as to how influential the *Malleus* really was. Its impact on English Protestant writers was limited, while we have noted how the council of that impeccably Catholic organization the Spanish Inquisition was sceptical about its value. The context within which the *Malleus* was written would, it must be repeated, repay further investigation; what is obvious is that arguing that it was representative of any hegemonic male view becomes difficult in the face of even a very basic level of contextual knowledge.[4]

The limitations of attempting to study the connection between witchcraft and women through demonological texts becomes even more evident when we turn from the *Malleus* to later English works of this type. Most of them discussed the problem of why so many witches were women, but their comments on the subject were normally brief and uncontroversial by contemporary standards, and contained little of that hysterical misogyny and sexual prurience which had marked the *Malleus*. Thus William Perkins mentioned the matter only very briefly. He noted that women were the weaker sex morally, that 'in all ages it is found true by experience' that most witches were women, and, like most writers, he traced the problem back to Eve. A fuller discussion appears in Alexander Roberts's *A Treatise of Witchcraft* of 1616. Here too, however, the tone was essentially conventional and calm. Roberts offered a standard list of female attributes which made women prone to witchcraft. They were credulous, and thus easily deceived; they had an over-developed sense of curiosity, and hence wished 'to know such things as be not fitting and convenient'; they had a softer 'complection [i.e. psychological framework]', and hence 'more easily receive the impression of the Divell' and, in converse cases, of 'good angels'; they had, since Eve, a 'greater facility to fall'; they had a greater appetite for wrath and a greater appetite for revenge; and they were 'of a slippery tongue, and full of words'. Such sentiments are, to modern eyes, without doubt misogynistic; yet they are far removed from the prurient fantasies of the *Malleus Maleficarum*.[5]

Since the 1970s, a number of writers have attempted to explain the fact that so many women were witches in terms which, while retaining an awareness of the realities of past gender relations, reject a simplistic model of male domination. Among the more important of these was a writer to whom we have already referred, Christina Larner, the great expert on Scottish witchcraft. Her interpretation, to recapitulate briefly, stressed the importance of the new type of Christianity being promoted by the Reformation and, in Catholic states, the Counter-Reformation. She regarded the more refined forms of Christianity thus produced not just as personal belief systems but also as 'validating ideologies', and argued that among the things they validated was moral purity, moral control and, by extension, law and order consciousness. This allowed her to link Christianization with another major theme of early modern history, state formation: the good citizen was now, in official thinking, equated with the good Christian, as officially defined. Campaigns for moral purity, or for law and order, tend to create deviants, and in this case the deviants in question were witches. In such a context, pre-existent misogynistic notions interacted with new religious, political and social processes.[6]

More recently, another approach informed by feminist theory has suggested further changes of focus. The Australian historian Lyndal Roper has carried out extensive researches into court archives dealing with German witchcraft cases. Her analysis of these sources, apparently richer than the English equivalents, has been informed by the application of modern psychological theory to witchcraft material, a connection which, as we have noted, a number of writers from Freud onwards have attempted to make.[7] Roper is aware of the difficulties inherent in this exercise, but argues that it does not 'endanger the status of the historical to recognize that some of its features are enduring: the importance of fantasy, the unconscious, the centrality of parental figures to psychic life, the way in which symbols or objects invested with deep psychic significance seep into more than one sphere of an individual's life'.[8] In attempting to follow through traces of such enduring features, Roper has suggested a set of connections between women and witchcraft which revolve around some of the dilemmas surrounding the psychic identity of womanhood. This, she argues, is a more fruitful approach than one which attempts to explain the connections in terms of the collective sociological characteristics of early modern women. The background lies, rather, in problems of attitudes to women's bodies, of their own psychic maps, of early modern concepts of the self and of the relationship between individual subjectivity and the wider culture.

Yet any generalizing theory about women and the witch craze encounters a major problem. Modern historians and the more sceptical of early modern observers alike have noted that the women accused of witchcraft were usually a very limited sample of their sex. In theory any woman might be accused of witchcraft, but in practice a disproportionate number of accused witches tended to be old, socially isolated, poor and to have an established reputation in their communities for being troublesome. John Gaule, writing in 1646, was just one of a number of writers who deplored the fact that

every old woman with a wrinkled face, a furr'd brow, a hairy lip, a gobber tooth, a squint eye, a squeaking voyce, or a scolding tongue, having a ragged coate on her back, a skull-cap on her head, a spindle in her hand, and a dog or cat by her side; is not only suspected, but pronounced for a witch.[9]

Recent attempts to explain why such women might so frequently be accused of witchcraft have focused on two, in large measure complementary, explanations. It has been argued that it was the economic marginality of such women which made their neighbours unhappy about them and led to their being accused as witches. We return to the contention that, in a period of harshening economic conditions for the lower orders, and of some moral confusion about how to deal with poverty, the old woman seeking alms was transformed from a proper object of charity to a threat to the stability of the village. A second strand of thinking would argue that such women, many of them widows or women otherwise living outside the conventional hierarchies of family or household, were not only perceived as poor but also as being outside normal patterns of control. Such women were anomalies in the patriarchal order and thus fit targets for the type of hostility which might lead to their being accused of witchcraft.[10]

Concern over uncontrolled or independent women might have been more intense in this period, irrespective of the phenomenon of witchcraft. It is now a commonplace that the century before 1650 was one in which concern over disorder was running at a high level. Educated contemporaries, many of them convinced that the millennium was at hand anyway, felt that they were living in a period when traditional social and political hierarchies were vulnerable to imminent collapse. Indeed, the cosmic threat that witches, as the devil's minions, were thought to pose to the ordered world fitted neatly into the patterns of thought which such concerns generated. One possible facet of these fears was worry that male domination, that central element of contemporary notions of hierarchy, was being threatened by female insubordination. In an age which was patriarchal, and in which the patriarchal family was seen as the basic unit and (for many) model of political authority, the spectre of the rebellious woman, most often found in the cultural stereotype of the scolding wife, was a disturbing one.[11] It is always difficult to gauge these matters, but there is at least some evidence to support the view that the early seventeenth century experienced an upsurge in misogynistic literature. Thus the notion that the Elizabethan and early Stuart periods experienced a crisis in gender relations, an aspect of a more general concern for the maintenance of social hierarchy and social order, might well have a bearing on why women, and women of a certain type, were accused of witchcraft.

Here as elsewhere, then, we suffer from no lack of theoretical positions as we continue our attempts to understand witchcraft. The issue, again as elsewhere, is to get to grips with the phenomenon as it was experienced in the past. One body of evidence which allows us to do this is a sample of depositions relating to witchcraft cases investigated by the Northern Circuit of the assizes over the second half of the seventeenth century. If we restrict ourselves to accusations in one county, we find eighteen such sets of depositions relating to Yorkshire, to which might be added two further cases from Yorkshire boroughs, one tried by the Doncaster sessions in 1605, the other at Scarborough in 1651.[12] These twenty relatively well-documented cases provide a total of thirty alleged witches, of whom twenty-seven were women and three men, the latter including two men who were married to suspected witches and a witch's son. In terms of the sex ratio, therefore, this sample, although small, seems to have been representative. Things become rather more unexpected when we turn to those who were the supposed victims of witchcraft and those who, although not themselves claiming to be victims of witches, gave evidence against them. Of those who claimed that they, their children or their animals had been bewitched, twenty-two were men and twenty-one women. Of those giving evidence, nineteen were men and twenty-seven women. A further eighteen women, along with others unspecified, were involved in the five occasions when searches were made for the witch's mark. It would be going too far to claim that the presence of women accusers and women witnesses negates the idea that the persecution of witches was somehow connected to the fact that early modern England was a male-dominated society. Conversely, the high percentage of women victims, the higher percentage of women witnesses and the active involvement of women in the search for the witch's mark suggest that there might be more to the accusation of women as witches than simple misogynistic attacks by men wishing to exercise domination. The point at least seems to be worth investigating further.

As the high percentage of women victims and witnesses in the Yorkshire sample suggests, many of the incidents which led to an allegation of witchcraft involved tensions between women. Such tensions surfaced in that most familiar aspect of allegations of witchcraft, the refusal of alms to a woman later accused of witchcraft. In the course of a tangle of accusations at Heptonstall in 1646, Henry Cockcrofte, a local yeoman farmer, described how a suspected witch 'as it seemed by his wife's relation', was displeased with the alms she gave her, while Richard Wood told how another suspected witch, 'as this informer's wife told him', when given alms of milk rather than the alms of wool she demanded, 'departed very angry'. Grace Johnson, a widow from Appleton Wiske, deposed how her maidservant had fallen into witchcraft-induced fits after giving alms to a woman at her door. Mary Mealbancke, servant to another family, recalled how Mary Waide, later accused of bewitching her employer's daughter, came begging for bread, '& this informer replyed that bread was no novelty at Christmas, whereupon the said Mary Wayde answered that your bread was a novelty at any time'. In another case, the intervention of a maidservant was crucial. Richard Wawne of Aslaby Woods, a butcher and grazier whose flocks were to be devastated by two Whitby witches, 'bid them begone, for they should not be served', when the two women came begging to his house, having been told by the maidservant that the women 'were ill thought of among their neighbours, & by some were accounted witches'.[13] Thus even that most familiar of backgrounds to a witchcraft accusation, the tensions generated over the giving and receiving of alms, frequently operated within the female domain.

A less familiar theme, located also in an allegedly female domain, which has been adduced to help explain the prosecution of women as witches is the repression of women healers as the male medical profession sought to establish a monopoly over medical care. Thus it has been claimed that the great majority of women accused as witches were 'lay healers serving the peasant population, and their repression marks one of the opening struggles in the suppression of women as healers'.[14] There does seem to be some evidence from our Yorkshire sample that women accused as witches had been involved in healing, although unfortunately for the usual arguments they seem to have been most frequently involved in curing animals (we await with interest attempts to link the witch craze with the rise of a male-dominated veterinary profession). Thus one Yorkshire witch admitted to curing cattle, while denying that 'she useth any unlawful art therein', while another had reportedly confessed to a justice of the peace that 'people did resort unto her for catell, to do them good, and that shee used certain prayers for that purpose'. More unusual is the case of Joan Jurdie of Rossington near Doncaster, accused of witchcraft in 1605. Jurdie, in the opinion of several of her neighbours, was a cunning woman. One woman deposed how, when she had sought Jurdie's advice on how to cure a child, she 'bade this examt [i.e. examinate, a person being questioned or giving evidence] . . . not to disclose it to her husband nor any person lest . . . I should be thought a witch'. Another woman, who six years previously had consulted Jurdie about a sick calf, deposed that she was now 'induced to suspect that the said Jurdie wife is a witch, because she doth take upon her to helpe such thinges'.[15]

Whatever the involvement of women in healing, one role which was definitely seen as predominantly female was child-rearing and child-care. As ever, we must be cautious in any discussion of the sexual division of labour in this period: women were involved in many forms of agricultural and industrial production, while the household's function as a unit of production meant that the distinction between the private and public spheres was less marked than it was to become. Nevertheless, most contemporary observers would probably have agreed that in early modern England, as in most societies, child-raising was seen as an activity proper to women. What should be deduced, then, as we attempt to understand the links between women and witchcraft, from the fact that twelve of our sample of twenty Yorkshire sets of depositions describe the bewitching of children or adolescents? Accounts of the young as victims of witchcraft, often with harrowing details of the torments they suffered, are one of the consistent themes in these depositions. Allegations of bewitching children also figured in the Church court records of the county in this period. In 1622, in the course of an altercation between two women at Almondbury, one cried to the other, 'away witche for thou bewitched Perkin's child that it never throve after then'. In another incident where two women were scolding each other, this time at Howden in 1637, one called to the other, 'hearest thou, queane, hearest thou, if my father Parke knew as much as I what end thou has made of fower of my barnes [bairns] he would hang thee all but the head'.[16]

The theme of the child as victim of witchcraft was not limited to our Yorkshire sources but recurs constantly. In 1712 the last woman known to have been
convicted for witchcraft at an English assize, Jane Wenham, stood trial in
Hertfordshire. Susan Aylott, one of the witnesses against her, remembered an
incident of several years before, when Wenham

came to this informant's house, and look'd upon a child which was in her lap, and
stroaked it: and said Susan, you have a curious child; you and I have had some words,
but I hope we are friends . . . then this informant lent Jane Wenham a glass, who went
away; and this informant was afraid of [i.e. for] her child, remembring she was thought
to have bewitched Richard Harvey's wife.

So many motifs present in one short passage: the ambivalent words, the loan,
the pre-existing tension, the reputation for witchcraft, but, most relevant for
immediate purposes, concern for a child. A child which, in fact, soon after 'was
taken in a grievous condition, stark distracted', and died.[17] Another striking
example of this type came in 1647, with one of the Isle of Ely accusations
which came towards the end of the Matthew Hopkins trials. Alice, the wife of
William Wade, told how she was in a shop with her child in her arms when
Dorothy Ellis came in to buy 'a half peniworth of salt'. Dorothy, 'laying the
hand upon the child's cheeke mumbled certaine words to herself', and after her
departure the child's eye 'fell a running'. Later that night the child 'fell a shriek-
ing out & would not sucke', and examination of its face by candlelight revealed
that 'the side Dorothy Ellis toucht [was] all swelled and one of her child's eyes
[was] out'.[18] Again we encounter the witch's terrifying power to do harm, once
more exercised on a child.

If many victims of the witch's power were children, and so many of the
accusers were their mothers, the fact that the stereotyped witch was an elderly,
post-menopausal woman introduces the possibility that one of the channels
along which witchcraft accusations ran might be inter-generational conflict between women. How children might help focus such conflict was demonstrated
by an incident in Morpeth, Northumberland, in 1675. Margaret Milbourne was
one of a number of women engaged in that other female occupation, washing
clothes in a stream. While she was so doing, her mother-in-law, also called
Margaret Milbourne, came and chastised her. The elder woman had been left
looking after the younger's child and claimed that she was too old to do so,
accusing the younger of being 'an ill housewife that can[n]ot be worth a groat in
her owne house'. The young Margaret answered back, the older woman made a
veiled threat and the younger fell ill a little after. What is striking is how this

altercation occurred in a female milieu: a domestic argument, revolving around caring for a child, between an older and a younger woman, taking place before other women who were washing clothes together.[19]

The Yorkshire material likewise demonstrates that the development of fears about witchcraft, and the determining of strategies in the face of a bewitchment of a child, might be predominantly female affairs. Consider Margaret Fish, a widow from Scarborough, who told in 1651 how John Allen's daughter, aged about four, was 'strangely handled by fits'. The child's mother, Anne Allen, was advised to go to a cunning woman, Elizabeth Hodgson, to 'looke or charme the said childe'. She went to Hodgson, who advised her that the child had been bewitched by a woman named Ann Hunnam alias Marchant. A servant girl, Mary Weston, told how she watched the child in its fits at the command of her employer, Anne Smallwood. Thus in this example the managing of a witchcraft accusation, prior to officialdom's involvement, rested entirely with women.[20]

Another such example was provided by the case of Joan Jurdie, the Rossington cunning woman. One of the supposed victims of her witchcraft was Janet, the wife of Peter Murfin. She had asked Jurdie to come with other women and attend to her while she was in labour, but Jurdie did not come until four days after the delivery of the child. When she did arrive, 'she would neither eate nor drinke with the said Murfin's wife . . . because the said Peter Murfin would not come to her house to drinke with her'. She went off, uttering threats according to one woman witness. Janet Murfin fell ill (her husband, the only man to give evidence in the case, told how the milk in her breasts turned to blood) and declared to another woman, 'I was never well since Satturday that Jurdie wife was here, for the same night I was ridden w[i]th a witch, & therefore I could never sup any meate since but supping meate.' Several women, as we have seen, mentioned Jurdie's skill as a cunning woman, while another, Jane Spight, told of the consequences of another breach of neighbourly conventions. Seven or eight years previously she had some guests come for 'a football play, and dined with her, and the said Joan Jurdie having likewise gesse [guests] at her house to dine with her, it was reported by one Wilbore's wife that the said Jone should say that it had bene better that this examt hadd provided no meet that day'. Six days later two of her husband's pigs had died suddenly, unexpectedly and inexplicably.[21] Such incidents take us a long way from ruling-class campaigns of terror directed against the female peasant population. What they suggest is that witchcraft tensions, witchcraft suspicions and witchcraft accusations were frequently one of the ways in which disputes between women were resolved, existing tensions being brought to a head by that most female of concerns, worry over a child's health. The persistent theme of the child as victim leads us into a world of jealousy, tension, competition and conflict in which women were likely to be the main participants.

Turning from the Yorkshire depositions to another court archive, we discover that the Home Circuit assize records provide a basis for some statistical insights into female involvement in witchcraft accusations. These records reveal that there were something like 1,207 calls for witnesses in witch trials in the counties covered by the circuit (Essex, Kent, Hertfordshire, Surrey and Sussex) between 1600 and 1702. Of these, 631 (52 per cent) involved men, and 576 (48 per cent) women. In individual cases, there might be a preponderance of women witnesses: fourteen women to three men in Kent in 1657, ten women to five men in Surrey in 1664, eight women and no men in an Essex case of 1650. In the South-East, as in Yorkshire, women seemed to have experienced no inhibitions about witnessing against other women before the courts. The significance of these figures is made clearer when they are compared with the sex ratio of witnesses for other offences. Thus, to take a random sample, in Hertfordshire between 1610 and 1619, 572 men and thirty-six women were called to give evidence in all types of felony case, a ratio of sixteen men to each woman. In the same decade ninety-two men and eighty-two women were called to give evidence in witchcraft cases over the Home Circuit as a whole: in other words, on one interpretation of these figures, women were fifteen times more likely to give evidence in witchcraft cases than they were in all felony cases. The simplistic connection between witchcraft accusations and male oppression collapses further, while, conversely, the impression that witchcraft accusations were somehow generated by disputes between women gains support.[22]

But we also find on a regular basis evidence of female involvement in witch prosecutions which goes beyond merely bearing witness against witches. This was the employment of groups of women to search suspects for the witch's mark. The presence of the mark, evidence of contact with the devil, was seen as confirmation of guilt in some fifteenth-century Continental trials, although the then current custom of shaving body hair from suspects does not seem to have been followed in England.[23] The first pamphlet account of a witchcraft trial, published in 1566, stressed the importance of the mark in proving a person to be a witch,[24] and as English trials progressed its importance remained central. It also gradually became accepted that the mark, with women, most commonly took the form of a teat-like growth in the pudenda, from which it was thought that the witch's familiar sucked blood. Contemporary usage dictated that the search for such a mark, of evident importance in helping establish guilt in all cases of witchcraft, should be carried out by women. The earliest known reference to the practice of appointing women to carry out such a task comes from an obscure enough source, the records of the court-leet of Southampton in 1579. The wording of the entry suggests that the practice was a familiar one. The leet jury directed that half a dozen honest matrons should be appointed to strip widow Walker and to determine if she had 'eny bludie marke on hir bodie which is a com[m]on token to know all witches by'. Three years later, the pamphlet account of a small-scale panic in Essex reveals that the systematic searching of suspected witches for the mark was an accepted practice in that county also, one such group of searchers being described as 'women of credite'. When, in 1588, the Puritan clergy gathered in the Dedham classis in the same county discussed how a witch might be known, 'some said she might be found out by serche in her bodie', although it is interesting, and perhaps indicative of the popular origins of such beliefs, that others 'thought that to be fancy in the people easilie conceiving such a thing and to be reproved in them'.[25]

The actual mechanics by which women were appointed to search suspected witches, and the degree of official sanction given to such searches, seems to have varied. Once more, Yorkshire material demonstrates the point. Edward Fairfax, in his account of two of his daughters' bewitchment in 1621–2, recorded that the women were 'by appointment [presumably by a justice of the peace] at the house of widow Pullein, at Fuystone, searched for marks upon their bodies'. Some years later Dorothy Rodes, another parent who thought her child to be bewitched, noted how the suspected witch, Mary Sikes, was 'searched by weomen appointed by a justice of peace'. A male witness in this case deposed how he went with one of Rodes's sons to Henry Tempest, a West Riding justice who seems to have been much involved in witchcraft cases in the 1640s, 'to procure a warrant for searching the said Mary Sikes and Susan Beaumont'. Six women, three married and three widows, were chosen. Another Yorkshire witness, Alice Purston, told in 1655 how she and other women were appointed to search Katherine Earle on the instructions of the constable of their township, who was himself acting under direction from a justice. Four years earlier another Yorkshire case involved a search simply directed by the local constable, while Frances Milles, deposing in the investigation of yet another Yorkshire witchcraft case, claimed that she was simply engaged to search the suspect by her neighbours in the parish of Thorpe.[26] By the mid-seventeenth century, then, searching was seen as a legitimate activity at both a popular and an official level.

One of the more remarkable pieces of evidence which we have for the recruitment of women searchers comes from the case of Elizabeth Sawyer, executed after trial at the Middlesex sessions in 1621. Sawyer's trial was rather hanging fire, with neither the trial judge nor the jury seeming to have much idea of what to do with the evidence before them, at which point Arthur Robinson, a justice who had taken a considerable interest in the case, intervened. He told the court that 'information was given unto him by some of her neighbours, that this Elizabeth Sawyer had a private and strange marke on her body, by which suspition was confirmed against her'. 'The bench,' we are told, 'commanded officers appointed for those purposes, to fetch in three women to search the body of Elizabeth Sawyer.' One of these was Margaret Weaver, 'that keeps the Session House for the City of London, a widdow of honest reputation'. She was joined by 'two grave matrons, brought in by the officer out of the streete, passing there by chance'. Sawyer resisted the searchers, behaving 'most sluttish and loathsomely towards them', intending thereby to prevent their search of her, but the women continued in their efforts, each of them deposing separately to the court about the results of the exercise. They found a teat 'the bigness of the little finger, and the length of halfe a finger', which looked as though it had recently been sucked. This evidence proved decisive and swung the jury against the accused.[27]

As this incident suggests, the credentials needed by the searchers might depend on good character rather than technical expertise. Other cases, conversely, suggested that women with some sort of relevant knowledge might be involved. Midwives were, of course, uniquely qualified to comment on irregularities of the female genitals. The exceptionally rich documentation generated by the Matthew Hopkins trials shows a number of them in action. A midwife named Bridget Reynolds searched one of the Essex witches, Elizabeth Harvey. Five women gave evidence against Joan Salter, one of the accused from the Isle of Ely, and deposed how they found three teats in her privy parts, 'which the midwive and the rest of these informants have not seen the like on the body of any other woman'.[28] Later in the seventeenth century, again in Essex, we find a midwife being appointed to search the body of a suspected witch 'in the presence of some sober women'. This she did, and informed the author of the account of the case that 'she never saw the like in her life: that her fundament was open like a mouse hole, and that in it were two long biggs, out of which being pressed issued blood: that they were neither piles nor emrods (for she knew both) but excrescences like to biggs with nipples which seemed as if they had been frequently sucked'.²⁹ Some midwives evidently felt themselves able to act as expert witnesses in witchcraft cases.

Not all the women searched, as the case of Elizabeth Sawyer demonstrates, submitted willingly, while a number of suspects claimed that the marks found on them were the natural consequences of childbirth or of injuries sustained earlier. But that the practice was widespread remains clear. Indeed, in one Oxfordshire case of 1687 we find a suspected witch actively seeking to be searched as a means of clearing her name. Joan Walker of Bicester, the widow of a gentleman, petitioned the county magistrates in that year to the effect that despite her good reputation and good conduct, 'severall wicked & mallicious persons enveing the good name, fame, credit & reputacon of your peti[tioner] have uniustly & without any ground or collo[u]r of reason given out in speeches that your peti[tioner] is a witch which odious name yo[u]r peti[tioner] utterly abhors & detests & all the works of the devill'. To clear herself, widow Walker requested that the magistrates should order that she 'may be searched by foure & twenty honest sober iudicious matrons & make report of their opinions at next sessions', and that the persons abusing her should be bound over to appear there. Admittedly, here we are looking at a late case, and one involving the gentry, but her suggestion that she should be searched by 'foure· & twenty' women is instructive. A criminal accusation at the quarter sessions or assizes would typically be screened by a grand jury of twelve or so men, and then tried by a trial jury typically consisting of another twelve. Walker obviously desired that the search that was intended to clear her name should mirror proper legal process as far as possible.³⁰ But here too we find a witchcraft accusation manifesting not merely male repression of women but rather a woman invoking standard procedures for investigating suspected witches in the hopes of ending such accusations.

And even when men were involved in witchcraft accusations, it is evident that many of them saw such accusations not as a means of repressing women but rather as something which was most likely to operate within the female sphere, something more or less peculiar to women. As we have seen from the Yorkshire depositions, many men giving evidence in witchcraft accusations simply repeated what their wives had told them. Let us take a final example. In 1651 depositions were taken about Margaret Morton, a woman who was thought to have bewitched the son of William Booth, a man from Warmfield in Yorkshire. Booth's wife, Joan, gave a detailed account of the illness, and told how the suspected witch was brought before the child to ask its forgiveness. Another woman gave supporting evidence, while a third, Frances, the wife of John Ward, gave an account of the results of a search for the witch's mark on Morton, told that she had long been suspected of being a witch and recalled that when two of her children had died two years previously, 'one of them said before it dyed, good mother put out Morton, who was then in the room where the child was'. William Booth was the only male witness, and what he had to say ran as follows: 'his child was greviously wasted and that he had a suspi[ci]on of the s[ai]d Margaret Morton to bewitch it by the rela[ti]on he hath had from his wife'.[31] As previously, we are left with the impression that detailed knowledge of the background to a witchcraft accusation was something to which women were thought to have privileged access. We must reiterate that it was not just that the people accused of being witches were women; it was rather that, in many cases, the whole business of deciding if an individual was a witch or if an individual act constituted witchcraft, how witchcraft should be coped with and how suspicions should be handled seems overwhelmingly to have been a matter which operated, initially at least, within the female sphere.

❑ It would be misleading to claim that the narratives on which we have concentrated here provide the only possible background to witchcraft accusations; in many cases men figured prominently as victims, accusers and witnesses. As ever when analysing early modern witchcraft, we do ourselves a disservice if we seek for monocausal explanations. But we have at least moved a long way from the positions sketched at the beginning of this chapter and have reminded ourselves that witchcraft was, in its gender aspects as so much else, a subject of considerable complexity. What has been demonstrated is that the close reading of contemporary archive material gives evidence on popular attitudes to the involvement of women in witchcraft accusations which is very different from that provided by an ill-informed reading of one or two demonological tracts. If nothing else, I hope I have shown that women were not the passive victims or dupes of patriarchy. They were, albeit within the limits set for them by a male-dominated culture, social actors with concerns and goals of their own.

Clearly, on the evidence presented here, the pursuit of these concerns and goals involved tension and competition between women. We are so used to seeing men and women as antagonists, as representatives of one of the great social polarities, that we tend to forget the possibility that women, like men, can be rivals with their own sex. I am reminded of an African woman who, when asked by an anthropologist why so many witches were women, answered 'because we are bad'. This badness, according to the anthropologist, lay in 'how the quarrels of children lead to rows among their mothers, about the frustrations of a barren wife, and the envy felt by a poor woman at the fine possessions of another'.[32] This anthropologist's informant, like the women upon whose depositions we have depended so heavily in this chapter, was clearly living in a society where female power was limited, and in which women were socialized to have a specific image of themselves. Yet it is precisely this contextual framework which has been missing in so much previous debate on the connections between women and witchcraft. Early modern society, even on the level of the individual village, was a complex and intricately ranked entity. One of the ways in which this ranking was achieved was through gossip and the evaluation of reputation, and it is evident from Church court defamation cases, from depositions about infanticide and from witchcraft cases that women were full participants.

The language used (admittedly most often in sources written by men) when witches and their opponents were described is well worth analysis. Thus we find that the women selected to search suspected women for the witch's mark were described as 'honest matrons', 'women of credit', 'a widdow of honest reputation', 'two grave matrons', 'some sober women'. As we have seen, the women suspected of witchcraft were of a different sort. Some idea of the divergence between 'women of credit' and the type of woman likely to be suspected of witchcraft is revealed by the case of Elizabeth Gregory, a Berkshire woman suspected of witchcraft early in the seventeenth century. The vicar of her parish was just one of a number of witnesses to describe her as a scolder, a swearer, an unquiet woman and a general nuisance among her neighbours. Interestingly, he added that she was 'such an one as the weomen of the towne where she dwelleth will not accept of her companye at churchinges, weddinges or at the labors and child birthes of weomen'. We return again to tensions within the female sphere.[33]

Yet we must not forget the probability that the parameters of this sphere were created by the ideological and practical constraints imposed, perhaps in large measure unconsciously, by a male-dominated society. As we have seen, witch accusations were not, as some have claimed, the outcome of straightforward woman-hating. Yet, as I have suggested, women's involvement in accusing, searching and giving evidence against other women suspected of being witches does not negate the fact that early modern England was a patriarchal society. What it does suggest is that we need to deploy a little sophistication in our discussions of what patriarchy was and how it operated, No political system, certainly none in the sixteenth or seventeenth century, could survive without at least the passive support of most of the ruled. Thus the patriarchal elements which helped structure social hierarchies, and people's perceptions of those hierarchies, in early modern England could work only if most women were willing to go along with them. It must have been very difficult for the women at the time to imagine alternative ways of how things might be ordered, or, even if they could imagine them, to discover ways of implementing changes. It is, therefore, hardly surprising that when male authority offered women a chance to participate in the system – for example, in searching a suspected witch for the mark – they should take it.

More generally, it is unsurprising that women, their access to so many avenues of social power blocked or limited, should direct many of their quarrels through such channels as *were* open to them. The point was well made by Peter Rushton in his discussion of Durham Church court defamation cases:

it could be that women were their own worse detractors because they lived in a social world where they had to compete in defending their own, and discrediting other women's, reputations, in the knowledge that only they had to defend themselves against attacks on particular issues, notably sexual honour and witchcraft. In other words, they were competing to prove themselves in the face of a generally misogynistic double standard applied by a male legal system.[34]

On the level of contemporary demonological theory, the connection between women and witchcraft can, perhaps, be interpreted as evidence of the misogynistic and patriarchal level ingrained in educated, and frequently clerical, male writers. On the level of the village accusation, the connection seems to have rested much more on how female power and female rivalries worked themselves out in a social and cultural framework whose values may well ultimately have been patriarchal, but which left ample room for women to interact, to argue, to come into friction with each other, to develop and to follow their own social strategies.

For there evidently was, in everyday life, such a thing as female power. The whole concept of 'power' was, as I have argued, central to popular notions of witchcraft, yet how it operated in the context of interpersonal, familial or community relations remains a difficult problem, which has so far been little investigated by historians. Such issues have been rather more studied by anthropologists, one of whom, Jill Dubisch, has opened up what may well be a useful line of approach in her discussion of what she terms 'negative power', the 'power to make trouble', which constituted 'a generally unacknowledged political act, aimed at achieving control over people'.[35] Here, perhaps, we encounter one element of the way in which the witch, and her sister, the scold, were thought to operate. At the very least, it would seem useful for historians to incorporate this notion of female power, or perhaps more accurately female struggles for local power, into their discussions of witchcraft accusations, and see the gender bias in these accusations not so much as the outcome of a war between the sexes but rather as a struggle between women for the control of female social space. As Christina Larner put it, 'where men might use knives, women used words . . . the cursing and bewitching women were the female equivalent of violent males. They were the disturbers of the social order; they were those who would not easily cooperate with others; they were aggressive.'[36]

The discussion of the role of women in witchcraft cases which has formed much of the subject matter of this chapter has, I hope, provided adequate illustration of this point. But to emphasize it, let us turn to a final illustration, preserved in the ecclesiastical court records of Cheshire for 1662. The case arose because of problems between Mary Briscoe and Ann Wright. A daughter of Wright, aged about twelve, had fallen ill and was 'sadly afflicted in a strange manner by fitts', in the course of which 'she would many times say that Mary Briscoe pricked her to the heart with pins and would have her heart and the like, and she did swell much in the body and soe died'. In consequence, so a witness named Cicely Winne deposed, 'the said Mary Briscoe was suspected by many neighbours to be the cause both of her afflictinge and a brother of hers who was sadly afflicted before that & dyed in a strange manner'.

On first sight, this case seems typical: the afflicted child, the allegations of witchcraft, the neighbourly evaluation and the launching of a defamation suit in the Church courts. But unusually full documentation allows the piecing together of something of the background of this very typical litigation. Neither woman was a stranger to trouble. Briscoe was described as a 'very troublesome and wrangling woman among her neighbours' and as a 'very wilfull and high spirited woman amongst her neighbours', whose husband, worried about the allegations of witchcraft against her, had told a neighbour that 'he was much troubled at it but he could not rule her, and he was very much afraid that she would come to the same end as her moth[er] did', adding that her mother 'fell to it [presumably witchcraft] till it brought her to her end'. But Wright, her accuser, had given birth to an illegitimate child just after the Restoration, and had refused both to identify its father and to do penance for it, while according to one witness she had accused Briscoe of bewitching her when the child was conceived. At about the same time her husband was in trouble for treasonable speeches against the restored Stuart monarch, and Ann was reported to have expressed her disquiet at having been forced to be a witness against him. Another woman claimed that Wright had defamed her for adultery, while it was also revealed that the two women were previously locked in a dispute over possession of a house, a dispute which had already spawned a suit which had been arbitrated by a justice of the peace. Wright and Briscoe were clearly both contentious women and, rather than being victims of a patriarchal legal system, were clearly willing and able to use the law in pursuit of their ends.[57]

Finally, there remain those problems of female psychology which, as was noted earlier in this chapter, have been identified as part of the connection between women and witchcraft. The subject is, perhaps, one which might best be set aside to await further research. At present, though, whatever reservations exist about the application of modern psychoanalysis to early modern people, it is clear that clues suggest the subject is worth pursuing.

Let us begin with a slightly unlikely source, a Roundhead propaganda news-sheet, *The Parliament's Post*, of 29 July – 4 August 1645. An anonymous writer in this journal turned his attention to the Matthew Hopkins trials, which were then raging in the eastern counties. The writer was obviously educated, referring to the works of 'the learned Francis Suarez', and aware of the debate which surrounded the possibility of spirits becoming a physical reality. Commenting on the current trials, he noted that 'we finde the divell in the shape of a personable man hath had carnall copulation with these women'. The writer then declared that the devil neither appeared 'in a reall body', nor, 'being a spirit', took any pleasure in 'the carnall acts', arguing rather, in what was then current vogue, that 'the female being the weaker sex, and the inclination of the flesh being prone unto lust, the divell maketh choyce by that way most to oblige his servants'. He (if we may assume the writer was male) then put forward something very like a psychoanalytical model of what was happening:

I am taught by the rule of phylosophy to affirme that it is onely a phantasticall body. But by the delight which these sorceresess doe receive from it, it should appear to be a reall body. However, the greatest delights in the act of lust consisting most in the imagination (as all philosophers doe affirme) why may not the divell abuse the imagination (the greatest faculty on which he workes) to apprehend those delights to be bodied and real, which indeed are but imaginery.

It would be crass reductionism to claim that all women 'confessing' to intercourse with the devil were indulging in fantasies arising from sexual frustrations or others arising from fixations on the father figure; but something other than the devil may have been working to 'abuse the imagination' of these 'witches'.[58]

Certainly, areas of female angst can be identified in witchcraft confessions. Let us consider Margaret Moore, a woman whose case has been studied in some depth. Moore was another of the Ely witches of 1647, who distinguished herself by confessing to her witchcraft both when initially investigated by local justices and at her trial. John Stearne told how Moore confessed to both making a pact with the devil and doing widespread harm by *maleficium*, and that 'she seemed to be very penitent, and sorry for it, for she wept at her tryall, and confessed herself guilty before the judge, bench and country'. She also, according to a witness, described the circumstances under which she met the devil. After the deaths of three of her children (a fourth survived), she

heard a voyce calling to hir after this, 'Mother, mother', to which the said Margaret answered, 'Sweet children, where are you, what would you have with me?' & they demanded drincke which the said Margaret answered that she had noe drincke. Then there came a voyce which the said Margaret conceived to be her three child[ren], & demanded her soule otherwise she would take away the life of her 4th child which was the only child she had left.

'Rather than shee would lose hir last child,' Stearne continued, 'she would consent unto the giving away of hir soule & then a spirit in the likenesse of a naked child appeared to hir & suckt upon hir body.' Margaret Moore's imagination, while operating in the wider context of a witch-hunt, was obviously being shaped by severe stresses arising from what was evidently a psychologically catastrophic bereavement.[39]

It is, perhaps, the insights given into the range of individual experiences – of personal frustrations and despair, which were clearly relevant to witchcraft accusations and beliefs but are so infrequently recorded in surviving documentation and so often lost in the necessarily schematic interpretations of the subject – that recourse to models drawn from modern psychoanalysis helps to provide. Further analysis of witchcraft sources using these models may well throw further light on the nature of accusations, and also on two key problems: the status of witches' 'confessions' and the linked issue of how far those accused of witchcraft believed themselves to be witches. Temperance Lloyd, one of three women executed at Exeter in 1682, confessed to sexual intercourse with the devil for nine nights in a row, to letting him suck from 'paps' on her body, to having been a witch for twenty years and to various acts of *maleficium*, including sinking ships at sea and killing their crews. Clearly, her confessions were shaped by the enthusiastic questioning of the mayor and justices of Bideford, where she was apprehended. But we are left to ponder what mental baggage she brought to her confessions, and what she made of it all as she stood at her trial 'perfectly resolute, not minding what became of her immortal soul', or as she went to the place of execution 'all the way eating, and seemingly unconcerned'.[40] We must also wonder in what way her experience, and that of others like her, was specifically female. At the very least, as Lyndal Roper has put it, 'willing or not, witchcraft trials are one context in which women "speak" at greater length and attract more attention than perhaps any other'.[41]

Whatever the psychic map of the individual witch, it is clear that witchcraft was something seen by contemporaries as appropriate to the female sphere. In much the same way, witchcraft might be seen by contemporaries as one of the ways in which women used their power and expressed themselves. Many must have felt that the use of violence or the use of the law as a means of gaining an end or gaining revenge was an unlikely remedy for the poor, elderly woman with a grievance. Witchcraft was more appropriate. On this level, it offered a source of power to the powerless.

Yet in our discussion of women and witchcraft we should not lose sight of one basic point: men were accused of witchcraft, and perhaps a closer investigation of such men as were accused would prove fruitful. The current interpretation would suggest that most men accused of witchcraft were related to a female witch, either through blood or through marriage, and much isolated evidence would seem to support this contention. Occasionally, however, it is possible to find a male witch who seemed to enjoy an individual career. One such was John Salmond or Smyth of Danbury in Essex, variously described as a beer-brewer or yeoman, who was first indicted for causing death by witchcraft in 1560, at a time when no statute covering witchcraft was in operation. He was acquitted, but was tried on two more counts in 1572, on one occasion with his wife, both of them being acquitted (he had, in the interim, been convicted for stealing rams in 1569). He was again indicted, on four separate charges, three of them involving killing people by witchcraft and one of killing a cow, in 1587. On this occasion his luck ran out and he was executed. Yet he had a career as a known witch which spanned twenty-seven years, and one is left to speculate on how many suspicions of *maleficium* other than those which surfaced in the official record surrounded him during this period.[42]

But consideration of male witches introduces a massive complication. As we have seen, most contemporary writers regarded the malefic witch as more likely to be female than male, and most runs of prosecution statistics from early modern courts seem to indicate that practice reinforced theory in this matter. Over 90 per cent of those accused between 1560 and 1675 of malefic witchcraft in Essex, to return to that well-documented county, were women. Of the cunning folk for whom records survive over the same period, however, some two-thirds were men, and John Stearne the witch-hunter commented that while 'hurting witches' tended to be women, 'those called white or good witches ... almost generally they be men'.[43] Obviously more detailed statistical work is needed, but a wide range of archival and printed sources would seem to support the contentions that there was no predominance of women among cunning folk and that the more learning or technique was demonstrated in the cunning folks' 'good' magic, the more likely it was that the practitioner would be male.

Given the virtual absence of contemporary opinion on the point (Stearne was one of the few demonological writers to put forward such a view), the significance of this finding remains uncertain. It would, however, seem to reinforce the commonplace of contemporary educated misogyny that women were more inherently evil, or at least more likely to give in to temptation to evil, than were men. If popular opinion tended to see malefic, 'hurting' witches as women, the female agents of a devil who was invariably portrayed as male, and 'good' cunning folk as potentially as likely to be men as women, we return to the problem of popular misogyny, and to some of the issues raised by women's movement writers in the 1970s, or at the very least to the need to probe male attitudes to the basic female attributes of menstruation, child-bearing and lactation. What we have demonstrated, however, is that if popular misogyny was a force behind witch accusations, its operations were far more complex and subtle than might appear on first impression.

CHAPTER 8

Possession

The model of witchcraft which stresses the significance of neighbourly disputes and village tensions has made an important contribution to our understanding of the subject. Yet, clearly, it does not provide a total explanation for witchcraft in early modern England. The time has
now come to examine what is perhaps the most important alternative model,
that provided by cases of possession. That human beings might be possessed
by devils was not, of course, a new idea in the sixteenth century,[1] while there
was no necessary connection between supposedly demonic possession and
witchcraft. Indeed, something very like possession could occur within the wider
phenomena of ecstatic religious experiences and other spiritual crises. But in
Elizabethan and Stuart England cases involving allegations of witchcraft following possession became more common, or at least became well publicized.
There is ample evidence, notably in the case books of doctors, that people believed that they or others they knew could be possessed or afflicted by the devil, by
demons or by other forms of evil spirit without the assistance or encouragement
of human intermediaries.[2] But many were ready to make the connection between
suffering as a result of supernatural causes and the presence of a malevolent witch.
This connection was to provide a major strand in English witchcraft beliefs.

Initially, let us return to two examples from the 1590s which attracted considerable attention. The first of these, at Warboys, affected a family of the
gentry, the Throckmortons, the main sufferers being five daughters of the
household. This incident was described at some length and in some detail in a
published work, which is a remarkable narrative of possession.[3] The other
concerned the activities of John Darrell. Darrell's career as an exorcist seems to

have been a long one, but there were four episodes in it which deserve special mention. The first was his role in the treatment of a seventeen-year-old girl named Katherine Wright at Mansfield in 1586. The second was his part in treating another adolescent, Thomas Darling, in Derbyshire about ten years later. The third involved his participation in the dispossession of seven children of a gentleman named Nicholas Starkie at Leigh in Lancashire in 1596–7. The fourth involved the possession of another adolescent, William Somers, at Nottingham. All of these cases were recorded in print,[4] and all of them led to allegations of witchcraft (indeed, the Somers incident almost precipitated a local witch panic), with the result that Darrell found himself in trouble with the ecclesiastical authorities.

The discrediting of Darrell did not end these cases of possession. In 1602 Mary Glover, the fourteen-year-old daughter of a London shopkeeper, was allegedly possessed after an altercation with an old woman named Elizabeth Jackson. The Glovers were a godly family and related to members of the capital's ruling élite, and the case attracted considerable attention. Some of London's leading doctors (among them Thomas Moundeford, seven times President of the College of Physicians) were brought in to examine the girl. Jackson was examined by one of the girl's relatives, William Glover, who was an alderman of London and a former sheriff, while Sir John Harte, a former lord mayor, also interested himself in the case. The business became a *cause célèbre* in the capital, with opinion divided between those who believed Mary Glover to be possessed and a sceptical faction which included the Bishop of London, Richard Bancroft. Mary's afflictions had begun in the April of 1602, and Jackson was eventually tried on 1 December, and sentenced to a year's imprisonment and four spells in the pillory. The trial was noted for its use of medical evidence, and indeed the case prompted the publication of a classic medical tract, Edward Jorden's *Briefe Discourse of a Disease called the Suffocation of the Mother* (1603). It also, by arousing the interest of so many members of the capital's élite, served to publicize such matters further and to provide more evidence of the gap in attitudes on how possession might best be handled which existed between popular godly preachers and the more sceptical élite of the Church of England.[5]

A few years later another noteworthy possession case occurred, this time involving another teenage girl, Anne, the daughter of a gentleman named Brian Gunter of North Moreton in Berkshire. The incident led to accusations of witchcraft against three women. One of them fled, but the other two stood trial at the assizes and were acquitted. Our detailed knowledge of this case rests on the allegations against the three women serving as the basis for a defamation suit at the Star Chamber, the surviving documentation for which is exceptionally rich. Anne Gunter, under interrogation, eventually retracted her charges, claiming that the accusations against the women were malicious and that she had simulated possession under pressure from her father. Her supposed sufferings attracted considerable attention. The girl was lodged for a time at Exeter College, Oxford, where her sufferings were witnessed by divines and medical doctors from the university, while subsequent investigations even involved James I, newly arrived from Scotland. Despite Anne Gunter's retraction, this well-documented case demonstrates how witchcraft beliefs might range from those local tensions and village beliefs which have become so familiar, through the social hierarchy to the monarch himself. The incident also demonstrates how possession as a culturally recognizable phenomenon was already firmly established in local society.[6]

Other references demonstrate how this recognition was widely diffused geographically. Let us take the example of just one county, Yorkshire. There we find that in 1601 Marmaduke Jackson, the son of a Mr Jackson of Bishop Burton, was allegedly thrown into fits after being bewitched by two women. In 1621–2 two daughters of Edward Fairfax of Fewston, a member of that clan which was to provide military leadership for Parliament's armies in the Civil Wars, were possessed. Their sufferings (and the trial and acquittal of the women who were thought to have bewitched them) were recorded at length by their father. Other cases are described in depositions in the Northern Circuit assize files, the best documented of these being the possession of Elizabeth Mallory, the daughter of a family of the gentry at Ripon, in 1656. A further remarkable case occurred immediately after the Restoration, when two daughters of another such family, the Corbetts of Burton Agnes, were possessed after being bewitched by two women. Their sufferings lasted for four years and resulted in two women being tried for witchcraft, one of whom was acquitted and the other reprieved after being condemned. The notion of possession, and the connection between that phenomenon and witchcraft, were therefore clearly matters of recurrent concern among the local gentry in the north of England throughout the seventeenth century.[7]

It is important to grasp that these and other such examples demonstrate that there was an established pattern to possession; it was something which people knew about. In one of the earliest known cases of this type, recorded at London in 1574, two teenage girls, Agnes Brigges and Rachel Pinder, admitted to simulating (or in contemporary phraseology 'counterfeiting') possession, and to falsely accusing a woman named Joan Thornton of having bewitched them. Many of the elements which were to recur with such regularity in later cases were already present: the fits and trances suffered by the two girls, the devil speaking through them in a strange voice, their vomiting of foreign bodies. The involvement of Protestant preachers in attempts to exorcize them, or at least in public prayer meetings around them, was also marked.[8] This standard pattern of behaviour among persons supposedly possessed spread rapidly and became a widely recognizable phenomenon. We have already seen how the pattern had spread among the Yorkshire gentry, and further proof of its wide diffusion is provided by another case which came to the Star Chamber, this time occurring at West Ham in Essex in 1621. Elizabeth Sanders, a yeoman's wife, told how she taught a young married woman named Katherine Malpas to simulate being possessed. Malpas, according to Sanders, was 'a fitt & apt scholler to learne the same counterfeite & dissembling traunces upon this de[fendan]te's first in-structinge of her therein'. The motive, Sanders confessed, was the 'expectation & hoape that much money would be given unto her . . . by such p[er]sons as shoulde come to see her in pittie & comeseration'. Malpas, it seems, not only proved a ready pupil but was also, according to Sanders, capable of elaborating upon the basic pattern of how possessed persons acted with variations of her own, while here too suspicions of witchcraft grew against another local woman.[9] Thus by the first half of the seventeenth century there was a clear and widespread knowledge about possession and its connection with witchcraft.

Despite the regular exposure of such frauds, the motif of possession re-tained its credibility over the seventeenth century. Indeed, the last decade of that century was to witness yet another controversy generated by a well-publicized case of possession. The episode involved Richard Dugdale, a nineteen-year-old gardener, whose sufferings began in 1689. Suspicions of witchcraft, although not entirely absent, were not of central importance here, but the incident demonstrated how both possession and exorcism were still live issues in the late seventeenth century. Dugdale, who lived at Surey in Lanca-shire, was seized with fits, began to speak in tongues and also, while possessed, ranted against the sinfulness of the locality. Helping him in his torments became a source of competition between the Catholics and the Nonconform-ists of the area, the latter staging fasts and prayer meetings to aid his recovery after the first had tried exorcism. When he eventually recovered, the Non-conformist clergy took the credit, although a full account of the incident was not published until 1697. This account attracted a counterblast from Zachary Taylor, the curate of Wigan and chaplain to the Bishop of Chester. Taylor had already written a tract against Catholic exorcists who had operated in his parish and now turned his attention to the Dugdale case, claiming that the youth was an impostor whose alleged sufferings had been exploited by the local Nonconformists. The resulting controversy, although less passionate and resulting in less active publication than that prompted by John Darrell, did show that possession and its remedies were as much a matter of theological debate at the end of the seventeenth century as they had been at its beginning.[10]

Indeed, the interest of the ecclesiastical authorities in these cases demonstrates how important they were in forming a cultural link between popular notions about witchcraft and those of educated élites. For the Church of England in the Elizabethan and Jacobean periods, the problems of how to interpret possession and deciding what to do about it were rendered all the more urgent because the Roman Catholic priests who entered the country illegally but in increasing numbers from the 1570s onwards claimed the power to exorcize. Protestant intellectuals might have written such claims off as yet more evidence of popish superstition, but there was always a fear that the public, particularly persons having family members who were thought to be possessed, might be less inclined to reject Catholic claims to be able to effect dispossession. In 1585–6 Catholic priests carried out a number of exorcisms in Buckinghamshire and Middlesex, and news of their activities caused some disquiet to the Privy Council.[11] The famous Pendle witch trials in Lancashire in 1612 were accompanied by the trial of three women from Samlesbury in that county, the girl accusing them of vexing her with fits having apparently been encouraged by a seminary priest.[12] A very well-publicized trial regarding the possession of a thirteen-year-old named William Perry, the 'Boy of Bilson', also involved a considerable Catholic input.[13] Clearly the Church of England could not afford to ignore such incidents; they became battlefields in the ideological struggle to establish right religion.

Yet as the Darrell case indicated, possession and exorcism presented the Church of England with internal problems, quite apart from the challenges offered by Catholic priests. There was a strand in early Elizabethan Protestant thinking which encouraged a desire to prove that the ministers of the newly, and still somewhat precariously, established religion were as effective at casting out devils as were their Catholic counterparts. But by the 1590s, the increasingly anti-Puritan mood in the upper reaches of the Church hierarchy meant that exorcism by Protestant ministers was viewed with growing suspicion. Thus Darrell found himself opposed by the Archbishop of Canterbury, John Whitgift, the Bishop of London, Richard Bancroft, and two anti-Puritan judges, Sir

John Popham and Sir Edmund Anderson. It was Bancroft's chaplain and a future Archbishop of York, Samuel Harsnett, who wrote the key tract attacking Darrell, while a further indication of the official mood came in the winter of 1602–3, when a number of sermons preached at St Paul's Cross attacked exorcism. The eventual tight controls on exorcism laid down by the 1604 canons demonstrated the triumph of the sceptical party in the Church. But the debate which preceded these canons in turn demonstrated how possession, and by association witchcraft, were very live issues of theological interest in the upper levels of the Church of England.[14]

These instances of possession also show how witchcraft in England, so often regarded as the product of neighbourly tensions among villagers, was also a live issue among the gentry. Time and again possession involved their children: the Throckmortons in Huntingdonshire, the Starkies in Lancashire, the Gunters in Berkshire, the Fairfaxes in Yorkshire. And, of course, in the possession of Mary Glover the central protagonist was related to London's aldermanic élite. There is the point that such episodes were more likely to be recorded, or at least receive full description, than were those involving husbandmen or agricultural labourers. But this very fact means that they provide us, admittedly on the basis of a limited number of examples, with a wealth of detail about how witches were supposed to afflict people, what could be done about such afflictions and, more broadly, what witches were meant to do and what remedies could be taken against their actions. Accordingly, these cases offer a distinctive line of approach to those attempting to understand the phenomenon of witchcraft.

❥ This contention is considerably strengthened by the fundamental point that in studying possession cases we are looking at very stereotyped patterns of behaviour. The descriptions of the sufferings of the possessed, if usually harrowing, are generally very similar. A typical example is the Cheshire Puritan gentleman John Bruen's account of the afflictions suffered by Thomas Harrison, a boy aged eleven or twelve, in 1602:

By his torments he was brought so low, weak and feeble that he was almost nothing but skin and bones, yet for the space of four and twenty hours every day – having only one half hour respite, which he called his awakening time and wherein they gave him a little food – he was of that extraordinary strength that if he folded his hands together no man could pull them asunder; if he rolled his head or tossed his whole body, as usually he did, no man could stay or restrain him. He would, to the great astonishment of the hearers, howl like a dog, mew like a cat, roar like a bear, froth like a boar . . . his legs were grown up close to his buttocks so that he could not use them. Sometimes we saw his chin drawn up so close to his nose that his mouth could scarce be seen; sometimes his chin and forehead drawn almost together like a bended bow; his countenance fearful by yawning, mowing, &c.[15]

Whatever the cause of such afflictions, the impressions they made upon those recording them, and upon the relatives, neighbours, friends and other interested parties who usually surrounded the bed of the sufferer, were profound.

The afflictions did not remain static: as such well-documented examples as that of Mary Glover or the children at Warboys demonstrate, the symptoms developed, often over a period of months. Typically, possessed persons would experience fits on the pattern described above, involving convulsions and considerable contortions of the body and face. They would also include quieter periods, when the afflicted fell into trances or what contemporaries described as 'melancholy fits'. In their convulsions the afflicted would show extraordinary strength, so that, as account after account informs us, as many as six grown men could not hold them down, while they might also become unnaturally heavy. The fits were intensified if the suspected witch was brought into the presence of the sufferer, or even came into the house where the sufferer lay; indeed, for the afflicted to go into fits when suspected witches were under the same roof unbeknown to the possessed was regarded as a proof that the possession was genuine. The possessed might also see the accused or their familiars in their fits and cry out against them. The devils inhabiting their bodies might speak to those present at the possession, and sometimes a full-scale dialogue might ensue between the possessing spirit and either the spectators in general or those members of the clergy who were so often present and taking a leading role in attempting to comfort the possessed. The afflicted also commonly vomited foreign bodies, most often pins, feathers and pieces of wood. Time and time again this repertoire of symptoms was reported by witnesses giving evidence about cases of possession or the pamphlet writers describing such cases.

Another recurrent feature was the age of the afflicted. In theory anybody could be possessed by the devil or by witchcraft, but in practice, at least on the evidence of those well-documented cases which are our main concern here, it seems to have been mainly children and adolescents. Most of those afflicted in the Throckmorton and Starkie households were in these categories, as were Thomas Darling, William Somers, Mary Glover, the Fairfax daughters and William Perry. The implications of this tendency will be discussed at a later point, but it does, at the very least, remind us that age, as well as gender and position in the social hierarchy, was an important variable in witchcraft accusations.

If the symptoms of possession were well known, and the possessed were often adolescents, so the narratives of possession followed a set pattern. Typically, the afflicted would fall into a strange illness, which from the start caused genuine puzzlement to their parents or other interested parties. Thus Fairfax's account of the bewitching of two of his daughters began on Sunday 28 October 1621, when his elder daughter Helen, who had been tending the fire in the parlour, was discovered by her brother William 'laid upon the floor, in a deadly trance'. Fairfax and his son tried to revive her, and then 'called her mother, and made use of many means to recover her, but in vain; for she laid several hours for dead'.[16] Frequently, as with the Fairfax children, at first natural causes were suspected. When Thomas Darling first fell ill, his aunt called in physicians, who could detect no illness 'unles it be the worms', and even when another doctor suggested witchcraft, the woman dismissed such an explanation as 'incredible', thinking it rather 'some strange yet a naturall disease'.[17] Worms were also suggested by the first doctor to examine Jane Throckmorton. Witchcraft was suspected only after another doctor, on seeing a sample of the girl's urine, suggested it as a more likely diagnosis than the falling sickness, which was the parents' suggestion. Even after this, the parents remained doubtful that their daughter had been bewitched.[18] Perhaps the most remarkable evidence of parental scepticism came from the Corbetts in Restoration Yorkshire, who, despite their daughters' insistence on the point, for several years rejected witchcraft as a cause of the girls' affliction, calling in doctors from York, Hull and Beverley and sending the girls to enjoy the country air with relatives at Pickering.[19]

Eventually, however, the search for natural causes would be discontinued and possession would be diagnosed. This step was usually followed fairly rapidly by suspicions of witchcraft falling on one or more local women. Usually, as in instances of village *maleficium*, the suspects would have an existing reputation for being witches, or at least for being difficult old women. Sometimes, as in the Mary Glover or Thomas Darling cases, an altercation with such a person might precipitate possession; in others, as in the Warboys case or the bewitching of Helen Fairfax, it might take time for suspicions to become focused, a process sometimes helped by the accuser claiming to see the suspected witch in their fits. The arrival of somebody claiming to have expertise in matters of witchcraft or possession might speed the process. Harsnett, in his attack on John Darrell's activities, was clear on this point: 'it seemeth to be a matter very pertinent to the dignitie of the exorcist,' he wrote, 'that he bee able to declare who sent the devill into his patient'. How the afflicted might act as a catalyst in provoking a large witchcraft panic was suggested by another of Harsnett's comments on the Somers case: 'as Somers named any to be witches, M. Darrell procured them to be sent for, for that they might be tried by Somers, whether they were witches, yea, or nay'.[20]

As Harsnett implied, the presence of a person thought to have special skill in dispossession or finding witches might be crucial in clarifying the situation for those who were confused or uncertain about possession. The role of such a person is demonstrated in one of the earlier cases of possession under discussion here, probably dating from 1573, involving the suffering of a youth named Alexander Nyndge. Nyndge suddenly fell ill, 'his father, mother, and brothers, and the residue of the household being present', and demonstrated those symptoms which were to become so familiar: 'his chest and bodie swellinge, with his eyes staringe, and backe bendinge inward to his bellie'. One of his brothers, Edward, an M.A., diagnosed possession by an evil spirit, and 'recomforted with him with mercifull wordes of the holye scriptures', and also demanded that the possessing spirit should 'declare the cause of that torment'. Alexander, racked with pain, asked his father 'to send for all the neighbours to help to praye for him'. The process continued, with Alexander suffering fits and convulsions, and at one stage looking 'much lyke the picture of the devil in a playe, with a horrible roring voice, sounding helbownd'. As family and neighbours prayed around him, his brother Edward and the local curate tried to conjure the spirit out. This they managed to do, after a sleepless night, at eight in the morning after the affliction first occurred. Although there was no mention of witchcraft, this episode demonstrates both how possession was already, in the 1570s, a recognizable phenomenon and also how an interested party might manage that phenomenon. And, of course, we are left to ponder how many other people had a mental image of the devil based on 'the picture of the devil in a playe'.[21]

Other cases similarly demonstrate how 'expert' advice might help to focus attention on the notion of possession and bewitchment. In the early stages of the Warboys episode, for example, a crucial role was taken by an uncle of the afflicted children, a Northamptonshire gentleman named Gilbert Pickering. It was Pickering who more or less forced Alice Samuel and her daughter to go to the Throckmorton household to confront the possessed girls. Clergy were also called in from an early date, among them Dr Dorrington, the minister of Warboys. Another uncle, Henry Pickering, 'a scholler of Cambridge', interrogated Alice Samuel in the company of other 'schollers'.[22] Thomas Darling was likewise offered expert advice and assistance at various stages in his suffering, the crucial intervention being that of John Darrell, described in the pamphlet account of his suffering as 'a faithfull preacher of the word'.[23] The Mary Glover case demonstrated another common theme, the subjection of the alleged witch or the supposedly possessed person to a series of tests, sometimes involving a confrontation between the two. In particular, the City of London's chief legal officer, the Recorder John Croke, staged what has been described as 'a remarkable set of rituals' to test whether Glover was indeed suffering from possession and bewitchment, and in the process moved away from his initial scepticism about her behaviour.[24] Every account of possession demonstrates how people outside the immediate family circle, whether other kin, clergy, local legal officials or local gentry, were willing to participate in attempts to aid the possessed. This is clear evidence of the widespread nature of interest in and knowledge about witchcraft and related matters.

We return to the contention that what happened in possession cases was not haphazard but was structured and culturally determined. Even what happened to many of the afflicted in their fits can be connected with the cultural context in which they lived. Consider Thomas Darling, whose afflictions were described in 1597. Darling had evidently internalized advanced Protestant beliefs: when he thought himself near to death during his afflictions, he expressed the wish that he 'might have lived to be a preacher to thunder out the threatenings of God's word'. 'Betweene his fittes,' the account of his sufferings tells us, 'he requested them to reade the scriptures, which ... they could not doe for weeping to behold his miserie.' When he was deprived of speech in his fits, 'hee would make signes of praying, with folded hands, sometimes lifting them up, and sometimes striking them upon his brest'. Later, the boy apparently entered into a dialogue with the devil in his fits, at one point crying out, 'Avoyde, Sathan. I will worship the Lord onely. Doost thou say thou wilt mitigate my torments, if I will worship thee? Avoyde Sathan, I will worship none, save onely the Lord God my saviour, my sanctifier and redeemer ... Do thy worst, Sathan, my faith standeth sure with my God, at whose hands I looke for succour.' Darling's interpretation of what was happening to him was evidently structured by his having been exposed to godly ideas. At another point, indeed, he treated his listeners to a lively description of hell, where he claimed to have been taken.[25]

More insights into how the sufferings of the afflicted might have been constructed can be derived from the troubles of Edward Fairfax's children. As the possession of Helen and her younger sister Elizabeth progressed, they gave elaborate descriptions of the spectres they saw in their fits and trances. Thus on 14 November 1621 Helen 'had an apparition of one like a young gentleman, very brave; and a hat with a gold band, and ruff in fashion; he did a salute with the same compliment, as she said, Sir Ferdinando Fairfax useth when he came to the house to salute her mother'. The young man asked her to marry him, 'and said he was a prince, and would make her queen of England and all the world if she would go with him'. She refused, noting that he seemed unhappy with the mention of God, and also that he tempted her to suicide. Mr Cooke, the minister of Leeds, then appeared to her, and at the girl's bidding drove the apparition away by reading prayers.[26]

The apparitions continued. On 31 December Helen saw a boy 'apparelled in scarlet breeches, a ruff in fashion, and a hat with a gold band, with whom she had much strange discourse'. On 10 January 1622 she saw 'a terrible monster with three heads, dropping with blood, a body and tail of a dragon, in the hand whereof a weapon with which it threatened to strike her'. The next day she saw 'one in stature not so high as a man, attired in white glistening garments', which set the pattern for a more elaborate spectre she saw on 13 January, when

one in bright clothing appeared to her, a man of incomparable beauty, with a beard, and his apparel shining; upon his head a sharp high thing, from which, and from his mouth, and from his garments streamed beams of light, which cast a glorious splendour about him. He spoke unto her and said he was God, come to comfort her; that the Devil had troubled her by God's sufferance, but she was so dearly beloved of God that he was come to comfort her.

Helen came out of her trance (the family had been praying with her) and declared that she believed the vision was God, 'or some angel sent to comfort her'. She was at first adamant in that opinion, although 'next morning with some difficulty we persuaded her to the contrary, by such reasons and scripture as our small knowledge could afford'.[27] Thereafter, the apparitions seen by Helen and her younger sister Elizabeth became less exotic, and tended increasingly to represent either the persons or the familiars of the suspected witches.

Throughout their fits, at least on their father's account, what the two girls claim to have seen provides a number of clues as to how the mind of a possessed, or pretended possessed, adolescent operated. For Helen, and to a lesser extent Elizabeth, did not just see a jumble of spectres in their trances: the images they saw, or claimed to have seen, were structured. Consider, for example, the arrival of the vicar of Leeds, Alexander Cooke, as Helen's spectral adviser in some of her early fits. The family had in fact lived in Leeds until about two years before 1621, and the two daughters would have had ample opportunity to listen to his sermons in Leeds Church. We have no way of reconstructing those sermons, but Cooke was an experienced controversist who had published a number of works against popery.[28] One can safely surmise that attentive listeners to his sermons would have had their sensibilities alerted to the wiles of the Antichrist. Similarly, the images of God which Helen recounted give us insights into how a young Puritan woman might see her creator, while it seems likely that the monster dripping with blood which she saw owed not a little to the Book of Revelation.

Helen and her sister also knew a fair amount about witchcraft. A young man who appeared to Helen in one of her trances on 1 January 1622 'took out of his poke a thing like a naked child and did beat it . . . he told her it was her picture, by which they did work upon her', demonstrating that she had heard of image magic. She was also familiar with the notion that if witches were imprisoned, they were incapable of doing further harm. She had some idea of the sabbat, declaring that 'all the witches had a feast at Timble Gill: their meat was roasted about midnight: at the upper end of the table sat their master, viz the Devil, at the lower end Dibb's wife, who provided for the feast, and was the cook'. And, of course, the witches' familiars, most often in the shape of cats, were central to the Fairfax daughters' accounts of what they saw in their trances. Interestingly, and again indicative of how this part of her mental world was constructed, Helen claimed to have driven off familiars in the shape of cats by reading that most famous of scriptural witchcraft references, Exodus 22: 18, at them.[29] If nothing else, Helen's accounts show us how far witch lore might enter the mind of the daughter of a godly and cultured gentleman.

Why should it have done so? It is impossible to tell to what extent such matters were discussed in the household before her affliction, but her father was clearly acquainted with both scriptural and classical texts relating to at least some aspects of witchcraft.[30] More telling, perhaps, are the clues given in his narrative to wider beliefs in witchcraft. Certainly, at the beginning of his account of his daughters' sufferings Edward Fairfax bemoaned the widespread belief in witches in his area and the custom, even among 'the best of my neighbours', of going to cunning folk.[31] Indeed, as we have already seen, in one remarkable passage he told how some of the members of his household sat in his kitchen and, in their discussion of Helen's and Elizabeth's afflictions, named a number of local cunning men and women and debated the success that those who had gone to them had had.[32] Moreover, Fewston is only twenty-five miles from Pendle Hill, scene of the famous Lancashire outbreak of 1612. Stories of witchcraft may well have spread across the county border, while in any case Fairfax noted that one of his neighbours, a Mr Robinson, had had his first wife killed by the *maleficium* of one of those executed in 1612.[33] That stories of witchcraft circulated in the area is further demonstrated by Fairfax's having heard of Mary Pannell, a witch from the West Riding village of Ledston, who had been executed in 1603.[34] Local gossip about witchcraft was obviously given added point when another local girl, Maud Jeffray, fell into fits a little before Helen and was taken to a cunning man, and when Fairfax's four-month-old daughter Anne died of a mysterious affliction at about the same time.[35] Helen Fairfax was clearly living in an intellectual and social milieu where gossip about witchcraft, knowledge of witchcraft and worry about witchcraft were commonplace. What she saw in her trances demonstrates how that experience interacted with the tensions of being brought up among gentry in a godly household.

❩ Despite a tendency for historians to make assertions on this point, our knowledge of the experience of childhood and, more narrowly, of adolescence in early modern England is as yet very limited.[36] Certainly as far as the experience of youth is concerned, most of what we know at present is confined to normative literature, interpretation of which is difficult. This literature, generally, emphasized youth's wildness and proclivity to sinfulness, and saw this stage in the life cycle as being, perhaps more than any other, the one in which the battle between good and evil inside the human personality would be intensified. Here at least we see a clear link with the theme of possession, where the afflicted was so often seen as being at the centre of a struggle between God and the devil.

This lack of knowledge of contemporary expectations about the experience of adolescence should make us nervous about applying modern concepts, and especially psychological concepts, to these narratives of possession in early modern England. Yet the connection does seem worth pursuing, and has certainly led to some fruitful thinking on similar cases in Colonial America. Marion Starkey's attempts to apply Freudian notions to the Salem prosecutions of 1692 now look rather dated, but she did at least ask some interesting questions. Subsequent work by John Demos on New England witchcraft cases has shown how an acquaintance with modern work on hysteria can provide useful insights into possession in the seventeenth century. And, even more recently, Lyndal Roper's work on German material has reopened the relationship between modern psychiatry and witchcraft in the past.[37] Even without dipping too deeply into modern models one point is obvious: however genuine the possession was to the afflicted person, being possessed or bewitched did allow young people considerable access to licensed misbehaviour and attention-seeking. As Joseph Klaits put it, writing of the Salem outbreak, the accusers

were adolescent girls living in a highly restrictive domestic environment that was ripe for interpersonal conflict, depressive states, and delusions. Possession allowed these young women to unconsciously act out forbidden fantasies and to relieve deep guilt feelings in the spotlight of benevolent concern from their superiors. For as long as they remained bewitched, they were not obscure village girls.[38]

Similarly Keith Thomas noted that a child who rebelled against religion on the grounds of being possessed by a witch or the devil would not receive the usual chastisement for ungodliness, but 'rather became the centre of a dramatic ritual of prayer and healing in which he was treated with affectionate concern. To be the victim of possession was a means of expressing forbidden impulses and attracting the attention of otherwise indifferent or repressive superiors.'[39] We need to know rather more about child-rearing, family life and attitudes to the age hierarchy in the past before we can be too secure in our acceptance of such interpretations. For the moment, however, they do seem to indicate some useful lines of inquiry.

Certainly, one of the most striking features of the accounts of possession was that they were usually very public affairs. One account of the sufferings of Mary Glover commented that 'it was an usual thing, daily, in times of her ordinarie fitts, to have manie beholders, coming in and going out, sometimes by troupes of 8 or 10 at once; and persons of worship and honour, which had waye made for them'. When a Hertfordshire girl fell into fits after being bewitched in 1669, people came from the adjacent villages to see her, 'some out of pitty, to help and comfort her, others out of curiosity to be ascertained of the truth of these relations, and some who were diffident of any such things as witchcraft or conjurations, who being fully satisfied in the truth of what is here set down, went home fully convinced of their errours'. Sceptics, of course, commented on how the presence of an audience seemed to encourage the afflicted to fall into their fits. 'It was an ordinarie course held by the keepers of the Boy of Burton,' wrote Samuel Harsnett in his attack on John Darrell's activities, 'that when any straungers came in, that desired to see him in his fits (as men desire to see monsters and strange beasts play their tricks)', the 'keepers' would read parts of St John's Gospel 'and straight way (forsooth) the devill must show himselfe, by casting the boy into some fitte'. Darrell himself noted a recent case (possibly that of Thomas Harrison, which was mentioned earlier) in which the Bishop of Chester, confronted by the possession of another boy, this time at Northwich, ordered the parents to allow no access to the afflicted 'saving such as are in authority and other persons of speciall regard and knowne discretion; and to have speciall care that the numbers alwayes be very smal'.[40]

These were not, despite Harsnett's disparaging comments, merely occasions for the idly curious to gather. The core of spectators usually consisted of the parents and other close relatives of the afflicted, near neighbours and ministers. These last normally came to the fore once it was decided that the problem was indeed one of possession and that medical doctors were otiose; they then had a clear idea of the importance of their presence. Thus Stephen Bradwell's account of Mary Glover's suffering told how once it was decided that 'corporall physicke' would be of no benefit to the girl, that it was thought 'a shame for Christians, to suffer a daughter of the church, thus to lye in the bonds of Sathan, themselves gazing thereat, but not applying themselves to such meanes as Christ hath left his church, and so in their hands, to use in her behalfe'. Accordingly, Bradwell continued, 'sundry godly ministers, and other devoute christians consulted, and agreed of a reverent assembling, and joynt humbling of them selves before the Lord, in prayer with fasting, on her behalfe'. The final dispossession of Mary, about a fortnight after the conviction of her supposed tormentor, Elizabeth Jackson, was seen as a battle between the forces of good and evil for the soul of the girl, the representatives of the forces of good being 'a company of such as feared God to the number of about 24, whereof 6 were preachers'. The tone of the meeting might be judged by how after a solid morning of prayer and exposition of texts by the ministers, 'diverse of the company called in the preacher still to be doinge, and not give the Lorde any reste untill he had heard us'.[41]

The combination of a central actor, a large and anxious audience and perhaps 'experts' who knew how to cure possession, or at least how to help the afflicted, could imbue cases of possession with a massive sense of theatricality. Consider the case of Elizabeth Mallory, aged about fourteen, suffering at Chidley Hall near Ripon in 1656. Witnesses told of her fits, her languishing for twelve weeks without use of her limbs and her vomiting of foreign bodies. At one point, in a typical piece of dialogue between the sufferer and the spectators, those present asked her who was afflicting her. When she replied that she did not know, those at the bedside suggested a list of names, and when that of William Waide was mentioned, 'she was paste holdinge, her extreamity was such & cryed out Will[ia]m Wayde thou terrifyer'. When William's wife, Mary, was brought before the girl, and asked her forgiveness after she was pressured into accepting that she had done her wrong, 'Elizabeth stood upp on her feete (although before her limbs were drawen upp yt she could not stir) & said she was well & walked upon her bed.' When Waide retracted her confession of guilt a little afterwards the girl immediately fell into her fits again. At a later point William was brought before the girl by Lady Mallory, and asked to beg her forgiveness 'and to repeat some wordes after hir or some other gentlemen [*sic*] w[hi]ch was then present', a technique which had been tried in the Warboys incident over sixty years before. William refused, but the attempt to orchestrate a confrontation between him and his supposed victim was typical of the dramatic quality which suffuses these accounts of possession.[42]

The possessed lay at the centre of these dramas, and the problem of how far their sufferings were genuine both exercised the more sceptical contemporary observers and remains a matter of uncertainty for the modern reader. Here, perhaps, future research might lean heavily on modern psychiatry. Certainly, possession cases seem to have much in common with that category of fictional psychiatric disorders which are frequently categorized as Münchhausen's syndrome. And this, of course, should not obscure the probability that many of those allegedly possessed as a result of witchcraft, as many contemporaries argued, were suffering from such familiar ailments as epilepsy or hysteria. At present, it seems safe to note that there was a complete range, from cases that were totally simulated to those where the afflicted was genuinely ill. In many instances, one suspects, the reality lay between these two poles. Afflicted children or adolescents may have suffered initially from a mild illness, either physical or mental, but found themselves dragged along by the logic of the situation into which they entered, and might eventually have believed that they were indeed suffering from that demonic possession which the adults surrounding them told them was afflicting them. Something of the process was described by Samuel Harsnett:

It falleth out sometimes, that divers children, having heard how such & such have been thus and thus troubled, they of themselves will begin to faine themselves sicke: if they bee boyes, peradventure because they would remaine from the schoole: if wenches, for that they would be idle, & both of them, that they might be much made of, and dandled . . . they are driven to counterfeite, and to fall to those trickes which they have heard of in others: wherein, if eyther their parents or maysters beginne to pittie them, then they runne on in their knaveries above measure: but especially if they begin to wonder at them, and devise some remedies for them.

Harsnett also noted how children, especially those aged between fourteen and eighteen, tended to react appropriately if exorcists were brought in.[43]

Whether simulated or not, possession, as we have noted, provided the op-portunity for licensed misbehaviour. Given that so many of the adolescents and children of whose sufferings we have descriptions lived in godly households, it is little wonder that this misbehaviour most frequently involved acts of rebel-lion against religion. The children of the Starkie household in Lancashire went into their fits, 'and thus they contynued all that afternoone, 3 or 4 of them gave themselves to scoffing and blasphemy, calling the holy bible being brought up bible bable bible bable and this they did aloud and often all or most of them ioyned together'. John Barrow, another youth who was possessed, when in his fits 'if any other did take the bible, and mention the word God or Christ in his hearing, he would roar and cry, making a hideous noise'. At one point in Mary Glover's fits, when the minister by her bed renounced Satan, she spat at him and at the people holding her arms. Similarly Hannah Crump of Warwick, possessed in 1664, struck and spat at those who prayed around her.[44] Sometimes the misbehaviour was more mundane. One of the Throckmorton girls evi-dently used her fits as an occasion for playing with her food: 'sometimes she hath merry fits putting her hand besides her meat, and her meate besides her mouth', the spirit possessing her, so the narrative of the episode tells us, 'making her misse her mouth, whereat she woulde sometimes smile, and some-times laugh exceedingly'.[45]

The Throckmorton children, indeed, used their possession as an ideal oc-casion for inverting normality and chiding adults. In one of their confronta-tions with mother Samuel they warned her of the hell-fire which awaited her if she did not confess her witchcraft to them, and then 'they rehearsed like-wise unto her, her naughty manner of lyving, her normall cursing and ban-ning of all that displeased her ... her negligent coming to God's service ... her lewde bringing up of her daughter, in suffering her to be her dame, both in controwling of her, and beating of her'. Elizabeth Throckmorton, aged about thirteen, delivered a similar verbal critique to Agnes, Alice Samuel's daughter:

Oh that thou hadst grace to repent thee of thy wickednesse, that thy soule might be saved: for thou hast forsaken thy God, and given thy selfe to the devill. Oh that thou diddest knowe what a precious thing thy soule was, thou wouldst never then so lightly have parted with it: thou hadst needs to pray night and day, to get God's favour againe, otherwise thy soule shall be damned in hell fire for ever ... thou art a wicked childe ...

Elizabeth continued by advising this 'wicked childe', in fact a young woman several years her senior, on the need for heartfelt prayer.[46] Faith Corbett extended this type of inversion to cheeking those members of the medical profession who were trying to treat her.[47]

While the misbehaviour was unfolding, sceptical observers might detect suspicious behaviour on the part of the possessed. One such, giving evidence about Anne Gunter's behaviour, told how at one stage a young man came to her bedside with a candle in one hand and a prayer written out on a piece of paper in the other: 'Ann Gunter suddenly lifting up one of hir legges in the bedd, stroke the candle into one of the young man's eyes . . . as he verily thinketh, att the instant of this accident he sawe the said Ann Gunter give a sudden smile turning her heade aside or rather as he remembreth putting her head under the cloathes.'[48]

Surprisingly often, however, the behaviour of the possessed was accepted. Even one of the most puzzling aspects of possession to the modern observer, the way in which contemporaries believed that the afflicted could pass quickly from suffering to normality, was rarely a source of sceptical comment. Thus a Northumbrian girl named Margaret Muschamp, again a daughter of the gentry, suffered a fit in court during the trial of her supposed tormentor, 'but as soon as she was out of her fit, did not know what was past, as all the beholders did see, onely an innocent bashfull girle, without any confidence at all when she was out of her fits'.[49]

A further element in the temptation towards misbehaviour is suggested by the occasional mentions of suspicion of a lack of affection between the parents and the suffering children. One of the witnesses in the Gunter case said that before his daughter fell ill Brian Gunter 'made verie little reckoning of her and disliked her soe much that beinge sicke at Oxford and makinge his will would have left her onlie tenn poundes for her portion',[50] while Edward Fairfax noted local opinion which thought that his daughters had simulated their fits 'to be more cherished'.[51] Some hints of tension also emerge in the account of the bewitching of the Corbett girls at Burton Agnes in Yorkshire. The two daughters of the house, even before their afflictions, faced parental disbelief of their allegations of witchcraft against two local women. As their sufferings developed and continued, they became increasingly petulant in their insistence that the medical remedies their parents persisted in employing were useless. At one point Faith Corbett declared 'all the doctors and physick in the world could do her no good, as long as these two women were at liberty; they would have her life, and she was contented, since she could not be believed'.[52]

We return, however, to the basic point that whatever family tensions might have underlain the behaviour of afflicted teenagers, and however we choose to explain their sufferings, it is clear that both they and those attempting to aid them in their possession were aware of a stereotyped view of what possession was about and how it was connected with witchcraft. And, although most of the evidence we have discussed here has come from families of the gentry, it is evident that this cultural patterning of possession was familiar among inferior social groups. Thus in 1658 there was the case of Abraham Hartley, a sixteen-year-old labourer's son from the remote parish of Baildon on the Yorkshire–Lancashire border. The young Hartley went through the standard pattern of fits, vomiting foreign bodies, including 'a horse shoe stubb & two crooked pins', and crying out against a suspected witch, Capp's wife, in his fits.[13] Throughout, as we have stressed, there is a sense that this type of possession was a widely recognized social and cultural phenomenon. At the base of this, as one can sense in, for example, the Fairfax case, is the feeling that, whatever the incidence of witchcraft prosecutions, witchcraft was something which was gossiped about and worried about. And considerable weight must have been added to this gossiping and worrying when people were able to see one of their neighbour's children undergoing the torments of possession.

There is also intriguing evidence that ideas about witchcraft were spread by tracts describing cases of possession. Harsnett, as might be expected, was familiar with the current literature on possession and was able in his critique of John Darrell's activities to cite a number of episodes which had been recorded in print.[14] Stephen Bradwell was able to make reference to the Warboys case in his account of Mary Glover's sufferings, and, indeed, it is probable that the attention this case attracted may have helped spread the stereotyped ideas of how possessed persons behaved. The investigations of Anne Gunter's possession included seeking evidence as to whether her father had caused a book describing the Warboys incident 'and other bookes of lyke argument' to be brought into his house 'to the intent that the same might be reade or reported to the said Anne'. Gunter claimed that such books had been brought to him by neighbours attempting to be helpful, while Anne confessed to having seen 'the book of the wyches of Warboys & some other bookes', the tract on Warboys having been brought to her father's house by a preacher named Weston. She could not remember reading any of these books, 'saving only the booke of the witches of Warboys, of w[hi]ch booke she learned the names of some spyryttes', which names she later applied to the familiars of the three women who were meant to be bewitching her. She also related how she learned from this book 'the manner of the fytts of Mr Throckm[or]ton's children. And the same kynde of fytes the depo[nent] dyd counterfett'. Her father had also evidently read this book. When, during the trial of two of the alleged witches, the assize judge refused to allow him to bring forward a piece of evidence in the same way as was mentioned in the printed account of the trial of the Warboys witches, Brian Gunter cried that 'his daughters could not have that justice w[hi]ch Mr Throgmorton's children hadd'.[55]

The phenomenon of possession was a multi-faceted one and our treatment of it has isolated a few main themes. The emphasis here should not obscure the fact that there are other aspects of the phenomenon which deserve further treatment, ideally in a book dealing solely with possession. Perhaps the most obvious is how possession presented challenges to the medical knowledge of the period, and how scepticism over the reality of possession helped change the medical view of matters relating to witchcraft. This medical opinion, of course, was not just concerned with the physical aspects of the phenomenon. The sense that modern psychiatry might throw light on these cases is a strong one, and at the very least an investigation of this type would also concentrate on early modern views on madness and mental health. Moreover, possession cases lead us into that most fascinating aspect of the cultural history of medicine, the history of attitudes to the body. For it was the body of the sufferer, contorting, vomiting foreign bodies, emitting stinking breath, screaming in strange tongues or strange voices, showing abnormal strength or abnormal weight, which lay at the centre of these incidents.

A second theme for future research, again signposted in this chapter, is the problem of how possession cases connected with the theological concerns of Protestant intellectuals and the upper reaches of the Church of England's hierarchy, and, indeed, with the wider history of religious experience. For the writhings of the possessed were obviously related to a much wider body of ecstatic religious experience, which comprehended medieval Catholic saints, seventeenth-century Puritans in spiritual turmoil and the fits suffered by many plebeian eighteenth-century Methodists as they came to a heightened level of religious experience. And if the child or adolescent supposedly suffering from possession could enjoy the privilege of a licensed critique of their elders, so could their equivalents undergoing religious ecstasy.

What has been made clear here is the significance of possession cases in spreading ideas about witchcraft, the way in which such cases followed a set pattern and the way in which possession, so often involving the children of the gentry, demonstrates that beliefs about witchcraft were not restricted to, and were certainly more complex than, village arguments between labourers, husbandmen and yeomen. With possession we confront a widespread and familiar phenomenon which brought the concerns of the learned and the godly into contact with the world of village *maleficium*. The case of Anne Gunter, to reiterate a point, involved a spectrum of people, from the servants of Brian Gunter giving him advice on local cunning men to that royal author of a demonological tract, James I. Moreover, as we have seen, a number of these possessions involved what was conceived of at the time as a battle between good and evil taking place around the contorted and writhing body of the afflicted. Narratives of possession, therefore, remind us of the sheer complexity of witchcraft as a cultural and social phenomenon in early modern England, while the phenomenon of possession itself remained firmly lodged in the popular and medical consciousnesses until well into the eighteenth century.

PART THREE

THE PROBLEM OF DECLINE

CHAPTER 9

The Growth of
Judicial Scepticism

⬤ One of the defining features of the European witch craze was that it
was essentially a judicial operation.¹ As we noted when describing the
origins of the craze, the religious input, which redefined scattered and
incoherent peasant beliefs about witchcraft as evidence for the existence of a
satanic sect of witches, was vital. But the extirpation of this newly defined sect
demanded the involvement of Europe's legal systems, the judges and court officials who ran them and legal commentators, while a large proportion of
what we know about witchcraft and witches in the late medieval and early
modern periods comes from legal records. Moreover, many of the demonological tracts of the period were written by judges: Kramer and Sprenger, the
Dominican inquisitors who wrote the *Malleus Maleficarum*, and Bodin, Remy and
Boguet, the authors of later works (indeed, that most English works of this
type were written by clerics rather than lawyers might indicate an important national peculiarity). And if the legal dimension was of vital importance to the
creation of the witch-hunts, it would seem logical, in tracing the decline of the
fear of witchcraft and of the desire to persecute witches, to consider relevant
developments in the courts and the legal profession.

Not all European legal systems were the same: there were important regional
variations, some of them to do with local court structures, others resulting from
the influence of the local ruler and yet others from what might be described as
the professional culture of the local legal establishment. It is, nevertheless,
possible to trace three main variables. Two of these resulted from the widespread influence of the Roman law, which by the fifteenth century had more or
less established itself as the law favoured by central governments in Western

and Central Europe. Criminal procedure under Roman law codes depended heavily upon the inquisitorial judge and the use of judicial torture in establishing proof. The judge, in this system, had an investigative role, which included constructing and directing the prosecution case. Obviously, a judge who was convinced of the need to extirpate witches would prepare the case against them more avidly than would one who was sceptical. Equally obviously, torturing suspects in criminal cases was a practice open to abuse. Most European law codes set strict theoretical limitations on the use of torture, but in many territories these limitations were dropped in cases of suspected witchcraft. Moreover, as might be imagined, a suspected witch being examined by a hostile judge allowing severe torture was extremely likely both to confess to all sorts of absurdities and to implicate others, who would then in turn be examined and tortured and by their own confessions add yet more names to the list of suspects. And the complexity of most European court systems added further opportunities for irregular proceedings against witches. Broadly, let us remind ourselves, the lower down a court system the investigation or trial of a witch took place, the more likely proceedings were to be in the hands of an unlearned judge who shared local prejudices about witches in general and, possibly, about the particular witch under investigation, and was likely to waive the rules limiting the use of torture and any other safeguards the accused might expect to enjoy.

England was outside the Roman law system, enjoying its own common law. Trial was by jury, theoretically with only minimal direction from the judge, while torture, although retained in treason cases until the reign of Charles I, was not generally used to prove the guilt of suspects or incriminate accomplices in criminal trials. There was a multiplicity of courts, but by and large these were unlikely to judge and convict persons suspected of having committed serious witchcraft. In general, the trial and sentencing of those accused of capital witchcraft offences were reserved for the assizes. And assize judges were drawn from the upper reaches of the legal profession, were sent out from Westminster and were usually above local animosities against witches. The ecclesiastical courts were still able to try lesser witchcrafts and sorceries, but normally ordered no heavier punishment than doing penance in a white sheet before the congregation in the parish church on a Sunday. The English might have been over-complaisant about their legal system, and it should be noted that some witches were convicted by English juries on 'evidence' that would not even have got them into the torture chamber in many of the better-controlled Continental legal systems. But it remains clear that a key factor in the relative dearth of large-scale witch panics in England was the existence of a legal system where investigation of malefic witchcraft was conducted without judicial torture and where witch trials were presided over by centrally appointed and well-qualified judges.

Despite these peculiarities, the legal process against witches in England was open to a number of practices which the modern observer would regard as abuses. Perhaps the main point to grasp is that, in the sixteenth and seventeenth centuries, trial procedures in general were not as formalized as they are under the current criminal justice system. The English criminal trial during those centuries, on the strength of such evidence as we possess, was a curious mixture of the ceremonial and the ramshackle. Yet we know tantalizingly little of what actually happened in the courtroom, of the confrontation between the accuser and witnesses and the accused, of the grounds upon which juries reached their decisions, of what was regarded as proper evidence in witchcraft or other criminal cases, of the degree of intervention by the judge. Such evidence as we do have suggests that the generality of criminal trials were less decorous and less smoothly conducted than the contemporary legal manuals would have us believe. Perhaps some notion of typical conditions may be conveyed by Mary Spencer, who at her trial for witchcraft in 1634 found that 'the wind was so loud and the throng so great, that she could not hear the evidence against her'. Similarly, John Aubrey noted that at the trial of a witch in 1653 'the spectators made such a noise that the judge could not hear the prisoner nor the prisoner the judge, but the words were handed from one to the other by Mr R. Chandler, and sometimes not truly reported'.[2]

Verdicts in criminal cases were, therefore, sometimes reached under confused conditions, although there is scattered evidence which gives us insights into how those verdicts were arrived at. First, despite the deference paid by all contemporary legal writers to the notion of trial by jury, it is clear that the influence of the judge could be decisive. Consider, for example, the intervention of Lord Chief Justice Sir Edmund Anderson in the Mary Glover case of 1602. Anderson was involved in a number of witchcraft cases around 1600, and was also a member of the committee which was to draft the 1604 witchcraft statute. In the Glover case he found himself faced by medical evidence suggesting what he considered to be insufficient grounds for concluding that the girl's sufferings were caused by natural disease rather than witchcraft. Anderson, after browbeating the doctor giving this evidence, addressed the jury in the following terms:

The land is full of witches; they abound in all places, I have hanged five or six and twenty of them; there is no man here can speak more of them than myself . . . Their malice is great, their practices devilish, and if we shall not convict them without their own confession, or direct proofs, where the presumptions are so great, and the circumstances so apparent, they will in a short time over-run the whole land.[3]

Anderson was extreme in his sentiments, and it was rare for an English judge to be so vocally hostile to witches. But his outburst did highlight what was to become a recurring theme in later trials, the problem of evidence. He was willing to suspend normal 'proofs' and convict on 'presumptions'. Moreover, as he went on to argue, the medical evidence offered on this as on other occasions was really no more convincing, or any more provable, than was the evidence offered to 'prove' witchcraft. It was useless, said Anderson, for divines and physicians to tell him that the suffering of Mary Glover was natural yet tell him 'neither the cause nor the cure of it'.

If the attitude of trial judges could be decisive, so could that of the justices of the peace, who were usually responsible for the initial screening of witchcraft accusations and the noting down of the initial evidence against alleged witches. They, of course, shared the feelings about witchcraft of the class from which they were drawn, the country gentry, and such feelings might run from the very hostile to the very sceptical. But it remains clear that if a justice wanted to use the system to attack witchcraft, he was in a position to do so. Thus the famous 1612 Lancashire trials were in large measure orchestrated by a justice named Roger Nowell, a sixty-year-old of considerable experience and local standing whose family had represented the Protestant and pro-Elizabethan interest in Lancashire in the later sixteenth century.[4] Thirty years earlier, even more direct evidence of a justice's input into a local witch panic had come from Essex. In 1582 the Essex justice Brian Darcy was heavily involved in investigating and organizing a local witch-hunt which originated with witchcraft accusations among his own tenantry. Eleven witches were subsequently tried at the assizes, although only two were executed. The long printed account of the incident contains details of how the interrogations of the suspects were conducted, with leading questions and frequent changes of tone in which threats alternated with promises of clemency in return for confession.[5] England may have lacked inquisitorial judges on the Continental model, but a combination of interrogating justices like Nowell or Darcy and trial judges like Anderson would have produced much the same effect in witchcraft trials.

Jurors likewise had their part to play. Sometimes, they might favour the accused: Reginald Scot, for example, in 1584 recorded a trial where an accused witch was acquitted due to the efforts of a juror who was 'wiser than the other'. More commonly, it would seem, jurors were likely to be hostile. Scot, indeed, noted that 'the name of a witch is so odious, and hir power so feared among the common people, that if the honestest bodie living chance to be arraigned therupon, she shall hardlie escape condemnation'.[6] Trial jurors (as opposed to the grand jurors, normally petty gentry, who sifted accusations before trial) were drawn from those very social strata which were most likely to provide accusers in witchcraft cases, and hence were likely to have few scruples in convicting witches. Something of the flavour of their deliberations is conveyed in a work of 1593, George Gifford's *Dialogue concerning Witches and Witchcrafts*. Gifford was an Essex clergyman and his *Dialogue*, although written as a fictional discussion, is widely regarded as an accurate guide to popular witchcraft beliefs. One of the characters in the *Dialogue*, a countryman named Samuel, recounted how he had been on a jury 'not many yeares past' which had tried a witch. Eight or ten people had given evidence against her, most of them with accounts of *maleficium*, but also 'two or three grave honest men which testifie that she was by common fame accounted a witch'. Samuel continued, 'wee found her guilty, for what could we do lesse . . . if she were innocent, what could we do lesse? We went according to the evidence of such as were sworne; they swore that they in their conscience tooke her to bee a witch, and that she did those things'.[7] Until either the existing set of beliefs about witches could be broken or something more by way of 'proof' was required by judges and juries, guilty verdicts would continue to be brought in witchcraft cases.

A witch, even under the English system, might suffer from being tried in an inferior court. Despite the pre-eminence of the assizes, local borough courts were involved in trying and executing witches in the Elizabethan and early Stuart periods, and occasional evidence demonstrates a lack of legal expertise in these tribunals. Thus in 1586 a woman named Joan Cason was tried at the borough sessions at Faversham in Kent. Cason was accused of killing a child called Joan Cook through witchcraft and of having familiars, but her protestations of innocence, saying that the accusation of killing the child was malicious, convinced the jury and the bench of town magistrates, presided over by the mayor. The jury, although unwilling to convict Cason on a capital charge, obviously thought there were some grounds for suspicion and wanted to find her guilty on a lesser charge of invoking spirits. The verdict was accepted, but a lawyer in the court then informed the mayor and the others present that, contrary to their wish and expectation, the charge on which she was found guilty was in fact capital. The mayor had no alternative but to sentence her to death, and at her execution she 'made so godly and penitent an end that many now lamented her death that were before her enemies'. The chronicle recording this incident contains the laconic marginal comment, 'the jury meant well'. Evidence of what could happen when borough authorities really decided to hunt witches came from Newcastle in 1650. There, as a by-product of the authorities' wish for a more Puritan town, a local witch panic occurred in which thirty people were accused and fifteen executed, a Scottish witch-pricker being imported to lend his expertise to the examination of witches.[8]

Torture, as we have noted, was not part of the English criminal trial process, but it is evident that accused witches could be subjected to a range of some-times very heavy psychological or physical pressures. Most often these were exercised outside, or on the fringes, of legal process, but they were no less severe for that. Perhaps the best-known form of 'neo-torture' was the swim-ming test, a practice designed to prove if a person was a witch by casting them into water. The standard method was to strip suspects to their shifts and tie their left thumb to their right big toe and their right thumb to their left. A rope would be placed to run under the suspects' armpits, each end to be held by a strong man. Suspects were then cast into a pond or river. If they sank, they were thought to be innocent of witchcraft, and the hope was that the men on either end of the rope would pull them out before they drowned. If they floated the assumption was that they were witches. The underlying rationale was probably that water, as a 'pure' element, would reject the tainted agent of the devil.

It should be stressed that the water test never enjoyed any formal legal status in England and that most judges and justices were opposed to it. The practice probably originated on the Continent; in 1653 the sceptical writer Sir Robert Filmer attributed its origins to the Germans, and something like it seems to have been used against suspected witches in France by about 1580. King James mentioned the test with approval in his *Daemonologie*, and it was probably this royal sanction which encouraged its introduction into England. The first re-corded use came in 1612–13, in cases in Northamptonshire and Bedfordshire, in the latter being suggested by a passing stranger from the North to a gentle-man thought to be suffering from witchcraft.[9] It was widely employed sub-sequently, although, as we have noted, officialdom was ambivalent or hostile towards it: during the Matthew Hopkins trials of 1645, for example, the swim-ming test was widely employed but immediately discontinued when assize judges arrived to take control of proceedings.[10] In general, this type of popular action against witches was something which judges abhorred: however hostile to witches, no trained judge would happily countenance the replacement of due legal process by mob justice or by the populace taking the law into its own hands. We have already seen how Oliver Heywood, the Yorkshire Nonconformist, recorded the likely outcome of such action in 1667, when he noted the execution of three men who had been convicted at the Yorkshire assizes for the murder at Wakefield of a woman they thought to be a witch.[11]

There are strong suggestions, however, that extra-legal pressure against witches was less likely to be regarded unfavourably if it was being exerted by the gentry rather than the common people. The point is well illustrated by a familiar case, that of the bewitchment of the children of the Throckmorton family of Warboys which began in November 1589. Mother Samuel, the chief suspect, was effectively held (without any legal sanction) as a prisoner in the Throckmorton residence for a period of several months. Samuel, along with her daughter and another woman, was more or less forced at an early stage in the case to confront the allegedly bewitched children in their parents' house by Gilbert Pickering, a relative of the afflicted family. At a later point she was examined by another relative, Lady Cromwell, in the presence of a Doctor of Divinity named Hall. Lady Cromwell, realizing that she was getting nowhere by 'good speeches', pulled off Mother Samuel's headscarf, cut off some of the woman's hair with shears and asked Mistress Throckmorton to burn it. After several months of this type of treatment, as well as being regularly forced to stand before the children as they cried out against her in their fits, Samuel, who originally held that the girls' fits were 'nothing but wantonesses', eventually broke down. She confessed to bewitching the children and to being a witch and to having given her soul to the devil. She was subsequently forced to repeat this confession before the congregation in her parish church, where the minister, Mr Dorrington, was another relative of the Throckmortons.[12]

Her subsequent retraction of her confessions meant that she had to be brought into contact with the legal system; informal pressure against her had obviously failed. She was made to repeat her confession in the Throckmortons' parlour, while Dorrington noted it down, and various neighbours hid outside an open window, listening so that they could stand witness if necessary. The woman was then examined by the Bishop of Lincoln, and she, her husband and daughter were committed to prison prior to standing trial at the Huntingdon assizes. The evening before the trial the presiding judge, Justice Fenner, interviewed one of the afflicted girls, Joan Throckmorton, in the Crown Inn, where she was lodging. The interview took place before 'a great assembly of justices and gentlemen', and the child, faced by so distinguished an audience, promptly went into fits. Agnes, the daughter of Mother Samuel, was brought in, confessed to her witchcraft before those present and was subjected to various tests (notably her ability to mention God or Christ) by the judge, Throckmorton and Dorrington. This can hardly have done anything other than prejudice the formal trial which began next morning, which ended with all three of the accused being found guilty.[13] The legal process against witches, we must reiterate, appears very informal to the modern observer.

➍ One aspect of this informality, as we have hinted, concerned the genuine problems encountered by judges and jurors when wrestling with how to prove witchcraft legally. Judges (one suspects even Fenner interviewing Joan Throckmorton and Agnes Samuel that night at the Crown in Huntingdon) were often perplexed in the face of accusations, anxious to punish the guilty, but equally careful not to convict the innocent. Consider, by way of illustration, the trial of Elizabeth Sawyer at Middlesex in 1621. The jury heard evidence against Sawyer, a key element of which was a man's declaration that his wife, on her deathbed, blamed Sawyer's witchcraft for her demise. 'This,' so the account of the trial runs, 'made some impression in their minds, and caused them due and mature deliberation, not trusting their own judgements, what to doe in a matter of such great import, as life.' The foreman of the jury turned to the presiding judge, Heneage Finch, Recorder of London, one of the leading legal figures of his day, a Member of Parliament from 1607, a man who was to be knighted in 1623 and who served as Speaker of the House of Commons. Finch, a man with legal training and considerable experience of worldly affairs, was as perplexed as were the jurymen. Asked by the foreman for 'direction and advice', Finch, 'christian-like, thus replyed, directly, Do in it as God shall put in your hearts'. The impasse was broken by a local justice of the peace who had been involved in collecting the pre-trial evidence against Sawyer and who suggested that she be searched for the witch's mark. This was done, the mark was found and Sawyer executed.[14] But what this incident illustrates is that the reaction of a court to a witchcraft accusation, even by 1621, was as likely to be puzzlement as any automatic assumption of guilt on the part of the witch.

This puzzlement, and the associated problems of legal proof, were to become consistent themes in accounts of witchcraft trials as the seventeenth century progressed. Indeed, they provoked a sceptical tract from an experienced justice of the peace with legal training, Sir Robert Filmer.[15] Filmer, probably born in the late 1580s, attended both Trinity College, Cambridge, and Lincoln's Inn, and was a friend of such important contemporary scholars as

Camden and Spelman. He wrote a number of manuscript tracts on politics and related matters for the perusal of other gentry in his home county, Kent, and in the Civil Wars supported the royalist cause, with the result that his manor house was plundered several times and he was imprisoned in 1644–5. He is best known, in fact, for his *Patriarcha*, a tract in support of absolute monarchy, unpublished until 1680, which achieved fame through being heavily attacked in John Locke's *Two Treatises of Government*. It is one of those ironies of the history of witchcraft that a second-rate thinker who is normally regarded as unprogressive in his politics should compose a text hostile to the persecution of witches.

Filmer's *Advertisement to the Jurymen of England*, published only a few months before his death in 1653, was written in reaction to the trial and conviction of witches at Maidstone the previous year. It was a short work of less than thirty pages, about half of which were devoted to that standard argument of sceptics, a refutation of the notion that the references to witchcraft and related matters in scripture had any bearing on the witchcraft of their day. The other half of the tract was taken up with a brief discussion of the 1604 statute, the definition of witchcraft and how witchcraft could be proved in a court of law. Filmer (a man with legal training and wide experience as a justice, it will be remembered) had difficulty in making sense of some passages in the 1604 statute and also made the interesting assertion that, by the time he wrote, judges 'ordinarily . . . condemne none for witches, unless they be charged with the murdering of some person'.[16] For his definition of witchcraft Filmer turned to William Perkins and Martin Del Rio, the Jesuit author of the *Disquisitionum Magicarum Libri Sex*, a work first published at Louvain in 1599 whose frequent subsequent reprintings made it one of the most authoritative demonological texts of the first half of the seventeenth century. It was, however, the work of the English Puritan Perkins which came in for Filmer's most sustained critique.

Apart from this critique, Filmer also (and perhaps here his scepticism got the better of him) argued that the witch should not be convicted for doing harm if, as was commonly held by learned writers, she 'doth not worke the wonder, but the Devill onely', for this would make 'the Devill . . . the worker of the wonder, and the witch but the counsellor, perswader, or commander of it, and onely accessory before the fact, and the Devill onely principall'. According to English law, as Filmer reminded his readers, an accessory to a criminal offence could only be convicted after the principal had been convicted, or at least outlawed, which, he wrote, 'cannot be, because the devill can never be lawfully summoned according to the rules of our common law'.[17]

This absurd image of the devil being summoned to an English court set the tone for the main passages of Filmer's thinking on the legal proof of witchcraft. Perkins, so Filmer claimed, mentioned eighteen 'proofes' of witchcraft, and the sceptical justice worked through these systematically, demolishing them in the process. In due course he came to Perkins's final proof, that of two witnesses confirming that the witch had either made a pact with the devil, had practised witchcraft, had invoked the devil or asked for his help. As Filmer pointed out, most people had 'invocated the devill, or desired his helpe', and that if such language constituted a formal pact, 'then whole nations are every man of them witches'.[18] As for the making of a pact, and the practising of witchcraft, both of these were essentially secret transactions and it was extremely unlikely that anyone should witness them. 'Thus at last when all other proofes faile,' wrote Filmer, Perkins was 'forced to fly to his eighteenth proofe, and tells us, that yet there is a way to come to the knowledge of a witch, which is, that satan useth all means to discover a witch: which how it can be well done, except the devill be bound over to give in evidence against the witch, cannot be understood'.[19] Filmer's comments were clearly sardonic, although it is probable that this combination of common sense and applied sarcasm might have constituted as convincing an argument against witch-hunting as 'scientific' refutations. But what they demonstrate is how a legally trained mind could expose the inadequacies of the formulae for legally proving witchcraft which one of the most celebrated English demonologists had offered.

Yet despite Filmer's critique, English courts seemed willing to carry on accepting very dubious 'proofs' in witchcraft cases, the basic maxim being that this was often the only way in which a conviction could be secured. Hearsay evidence about the reputation or 'fame' of supposed witches was given due attention. Children were allowed to give evidence, notably in the 1612 Lancashire trials.[20] That same year, in a related case which was tried over the county border in Yorkshire, Jennet Preston, accused of killing by witchcraft, was convicted partly on the strength of the tradition that the corpse of a murdered person bled if touched by the killer.[21] Judges and juries were regularly confronted by allegedly bewitched persons falling into fits and screaming and contorting when faced by the accused witch in court. And judges frequently had recourse to a number of 'tests' in their efforts to 'prove' witchcraft. Old women, probably already frightened and bemused by the experience of standing trial, were invited by judges to repeat the Lord's Prayer or the creed in court. These tests were already circulating in the 1590s. Mother Samuel, one of the witches of Warboys, was unable to repeat the Lord's Prayer or the creed as she stood at the gallows in Huntingdon in 1593, while the Derbyshire witch Alice

Gooderidge proved herself to be similarly ignorant in 1597 when challenged to do so by the relatives of a boy she had allegedly bewitched.[22] The first known use of this test in a court of law seems to have come in a trial we have already encountered, that of Mary Glover's tormentor, presided over by Lord Chief Justice Anderson in 1602. Here the accused witch, Elizabeth Jackson, set the pattern for later trials when she was unable to repeat the 'forgive us our trespasses' and 'lead us not into temptation' passages in the Lord's Prayer and bungled the creed.[23] She was convicted, but suffered the lesser penalties of imprisonment and the pillory rather than death.

Indeed, at about the same time as Filmer was writing his sceptical tract, one of the more bizarre forms of proof in witchcraft cases, spectral evidence, was enjoying increasing currency. The key element here was that supposedly bewitched persons claimed to see the 'spectre' of the person thought to be afflicting them, either in their own, human, form or in an animal one. Obviously, people who genuinely thought themselves to be bewitched and were consequently in a somewhat stressed state might easily convince themselves, in all honesty, that they could see the apparition of their tormentor as they suffered their fits and hence confirm their suspicions about the origins of their afflictions. The status of spectral evidence as a means of establishing legal proof is immediately dubious and even so rabid a witch-hunter as John Stearne expressed his doubts about it.[24] Yet instances in which this evidence was advanced proliferated from around the middle of the seventeenth century. As early as 1621–2 the afflicted daughters of Edward Fairfax repeatedly saw the spectres of the women they thought to be bewitching them. In another Yorkshire case, investigated by the justice Henry Tempest in 1650, Sarah Rodes, a supposedly bewitched child, woke from her sleep in a fright and told her mother that Sikes's wife had taken her by the throat. In Exeter in 1660 Margaret Lake, incapacitated after an altercation with the suspected witch Bridget Wooton, deposed that she had 'conceived that she hath seene the person of the said Brigett in a corner of the informant's mother's chamber where she this informant then laie sicke'. In much the same way, and at about the same time, young James Johnson, a yeoman's servant from Thorne in Yorkshire, thought he saw Helen Grey sitting by the chimney in his master's house, 'when he was in extreame paine sitting in the chimney corner'.[25]

That running witchcraft trials could cause technical problems for even the best legal brains of the mid-seventeenth century is demonstrated by an incident in the career of Sir Matthew Hale. Hale (1609–76) was the son of a barrister, but his father had died when Matthew was only five and his own decision to

enter the law came relatively late in life. He had originally pursued other interests while a student at Magdalen Hall, Oxford, but entered Lincoln's Inn in
1628, where he became a protégé of Noy, one of the most influential lawyers of
the time. Hale was typical of those who, although probably ultimately royalist in
sympathy, managed to survive the 1640s and 1650s successfully. He practised
law throughout the period and in the 1650s swallowed whatever reservations he
had about the status quo sufficiently to sit as a Member of Parliament. He also
survived the Restoration, sitting in the Convention Parliament from April 1660,
served the new regime in a variety of ways and was a friend of such leading
clergymen as Tillotson, Wilkins, Ussher and Stillingfleet. He enjoyed a reputation for strict integrity as a lawyer, hostile to the contemporary practice of
accepting presents from suitors, and was also known for his industry, technical
knowledge and learning. Hale published extensively on legal and other matters
and was remembered after his death as a major figure in the English common
law tradition.[26]

In March 1662 Hale, by that time a knight and Lord Chief Baron of the
Court of Exchequer, found himself on the Norfolk Circuit of the assizes,
trying felonies at Bury St Edmunds in Suffolk. Among the accused were two
widows from Lowestoft, Rose Cullender and Amy Duny, who were accused of
bewitching various children, notably those of Samuel Pacy. They had been
examined by a local justice of the peace, Sir Edmund Bacon, and had been
searched for the witch's mark by six women, who had found teats on Cullender.
They stood indicted on thirteen separate charges of bewitching eight people,
witnesses at the trial remembering earlier incidents of *maleficium* going back to
1657. The more recent accusations included the bewitching of Jane Bocking by
Cullender and Duny. The child was too sick to give evidence before the court,
so her mother came to do so on her behalf. Jane had allegedly vomited crooked
pins (a common symptom of having been bewitched by that date), some of
which were produced in court, had seen spectres in her fits and had also cried
out while afflicted against Cullender and Duny. Other witnesses gave evidence
about the strange deaths of horses, cattle and pigs, infection by lice and the
overturning of harvesting carts.[27]

The two women were convicted and hanged, and the case has usually been
regarded as demonstrating Sir Matthew Hale's credulity in such matters, a blot
on the reputation of one of the heroes of the common law. A more sensitive
reading of the account of the trial suggests that a fairer conclusion might be
that the trial demonstrated the continuing problems in proving guilt in witchcraft cases. The initial point to be grasped is that there was a substantial body of

local opinion which held that the two women were witches. Over ten people gave evidence, and their statements were complemented by the medical opinion of 'Dr Brown of Norwich', in fact Sir Thomas Browne, author of the *Religio Medici*, a man as distinguished in medicine as Hale was in the law. Browne assured the court of the probability that the afflictions suffered by the supposed victims were caused, or at least exacerbated, by witchcraft, and alluded to a recent case in Denmark in which bewitched persons, like their Suffolk equivalents, had spat pins and other foreign bodies.[28]

So local opinion and expert medical advice had been consulted, and both pointed strongly to the guilt of the two women. The judges (three serjeants-at-law were present, as well as Hale) also tried a number of tests. Some of the afflicted children were carried into court and touched by Rose Cullender while they were in their fits. They shrieked out and opened their fists, which had previously been so firmly closed that strong men were unable to open them. 'An ingenious person' present in court suggested that the children 'might counterfeit this their distemper', and to test the matter further Lord Cornwallis, Sir Edmund Bacon and Serjeant Keeling repeated the experiment, this time blindfolding one of the children with her own apron, bringing Amy Duny to her, but having another woman touch her. The allegedly afflicted child acted as she had done when Cullender touched her, which should have supported the notion that her reactions were simulated. But Mr Pacy, father of two of the afflicted children, suggested that 'possibly the maid might have been deceived by a suspition that the witch touched her when she did not'. Curiously, this seemed to assuage the doubts of those present.[29]

Indeed, throughout the trial the involvement of the supposed sufferers had added a dramatic intensity to proceedings. Three of them had been 'brought to Bury to the assize and were in reasonable good condition', but when they were brought into the hall where the court was sitting 'to give instruction for the drawing of their bills of indictments 'they fell into strange and violent fits . . . so that they could not in any wise give any instructions to the court who were the cause of their distempers'.[30] Nevertheless, they were brought into the court and the evidence of their reactions when touched by the alleged witches was noted. The morning after the trial the three children recovered, although one of them, Susan Chandler, 'by reason of her very much affliction, did look very thin and wan', and told the court that they had felt better half an hour after the conviction of the witches. They 'affirmed in the face of the country [i.e. jury] and before the witches themselves, what before hath been deposed by their friends and relations, the prisoners not much contradicting them'.[31] Hale then passed sentence of death, and Duny and Cullender were hanged a few days later.

As we have noted, Hale was assisted in his deliberations by three other lawyers, and these were obviously split on how to interpret the evidence. One of them, Serjeant Keeling, was clearly unhappy with the case and argued that the evidence was insufficient to obtain conviction. He accepted 'that the children, were in truth bewitched', but that the guilt of the accused depended 'upon the imagination only of the parties afflicted', and if that, and especially the spectral evidence being offered, were accepted, 'no person whatsoever can be in safety, for perhaps they might fancy another person, who might altogether be innocent in such matters'.[32] Hale, in his summing up, was somewhat equivocal. Witches existed, he argued, because 'the scriptures had approved so much', because 'the wisdom of all nations had provided laws against such persons' and because the laws of England had condemned them. He refused to run over the evidence which had been given for the benefit of the jury, fearing that he might prejudice them in either direction, but 'desired the great God of Heaven to direct their hearts in this weighty thing they had in hand'. For, as he reminded the jury, 'to condemn the innocent, and let the guilty go free, were both an abomination to the Lord'.[33] Hale probably felt that the court's proceedings had reviewed the evidence as fully as was humanly possible and that the decision over the verdict could properly be handed over to the jury.

⊃ The Bury St Edmunds trial of 1662 demonstrated how, even in the face of a court willing to entertain the possibility of deception, and anxious to subject a witchcraft accusation to as many of the known tests and methods of proving witchcraft as possible, the accepted standards of proofs in witchcraft trials were still difficult to reject. Yet as we have noted, by the Restoration it was rare for a conviction to be found. All extant assize records, in particular those of the Western Circuit, demonstrate that although indictments for witchcraft were still being brought to court well into the 1670s, relatively few alleged witches were executed. The last known witch to suffer the death penalty was Alice Molland, sentenced to death at the Devon assizes in 1685. The last instance in which it is possible to confirm that execution had actually taken place, however, came in the same county three years earlier, when Temperance Lloyd (who had already been unsuccessfully tried as a witch in 1671), Susanna Edwards and Mary Trembles were convicted for bewitching four women. As we have already seen, the incident was deemed noteworthy enough to be commemorated in three pamphlets and a ballad.[34] The case is another of those which would repay detailed examination, but what comes through very clearly from the various accounts is the heavy local pressure against the women, perhaps shown most clearly when, with the full connivance of the local élite, they underwent a dramatic public confrontation with their alleged victims in Bideford Town Hall.

But as a demonstration of how a different court might come to a different conclusion at the same time, let us turn to Joan Buts, tried in Surrey, again in 1682. The accusations made against her were in no way unusual, involving the possession of a child. The judge was sceptical, and there does not seem to have been the degree of popular hostility that appeared in the Devon case. Even so, nineteen or twenty witnesses were heard in a trial that lasted three hours, with the judge sifting their evidence very carefully. The jury brought in an acquittal, although the comments in one of the pamphlets describing this incident show how witchcraft was still very much a contested issue: 'The jury having been some time out, returned and gave in their verdict that she was not guilty, to the great amazement of some who thought the evidence sufficient to have found her guilty; yet others who consider the great difficulty of proving a witch, thought the jury could do no less than acquit her.' It should be noted that it was not the complete rejection of witchcraft which was the issue, but rather the 'great difficulty of proving a witch'. A decade after this case, the senior justice of the peace, addressing jurors at a meeting of the Surrey quarter sessions, could remind his listeners that witchcraft was 'a sin of a very deep die, being directly againt the first Commandment', and that it was punishable by death both by divine law and by the 1604 statute. He suggested that when 'clear and undeniable' evidence was available, the jurors should 'proceed according to your oaths', but that generally witchcraft 'was so hard a matter to have full proof brought of it, that no jury can be too cautious and tender in a prosecution of this nature'.[35] Like this justice of the peace, few justices or judges were able to reject witchcraft totally, yet it would seem that the gradually growing scepticism of judges when trying particular alleged witches, their increasing practice of subjecting the proofs offered by accusers and witnesses in witchcraft cases to careful scrutiny in court and the tenor of their summings up must have had the cumulative effect of encouraging a wider scepticism.

This scepticism was clearly affecting the views of one judge by 1701. In that year a young man called Richard Hathaway was indicted at the Surrey assizes for falsely accusing a woman named Sarah Moordike or Moorduck of witchcraft.[36] The background to the trial demonstrated how strongly belief in witches was still held among the population of the metropolitan area. Moordike had been tried at the assizes at Guildford and acquitted, but both before and after the trial

Hathaway had been able to mobilize opinion against her. The minister of his parish in Southwark took an interest in the case, and supervised Hathaway's scratching of the woman. Moordike was also 'abused by the rabble' and refused protection from this mob violence by a justice from whom she sought help. Collections were raised on Hathaway's behalf 'to support his spirits under the disappointment that he met with in her being acquitted', while before the trial bills were posted in a number of churches in the area asking the congregations to pray on his behalf. Such was the fury of the mob that they attacked Moordike in the street, and 'used her so barbarously, she was forced to leave Southwark, where she had lived many years, and also her employment, which had been profitable to her'.[37] She went across the Thames to London, but was pursued there by Hathaway, who, at the head of a mob which included soldiers, broke into the house where she lodged. A local constable intervened and she was taken before a London alderman, who ordered her to be searched for teats and other marks, permitted her to be scratched by Hathaway and committed her to prison to await trial.[38]

Our knowledge of these background incidents is unusually detailed because we possess a very full account of the trial of Hathaway. In this instance the senior judge present was another leading figure in the English legal pantheon, Chief Justice John Holt, aided by Baron Hatsell. The judges were sceptical and gave a very strong lead to the court's deliberations. Detailed accounts were given, clearly with due judicial encouragement, of how Hathaway had counterfeited the symptoms of possession, among them going for long periods without food and vomiting pins and other foreign bodies. The evidence was far from one-sided and a good number of witnesses were convinced that Hathaway had been bewitched, although even many of these, under cross-examination, became convinced that his symptoms might be natural or simulated. Holt, in particular, proved an adept questioner, keeping his temper, for example, when examining a woman who claimed that she knew about witchcraft as a result of having been bewitched herself when she was a girl, during which experience she had levitated.[39] Holt also asked a doctor, named Hamilton, if it was possible for a man to live for two weeks without eating, as Hathaway had claimed to have done while he was bewitched, and if 'all the devils in Hell' could 'help a man fast so long', the reply to both questions being negative.[40] In his summing up, Holt took a sceptical line and returned to the alleged fasting, asking the jury 'to consider with yourselves, whether you have any evidence to induce you to believe it to be in the power of all the witches in the world, or of all the devils in Hell' to enable a man to go without food 'beyond the normal time that nature will allow', adding that witches 'cannot invert the order of nature'. He also drew the jury's attention to the damaging evidence which had been given about Hathaway simulating the vomiting of pins.[41] The jury found Hathaway guilty of false accusation against Moordike without leaving the court and he was sent to gaol until he could find sureties for his good behaviour.

The last known conviction of a witch before an English assize court, at Hertfordshire in 1712, demonstrates how this process of judicial scepticism had continued, albeit in the face of a widespread continuation of belief in witches and witchcraft. The case, involving a woman called Jane Wenham from the parish of Walkerne, provoked a lively pamphlet debate and had a number of broader overtones.[42] The debate, and the broader overtones, will be considered in the Conclusion. For our immediate purposes, the circumstances seem straightforward enough. John Chapman, a farmer at Walkerne, attributed the strange death of up to £200 worth of cattle and horses in the area to Wenham's witchcraft, 'but not being able to prove any thing upon her, he did not inform against her, but waited till time should present a favourable opportunity of convicting her'.[43] Other people in the area began to suspect Wenham of witchcraft, and she was held responsible when a servant girl named Anne Thorne, aged sixteen or seventeen, began to show strange symptoms. She was found 'stript to her shift-sleeves, bawling and wringing her hands in a dismal manner, and speechless', and also began to run randomly around the village; 'she found a strange roaring in her head (I use her own expression), her mind run upon Jane Wenham, and she thought she must run some whither'.[44]

Even before Thorne's supposed bewitchment, Chapman's suspicions against Wenham had been aired at an official level. One of his servants, a youth named Matthew Gilston, had been strangely afflicted after refusing to give Wenham some straw. Chapman, meeting with the woman a little after this, had fallen into an altercation with her, 'and in the heat of his anger call'd her a witch and a bitch'. Wenham applied to a justice of the peace, Sir Henry Chauncy, for a warrant against Chapman for this defamation, 'expecting not only to get something out of him, but to deter other people from calling her so any more'. Chauncy got wind of Wenham's bad reputation and decided to refer the case to the arbitration of any neighbour whom Wenham should choose. She, perhaps a little surprisingly, chose the minister of the parish, a Mr Gardiner, who 'having heard her complaint, advis'd them to live more peaceably together, and ordered John Chapman to pay her a shilling, but would allow Jane Wenham no further satisfaction'. Thus an opportunity to defuse the situation was lost and Wenham 'went away in a great heat, saying, if she could not have justice here she would have it elsewhere, or words to that purpose'.[45] But as Anne Thorne's symptoms developed, so did suspicions against Wenham, because, as so frequently, the girl's sufferings took place 'before a multitude of witnesses, who could not be impos'd on'.[46]

Jane Wenham was committed to prison, and on 4 March 1712 stood trial before Sir John Powell, a judge who was evidently unconvinced of the reality of her witchcraft. He expressed surprise when Thorne went into fits in court, he expressed dismay that some curious cakes of feathers, thought to be a means of conveying witchcraft, had been burnt rather than being retained as evidence and rejected the usefulness as proof of witchcraft of a number of bent pins said to have been vomited by Thorne. After Thorne had recovered from her fits in court, a clergyman read the office for the visitation of the sick over her, which led Powell to comment acidly that he had heard that the papists used exorcism but had never heard of it in the Church of England.[47] He also bullied prosecution witnesses. A woman named Elizabeth Field recounted how, nine years previously, a child in her care had been afflicted by Wenham's witchcraft, but that she was unable to bring a prosecution against her because 'she was a poor woman, and the child had no friends, able to bear the charges of such a prosecution'. In response, Powell asked her mockingly 'if she had grown rich since'.[48] And it was at this trial, according to tradition, that the judge, confronted by claims that the witch was accustomed to fly, retorted that there was no law against flying. Despite Powell's attitude, the jury found Wenham guilty, but the judge rapidly gained a reprieve, and Wenham subsequently passed under the protection successively of a local gentleman and of a Whig magnate resident in the area. This case demonstrates clearly how a learned, if in this case not particularly distinguished, judge could, by the early eighteenth century, be entirely out of sympathy with the traditional view of witchcraft.

Yet the pamphlet description of the trial also demonstrates just how entrenched that traditional view was. Wenham's neighbours, for example, attempted to establish her guilt by a number of unofficial means. At an early stage, Chapman burnt a bundle of sticks thought to have magical properties, 'alluding to a receiv'd notion, that when the thing bewitch'd is burn'd, the witch is forc'd to come in'. Wenham was later brought before Thorne in order to be scratched by the girl, 'that the noise of her nails seemed to all that were present as if she were scratching against a wainscot, yet no blood followed'. Wenham herself, under the pressure of the crowd around her, 'protested that she was innocent, and offered to be try'd, by searching her body, to see whether she had any teats, or by throwing her into the water'. One of those present declared that there was no need for that, but suggested that she be invited to say the Lord's Prayer, which she was unable to do, even proving incapable of repeating it as it was recited to her sentence by sentence.[49] Examined by Justice Chauncy a few days later, Wenham continued to protest her innocence and reiterated that she was 'ready to submit to the water experiment'. Chauncy, as was proper, 'would by no means allow of that sort of trial, it being illegal, and unjustifiable'. A minister present, Mr Strutt, then asked her to repeat the Lord's Prayer, which she was able to do, until (as was so frequent on these occasions) she came to the 'forgive us our trespasses' passage. Under considerable pressure at this point, Wenham confessed to having been a witch for sixteen years, implicated other local women as witches and admitted to having bewitched Thorne, although she gave evasive answers when asked if she had made a pact with the devil.[50]

For a final demonstration of how, by the later seventeenth and early eighteenth centuries, judicial attitudes might differ from popular ones, let us turn to the writings of Roger North.[51] North (1653–1734) was a lawyer and historian who, finding the 1689 political settlement not to his taste, turned his back on a legal career to lead the life of a scholar-gentleman in the country. He came from a dynasty of lawyers, however, and in his notes on his family recorded a number of witchcraft cases in which they had been involved or which he had witnessed. One such was his account of the trial of two witches at Exeter (possibly, in fact, the three executed in 1682) presided over by Sir Thomas Raymond. North noted that 'it is seldom that a poor old wretch is brought to trial on that account, but there is, at the heels of her, a popular rage that does little less than demand her to be put to death', and if the judge should resist this demand, the people would declare that 'this judge hath no religion, for he doth not believe witches'. In this case there was a large amount of 'popular rage', and Exeter 'rang with tales of their preternatural exploits, as the current of tattle useth to overflow'. The accused 'were brought to the assizes with as much noise and fury of the rabble against them as could be shewed on any occasion', while 'the stories of their acts were in everyone's mouth'. North noted that 'a less zeal in a city or kingdom hath been the overture of defection and revolution, and if these women had been acquitted, it was thought that the country people would have committed some disorder'. Judge Raymond, on North's account 'a mild, passive man, who had neither dexterity nor spirit to oppose a popular rage', gave in to the popular pressure and the accused were executed.[52]

Raymond's conduct of this trial was compared unfavourably by North with the methods employed by one of his relatives, when, in one version of the story as recounted by North, he was trying a male witch. The man was accused of bewitching a thirteen-year-old girl who, in the standard pattern, 'had strange and unaccountable fits, and used to cry out upon him, and spit out of her mouth straight pins', these fits and the spitting of pins intensifying whenever the suspected witch was brought before her. The judge was sceptical, but worried about giving offence to the jury if he showed this too clearly. The accused gave his own defence, which he did, according to North, 'as orderly and well expressed as ever I heard spoke by any man, counsel, or other'. He claimed malice and imposture in the girl and called witnesses who gave evidence to that effect. The judge 'was not satisfied to direct the jury before the imposture was fully declared, but studied, and beat the bush awhile'. He cross-examined witnesses and the justice of the peace who had taken the pre-trial depositions against the accused, who declared that the girl was faking the spitting of pins. The judge's efforts bore fruit: 'this cast a universal satisfaction upon the minds of the whole audience and the man was acquitted'. As a final touch, as the judge was leaving the courtroom, 'a hideous old woman' cried, 'God bless your lordship.' When asked what the matter was, the woman replied, 'fifty years ago, they would have hanged me for a witch, and they could not: and now, they would have hanged my son'.[53]

In North's accounts of these two trials we confront what must have been one of the constant issues at stake in court when a witch was tried: what might be termed, at the risk of over-simplification, the conflict between élite and popular culture, the gulf between the lower orders who accused witches, subjected them to 'tests' like scratching or swimming and sat on juries, and the learned judges presiding over the court.[54] Something of this can be sensed from the accounts of the trials of Richard Hathaway and Jane Wenham. It is also evident when we consider the terminology used in North's accounts: the 'popular rage', the 'current of tattle', the fear of disorder in the Exeter mob, the tendency for the country folk to declare that sceptical judges had no religion. North's description of the depositions in the case presided over by Raymond showed how far distant he was from the beliefs of what he termed 'the common sort': they were 'mere matter of fancy, as pigs dying, and the like'.[55] This cultural distancing, as North's account suggests, was heightened by the popular action which so often accompanied a witch trial: the mob pressure, sometimes in the very courtroom, the swimmings, the scratchings, the burnings of thatch. Judges did not need to reject all belief in the existence of witches to be able to refuse to convict in the face of such practices and to regard the witch beliefs of the common people, to some extent still shared by the parish clergy and the country gentry, as so much vulgar superstition.

This cultural differentiation helped judges reject the validity of the confessions of witches. Adherents of witch-hunting had always regarded the 'voluntary confessions' of suspected witches as a major source of ammunition against sceptics. The counter-arguments were self-evident and had, in fact, been stated by Reginald Scot in 1584. Witches might be brought to believe by pressure that the accusations against them were true, while, more generally, confused, 'melancholike' old women were prone to confess to having committed impossible acts.[16] By the time in which North wrote, educated opinion had moved firmly in the direction signposted by Scot a century earlier. Referring to the Devon case tried by Raymond, North declared that he found the witches' confessions to be 'mean and ignorant, the proceed of poverty and melancholy, and in the style of the vulgar tradition of sucking teats, &c'. He continued, 'It is not strange that persons of depauperated spirits should be distract in their minds, and come to a faith of mere dream and delusion. What hath been the discourse of the sleepy chimney, with silent dull thinking, takes place as if the old stories were realities, and then pride and self conceit translates all to their own persons.'[17] 'Dull thinking' around 'the sleepy chimney' was evidently something which, by the late seventeenth century, was far removed from the cultural milieu of leading jurists.

Thus an examination of the judicial grounds for scepticism again demonstrates the sheer complexity of witchcraft beliefs. Our first point must be to reiterate that on the Home Circuit, even including the period of steady prosecution in late Elizabethan times, conviction rates in witchcraft trials were low: only a third of those accused, of which nearly a third again suffered lesser penalties than death. From the outset, on the evidence of records of that circuit, English assize judges must have been more aware than were many of their counterparts in other areas of the difficulties involved in trying witches, and of the need to distance themselves from the local tensions and malice which, even demonological writers accepted, might often accompany a witchcraft accusation. But by the later seventeenth century this distancing process, for judges as for so many educated people, had become much more marked. There was a general change in élite attitudes, a whole set of intellectual shifts which coincided with a deepening rift between élite and popular culture. Many, like the local justice of the peace or the parish clergy caught up in the Wenham trial, were still occupying a sort or disputed territory between these two cultures. But Roger North was able to dismiss popular witchcraft beliefs as 'mere matters of fancy' held by 'the common sort'. Even those of his class who were unable to reject witchcraft totally as a philosophical possibility were happy enough to go thus far and dismiss the generality of witchcraft accusations as popular superstition. Accordingly, the successful prosecution of a supposed witch before a court of law became a near impossibility. And, one suspects, the following of one acquittal of a suspected witch by another in the later seventeenth century must have had a cumulative effect in reinforcing the growing tendency towards scepticism in matters of witchcraft among those caught in that disputed cultural territory to which we have alluded.

CHAPTER 10

A Changing Religious Context

Elizabeth Livingstone was the daughter of Sir James Livingstone, Viscount Newburgh in the Scottish peerage. Her father had royalist leanings (he was, in fact, married to the widow of a cousin of Charles I). When Elizabeth was born, probably in October 1649, her family's fortunes were, as might be expected, not at their strongest. But Newburgh established himself in émigré royalist circles as an expert on Scottish affairs and after the Restoration became influential in Scotland. He also continued to pursue the lifestyle of an archetypical cavalier, given to good living and fine clothes, eventually declining into 'corpulency and goutishness'. His wife had died in 1650 and his daughter was brought up at Nocton in Lincolnshire by her aunt, Lady Stanhope. Elizabeth was to marry twice. Her first husband, Sir Ralph Delaval of Seaton Delaval in Northumberland, died in 1682, after which she married an obscure Lincolnshire gentleman fourteen years her junior. Unfortunately, she chose the wrong side at the time of the Glorious Revolution and from 1689 until her death at Rouen in 1717 lived on the Continent as an émigrée Jacobite.

As this brief sketch suggests, Elizabeth's life was an interesting and eventful one, and the impression she leaves is that of a strong and independently minded woman. She also, as a teenager in her aunt's household, developed a strong taste for religion. Motherless, and with an absent father whose lifestyle the girl appeared to find increasingly distasteful, she formed a close friendship with Mrs Corny, one of her aunt's circle and the wife of an Anglican clergyman, and it is probably under her influence that Elizabeth's religious sensibilities developed. The girl recorded her prayers and meditations in a sort of spiritual diary, a good example of that process of godly self-examination to which the literate

Protestant was prone, and which provides numerous insights into the religious experience of the age. One such insight, of a slightly unexpected nature, was provided by a meditation 'writ in my 17th yeare [i.e. about 1666] ... upon the haveing wormes in my gums and the takeing of them out'. Elizabeth was apparently suffering from a very severe gum infection ('my head, my eye, my teeth and my neck are most miserably tormented with rageing paine'), and in the absence of better-qualified help she turned to a 'poor unlearn'd woman' living nearby. She effected a cure, removing 200 small worms from the girl's gums, but Elizabeth was troubled by her helper's reputation, 'amongst the gidy mulltitude', of being a witch (she noted that 'the more sober sort' thought her to be a cheat).

After some agonizing, Elizabeth decided that the woman was neither witch nor cheat, but had cured her by natural means. Her reasons for rejecting the suspicion of witchcraft were interesting. First, she wrote, 'God forbid I shou'd ascribe such power to a wicked creature, as is onely due to our glorious creator', noting that 'tis at his word that the strong winds arise and not at the command of a witch (as some people do foleishly imagine), and tis God alone that can still the rageing of the sea'. She continued, 'we were certainly in a most miserable condition iff a profess'd servant of the Devill's cou'd at her pleasure cause sorow, paine, or sicknesse to seaze us'. God, she concluded, would 'preserve us from such sad evills and himselfe corects us, but with judgement not in his anger least we shou'd be consumed and brought to nothing'. Her account of the incident was followed by thirteen appropriate prayers, largely on the theme of God's justified chastisement of sinful humankind in general and of Elizabeth Livingstone in particular.[1]

Ↄ The intense forms of Christianity disseminated after the Reformation and Counter-Reformation were, as has long been recognized, crucial in explaining why witches were persecuted in the early modern period. This influence has been interpreted in a number of ways. Early Enlightenment writers, tinged with anti-clericalism, found it all too easy to attribute witch-hunting in large measure to priestly bigotry. Many later observers have followed this path, perhaps most recently those writers from within the women's movement who have seen the Church's input into the construction of late medieval demonology as a key facet of the misogynistic thinking of the period. And, more soberly, a number of recent studies, of which Christina Larner's work on Scotland is perhaps the most familiar,[2] have argued that the quest for doctrinal purity which so many governments and churches pursued after the Reformation was a vital factor in

constructing the ideological bases for large-scale witch-hunting. Thus the notion
that Christianity between the fifteenth and eighteenth centuries was an oppres-
sive ideology which, *inter alia*, fostered the persecution of alleged witches has
become a well-established one. And yet we are confronted with Elizabeth
Livingstone, a young woman with an impeccably godly world view, rationally
appraising whether suspicions of witchcraft against a woman were justified and
deciding, on theological grounds, that they were not. Evidently the connection
between profound Christian belief and the persecution of witches is a little less
certain than may have been thought.

One area of argument which must be addressed, if only to be quickly set
aside, is whether Catholic or Protestant countries were more active in prosecuting witches. The issue generated considerable heat as nineteenth-century lib-
erals came to associate Protestantism with progress and hence saw the persecution of witches as yet another symbol of Romanish backwardness. Recent
studies of areas where there were a number of adjacent states with different
religious allegiances (notably south-western Germany and what are now the
Franco-Swiss borderlands) have revealed little by way of a clear-cut division in
the intensity of witch prosecutions along religious lines. In south-western Germany, for example, there appears to have been a roughly equal level of intensity
of prosecutions in Catholic and Protestant states before about 1600, after
which date, perhaps significantly, some of the Catholic territories pursued a
harder line. Perhaps the fairest conclusion to draw was that some areas, like
Catholic Würzburg or Protestant Lowland Scotland, were capable of staging
heavy bouts of witch persecution, while in others, like Catholic Venice or the
Protestant Dutch Republic, witch trials were very infrequent. Neither side of
the religious divide was able to claim at the time, or should be denigrated by
later observers for having possessed, a unique propensity to persecute witches.[3]

In large measure this was the outcome of there being, throughout the period
of the craze, a number of positions which theologians could maintain concerning witchcraft. Research on south-western Germany, where, in Protestant states
at least, theology faculties of universities were regularly asked for their opinion
on witchcraft cases, illustrates this point as surely as do Elizabeth Livingstone's
meditations. In the German South-West, Catholic, Lutheran and Calvinist
writers, theologians and jurists alike all developed their ideas on witchcraft
somewhere between two positions. The first, derived from the *Malleus Maleficarum*, was one which saw witchcraft as all-pervasive, as a diabolically inspired
rebellion against God and as a constant threat against humankind which, following the advice of Exodus 22: 18, had to be extirpated. The other was derived

from the *Canon Episcopi*. This, while not denying the existence of witches or their diabolical connections, stressed the role of divine providence in everyday life. Thus if general calamities like storms occurred, or the more individual ones that so often formed the basis of witchcraft accusations, believers should seek the explanation in their own sinfulness, rather than take the morally distracting line that witchcraft was to blame. God controlled the uncertainties of human existence, not the devil or his agents, and the proper response to the misfortunes that might accompany those uncertainties was prescribed in the Book of Job. The conclusions which Elizabeth Livingstone was reaching about the spiritual dimensions of curing her gum infection were very much in line with those reached on a more general scale some years previously by theologians at Württemberg and Tübingen universities.[4]

There were, interestingly given the contemporary religious divide, a number of incidents in late Elizabethan and Jacobean England, some of which we have referred to in other contexts, which suggest that Roman Catholic priests may well have made a decided input into the development of English witchcraft beliefs. In 1585–6 a group of priests under the direction of a Jesuit named William Weston sought to demonstrate that they, and not the clergy of the Church of England, were Satan's true opponents by carrying out a number of exorcisms among recusants and others. In 1620 a thirteen-year-old youth, William Perry, the 'Boy of Bilson', accused a woman named Joan Cocke of witchcraft and she was tried at the Staffordshire assizes. Here too there was a heavy Catholic input, as priests attempted to exorcize the three demons which Perry claimed Cocke had caused to enter his body. And, perhaps most remarkably, in 1612, at the same time as the better-known Pendle witches were being tried at Lancaster, three women, the 'Witches of Samlesbury', were also tried there for witchcraft, on the evidence of a fourteen-year-old named Grace Sowerbutts. Grace's accusations included accounts of cannibalism, with the eating of an exhumed dead child, and a sabbat which included the transportation of witches, feasting and sexual intercourse between human beings and demons. The judge suspected the veracity of the girl's story and under questioning she admitted that her evidence was a fabrication, the details having been taught to her by a recusant priest named Christopher Southworth. In all these cases, Catholic priests trained in Continental seminaries, and probably exposed to the ideas of Continental demonologists, played a leading role. The exact links have yet to be established, but the influence of these and other Catholic priests may well have constituted an important route for the entry of 'Continental' notions about witchcraft into the English popular consciousness.[5]

A more general explanation for the increase in concern about witchcraft in sixteenth-century England lies in the impact of the Reformation and of Protestantism. Keith Thomas, in fact, has argued that the decline of what he describes as 'the Magic of the Medieval Church' was an important element here. In particular, he isolated two areas: the sharper line between 'religion' and 'magic' drawn by Protestant theologians; and the notion that the Protestant clergy's resulting unwillingness to offer what were seen as 'magical' forms of assistance in the face of misfortune made the population feel both more vulnerable in the face of supposed witchcraft and more likely to resort to cunning folk as appropriate alternative sources of assistance. Without doubt both of these elements were present, but as some of Thomas's commentary does imply, they are perhaps best considered as facets of those broader processes of change which were taking place in Western Christendom. We return to that great theme of the emergence of a more internalized, intellectualized Christianity which was gradually supplanting the older style of Christian belief which, on a popular level, stressed the importance of involvement in communal ritual, of 'Christian charity' expressed through good neighbourliness and of a ready prevalence of a 'quasi-magical' interpretation of the Church's powers. This 'superstitious' mode of religious belief was one which attracted the opprobrium of English Protestant writers on witchcraft.[6]

This helps explain the attention which has been devoted to the possible connections between Puritanism and witch-hunting in England. Earlier historians, notably G. L. Burr and R. Trevor Davies, sought to demonstrate this connection by focusing on the apparently greater tendency to prosecute witches in Puritan areas like Essex, and the supposed influence of the Calvinist royal demonologist James VI of Scotland after he came to the English throne in 1603.[7] The understandable tradition that returned Marian exiles, attracted to a more extreme Protestantism and imbued with 'Continental' notions about witchcraft, were largely responsible for the 1563 witchcraft statute lent further credibility to this notion. Moreover, it is undeniable that most of the authors of English demonological tracts were Puritan clerical intellectuals, among them the towering presence of William Perkins and such respectable ministers of the word as Richard Bernard. Given the Puritan emphasis on humankind's sinfulness and the need for warfare against the devil, it would seem logical that these hotter Protestants should be eager to destroy the witch, who had, in their eyes, broken her baptismal covenant with God and had thus become both an affront and a threat to the well-ordered godly commonwealth.

As we have already seen, the works of the learned Protestant demonologists of the late Elizabethan and early Stuart periods, as well as the sentiments voiced in at least some of the witchcraft pamphlets of those periods, would support such an opinion. The authors of these works took the perfectly orthodox view, equally common among Continental demonologists, Protestant and Catholic alike, that witchcraft was made possible by the three elements of divine permission, satanic power and the human agency of the witch. Yet equally, as we have seen with Reginald Scot, there existed a strand within Christian thinking which encouraged a rather different interpretation of witchcraft. This position owed much to what the twentieth-century mind would describe as common sense, allied to a reading of other authorities than those cited by the witchcraft writers and an attachment to the tradition of the *Canon Episcopi*. William Perkins, with the aid of Scripture, was able to construct a theory of witchcraft in which God permitted a combination of a powerful Satan and weak but wicked men and women to chastise a sinful mankind. Other English Protestants, among them the obscure young gentlewoman Elizabeth Livingstone, took a rather different view, again on the basis of their reading of Scripture and other authorities. For them, the power of Satan was downgraded and a belief in the majesty and sovereignty of God emphasized. The misfortunes allegedly caused by witchcraft were wrongly attributed: they were more properly the outcome of divine providence.

For those holding such a view, to attribute too much power to Satan was to make a mockery of God's justice, while to assign vast powers to the witch, and hence elevate the creature's powers to those of the creator, was worse. Following this line of argument, the theoretical ability of witches to do harm became very questionable. To the English Protestant of this period, the age of miracles was past. Miracles had been useful in the early stages of the establishment of the Church, but by the seventeenth century Christ, to the mainstream Protestant at least, was no longer walking on the earth, and whatever was needed to encourage belief and achieve salvation was to be found in Scripture. The exact extent of the power of witches had always been something of a problem for demonologists. Most, like the authors of the *Malleus Maleficarum*, resorted to a fudge which attributed some phenomena directly to witchcraft but held others to be illusory, these latter, in so far as they were the outcomes of dealing with Satan, being sinful and worthy of punishment. But more sceptical writers could, on perfectly sound theological grounds, fall back on one of two positions. They could argue that God was omnipotent, and that too active a belief in the powers of the witch elevated the power of the devil too high, and that persecution of the suspected witch was otiose, given that the real problem lay in contemplating the omnipotent God's desire to chasten humankind. Or they could argue that, since the age of miracles was past, and that in any case only God could perform them, notions that witches could do harm at a distance, change their shapes or fly to the sabbat were implausible. Hence various strands within English Protestantism could lead some learned and devout English Protestants to argue for a more active prosecution of witches and others, equally learned and devout, to regard witchcraft as a very marginal issue.

A full appreciation of clerical attitudes to witchcraft is difficult to construct, since the relevant evidence is of a very diffuse nature. We have tended when discussing demonology to concentrate on immediately relevant tracts, but references to the devil can be found in almost any theological tract of the early modern period, while references to witchcraft are also widespread. To take an interesting line of approach, it will be remembered that in 1538 John Bale portrayed idolatry as an old witch. Later writers dealing with idolatry were prone to include witchcraft under that heading. Gabriel Towerson, in his commentary on the Decalogue of 1676, mentioned the common practice of using 'charmes, or spells, or amulets', and declared that the diabolical pact was proved by 'so many authentick stories which have been publish'd to the world concerning it, the free confession of the accused parties, and the sentences of grave and sober judges'. James Durham, whose 'practical exposition' of the Ten Commandments was published a year previously, reproved the use of charms and resort to cunning men, and noted that 'witchcraft, charming, covetousness, judicial astrology &c' drew human affections 'away from the living God'. The tendency for references to witchcraft to crop up in unexpected places is further demonstrated by the Oxford theologian Zachary Bogan, who in his *View of the Threats and Punishments recorded in the Scriptures* of 1653 included in his treatment of blasphemy mention of 'the use of the names of Paul and Peter at the turning of a sive' in order to find lost or stolen goods in his native Devon.[8]

However widespread such references were, the actual involvement of the clergy in witchcraft accusations was ambivalent. On a number of occasions ministers might play a key role in the prosecution of a witch. In the Warboys case, for example, the local clergyman, Dr Dorrington, was one of the leading figures in the campaign against the Samuels. Other clergymen were the authors of pamphlets against witches, among them Alexander Roberts of King's Lynn, who appended an account of the witchcraft of Mary Smith to his short demonological tract of 1616, and Henry Goodcole, who published an account of the witchcraft, trial and confession of Elizabeth Sawyer, the witch of Edmonton.[9] At the very least, the clergy were seen as appropriate people to consult when witchcraft was suspected. When the children of Nicholas Starkie of Leigh in Lancashire fell ill in 1597, their father, suspecting witchcraft, consulted John Dee, then resident in Manchester. Dee, perhaps aware of the danger he might fall into should he involve himself in the case, said that he would not meddle with it, but advised Starkie 'that settinge aside all other helpe, he should call for some godlye preachers, with whom he should consult concerning a publicke or private fast'.[10]

The outcome of such involvement would not necessarily be that the clergymen in question would combine to harry the witch. Alan Macfarlane, analysing witchcraft prosecutions in Essex, could find little evidence of the influence of a persecuting clergy.[11] Indeed, the diary of one Essex clergyman shows how a country minister might inhibit an accusation. Ralph Josselin, vicar of Earls Colne in that county between 1641 and 1683, was a fairly typical minister of a mildly Puritan disposition. He noted how in 1656 one of his flock, a man called Biford, was 'clamoured on as a witch', a gentleman of the parish thinking his child to be bewitched by him. Josselin took Biford for a walk in the fields, 'and dealt with him solemnely, and I conceive the poore wretch is innocent as to that evil', his diary recording no further allegations against the man. In the following year the vicar of the neighbouring parish of Gaines Colne told Josselin that he had seen Ann Crow, a woman 'counted as a witch', behaving suspiciously near a grave, and had also seen an animal 'in shape like a ratt, only reddish and without a tail', running away from her. Josselin subjected the woman to questioning, noting, 'I pressed her what I could; she protests her innocency', and once again the matter seems to have gone no further. Thus by the late 1650s Josselin, a country clergyman of some experience, accepted the possibility of witchcraft, yet in two cases in which he was directly concerned treated the notion that the two specific individuals involved were witches with some caution.[12]

This sceptical clergyman was perhaps best illustrated by John Gaule. Gaule, dismissed by one nineteenth-century writer as 'an unlearned and wearisome ranter', was, in fact, typical of that stratum of minor clerical controversists who flourished at the time. The author of a number of tracts, he had preached a Paul's Cross sermon in 1628 and was to preach an assize sermon at Huntingdon in 1647. By 1646 he was vicar of Great Staughton in that county, and was moved to write a tract against the witch-hunting activities of Matthew Hopkins. Adopting what was the standard sceptical position, Gaule accepted that 'there have been; so there are, & will be witches unto the world's end', but set himself very firmly against what he termed 'the observations, traditions, opinions, affections, professions, proverbs, occupations and conversations of the vulgar' concerning witchcraft and other superstitions. With an eye to more immediate issues, he also set his face very firmly against witch-hunting, 'a trade never taken up in England till then', and deplored the way in which 'the witch-searchers' both encouraged and depended on the superstitious hostility to witches among 'the under sort'. What is perhaps remarkable, however, is that this counterblast to witch-hunting was written not by a major figure in a seat of advanced learning, but rather by an undistinguished clergyman in an obscure rural parish.[13] A certain scepticism concerning matters of witchcraft was evidently widespread among the country clergy.

❥ It has been customary to see the later seventeenth and early eighteenth centuries as an era of relative calm in the history of Western Christianity. After the century and more of strife which followed the Reformation, and which is seen by traditional historiography as ending with the close of the Thirty Years War, the period which began in about 1650 has often been portrayed as a comparatively placid era, free of the quarrels about religious dogma which had characterized the previous 100 years. With the post-Reformation upsets safely out of its system, Europe, according to this interpretation, was now on course for the Age of Reason or the Enlightenment of the eighteenth century. In such a spiritual environment, interacting as this rational Christianity did with the new certainties of Cartesianism or Newtonianism, belief in witchcraft, along with other categories of what the modern mind would describe as superstitious beliefs, would quickly disappear. Thus a recent writer on the history of Christianity in this period could claim that the later seventeenth century experienced a 'silent revolution' in which the active persecution of witches was discontinued and witchcraft itself redefined as one of the many facets of peasant credulity.[14]

Writing history involves making generalizations and, in the last resort, it seems incontrovertible that the discontinuation of belief in witchcraft among educated people in England was one aspect of some major intellectual shifts. Yet it should be emphasized that these shifts were not as sudden, straightforward or complete as might at first be thought. Nor was the religious terrain of the late seventeenth century as calm and as uncontested as some accounts of a linear progress towards an Age of Reason might have us believe. Across the Channel, the regime of Louis XIV, which had more or less put an end to witch-hunting in 1682, in 1685 then launched, with the Revocation of the Edict of Nantes, a period of intense religious persecution. In England, at a time when indictments against witches were waning and executions for witchcraft were almost unknown, the years after 1679 saw an explosion of religious bigotry against a mythical 'Popish Plot'. The relative placidity which so many historians claim to have found in pre-Enlightenment Christianity must have seemed considerably less certain to those living at the time. Indeed, the experience of the turmoil of the 1640s and 1650s was of fundamental importance for most English intellectuals, clerical or lay, who came to maturity in the years after 1660. The effects of this experience are only gradually becoming apparent as research progresses on the religious and intellectual history of late seventeenth-century England. What is already evident is that discussion of witchcraft at that time took place in a mental environment where consensus was valued, where the dangers of religious heterodoxy had been demonstrated by recent experience and where theological debate interacted constantly with the strain of maintaining a new political equilibrium and with the problem of absorbing the complexities of a new science.

Indeed, some have argued that this desire for a less fraught religious situation prompted the emergence of a new strand in Anglican thought, Latitudinarianism. Briefly, the Latitudinarians were thought to have represented a middle course between superstitious religion and popery on the one hand and sectarian enthusiasm on the other. This middle course encouraged open-mindedness and toleration, and hence clergy of a Latitudinarian cast of mind were likely to encourage and enjoy intellectual contacts with the new scientific thinking of the period. Detailed recent research has challenged this notion of a coherent 'Latitudinarian' line of thought, another example of how the old certainties about the religious and intellectual life of the later seventeenth century are currently under revision.[15] What this challenge has underlined, however, is the sheer complexity of religious and intellectual life, and the number of intellectual positions and tendencies which were present.

Given these complexities, it is hardly surprising that the decline of witchcraft beliefs in post-Restoration England cannot be interpreted as any simple triumph of reason over superstition or science over theology. The complexities become manifest when we consider some of the major protagonists in the controversy over witchcraft, which was one of the intellectual sub-plots of the period. Consider, for example, Joseph Glanvill (1636–80), one of the leading defenders of the reality of witchcraft in post-Restoration England. He was born at Plymouth and entered Oxford in 1652, taking his B.A. and M.A. He was, however, attracted to the Neoplatonic ideas which were circulating in Cambridge and, in particular, was an admirer of Henry More. Glanvill became a conforming minister after 1660 and, following a brief spell as rector in an Essex parish, held various livings in Somerset. He attracted the attention of Charles II, becoming a Chaplain in Ordinary to the King in 1672, but also retained his interest in progressive intellectual and scientific activity, becoming a Fellow of the Royal Society in 1664. His interest in advanced scientific thinking did not prevent him from believing in witchcraft and his *Saducismus Triumphatus*, first published in 1668, was a full-scale attack on sceptics. Yet Glanvill's wider interest in science, his position as a respected religious controversist and the rational and moderate tone of his arguments make it impossible merely to write him off as the benighted proponent of an obsolete ideology.[16]

Similar complexities are suggested by the career of Henry More, who, as we have noted, was such an influence on Glanvill. Born at Grantham in 1614, More was the seventh son of a Puritan family of the gentry who proceeded through the local grammar school to Christ's College, Cambridge. He became a fellow of the college, and was affected by the Christian Platonism which was then fashionable at Cambridge, an influence which probably underlaid his enduring attachment to a belief in the reality of the spirit world. He also, in a neat demonstration of the impossibility of pigeon-holing the thinkers of this period, read deeply into the works of Descartes, and, although he was unable to accept the Cartesian system fully, the French writer's influence on his understanding of the physical world was of fundamental importance. More survived into the Restoration period, despite being regarded as suspect by a number of royalist clerics, and continued to publish theological works, while also entering into the scientific debates of the period. Towards his death he turned again mainly to theological matters, especially biblical prophecy, which had interested him throughout his life. His devotional mystical theology gave him an almost saintly aura to a circle of younger scholars and it is clear that he was one of the most influential thinkers of his time.[17]

Glanvill's arguments about witchcraft were complex, addressing, for example, the fundamental if difficult problem of the nature of matter. His theological premises, our immediate concern here, can be relatively easily stated. He sought to counteract the tendency by which, he claimed, 'men, otherwise witty and ingenious, are fallen into the conceit that there is no such thing as a witch or apparition, but that these are the creatures of melancholy and superstition', a notion that was fostered by 'ignorance and design'. To Glanvill, the question of whether witches existed was 'not matter of vain speculation, or of indifferent moment', but rather 'an inquiry of very great and weighty importance' on both legal and theological grounds. He sought to prove witchcraft from Scripture, and to give proof of apparitions, spirits and witches from 'a choice collection of modern relations'. This collection, drawn mainly from the West Country, involved accounts of witchcraft and of such related phenomena as a poltergeist at Tedworth in Wiltshire. Central to Glanvill's concerns were fears that atheism was on the increase and that denying witchcraft might be a first step towards denying the existence of the devil and subsequently of God. If a Christian did not believe in witchcraft, Glanvill argued, 'then all religion comes to nothing'.[18]

Similarly Henry More, in his *Antidote against Atheisme* of 1653, enlisted a number of accounts describing incidents 'that cannot be resolved into any naturall causes, or be phansyed [fancied] to come by chance, but are so miraculous' in his efforts to prove 'the presence of some free subtile understanding being, essence distinct from the brute matter and ordinary power of nature'. These included the cure of a horse by magical means, finding the mark of a hand on the shoulder of a man who had died after claiming to have been struck by a hand while out walking, and the blast of wind felt at a gallows when a condemned felon renounced God. To these tales were added a number of stories about witchcraft, stories which concentrated on 'the supernaturall effects observ'd on them that are bewitch'd and posses'd'. These accounts included some from the Continent (More was anxious to refute Weyer), the Warboys case, other English cases in print and a number of East Anglian cases which More had observed at first hand.[19] More's objective in presenting these narratives to his readers anticipated Glanvill's. He felt that they provided ammunition against scoffers and atheists, and it is interesting to note that within a generation this point had been taken up by the authors of witchcraft pamphlets. One such, describing the possession of a young woman at Orpington in 1679, claimed that the details of the case were 'of sufficient validity to confirm the most staggering and unresolved Christian, and to convert the most impudent and incredulous atheist in the whole world'.[20]

The atheism so feared by More, Glanvill and other defenders of the belief in witchcraft was hardly widespread before the mid-eighteenth century, and even after that date few totally rejected the reality of Christianity. By about 1700, however, a number of thinkers were attracted to deism, and it was at these that the orthodox increasingly aimed their criticism. Deism was a somewhat ill-defined position. Its essence was that positive religion should be rejected, and all that needed to be acknowledged was an abstract divinity which presides over the natural order and should be worshipped by conformity to that order. As might be imagined, the deists of this period were a varied group, coming from different social strata, having different levels of intelligence and adhering to different theological emphases. For our immediate purposes, however, one of their key positions needs to be noted. They shared a rejection of the necessity of revelation for belief, holding that an acceptance of natural religion was sufficient. They thus took the concepts of 'reason' and 'nature' in religious matters to extremes, tending to reject any signs of 'enthusiasm'. An objection to witchcraft was not a central element in the deist position, but the spread of deism in the early eighteenth century was another intellectual development which rendered the belief in witchcraft increasingly untenable among the educated.

As we have seen, neither Glanvill nor More restricted his arguments solely to witchcraft. Both, in their attempts to demonstrate the reality of the spirit world, had recourse to accounts of ghosts, apparitions, poltergeists and related phenomena. This interest, as we have suggested, involved them in debates about the nature of matter and of the physical world. It also led them into one of the major sources of contemporary theological debate, the status of miracles. Witches, it will be recalled, were thought able by the writers of demonological tracts to perform not true miracles, *miracula*, but rather lesser wonders, *mira*. Yet even these lesser wonders, and hence the whole question of the power of witches, became an interesting side issue as the question of miracles was discussed in a succession of tracts. For if the age of *miracula* was thought to have passed, the notion that the devil's agents could perform *mira* would be difficult to sustain. And, more generally, the idea that a spirit world existed in such a way as to impinge regularly on the physical world would likewise become increasingly untenable. Glanvill was correct in his fear that denying the validity of one aspect of the supernatural world might all too easily pave the way for a more general attack.

Recent research has shown that the debate over miracles, so distant to the modern mind, was one of the major areas of concern among early-eighteenth-century writers, with a wide variety of theologians, philosophers and men of letters more generally putting their thoughts on the subject into print.[21] Thus Thomas Woolston's tracts on miracles, published in 1727 and 1728, sold (according to Voltaire) 30,000 copies in England and prompted the publication of over sixty replies.[22] Most modern observers have tended to interpret the debate, once again, in terms of the triumph of 'rationalism' (in this case signposted by David Hume's essay 'On Miracles' of 1749) over outmoded religious beliefs. As ever, the situation was more complex. More confusingly, the stress on the importance of miracles was a novel feature in post-Restoration England, and was frequently argued for by advanced thinkers in touch with the best of contemporary scientific thought (we return to Glanvill). Those sceptical about the status of miracles, conversely, were not advanced 'rational' thinkers, but tended rather to argue from traditional theological positions. What might be described as the mainstream Church of England position was set out by Edward Stillingfleet, the future Bishop of Worcester, in his *Origines Sacrae*, first published in 1662 and subsequently frequently reissued. For him, miracles undoubtedly existed in biblical times, and the accounts we have of them in the Old and New Testaments were true. But in Restoration England the proof of religious truth did not depend on new miracles: 'we cannot in the least understand to what end a power of miracles should now serve in the church . . . we see no reason in the world for miracles to be continued where the doctrine of faith is settled'.[23] To deny the reality of the miracles recounted in Scripture was atheistic, but to seek too fervently for new divinely inspired wonders was to enter the world of papists and Nonconformist 'enthusiasts'.

Any discussion of this issue must reject the notion, so dear to nineteenth-century 'liberal' intellectuals, that there is a necessary conflict between 'religion' and 'science'. Most of those involved in scientific endeavour in late Stuart England were convinced Christian believers, happy in general to remain within the fold of the Anglican Church. They saw no tension between their scientific work and their religious beliefs. Indeed, many of them, as they increased their knowledge of the universe, felt increasing awe as they deepened their comprehension of God's creation. Scientifically, they were attached to what has been described as a 'moderate empiricism', to the notion that what might be termed 'moral' probability judgements were as likely to indicate the truth as were mathematical or what we would term 'scientific' ones. Above all, as was appropriate as the knowledge of the physical world increased in the later seventeenth century, they maintained a flexible and open-minded approach in which nothing, least of all the type of evidence of the spirit world advanced by Glanvill and More, was rejected out of hand. Thus Robert Boyle, one of the leading exponents of the new science, could argue that a philosopher observing 'the wonderful providence, that God descends to exercise for the welfare of inferior and irrational creatures', had an advantage over those 'not versed in the works and course of nature' in accepting Christianity, and that 'the consideration of God's providence, in the conduct of things corporeal, may prove to a well disposed contemplator a bridge, whereon he may pass from natural to revealed religion'.[24]

Some of the complexities present in the Restoration period were demonstrated by the career of Valentine Greatrakes, the 'Irish Stroker'.[25] Greatrakes, born in 1628 into the petty gentry in Ireland, led a fairly normal life for a member of his class (including a spell as an officer in Cromwell's army) and was settled on his family estate when, in 1662, he underwent a fit of religious enthusiasm and suddenly decided that he had a gift of healing, being especially equipped to cure scrofula, the 'king's evil'. Greatrakes's reputation as a healer spread rapidly in the area around his home and people began to come to him in large numbers for help with scrofula. His move to carry on with his thaumaturgic activities at the port of Youghal meant that English sufferers were added to his Irish clientele, and despite a prohibition from the local ecclesiastical authorities (the bishop was alarmed to hear that he was healing in the name of Jesus), he eventually extended his curing to Dublin. By this time he had been heard of in England, and he was invited by Viscount Conway of Ragley to come over in the hopes of curing his wife of migraine. Anne, Viscountess Conway, was a woman heavily involved in religious and philosophical speculations, and included Henry More among her circle. The Conways' interest in Greatrakes provided his entrée into scientific circles in England and he carried out numerous cures in that country during 1666, eventually being invited to perform them before the king at court.

There was a general acceptance that Greatrakes could cure, but commentators on his activities varied greatly in their opinions of where that ability came from. Faith-healing was typical of those lesser wonders with which writers on miracles were concerned, an activity as worrying to ecclesiastic officialdom as it was welcome to the population at large. Greatrakes himself was convinced that his abilities were miraculous, derived from God and designed to convince the atheists and unbelievers of the age of God's glory. Others attributed his cures to natural causes, or regarded him as a fraud or a demonic agent. Henry More was favourable to Greatrakes's activities and stressed the man's godliness. He thought that the cures had a natural explanation, but added that 'they may be the special gift of God in nature, especially in regenerate nature . . . wonderful at least, if not properly called miracles, as the Church of Rome in no age could ever produce for their religion'.[26] Sceptics urged that God would not display his power in such 'mean offices' as Greatrakes involved himself in, which diluted divine providence. Another area of attack was opened by David Lloyd, a high churchman and ardent royalist, who in 1666 published his succinctly entitled *Wonders no Miracles*. Lloyd held that true miracles were limited to those described in Scripture and that Greatrakes's cures were not only ungodly but also politically suspect. By touching for scrofula he was usurping powers reserved for the monarch, while, more generally, the popular response to his curing smacked of rabble-rousing and encouraging that enthusiasm which was thought so redolent of the social disruption of the 1650s. To Lloyd, Greatrakes's claim that his powers came from God was both theologically unsound and potentially socially and politically subversive.[27]

The debate on miracles and Greatrakes's cures have, perhaps, led us a little away from the theme of witchcraft. But they demonstrate how far witchcraft beliefs were embedded in a much wider cultural acceptance of what we would call the supernatural, and how changes in those wider cultural issues affected. the status of the existence of witchcraft. To illustrate this connection, let us turn to one of the last works in the debate on miracles, Conyers Middleton's *A free Enquiry into the miraculous Powers* of 1749. Middleton's book received considerable attention at the time (David Hume, whose own thoughts on the subject were published in the same year, was miffed at how Middleton's book eclipsed his own). It took a critical view of the miracles of the early Church and was widely thought to be a disguised denial of the reality of the miracles recounted in the New Testament. Unusually, at one point Middleton, a veteran of religious controversy, illustrated his argument by reference to witchcraft. 'There is not in all history,' he wrote, 'any one miraculous fact, so authentically attested as the existence of witches. All Christian countries whatsoever have consented in the belief of them and provided capital laws against them: in consequence of which, many hundreds of both sexes have suffered a cruel death.' But by the time of his writing, he observed, 'the belief of witches is now utterly extinct, and quietly buried'. In Restoration England, most clerical intellectuals held that the age of miracles was past. By the mid-eighteenth century, a writer on miracles could hold that the age of witch beliefs was past and that the ability of previous ages to entertain such beliefs was a demonstration of how established opinions could be wrong. Clearly an intellectual shift had taken place.[28]

❯ So for the learned the notion that miracles were a proof of revealed religion was becoming increasingly difficult to maintain by the mid-eighteenth century. It seems likely that such a shift, and a consequent retreat in belief in witchcraft, were much less definite on a popular level. The 1640s and 1650s had seen a flourishing of those publications describing miracles, apparitions, monstrous births, disasters and witchcraft which had been a feature of the popular press since the Elizabethan period. The intent of these mid-seventeenth-century tracts, like those which came before and after them, was to demonstrate that God was angry with the sinful English, that his providences affected the affairs of the physical world on a regular basis and that strange forces were at work in that world. In the mental world which accepted such a situation, there was no problem in accepting that the normal rules of nature might be suspended and that freaks of nature might somehow become symptoms of the more general abnormalities of the times. Conditions in England during the Civil Wars and Interregnum encouraged the making of these connections between general instability and the individual wonder. After the Restoration, however, this literature of wonders, of 'strange news', continued.[29]

The popular literature of the later seventeenth and early eighteenth centuries remains one of the great unworked sources for English social history. But even a superficial trawl through this material reveals that the taste for the old literature of wonders and prodigies remained undiminished. Merely listing the titles of some of the ballads of the period helps convey the flavour: 'News from Hereford, or a wonderful and terrible earthquake'; 'Nature's wonder, or a true account how the wife of John Waterman of Fisherton-Anger was delivered of a monster'; 'The world's wonder, or the prophetical fish'; 'The disturbed ghost, or the wonderful appearance of the ghost or spirit of Edward Aron'; 'Strange news from Staffordshire, or a dreadful example of divine justice'; 'The strange and wonderful storm of hail which fell on London on May 18, 1680'.[30] And, as some of the titles suggest, these wonders were still being presented as part of the divine scheme of things, as warnings to the sinful English of God's power. Consider the moral drawn from a story told in a ballad of 1665, in which the devil attacked and killed a woman who called on him in the course of an altercation with her employer:

> So to conclude remember still,
> Swearing and cursing ends in woe,
> If you let the devil have his will,
> Hee'l prove the worst & greatest foe.[31]

If tales of divine warnings and divine providence were still current in popular literature, so too was a literal belief in the devil.

Such a straightforward belief in the nature of the moral universe was, however, being seen as more appropriate to the lower orders by the Restoration. Once again, we encounter the split between élite and popular culture. The general population believed in the immediacy of divine wrath and the concomitant dangers presented by the devil's powers, along with a host of associated beliefs which educated opinion, the efforts of Glanvill and More notwithstanding, was coming to marginalize as 'superstition'. A related process of marginalization was taking place as religiously based enthusiasm for hunting witches came to be associated with Nonconformity. One of the legacies of the 1640s and 1650s was that after 1660 Anglican clergy and their gentry supporters alike associated 'enthusiasm' in religious matters with the allegedly lower-class sectarians who had attempted to subvert the social hierarchy during the Interregnum. For a good half-century after the Restoration, Protestant Nonconformists were therefore regarded as potentially subversive by mainstream opinion, and were also thought of as more likely to adhere to the old traditions of literal approaches to Scripture and acceptance of signs of divine providence in the events of everyday life. Such people could be portrayed as especially likely to adhere to popular ideas on witchcraft. The tone was set shortly after the Restoration by Samuel Butler's *Hudibras*, a satire against sectarianism which included among its targets the witch-hunting of Matthew Hopkins, and evidently endured. Thus in 1682 we find Lord Chief Justice Sir Francis North commenting in a letter to central government on the Exeter witchcraft trials of that year. He noted the opinion that it would have been disadvantageous to have acquitted the three accused because 'it may have given the faction occasion to set afoot the old trade of witch finding, which may cost many persons their lives, which this justice will prevent'. The execution of three women would defuse a situation which could have led to mass panics and challenges to the Anglican orthodoxy.[12] But the adoption of a 'rational' Christianity was something which seems to have taken root more firmly among the educated than among the population as a whole. If belief in witches and cunning men ran more strongly among the common people, so did the taste for a more immediate and more intense religious experience.

That this taste never entirely disappeared, and continued to be a concern for the educated, is demonstrated by a number of episodes in the eighteenth century. Perhaps the most instructive of these was the affair of the 'French Prophets', a group originally clustered around three Huguenot refugees from religious guerrilla warfare who arrived in London from Languedoc in 1706.[33] By 1708 the Prophets exercised an influence on those sections of the public who were still willing to interpret godly possession, faith-healing and miracle-working as evidence of both God's providence and the approaching millennium. Regarded with suspicion by the mainstream Huguenot churches in London, the French Prophets began to announce the apocalypse and to call Londoners to repentance. In the summer of 1707 one of their English adherents, John Lacy, · began to talk in tongues (admittedly the fact that the tongue in question was Latin did not impress sceptics), to levitate and to demonstrate the gift of healing, curing a sixteen-year-old girl, Betty Gray, of blindness. In the spring of 1708, with James the Old Pretender sailing on Scotland, the Prophets variously predicted that fire and brimstone would fall upon the wicked and that England would be smitten by a famine.

Neither fire, brimstone nor famine came, and it is all too tempting to dismiss the French Prophets as yet another odd sect. But contemporaries did not see it that way. The activities of the Prophets attracted considerable interest and debate, which resulted, between 1706 and 1710, in the publication of about sixty books, tracts and pamphlets, among the authors of which were a number of Huguenot ministers, a range of Anglican clergy which included Edward Fowler, the Bishop of Gloucester, a Scottish Presbyterian and Daniel Defoe. But as the resultant debate demonstrated, by the time of the Prophets the advance of 'rationality' meant that most educated people felt religion should be as free as possible of 'enthusiasm', while if spiritual forces did work on the physical it was through the emotions or the soul rather than exterior forces. But if the old, 'enthusiastic' attitude to religious experience was losing its hold on theologians and philosophers, it continued to be current among the population at large and surfaced occasionally even as the Age of Reason advanced. Their resilience was demonstrated fully when popular religious enthusiasm was unleashed in a decisive manner with the advent of Methodism.

John Wesley himself was convinced of the reality of witchcraft, taking broadly the same position as Glanvill had in the previous century: denying witchcraft implied denying the reality of the devil, which in turn implied denying the reality of God. As late as 1785 we find Wesley writing, 'while I live I will bear the most public testimony I can to the reality of witchcraft', adding that denial of it 'springs originally from the deists'. In 1776 he noted, 'I cannot give up to all the deists in Great Britain the existence of witchcraft till I give up the credit of all history, sacred and profane', adding that 'at the present time I have not only as strong, but stronger proofs of this, from eye and ear witnesses, than I have of murder, so I cannot rationally doubt of one any more than the other'. In 1774, while writing to his brother Charles, he reaffirmed his belief in witchcraft, stating that he had no doubt of the substance both of Glanvill's narratives and of those of Glanvill's New England contemporary the clergyman Cotton Mather.[34]

With accounts of early Methodist conversions we find ourselves returning to the world of convulsions, possession and the idea of the body and soul of the Christian as a battleground for the forces of good and evil. In 1739 Wesley recorded a number of such cases in the Bristol area. One involved Sally Jones, a woman aged nineteen or twenty living at Kingswood. Wesley first found her 'on the bed, two or three persons holding her. It was a terrible sight. Anguish, horror and despair, above all description, appeared on her pale face. The thousand distortions of her whole body showed the dogs of hell were gnawing at her heart.' Sally was apparently convinced that the devil had possession of her, declaring to Wesley, 'Six days ago you might have helped me. But it is past. I am the devil's now. I have given myself to him. His I am. Him I must serve. With him I must go to hell.' Her fits and convulsions continued, and when Wesley visited her again a few days later 'her pangs increased more and more; so that one would have imagined, by the violence of the throes, that her body must have been shattered to pieces'. One of those present, 'who was clearly convinced that this was no natural disorder', said, 'I think Satan is let loose. I fear he will not stop here.' Although no connection with witchcraft was made in this instance, it is evident that the notion of demonic possession was still alive.[35]

It was still alive in 1762, when Wesley recorded another such case, this time at Halifax in Yorkshire, involving a young woman aged twenty-two. He described 'the change of her countenance, which was horrid and dreadful, yea, diabolical, as long as the fits were upon her, but was remarkably pretty and agreeable as soon as she came to herself'. On this occasion doctors were involved, and Wesley noted with some surprise that although he 'should have imagined the physicians would have supposed all this to be counterfeit', in fact they accepted it as genuine, 'as she could have no motive to feign, since she gained nothing thereby, living on the fruit of her own and her father's labour'. Wesley asked one of the physicians, 'old Dr Alexander', what the disorder was. He replied, 'It is what formerly they would have called being bewitched.' 'And why should they not call it so now?' wrote Wesley in his journal, answering himself, 'because the infidels have hooted witchcraft out of the world; and the complaisant Christians, in large numbers, have joined with them in the cry'. He continued that in 'speaking so dogmatically' against witchcraft, the sceptics defied 'what not only the whole world, heathen and Christian, believed in past ages, but thousands, learned as well as unlearned, firmly believe at this day'. Witchcraft, well into the eighteenth century, was evidently a live issue for John Wesley, and one suspects that he was not alone in this.[36]

But the very debate stirred by Methodism leads us back to the divide between the rational Christianity of the Enlightenment and what many educated observers saw as the religious enthusiasm, and related taste for superstition, of the lower orders. Thus Lady Mary Wortley Montagu, that splendid exemplar of eighteenth-century aristocratic sentiments, wrote of her childhood nurse that 'she took so much pains from my infancy, to fill my head with superstitious tales and false notions, it was none of her fault that I am not at this day afraid of witches and hobgoblins or turn'd Methodist'. In 1743 Charles Wesley had written to his brother John, describing the progress of conversions at Newcastle, and noted that 'many more of the gentry come now that the stumbling block of fits is taken out of the way'.[37] For the educated, belief in witchcraft, like acceptance of the reality of wonders, faith-healing and the experience of religiously or demonically inspired possession, could be rejected on intellectual grounds. But the knowledge that acceptance of such matters was still current among the lower orders meant that intellectual positions were heavily reinforced by social prejudice.

CHAPTER 11

Science and the
Decline of Witchcraft

Most commentators on the history of witchcraft have taken it as axiomatic that the decline in the belief in witches and magic, certainly in educated circles, owed much to what could be described, perhaps a little ironically, as the rise of science. The seventeenth century has been portrayed as the period of the 'Scientific Revolution', in which the main elements of the modern lay view of physics and the cosmos were established. Once generalities are left behind, however, the exact nature of the relationship between the decline of witchcraft and the rise of science is a little difficult to demonstrate. It is, for example, hard to see exactly why Isaac Newton's thoughts on the paths of moving bodies, as set out in his *Principia* of 1687, should make assize judges less likely to convict witches, let alone why they should make villagers less willing to launch witchcraft accusations against each other. Indeed, on closer examination it becomes evident that the supposed impact of science in the seventeenth century owes more to a way of thinking engendered by the eighteenth-century Enlightenment, with its stress on rationalism, and the subsequent anti-clerical, progressive and technologically oriented liberalism of the nineteenth century, than to the reality of the mental world of the late seventeenth century. According to this paradigm, scientific rationalism and the experimental method defeated the ignorance and superstition of a belief system based on religion and the acceptance of established authority. Thus, on this reading of intellectual change, both religion and such magical elements as educated people accepted were ousted over the eighteenth and nineteenth centuries by a series of scientific and technological developments which had their origins in the seventeenth.

For a demonstration of how this thinking worked, we can do no better than turn to that hero of the Enlightenment, Voltaire. Consider his encomium on the English contribution to scientific advance:

But it is in philosophy that the English have particularly had the mastery over all other nations. Ingenious and speculative notions were out of the question. The fables of the Greeks had long been laid aside, and those of the moderns were to appear no more. Chancellor Bacon first led the way, by asserting that we should search into nature in a new manner, and have recourse to experiments. Boyle employed his whole life in making them ... After three thousand years of vain enquiries, Newton was the first who discovered and demonstrated the great law of nature, by which every part of matter tends towards the centre, and all the planets are retained in their proper course. He was the first who truly beheld light; before him we knew not what it was.[1]

Here we have what was to become the standard textbook approach: a mention of past ignorance (the fables of the Greeks, the three millennia of vain inquiries), a nod at experimental method and a roll-call of selected names from the pantheon of great scientists, and the scientific advances of the seventeenth century could neatly be included in that most complacent of intellectual activities, the writing of the history of progress.

But this 'triumphalism' is no longer accepted by specialists working in the field of the history of science, a highly technical branch of historical endeavour which has established itself over the last fifty years or so.[2] Ultimately, of course, 'scientific' ideas did change, and, more specifically, the best thinking in what we would describe as 'physics' did alter perceptibly in the decades around 1700. But recent rethinking on these processes has suggested two complications which create difficulties for any simple model of scientific advance. The first is that the changes in 'scientific' thought were neither as total nor as rapid as previous generations have assumed: in the second half of the seventeenth century, even very intelligent and very educated people showed an understandable inability to jettison the belief systems in which they had been raised intellectually. And second, it remains very uncertain to what extent the new scientific thinking, at least before the early eighteenth century, was disseminated. If we return to Newton's *Principia*, we discover, if a recent biographer of that great scientist is to be trusted, that there were perhaps seven people in the whole of Europe who were qualified to comprehend it.[3] The propagation and popularization of Newtonian ideas and the other concepts of the 'Scientific Revolution' are fascinating subjects to which a number of recent scholars have turned their attention, but it can hardly have been a rapid process, and certainly postdated the decline in belief in witchcraft and magic in educated circles.

And there is an additional problem: witchcraft was not of central importance to most of the scientific debates of the period, which renders tracing the direct impact of new scientific ideas on witchcraft beliefs even more difficult. Certainly, as the historian Stuart Clark has suggested, demonology did, in the late sixteenth and earlier seventeenth centuries, enjoy a 'scientific' status.[4] It involved the construction of what might be described as a 'natural science of demons': of how far the effects which demons (and by extension witches) created were worked by natural causes. Not even the most rabid demonologist accepted all the popular or classical beliefs about the powers of witches, and all demonologists held that a number of the phenomena attributed to witches and demons were, in fact, attributable to natural causes. So the issue became one of subjecting instances of witchcraft to close scrutiny, and this sometimes very precise process led to some of the more arcane speculations of the writers of demonological tracts and, indeed, their critics. The status and categorization of preternatural phenomena hence assumed a crucial importance, and the areas of debate impinged on problems which the modern mind, albeit reluctantly, would accept as 'scientific'. Discussion of shape-changing by demons, for example, and of the possibility of sexual intercourse between human beings and demons engendering children led directly to one of the central concerns of seventeenth-century scientists, the nature of matter.

If we are to spend some time discussing the impact of 'new' scientific notions, it is perhaps worthwhile to ponder briefly the nature of traditional ones. Perhaps most widespread in 1600 was that system which historians label 'Aristotelianism'.[5] Aristotelianism, as we have noted, was developed from its roots in classical Greece. Perhaps the most important stage in this development, and the most important in the study of witchcraft, was that fusion of Aristotelian science with Christian thought which was one of the major intellectual achievements of the Middle Ages, a key figure here being St Thomas Aquinas, an authority who was still widely cited in theological works, demonological tracts among them, well into the seventeenth century. The resulting intellectual system, frequently referred to as Scholasticism, was a rich and complex one which it is difficult to summarize. Briefly, Aristotle and subsequent thinkers working within an Aristotelian framework were concerned with understanding what common parlance would describe as the 'real' world: that is, the one which we can understand through our senses. In pursuit of this understanding, Aristotle wrote a number of empirically based, systematic and (if his initial premises were accepted) logical and consistent works which provided the basis for a general view of the world, and indeed the universe, within which human beings found themselves. To the modern observer, there is much in the Aristotelian system which seems bizarre, but the strength of its inner logic and the attraction of its comprehensiveness have to be acknowledged: it provided a means of categorizing all physical phenomena, whether animal, vegetable or mineral, and explained such basic issues in physics as motion in terms which comprehended both the movement of the planets and the flight of a javelin thrown by a human being. It was, moreover, an intellectual system which was very much alive, and being adapted to help provide answers to new problems, in the decades around 1600.

As might be imagined, breaking out of this intrinsically logical, theologically acceptable and time-honoured intellectual framework was difficult. Even somebody working in the new natural philosophy of the later seventeenth century, Joseph Glanvill, advised a respectful attitude towards the ancient writers. The thinkers of his time, he wrote in 1668, were 'very ready to do right to the learned ancients, by acknowledging their wit, and all the useful theories and help we have had from them'. But, he continued, they were 'not willing that those, however venerable sages, should have an absolute empire over the reasons, of mankind. Nor do they think, that all the riches of nature were discovered to some few peculiar men of former times.'[6] A generation earlier, things were perhaps less equivocal. John Aubrey remembered how, when he first began to interest himself in natural philosophy, he sought advice on works to read from William Harvey. Harvey is best known for his demonstration of the circulation of the blood, and is normally included in that roll-call of great scientists who helped progress. He also plays a part in the history of witchcraft because of one celebrated occasion when, in a demonstration of the attachment to the experimental method, he dissected a toad which was allegedly a witch's familiar. His reaction to Aubrey's request is, therefore, instructive: 'he bid me goe to the fountain's head, and read Aristotle, Cicero, Avicenna, and did call the neoteriques [i.e. modern writers] shitt-breeches.' Harvey was by no means the only eminent scientist who still found the Aristotelian intellectual framework a satisfactory one in the early seventeenth century.[7]

Although it was the new mechanical school of thought which was to dislodge Aristotelianism, most Aristotelian thinkers in the period c. 1500–1650 would have regarded the main threat to their position as coming from that intellectual system which historians have labelled Neoplatonism.[8] As we have already noted, this system had its origins in the thinking of Plato (428–348 BC). His ideas, considerably developed by later thinkers, were passed down to subsequent generations in a body of writings which set a moral as much as an intellectual agenda. If Aristotle was concerned with understanding and analysing the real world, Plato was concerned with the world of the spirit and held that ultimate reality lay not so much in the physical as in the spiritual. However well known they may have been earlier, Platonic ideas seem to have enjoyed a wider currency from the late fifteenth century. A major figure in this process was the Italian scholar Marsilio Ficino, who from 1462 devoted a prodigious amount of energy to translating Platonic and Hermetic works, writing commentaries upon them and composing a number of original treatises.

Neoplatonism (as befitted a tradition based on Plato's writings) was essentially an open-ended system of beliefs whose emphasis upon the spiritual and the occult permitted the assimilation of the mystical mathematics of the Jewish cabbala, the occult lore of alchemy and the technicalities of astrology. Perhaps two features of Neoplatonism need to be stressed here. The first was that it was essentially a belief system for adepts: the alchemist and the cabbalistic scholar, in their searches for the meaning of the universe or inner perfection, were dismissive of the common multitude. The magus was, ideally, well born, cultivated and spiritually pure. Only a very superior person could acquire that superior knowledge, and perhaps superior power, which the pursuit of the occult might bring (readers of Shakespeare will think immediately of Prospero in *The Tempest*). And second, the main thrust of Neoplatonism was an optimistic, idealistic one. The search was not just for an understanding of the physical world but also for spiritual enlightenment and fulfilment. Neoplatonism and the tradition of occult knowledge which it in some measure comprehended were both, it must be reiterated, untidy and variegated bundles of beliefs and intellectual speculations; yet at their basis lay the notion that the physical world was governed and animated by spiritual forces at whose centre lay the *spiritus mundi*.

Both Aristotelianism and Neoplatonism were dislodged, over the seventeenth century, by a new intellectual system which is described as corpuscular, or perhaps more familiarly mechanical, physics.[9] Perhaps the most celebrated proponent of the new mechanical approach was the French scholar René Descartes (1596–1650). Descartes's lasting contribution was perhaps more strongly marked in philosophy than in physics, but he made an important contribution (already signposted by Galileo) to the latter discipline by demonstrating that there was no fundamental distinction between motion in the heavens and motion on earth: both celestial and terrestrial bodies obeyed the same set of physical laws. This insight, central also to Newton's thinking, challenged both the Neoplatonic axiom that the terrestrial sphere, being composed of baser matter, operated under different laws from the stellar one, and the Aristotelian distinction between the sub-lunary sphere and the starry universe beyond. And, of course, adherence to such a set of physical laws made literal belief in the existence of spirits and demons rather more difficult.

Knowledge of Continental ideas was facilitated in this period by the international nature of scientific debate, and leading natural philosophers operating in England such as Robert Boyle (1627–91) and Isaac Newton (1642–1727) were fully aware of the new mechanical physics. Yet there existed important differences between the mainstream of thinking in England and the Continental adherents of the mechanical philosophy. First, many English-based natural philosophers, not least Boyle and Newton, were concerned that the Cartesian system wrote God out of the scheme of things: the supposed antipathy between 'science' and 'religion' which became axiomatic in post-Enlightenment thinking was not yet present in late seventeenth-century England. And many of the Continentals, so anxious to banish occult forces and innate qualities from their analysis of the physical world, were dismayed at the apparent inability of even the best English writers to divest themselves fully of such notions. Thus gravity, for whose 'discovery' Newton is so celebrated in English history books, was regarded as a suspect concept by some Continental scientists: it was rather too akin to one of those occult forces which had been so fundamental to Neoplatonism.[10]

But as these Continental suspicions of intellectual untidiness indicate, modern attempts to put neat labels on early modern natural philosophers can be misleading: most of them unconsciously entertained elements of what, on the strength of modern categories, look like competing belief systems. The point is well illustrated by a recent biographer of Robert Fludd, one of the key figures in the history of alchemy in England. Fludd's biographer, William H. Huffmann, characterized his thought as 'Renaissance Christian Neoplatonism', but admitted that the intellectual synthesis which his subject attained could more accurately, if less handily, be described as 'Gnostic-Pythagorean-Platonic-Neoplatonic-Hermetic-Cabalistic-Judeo-Christian', with some Aristotelian elements thrown in.[11] The modern reader has to come to terms with the evident lack of inhibition which seventeenth-century intellectuals experienced when using ideas from a number of intellectual traditions. It is possible to find Hermetic, mechanical, Aristotelian and Neoplatonic terminology used in one book, which suggests that the divisions between these traditions were much less watertight to contemporaries than our modern categorizations might allow. Indeed, as is now familiar to all historians of science, even that hero of the 'Scientific Revolution', Isaac Newton, demonstrated how the new 'scientific' thinking could coexist with older areas of intellectual speculation. Newton maintained, at least until the mid-1690s, an active interest in alchemic studies, while throughout his life he immersed himself in theology and biblical scholarship.[12]

❥ In July 1662 the Royal Society obtained its first charter, from which point natural philosophers in England had a secure institutional base.[13] The Society had its immediate origins in groups of scholars who had come together over the previous two decades, although there were longer-term processes in operation. Most historians of science in England acknowledge the influence of Francis Bacon (1561–1626), a prominent statesman before his disgrace in 1621, but also a scholar who combined the grandiose notion of a 'Great Instauration', a general reform of the world, with a more prosaic insistence on inductive thinking, on the observation of facts and on the experimental method. Most historians have also asserted the importance of Gresham College, founded in London in 1597, as a centre for scientific studies. More immediately, however, the impetus which led to the formation of the Royal Society came from a number of groupings of intellectuals with an interest in new trends in natural philosophy. There was a circle of Anglo-Irish scholars, known as the Invisible College, whose most famous member was Robert Boyle. There was also a group of scholars at Oxford who gathered around John Wilkins, from 1648 Warden of Wadham College. Other groupings were found in Cambridge, where there was a circle of Neoplatonist thinkers, and in London.

With the coming of the Royal Society, we might be excused for thinking that the rapid triumph of new scientific ideas was assured and the destruction of belief in witchcraft made inevitable. To employ modern concepts, the line between 'science' and 'magic' would now be clearly defined along lines acceptable to us today. The 'magical' elements in early modern science, not least the acceptance of the existence and operation of occult forces, would be marginalized, and hence belief in the reality of witches, apparitions, poltergeists, ghosts and all the other denizens of the spiritual world would be banished from the intellectual framework of the educated. As Charles Webster, one of our leading historians of science, has put it, if it happened, this shift 'would constitute one of the major contributions of the Scientific Revolution towards the modernization of belief systems. Once freed from the ancient shackles of demonology, the way was clear for the more scientific investigation of many of the phenomena associated with witchcraft, and the more humane medical treatment of the persons affected.'[14] Yet, as recent research by Webster and others has demonstrated, the situation was considerably less clear-cut.

There were two main elements in the new science which have been identified by older generations of historians as permitting a decisive break with existing thought. The first was a rise of an empirical, 'experimental' style of scientific investigation, which was held to have made manifest the vacuousness of the traditional method of arguing from existing authorities. The second was that rise of mechanical philosophy to which we have referred. Both these phenomena were of course present, and important, in post-Restoration scientific thinking, but in neither case was their impact quite so decisive as has been argued. Empiricism and experimentalism are both at the heart of what the modern non-specialist would regard as sound 'scientific method', but even some initial thoughts on the demystification of scientists suggest a few problems. Ultimately, the emphasis on new methods of validation, on the need for quantitative precision when supporting scientific argument, did represent something novel. Yet historians of science are now aware of the problem of reading into these methodological changes too much of the methodologies of which they themselves approve, while there is also a growing sensitivity over the possible divergence between what seventeenth-century scientists said they were doing as they went about their business and what they actually did. And, of course, these seventeenth-century scientists lived, as do their modern equivalents, in a wider cultural context. Thus a recent study of a very famous set of experiments carried out by no less a figure than Robert Boyle has shown that they were marked not by a value-free 'experimental method', but rather by an experimental method appropriate to Boyle's perceptions of the cultural, political and religious needs of Restoration England. And, as the criticisms made of Boyle's method by Thomas Hobbes and Henry More demonstrated, scientific experimentation was still disputed territory in the 1660s.[15]

The mechanical philosophy, certainly in its Cartesian variant, did not, as we have noted, enjoy the same ascendancy in England as it did on some parts of the Continent, but its main tenets passed to later centuries as major components of a 'scientific' view of the world. Nature was not alive, animated or directed towards some higher moral purpose, but was rather the outcome of the random motion of material particles. A thoroughgoing mechanism would certainly have made belief in witches and spirits, or indeed in any part of that 'natural magic' which was so much a part of early 'scientific' thinking, extremely difficult: there was no place for immaterial forces or animistic powers. Yet two major difficulties remained for contemporaries when confronted by the mechanical philosophy. The first was that many found the sometimes complex explanations offered by mechanical philosophers, especially of everyday phenomena, unconvincing. Aristotelianism, not least as conceived of by the average educated person, at least had the virtue of appearing to be consistent with common-sense experience. Some of Descartes's notions did not. His insistence that animals were mere automata, equivalent to machines, brought adverse comments, even in the phase when he was most influenced by the French philosopher, from Henry More, and the consequent indifference to animal suffering shown by Descartes's followers during vivisections revolted the English naturalist John Ray.[16] And second, we return to that great worry most English natural philosophers experienced with out-and-out mechanical philosophy: it appeared to leave very little space for God.

The problem is well illustrated by the reception of the ideas of Thomas Hobbes. Hobbes (1588–1679) is best known today as a political theorist, but in his lifetime he was regarded as a leading mechanical philosopher, on a par with Gassendi and Descartes. Hobbes's most famous political work, his *Leviathan* of 1651, contained a forthright denial of the existence of witches. He attributed 'the opinion that rude people have of fairies, ghosts, goblins, and the power of witches' to the 'ignorance of how to distinguish dreams, and other strong fancies, from vision and sense'. While Glanvill and More collected testimonies providing evidence of apparitions, poltergeists and other supernatural phenomena, Hobbes wrote such reports off as either the 'fancy' of the people claiming to see them 'or else the knavery of such persons as make use of such superstitious fear, to pass disguised in the night, to places they would not be known to haunt'. 'As for witches,' Hobbes wrote, 'I think not that their witchcraft is any real power; but yet that they are justly punished, for the false belief they have that they can do such mischief.' But Hobbes, the mechanical philosopher and rejecter of witchcraft, was not hailed by his contemporaries as a welcome bearer of enlightened ideas. In the Restoration period he was widely excoriated as an atheist, his *Behemoth* of 1668 was banned from publication and the bishops prevented the reprinting of *Leviathan*.[17]

As mention of Hobbes's reputation reminds us, one of the features of scientific endeavour during this period was the wide array of contacts which scholars enjoyed, a pan-European network along which ideas and information were exchanged and controversies conducted. In England, two émigré scholars played a vital role in keeping these networks going. Perhaps the better known was Henry Oldenburg (?1605–77). Originally from Bremen, Oldenburg had come to England as an ambassador for that city in the 1640s and subsequently settled there. Despite his associations with the Republican and Cromwellian regimes, he survived the Restoration and shared with John Wilkins the responsibility of the early secretaryship of the Royal Society. His assiduity in this role is demonstrated by the massive correspondence he engaged in from 1663.[18] But this type of contact had already been established somewhat earlier by Samuel Hartlib (d. 1670), a refugee from Prussia, who was at the centre of extensive correspondence networks in the 1640s and 1650s.

Although Oldenburg's correspondence is relatively quiet on such matters, with Hartlib we are plainly still in a world where interest in the scientific involved an interest in the magical. Witchcraft is mentioned directly at several points in his papers, for example when a correspondent told Hartlib about witches in Lapland in 1652 or when heavy rains on the coast of Denmark and Holstein were attributed to the malevolence of witches. Henry More wrote to Hartlib about prodigies that had been seen in England and Germany, 'such as men fighting in the ayr and such like', noting also that 'the Divell or some spiritt doe visibly appear to the Americans'. John Beale was another of Hartlib's contacts who regularly mentioned the supernatural. In 1657 he was giving Hartlib his opinions about the contacts which Christ allowed between angels, and 'some of his holy people for their guard, comfort & information', and a year later stated his belief in a 'Prince of Devills', who, with his own 'Angells', was doomed to everlasting hell-fire, but who 'doth at this time exercise a very powerfull dominion over the princes & nations of the earth'. Beale also, at about the same date, sent Hartlib a letter of 'Prognostiques, Apparitions', where he described being visited at night by 'a satanicall horror in the shape of a greate dog with flaming eyes' while a teenage schoolboy at Eton.[19]

This concern over spirits, demons, witchcraft and the supernatural more generally continued to exist on the fringes of scientific debate until well into the 1680s. In the two or three decades after the Restoration many of the writers discussing the reality of witchcraft, even if not themselves established natural philosophers, at least paid some attention to the unfolding scientific context of the debate in which they were participating. We have already met Henry More and Joseph Glanvill, two scholars who were able to defend belief in the reality of witchcraft from a distinctive synthesis of Christian and, more specifically, Anglican ideas and the tenets of the new natural philosophy. Another such was Meric Casaubon, son of a Protestant émigré from France. The younger Casaubon came to England in 1611, was educated at Eton and Oxford, and subsequently became a minister of the Church of England. His *Of Credulity and Incredulity in Things natural, civil and divine* of 1668 stated what was becoming the standard moderate view on witchcraft and related matters. Casaubon was aware that matters of witchcraft were difficult to prove and that accounts of them had to be treated with caution. He also, interestingly, showed himself aware that knowledge was shifting and that phenomena which were regarded as supernatural when he wrote might, at some future point, be capable of a natural explanation. Yet he couched his defence of belief in witchcraft not in 'scientific' terms (in fact, he seems to have been indifferent or hostile to the new science), but rather followed two well-worn themes. First, the familiar one that rejection of belief in witches was the first step on the downward path to atheism. And second, that whatever reservations one might have about particular cases, the weight of evidence in support of belief in witchcraft was so overwhelming as to be incontrovertible. Clearly even for this well-read and eclectically minded author, the new natural philosophy had little bearing on the problem of witchcraft.[20] And in 1684, the appearance of a large work written firmly in the More–Glanvill tradition, Richard Bovet's *Pandaemonium*, demonstrated that an awareness of the new natural philosophy was not inconsistent with serious argument in support of the reality of witchcraft.[21]

Perhaps, however, we are wrong to look for objections to witchcraft in reasoned argument, but should rather seek them in mockery. As long ago as 1911 Wallace Notestein commented that 'it was natural that those who disbelieved should resort to ridicule ... and there was a class in society which would willingly have laughed witchcraft out of England'.[22] Certainly, by the Restoration period it was common for those arguing for the existence of witchcraft to claim that a shallow fashion for 'scoffing' aided their opponents: Meric Casaubon, for example, denounced 'that mocking and scoffing at religion, and at the Scriptures', which was 'so much in fashion', and characterized such people as atheists, or 'confident illiterate wretches'. A work published thirteen years after Casaubon's, however, could make the converse statement that those professing a belief in witchcraft would be greeted 'with loud laughter and a supercilious look', while recent work on John Wagstaffe, author of a sceptical tract of 1669, has argued that he was motivated mainly by a mocking vein of free thought.[23] Once more we enter the problem of broader cultural changes, but it seems implausible that the wits and rakes who adorned the court of Charles II would take very seriously the tales of ghosts, witches and apparitions so eagerly sought by More and Glanvill.

It is, therefore, notable that only one debate over the existence of witches has so far been accredited with the status 'scientific'. This involved, on the one hand, Joseph Glanvill, with More and Casaubon involved by implication, and, on the other, John Webster (1610–82). Webster was a North Country man. Born at Thornton in Craven in Yorkshire, he was ordained as a priest and took a

Yorkshire living in 1632, but after a short spell of schoolteaching and subsequent service in the late 1640s as a surgeon with the parliamentary forces
during the Civil Wars, he subsequently practised medicine at Clitheroe in Lancashire. He had a Nonconformist religious background and was also apparently
well versed in science, supplementing his interest in medicine with a knowledge
of metallurgy, chemistry and astrology. In 1677 he published a major sceptical
tract, *The Displaying of supposed Witchcraft*, which superficially appears to be a
'rational' attack on an outdated belief system. Once again, however, things are
not quite as they appear.[24]

Webster was writing from what has been described as a Paracelsian-
Helmontian position, one which, whatever his views on malefic witchcraft,
accepted certain areas of occult agency. The events of the 1640s and 1650s had
equated this position with Nonconformity, and for a certain strand of Anglican
writer in post-Restoration England, radical Nonconformity and the radical
occult science of the sixteenth century were seen as equally suspect and as
much a part of the devil's work as witchcraft. Thus Webster's attacks on
witchcraft beliefs were not written as part of a purely 'scientific' debate, but
rather in the face of the attempt by Glanvill, More and others to construct an
Anglican natural theology in which spirits, the devil included, would play a
part. Webster's objective was much more to deny the presence of the devil in
occult happenings than to deny them altogether. His lengthy defence of the
tradition that the body of a murdered person bled if approached by the murderer suggests Webster's unsuitability as a representative of a new scientific
rationality.[25]

Much of Webster's argument, indeed, reflected theological concerns. He
regarded 'the scriptures and sound reason' as the surest guides to proof in
matters of witchcraft, and held that Scripture was a surer guide than 'the vain
lyes and figments of the heathen poets, or the dreams of the Platonick school,
either elder or later, nay better than all the natural and groundless speculations
of the schoolmen'.[26] Working from Scripture, he reached what we have already
identified as a theologically sustainable sceptical position: biblical references to
witchcraft had little bearing on seventeenth-century debates, and in any case
involved mistranslation, while the notion that witches were empowered to carry
out their actions by divine permission cast serious and unworthy doubts on the
dignity of the Almighty.

Webster was, however, fully aware of the implications of recent advances
in scientific knowledge and techniques, and argued that, given the many gaps
in human knowledge, it was better to wait for a natural explanation than to

attribute the inexplicable to demons. For, by the time Webster wrote, at least one body of opinion was becoming convinced that, given the gradual advancement of knowledge, such natural explanations might be forthcoming. 'I have known some years ago,' he declared, 'that a person for owning or maintaining the circulation of the blood, should have been censured and derided as much by other physicians, as one should be now for denying the same.'[27] He was also in favour of the experimental method, which helped make him suspicious of the type of eyewitness accounts favoured by More and Glanvill. The testimony of 'eye and ear witnesses', he thought, was invalid in 'the balance of justice or right reason', because they could be 'corrupt in point of interest, and so have their judgement misguided and biassed by the corruption of their desires and affections, or relate things out of spleen, envy or malice'. This general scepticism was reinforced by his experiences as a medical practitioner, which had included treating allegedly possessed persons. He remembered, for example, encountering a youth aged sixteen or seventeen who fell into an ague, 'in the declination of which he seemed taken with convulsion fits, and afterwards to fall into trances, and at the last to speak (as with another small voice) in his breast or throat'. His family and neighbours were 'perswaded that he was possest, and that it was a spirit that spoke in him'. Fortunately, however, a kinsman of the afflicted, a gentleman 'of great note and understanding', sent for Webster, who was able to disabuse the family about the nature of the young man's affliction.[28]

The so-called Glanvill–Webster debate thus demonstrates the limitations of the 'scientific' attack on witchcraft beliefs in late-seventeenth-century England, or perhaps more accurately demonstrates the limited applicability of the modern category 'science' to early modern thought. On the one hand, Webster was anxious to deny the devil's agency in the physical world in order to ensure the legitimacy of occult scientific practices. On the other, Glanvill adapted elements of the new natural philosophy in order to help demonstrate that spirits existed in nature and thus help maintain an Anglican natural theology. The problem for both writers was not a purely 'scientific' one in the modern sense of the word, but rather how to define the balance between the natural and spiritual worlds. Thus the Anglican position allowed the rejection of Neoplatonic and Paracelsian thinkers, who merged the natural and the supernatural, and the rejection of thorough-going adherents of mechanical philosophy, like Thomas Hobbes, for separating the two too thoroughly. We return to the conclusion that witchcraft as an intellectual problem was still a live one in post-Civil War England, and that even those accepting the best 'scientific' thought of the period did not necessarily have to reject witchcraft beliefs as a consequence of that acceptance.

❷ So even by the 1680s the ideas of the 'Scientific Revolution' had not penetrated the educated culture of England sufficiently to allow them to be drawn on to any deep degree by writers on the reality of witchcraft. Yet over the next generation or so, acceptance of this reality became impossible in the best intellectual and social circles, and the positions maintained by More, Glanvill, Casaubon and Bovet were no longer tenable there. But, it must be reiterated, this transition was neither rapid nor straightforward. There was no decisive argument, debate or great work which ended the possibility that the educated man or woman might believe in witchcraft. Indeed, the erosion of the foundations for such a belief seems to have been the result of changing fashion rather than of the triumph of decisive, reasoned arguments. In natural philosophy, as with theology and with concepts of legal proof, such intellectual shifts as did occur are best interpreted as a gradual chipping away at witchcraft beliefs, a gradual process of marginalization, rather than a dramatic overturning of existing belief systems.

The gradualness of this process owed at least something to contemporary reservations about the new science. The general tendency to write history in terms of progress, and to disparage the opinions of those who seemed to be on the wrong side, has tended to obscure the extent to which the activities of natural philosophers in the later seventeenth century were not viewed with universal approbation. The experimental method, of which the writers of textbooks have made so much, was open to criticism which went beyond debate over Boyle's findings with the air pump. Thus Henry More, his mind fixed on higher truths than the experimental method could demonstrate, referred to 'that more mechanical kind of genius that loves to be tumbling of and trying tricks with the matter (which they call making experiments)'.[29] Others took a more satirical, mocking line. If Restoration wits could find much to scoff at in tales of apparitions and witches, the sometimes bizarre activities of the natural philosophers also gave them cause for merriment. This spirit was encapsulated in 1676, when Thomas Shadwell published a play entitled *The Virtuoso*. The hero (if that is the word) of this comedy was Sir Nicholas Gimcrack, a gentleman amateur scientist whose experiments and intellectual interests were a series of neat parodies of the activities of the Fellows of the Royal Society: investigating the swimming action of a frog, investigating respiration, transfusing blood from one animal to another, transfusing blood from a sheep to a human being, dissecting ants' eggs with the aid of a microscope and attempting a taxonomy of the spider population of England.[30]

But significant intellectual shifts were taking place, shifts that challenged the broader belief system which provided the context within which an educated acceptance of witchcraft could exist. Let us take astrology as an example.[31] As we have argued, this was one of the most widespread of those 'occult' areas of quasi-scientific activity which abutted on magic and witchcraft beliefs, its findings accepted in the later sixteenth century by kings and statesmen. In England, the heyday of astrology came late, in the troubled decades of the 1640s and 1650s, and is especially associated with a great practitioner of the astrologer's art, William Lilly (1617–92). Lilly was an outstanding example of how astrology could straddle the supposed gulf between élite and popular culture. He had learned much of his art from a cunning man called John Evans, resident at Gunpowder Alley in London, but he was to go on to write a number of technical works on astrology and to have his talents for prediction and divination mobilized by the parliamentary war effort. The mid-seventeenth century was to witness the flourishing of a number of other astrological practitioners, among them Lilly's great rival, the royalist astrologer and almanac writer John Gadbury (1628–1704), and Thomas Streete (1621–89), whose *Astronomica Carolus* of 1661 was to be a standard textbook for many years, helping to spread Kepler's ideas to a wider audience, which may have included Isaac Newton.

Yet the Restoration of Charles II in 1660 was to see the beginning of the decline of the acceptance of astrology in educated circles. Again, part of the reason lay in the nature of Restoration politics. Astrologers, who had flourished so markedly in the 1650s, were now, like religious sectaries, tainted with radicalism and republicanism, while the somewhat shaky nature of the Restoration regime helped foster a nervous attitude towards prediction and prophecy in political matters. Gradually, astrology came to be regarded as obsolete and vulgar. A few practitioners struggled against the current. Joshua Chidley (1625–70) attempted to reform astrology and to fit it into an Anglican, heliocentric belief system, while in 1699 Francis Moore (1657–1714), a pro-Whig astrologer in London, produced the first edition of an annual publication which is still with us in the form of *Old Moore's Almanac*. But by 1700 those Fellows of the Royal Society who were sympathetic to astrology were dead, and in 1704 John Gadbury, who in any case had been turning away from astrological prophecy, also died. Thereafter a network of provincial astrologers, whose activities await detailed research, continued to practise, but they became increasingly marginal to the scientific advances of the period. And, as the sales of almanacs testify, at the same time as astrology was losing its position in educated circles, it remained, albeit perhaps in an intellectually diluted form, firmly entrenched in the popular mentality. As we shall see, much the same was true of witchcraft.

In the field of medicine changes were taking place which reflected more directly upon witch beliefs. The medical dimensions of the history of witchcraft still remain one of its great uncharted areas, but it is clear that local doctors were regularly involved in suspected witchcraft cases. It is, therefore, instructive to note the opinions of Richard Mead, one of the most important medical practitioners in mid-eighteenth-century England, who in 1755 published his *Medica Sacra*, a commentary on diseases described in the Bible. By the time he wrote, Enlightenment values had been thoroughly internalized and the learned doctor was able to provide rational explanations for those cases of possession and other diseases noted in Scripture which earlier generations had used as authoritative evidence to demonstrate the reality of possession by witches and demons. Such beliefs, for Mead, were merely 'vulgar errors . . . nothing more than the bugbears of children and women'.[32] Mead commented on witchcraft:

my soul is seized with horror on recollecting, how many millions of innocent persons have been condemned to the flames in various nations since the birth of Christ, upon the bare implication of witchcraft: while the very judges were perhaps blinded by vain prejudices, or dreaded the incensed populace, if they acquitted those, whom the mob had previously adjudged guilty.

Mead was able to 'most heartily rejoice, that I have lived to see all laws relating to witchcraft entirely abolished' in Britain, and was able to ascribe the persistence of such laws in some foreign states to 'their ignorance of natural causes'.[33]

Such opinions might have been appropriate to leading medical practitioners in 1755, but for many provincial physicians witchcraft accusations had barely ceased to be a live issue by that date. As early as the 1650s mainstream medical opinion was turning against the explanation of medical problems by witchcraft or demonic possession, but the issue was much less clear in the localities, where the provincial physician might find any diagnosis of an ailment based on a natural explanation disputed by Catholic exorcists, Nonconformist ministers and local cunning men and women.[34] Indeed, for the Nonconformists of that first, embattled generation which followed 1660, belief in divine providence, in an explicitly eschatological interpretation of the world around them and in the inspirational power of extempory prayer made acceptance of the devil's hand in a spectacular illness all too plausible. Yet even for them, as the memory of the religious upheavals of the 1650s receded, the devil became marginalized.

One provincial physician whose firsthand experience of popular ideas on witchcraft had led him to a sceptical position was, as we have seen, John Webster. In one part of his *Displaying of supposed Witchcraft* Webster discussed the efficacy of amulets, seen as essential in medical treatment two generations previously by practitioners as disparate as Richard Napier and village cunning folk. Webster pointed out that he had practised medicine in the North, where, he claimed, 'ignorance, popery and superstition doth much abound', and where the common people suffering from any sort of 'epilepsy, palsie, convulsions and the like' were very prone to 'perswade themselves that they are bewitched, fore-spoken, blasted, fairy-taken, or haunted with some evil spirit, or the like'.[35] Trying to convince such people that they were not suffering from supernatural, but rather natural, problems was, according to Webster, pointless:

say what you can they shall not believe you, but account you a physician of small or no value, and whatsoever you do to them, it shall hardly do them any good at all, because of the fixedness of their depraved and prepossessed imagination. But if you indulge their fancy, and hang any insignificant thing about their necks, assuring them that it is a most efficacious and powerful charm, you may settle their imaginations, and then give them that which is proper to eradicate the cause of their disease, and so you may cure them, as we have done in great numbers.[36]

This quotation provides a neat illustration of one area of that divergence between learned and popular culture to which I have referred frequently. But it also demonstrates how at least one doctor in post-Restoration England was able to separate natural, rational effects from those which earlier generations might have regarded as sympathetic magic. A cultural divergence was coinciding with an intellectual divergence between old practices and a burgeoning view of 'the natural' which was rendering earlier ways of viewing the world redundant.

For in the second half of the seventeenth century the best minds were challenging one of the old ways of categorizing knowledge. Historians have made much of the rise of 'experimental method' over the century, of the triumph of the observation of empirically provable 'facts' over venerable tradition. This process, carrying with it as it did the possibility of new forms of 'proof', was important, and had implications in both the legal and the intellectual treatment of witchcraft.[37] But connected with it, if perhaps more difficult to delineate, was a process whereby the way in which thinking was organized, the way in which knowledge was compartmentalized, altered. John Ray the naturalist wrote in 1678 that in his account of animal species he had 'wholly omitted what we find in other authors concerning . . . hieroglyphics, emblems, morals, fables, presages or aught else appertaining to divinity, ethics, grammar or any sort of human learning; and [would] present . . . only what properly relates to natural history'.[38] As we noted earlier, scholarship in the early modern period was essentially polymathic, and as our brief sketch of Newton's mental world suggests, or as the presence of such wonderfully eclectic scholars as John Aubrey or Elias Ashmole in the Restoration period demonstrates, this tradition was far from dead in the later seventeenth century. But as Ray's comment implies, there was a gradual process afoot which made the old mental world of correspondences, of the microcosm and the macrocosm, of sympathetic action, less sustainable. And this process, by driving wedges between the scientific and the occult, and between the natural and the spiritual, contributed to the marginalization of magic and witchcraft.

Although it is difficult to chart, there was thus a gradual mental shift which seems to have helped the educated jettison an acceptance of the reality of witchcraft. Yet even a generation after Casaubon and Bovet, it is still difficult to find sceptical writers rejecting witch beliefs explicitly on the grounds of the new scientific discoveries. Francis Hutchinson, author of a major sceptical work first published in 1718, was willing to nod at the impact of the new science and the Royal Society, but was unable or unwilling to follow this line of approach through.[39] Equally, the sceptical works published at the time of the Jane Wenham case in 1712 manifested scant dependence on new scientific ideas. There was some comment on medical proof and argument for natural rather than diabolical interpretations of illness, but more commonly there were the standard, non-scientific lines of sceptical argument: a stress on mistranslation of Scripture, a common-sense scepticism about the 'proofs' of witchcraft, the knowledge that this accusation, like so many others, arose from neighbourly hostilities, scepticism over the validity of the witch's confession, all now couched in the rhetoric of early-eighteenth-century rationalism.[40] And part of that rhetoric was that disparagement of the irrational beliefs of the lower orders which we have already encountered: if witchcraft accusations were rejected by judges, wrote one author in the Wenham debate, 'hereafter we may not have that waste of humane blood in every village, upon the wild testimonies of a parcel of brain sick people, who often stand in need of dieting and shaving themselves'.[41]

For a final indication of the lack of direct evidence between scientific advance and the rejection of witchcraft beliefs among the learned, let us turn to a printed version of a sermon preached in 1736, by a happy coincidence the year in which the English (and Scottish) witchcraft statutes were repealed. Its author was a Leicestershire clergyman, Joseph Juxon, and it was preached after a suspected witch was subjected to the swimming test at Twyford in that county.[42] Juxon was firmly opposed to the practice of swimming witches, and in fact denied the existence of witchcraft altogether. His grounds for so doing are instructive. In part, they were social. He noted, as Reginald Scot had a century and a half before him, that persons suspected of witchcraft were typically 'such as are destitute of friends, bow'd down with years, laden with infirmities; so far from annoying others, as not to have it in their power to take care of themselves'.[43] Yet 'there is so much superstition and fear, and this is so deeply rooted [that] whenever the alarm is given, there is always a party formed, a very powerful one too, against these poor, ignorant and helpless creatures'. Accusations against such people had to be nipped in the bud, for though 'persons of ill fame be accused at first . . . yet the suspicion may fall at last upon those of unblemish'd character and reputation'. Juxon remarked that 'in our own country we have in former times had some few instances of terrible executions on this account', and noted one foreign episode of witch-hunting (unfortunately unspecified) where there was 'such havock made [that] there was no peace to be had, 'til an effectual stop was put to such unrighteous accusations'.[44]

In addition to this disquiet at the social breakdown which might ensue if witchcraft accusations were allowed to flow unchecked, Juxon also mobilized what were by then the familiar theological arguments for scepticism. There was no scriptural basis for the witchcraft beliefs current among the population at large, these being founded rather upon 'the very dregs of heathenism and popery' and 'such lying legends, which have been propagated only by weak and credulous people, and beleeved by none but those, who are weak and credulous as they'. The good man was under God's care and protection and had no need to fear witches. To ascribe too much power to the devil was to deny both divine control of the natural world and the operation of divine providence within it. The evils popularly ascribed to witchcraft, wrote Juxon, 'are such as may proceed from natural causes, and are common unto men'.[45] The arguments, although voiced in the restrained tones of the early Enlightenment rather than the more pungent ones of mid-Elizabethan England, were essentially the same as those put forward by Reginald Scot in 1584. There was little sign in Juxon's sermon of any reception of new scientific ideas, or any application of the new natural philosophy to the problem of witchcraft. The arguments against witchcraft to which Juxon had recourse were, by 1736, more or less standard ones; what had changed, for educated opinion if not for the villagers of Twyford, was the willingness to accept them.

Thus, for the generality of the educated public, it would seem that the direct contribution of the 'Scientific Revolution' to the decline of belief in witchcraft was minimal. Possibly awareness of the advance in scientific knowledge helped create an intellectual and perhaps psychological context in which witchcraft beliefs could be steadily eroded and marginalized, but it is difficult to see anything like a direct and open assault. One of the implications of the new physics with which Newton was associated was that the physical universe, the earth included, was now seen as operating under predictable rules, while there may have been a corresponding growth in optimism about humankind's ability to know, and perhaps even control, the natural environment. If this optimism was in existence, it coincided with the growth of a new, more measured form of Christianity, and also, perhaps, with a rather less apprehensive view of the possibilities for the survival of civil society – a shift, as it were, from Hobbes's view of a war of all against all to Locke's notion of a social contract. This latter might have been no less of a fiction than the first, but it was a good deal more reassuring. Such a mental world left rather less room for angels, demons and other supernatural forces, and, perhaps more importantly, was one in which the ubiquitous power of Satan was no longer quite such a matter of concern among educated people. Arguably, the emergence of a recognizably 'modern' or 'scientific' approach to the study of nature was as much a symptom of these intellectual and cultural changes as a cause of them. But it is undeniable that in the long run, however uncertainly and tangentially, that swirling mass of intellectual endeavour which historians refer to as the 'Scientific Revolution of the Seventeenth Century' contributed to the process of the gradual invalidation of witchcraft beliefs.

Conclusion

The Reverend John Christopher Atkinson became vicar of Danby in North Yorkshire in 1847. Born at Goldhanger in Essex in 1814, he attended school at Kelvedon in that county and subsequently went to Cambridge. Ordained in 1841, he made good early progress in his chosen profession, but after being appointed to his North Country living was to hold it until his death in 1900. Over that period, punctuated as it was by three marriages and the fathering of thirteen children, Atkinson seems to have grown into the ideal Victorian parson: learned, professionally competent, but experiencing a genuine interest in and affection for his parishioners. His broader interest in his adopted region led to his publishing a number of works in the best traditions of Victorian antiquarian scholarship: a glossary of the Cleveland dialect, a history of Cleveland, a history of Whitby, editions of local documents (including the seventeenth-century North Riding Quarter Sessions rolls), numerous papers to archaeological societies and, as if to balance this serious output, a number of books for children.

Perhaps Atkinson's best-known book is his reminiscences of his time at Danby, his *Forty Years in a moorland Parish*. And one of the greatest surprises this book contains for the modern reader (obviously a reflection of something which considerably surprised the Reverend Atkinson) was the degree to which the villagers of Danby, at least in 1847 and the years immediately following, believed in witchcraft. Atkinson, writing in 1892, assured his readers:

I have no doubt at all of the very real and very deep-seated existence of a belief in the actuality and the power of the witch. Nay, I make no doubt whatever that the witch herself, in multitudes of instances, believed in her own power quite as firmly as any of those who had learned to look upon her with a dread almost reminding one of the African dread of fetish. Fifty years ago the whole atmosphere of the folklore firmament in this district was so surcharged with the being and the works of the witch, that one seemed able to trace her presence and her activity in almost every nook and corner of the neighbourhood. But this is far too wide and deep and intricate a subject to be entered upon at the close of a section already quite sufficiently long.[1]

In fact, despite the disavowal at the close of this quotation, Atkinson did provide his readers with a review of witchcraft beliefs which would not have been out of place in the seventeenth century: concern over the health of cattle, a belief in shape-changing, the problems of power and reputation, the ready recourse to cunning folk. Atkinson's account makes interesting reading when set against that of another clergyman with an interest in popular beliefs, George Gifford, who wrote, it will be remembered, in the late Elizabethan period.

It might also be remembered that we opened this book with an account of the killing of a witch in 1751 and commented on how the schoolbooks so often portray the mid-eighteenth century as an age of progress. How much more is this true of 1847 and the forty years which followed it. A book published in 1849, celebrating the 'Thirty Years Peace' of 1816–46, ended on a note of early Victorian confidence, listing such technological developments as the electric telegraph and early photography, and such social advances as improvements in medical provision and sanitation, the early stages of state education and the abolition of slavery in the British Empire.[2] And in the decades after 1847 during which Atkinson tended his flock in that remote corner of North Yorkshire, Britain registered a formidable set of achievements: it became the world's 'First Industrial Nation'; it lay at the centre of a massive empire, covering a substantial proportion of the world's surface; it developed, notably through the extension of the franchise in 1867 and 1884–5, something like a parliamentary democracy; and it also, through both state intervention and private initiatives, demonstrated that none of these other achievements was incompatible with the existence of a concept of society in which at least something was done to aid the less fortunate and to protect the relatively weak from the relatively strong. And yet, at least at the early stage of this most progressive and exciting of periods, if Atkinson's account is to be trusted, the belief in witchcraft was still firmly adhered to in country areas.

A book waits to be written (fortunately another book than this one) on the extent, content and functions of these nineteenth-century beliefs, something along the lines of a fascinating work which has been published on similar beliefs in nineteenth-century France.[3] But even a preliminary reading of a wide variety of sources, produced mainly when country clergymen and folklorists began to take an interest in matters which had been ignored since the witch trials had ended over a century earlier, indicated the extent and variety of witchcraft beliefs. There is a tremendous problem, as with the sixteenth and seventeenth centuries, in determining the content of these beliefs and their significance. It seems likely, for example, that even in remote country areas belief in witchcraft was less pervasive in the nineteenth century than it was in the seventeenth, and how these beliefs could coexist with others which were entering the popular mind is more problematic. What seems unhelpful is to describe these beliefs as 'survivals', a term which at once marginalizes and minimalizes them as remnants of some earlier belief system which was destined merely to wither. Over the long term, perhaps, this interpretation is accurate, but even a superficial acquaintance with these later witchcraft beliefs demonstrates their vitality, their adaptability and their continued relevance to the lives of many people. And if we direct our attention back to the later seventeenth and earlier eighteenth centuries, we find clues which indicate that plebeian witchcraft beliefs were developing and becoming more elaborate at much the same time as the social élite was gradually distancing itself from the idea of witchcraft.

A set of such clues survives in depositions among the assize records of the Northern Circuit given in 1673 by Anne Armstrong, a servant girl living near Birchen Nook in Northumberland.[4] Early that year the young woman managed to place herself at the centre of a web of witchcraft accusations. She told how, in the course of bargaining over eggs with a woman called Anne Forster, Forster 'look't' her head. Three days later a man in ragged clothes came to her, and told her that Forster 'should be the first made [i.e. to make] a horse of her spirit' and ride her, and went on to give her an account of what would happen to her at what was obviously a plebeian version of the sabbat. After he left, Armstrong, on her own testimony, fell into a trance and suffered a series of fits spread over several days. On one occasion, in Armstrong's imagining, Forster came and put a bridle on the girl and rode her cross-legged until they came to a gathering at nearby Riding Mill. And there indeed the young Armstrong, so she claimed, had her first experience of the sabbat.

She told the examining justices of the peace how she had remained in the shape of a horse until Forster removed the bridle from her, and then she saw thirteen women and a tall black man whom the women called their Protector. The others danced in the shapes of hares, cats and mice, and Armstrong sang, and was then bridled again and ridden home. On another occasion she attended another such meeting where the Protector was sometimes described by those present as their God, and sat at the end of a table in a golden chair. Everyone touched a hanging rope three times and this caused all the provisions they desired to be brought to the table. She gave her first depositions in February, others followed in April and May, by which time her tales of the sabbat had become more elaborate: she had ridden there on wooden dishes and eggshells, and had danced before the devil in various animal forms. At each of the meetings the witches pulled on ropes and these produced what was probably the limits of what a Northumbrian country girl could imagine as fine food: capon, 'ye plum broth ye capon was boyld in', beef, mutton, cheese, butter, wines and ale. Those present reported their misdeeds to the devil, who made much of those who had performed the most wickedness and beat those who had no evil-doing to report. Anne was offered a lease on her life to run for sixty years, during which time she would never want for money and one cow would give her as much milk as ten would normally. By the end of April and early May she was telling of how the witches at the sabbat came together in 'coveys' of thirteen, said the Lord's Prayer backwards and attended in ever increasing numbers.

Armstrong's depositions are among the most remarkable texts in the history of English witchcraft; they are, in fact, currently being subjected to detailed research. Yet even on a superficial level they demonstrate the fertility of plebeian witchcraft beliefs. Obviously, Armstrong's depositions require detailed textual analysis, and attempting to determine where her ideas came from would entail some fascinating cultural detective work. What is evident, however, is that here we have not the sabbat of the learned demonologists, but rather a view of the witches' meeting which was based on local traditions. The devil presided, sometimes sitting at the head of a table, receiving his minions' reports of the evil they had done. There were no cannibalistic feasts or promiscuous sexual couplings here, but rather country dancing and gorging on the best food that a servant girl in remote Northumbria could imagine. There was that shape-changing, so central to later English witchcraft beliefs and clearly conflated with notions about familiars. The idea that witches rode humans to the sabbat, in much the same way as they might ride horses, was evidently gaining ground. And the more familiar tales of *maleficium*, sick animals and the suffering of violent fits all made their appearance when other people living in the area began to give the justices their own tales of witchcraft as the stories and accusations spread. Indeed, some of the depositions suggest that Armstrong was gaining a local reputation as a witch-finder and that the potential for a large-scale witch-hunt was present in the area. As we have suggested, breaking down Armstrong's tales into their component parts would prove an intriguing exercise: at the very least there are some interesting parallels with that other plebeian account of the sabbat given by young Edmund Robinson in Lancashire in 1634. But Armstrong's descriptions, coming as they did forty years later, are strongly suggestive of a popular idea of witchcraft which was developing and becoming more complex.

If Armstrong's depositions are suggestive of a broadening of the popular witchcraft agenda, a case from over sixty years later demonstrates that agenda's longevity. In November 1736 (ironically, a few months after the repeal of the witchcraft statutes) Margaret Goldsbrough, an inhabitant of the isolated village of Baildon, requested the justices of the West Riding of Yorkshire to bind over three of her neighbours, Mary Hartley, John Hartley and 'one other John Hartley called Red John', to keep the peace with her. Goldsbrough told how she had been selling besoms in the village with her mother, Bridget, and the older woman had fallen into an altercation when they visited the Hartley household. Mary Hartley had begun to accuse Bridget of being a witch and of bewitching her son John. Hartley pursued the two women into the street, where she and the two John Hartleys began to shout at them, accusing them of being witches and calling out 'kill them and let them live no longer'.

The content of the accusation of witchcraft, especially in the light of what we have said of Anne Armstrong's depositions, is interesting. Mary Hartley told Bridget Goldsbrough, 'I wou'd have you let my barn [i.e. bairn] alone, he works hard for his living and cannot bear to be disturbed at night.' When Bridget asked what Hartley meant by this, the indignant mother replied that the two Goldsbrough women were witches, the previous night they had ridden her son to Pendle Hill (Baildon is just over the border from that part of Lancashire) and 'Margaret brought a saddle and bridle and wou'd put the bridle into his mouth but that the bitts were too large'. Other allegations involved shape-changing. Sarah Brooks and her husband, John, both told how the Hartleys had spread stories that Bridget Goldsbrough turned herself into two grey cats. But it was the notion of witches riding their victim through the night, presumably to a sabbat, which was crucial, for it was clear, given Armstrong's earlier use of the motif, that this was by now a central element in popular ideas of what witches did, at least in the north of England. It is also significant that the objective of the journey was Pendle Hill. Clearly, well over a century after the celebrated 1612 trials, that topographical feature still enjoyed associations with witchcraft locally. There are also, as so often, overtones of wider social tensions. The

Goldsbroughs and the Brooks were among the more substantial families in the township (in fact, Bridget Goldsbrough and Sarah Brooks were sisters), while the Hartleys were a poorer and more obscure family. Yet it may not be without significance that a youth called Abraham Hartley, son of (presumably) another John Hartley, was allegedly bewitched at Baildon in 1658. The surname is not so uncommon as to allow certainty, but it is at least worth speculating on the presence of a family tradition of witchcraft.[5]

If we go back half a century, and to the opposite end of the country, we gain sight of another direction in which popular beliefs were developing. In 1687 the Essex justice Sir William Holcroft noted another of those cases which give us tantalizing glimpses of the plebeian mental world. In that year he recorded the apprehension of a woman named Ann Watts, a fortune-teller normally resident on the fringes of London, who had apparently been sleeping rough in the woods of one of Holcroft's gentleman neighbours. Holcroft recorded that she was brought before the local petty sessions, and although we do not know what happened to her (presumably an admonition and a light penalty), we know that certain books in her possession were ordered to be burnt. The volumes in question were two works by Cornelius Agrippa, one of them being his *Occult Philosophy*; Scot's *Discovery of Witchcraft*; a 'tutor to astrology'; and what was probably one of the long series of *Ephemerides*, published by that highly successful astrologer John Gadbury. Here we have a rare (or at least rarely documented) example of an itinerant fortune-teller who was clearly operating in the frontier territory between élite and popular magical culture. Reginald Scot we have already met several times in this book, and it is probable that Ann Watts valued his work for the details it contained of how to perform conjuring tricks. Similarly, one of Gadbury's almanacs and a teach-yourself astrology book were of obvious use to her. But Cornelius Agrippa was a renowned Renaissance magus of the earlier sixteenth century and his *Occult Philosophy* had been a key text for those interested in learned magic. It is interesting to note that this text was in the possession of a plebeian fortune-teller at just that point when it had been more or less marginalized by learned natural philosophy.[6]

Recent research has demonstrated, as Ann Watts's books suggest, that by the later seventeenth century astrology was very much a 'pseudo-science' which operated over a variety of social and cultural levels, the 'death' of which after 1660 has been much exaggerated. Victorian folklorists were to find masses of astrological lore embedded in popular thinking, while painstaking historical investigation is beginning to uncover networks of judicial astrologers operating in provincial England, and catering for the middling levels of society, in the eighteenth century. Again, the issue is not just one of 'survival'. Patrick Curry, the leading historian of English astrology, has argued that what occurred over the late seventeenth and eighteenth centuries was a refashioning of astrological ideas for the benefit of consumers from the middling and plebeian levels of society. The popular enthusiasm for eclipses, comets and other astronomical phenomena lived on, as did the taste for prediction, prophecy and fortune-telling.[7] Thus for the common people witchcraft continued to exist in much the same way as it had for the educated in the sixteenth century: as part of a wider belief system which, however irrational it might appear to the modern observer, helped many people make sense of the world and cosmos in which they existed, and helped them deal with at least some of the problems they experienced. Charting the dimensions and component parts of this belief system, let alone attempting to delineate ways in which it changed, is an historical exercise which has as yet barely begun.

Certainly, as far as witchcraft is concerned, this is true of the eighteenth century; for the seventeenth century we have the records of witch trials and the stories collected by learned writers, while by the nineteenth century, as the Reverend Atkinson demonstrated, witch beliefs were being collected by folklorists and clergymen of an antiquarian disposition. Whatever the common people may have believed in the eighteenth century, it is obvious that not many people were interested in noting it in any very systematic way. Yet a few traces of witch belief survive: an entry in the parish register of Coggeshall in Essex, for example, of the burial of John Man, 'a reputed witch', on 6 July 1755, or the case in 1788 when a Sheffield labourer had stolen money returned to him when the town crier had announced that he had gone to a cunning man to identify the thief.[8] But perhaps the most consistent evidence comes from recorded examples of the swimming of witches, one aspect of popular witchcraft beliefs which was public enough to impress itself upon genteel observers. We began this book with the story of Thomas Colley and Ruth Osborne at Tring in Hertfordshire in 1751. Other swimmings occurred (this list is not exhaustive) in Kent (1735), Leicestershire (1736), Bedfordshire (1737), Norfolk (1748), Suffolk (1752), Leicestershire again (1760 and 1776), Cambridgeshire (1769), and Suffolk again (1795).[9]

As we have suggested, the emergence of folklore as a matter of interest among the educated means that we have far more information about witchcraft beliefs in nineteenth- than in eighteenth-century England. Middle-class observers were collecting information about witchcraft along with other aspects of popular belief, and there was evidently a great deal to be found. For a typical, if well-documented, example let us turn to Essex, where evidence of witchcraft is so plentiful from Elizabethan and Stuart times.[10] As late as the 1890s, people in the remote, rural areas of that county continued to believe in witches and witchcraft. Witches, still conceived of as isolated individuals, by now thought to be working through the power of the evil eye, performed the traditional acts of *maleficium*: they inflicted plagues of lice on people, they stopped the wheels of wagons, they caused a whole range of illnesses, they paralysed people. There were some new touches too. The wheels of bicycles as well as those of wagons might now be stopped from turning. Nelly Button, a notorious witch living at Hockley in the 1860s, was reputed to have caused the concertina of a man who had offended her to play every night of its own accord until he was almost demented. Another, in this case male, Essex witch, in dispute with the farmer employing him about the length of his lunch-break, used his powers to stop a threshing machine from operating until he had finished his meal. There was still a widespread belief in familiars, and people still went to the cunning man or woman when they were ill, wanted to find stolen goods or felt they needed exceptional help against witchcraft. And, when the help needed was not so exceptional, they still made use of counter-magic against the witch: scissors and knives were put under doormats to impede the witch's entrance into a house, while labourers going out to work might tuck a manuscript copy of the Lord's Prayer into their boots to ward off *maleficium*.

Evidence from other areas demonstrates that the population of rural Essex was not unique in its late adherence to witchcraft beliefs. The situation in North Yorkshire, as described by Atkinson, was basically similar, with some regional variations. 'Witch wood' was widely used as a charm against witchcraft, women would say a charm before they churned butter and a more serious threat from witchcraft, such as the sickness of animals, would necessitate the more elaborate remedy of burning a sheep's heart with nine new pins, nine new needles and nine small nails.[11] Atkinson, indeed, had the bracing experience, three centuries after the Reformation, of being told by a woman whose request to exorcize her he had refused, that the priests of the 'au'd [i.e. old] church' were 'more powerful conjurers than you church priests'.[12] North Yorkshire also saw the practice of building carved witch posts into the structure of farmhouses to ward off witchcraft. Detailed research would doubtlessly reveal cognate practices throughout rural England during the nineteenth century.[13] Even an initial survey of popular introductions to county folklore reveals witchcraft beliefs in areas as disparate as Hampshire, Hertfordshire, Somerset, Wiltshire and the Lake District.[14]

As with their social superiors two centuries earlier, the exact reasons why widespread belief in witchcraft died out on a popular level around the end of the nineteenth century remain elusive. Flora Thompson, remembering her Oxfordshire childhood of the 1880s, recalled an elder tree near her home into which, as tradition had it, a witch had changed herself when chased by a village mob. She asked her mother if witches still existed and received the reply, 'No, they seem to have all died out. There haven't been any in my time: but when I was your age there were plenty of old people who had known or even been ill-wished by one.'[15] The reasons why witches 'seemed to have died out' in popular belief have yet to be examined in detail. But interestingly, at another point in her recollections, following a more general discussion of superstitions, Thompson discussed the cultural changes which were affecting even the rural poor by the 1880s:

the world was at the beginning of a new era, the era of machinery and scientific discovery. Values and conditions were changing everywhere. Even to simple country people the change was apparent. The railways had brought distant parts of the country nearer, newspapers were coming into every house; machinery was superseding hard labour, even on the farm to some extent; food bought at shops, much of it from distant countries, was replacing the home-made and the home-grown. Horizons were widening . . .[16]

As with the standard accounts explaining the rejection of witchcraft and broader 'superstition' among the educated at the end of the seventeenth century, we find an explanation based on technical change and a wider intellectual view. And with those more familiar accounts, we might be excused for feeling that this is not the whole story; but once again we have a sense of witchcraft beliefs gradually being marginalized, gradually being rendered obsolete, as the competition from alternative views of how the world worked became overwhelming.

❯ A belief in witchcraft, it would thus seem, continued to flourish among the lower orders of rural England until the mid- or late nineteenth century. Among their educated betters, so all the evidence suggests, belief in witchcraft, witches and magic collapsed in the early eighteenth century. Yet even here the story is more complex and less certain than might appear at first sight.

There is no doubt that full-scale defences of the reality of witchcraft were rare after 1700. What is generally regarded as the last by a respectable scholar came in 1715, in the shape of Richard Boulton's *A compleat History of Magick, Sorcery and Witchcraft*. Boulton, a relatively obscure doctor whose other publications included a number of books on medical matters and an epitome of Robert Boyle's works, argued along what were by that date traditional lines, and such passages as those describing how the devil came most readily to persons in a state of despair and how magicians were attracted by 'too eager desire and pursuit of knowledge' were very similar to their equivalents in demonological tracts of the later sixteenth century.[17] Boulton also emphasized the importance of the swimming test and the witch's mark in establishing proof, and cited as evidence details of witchcraft trials running from the Elizabethan Warboys case to more recent episodes such as the trials at Salem, Massachusetts, in 1692 and the possession which began in 1689 of Richard Dugdale, the 'Surey Demniack', in Lancashire.[18] He argued, like so many others taking his position, that 'it would be absurd and unreasonable to deny the truth of such relations, as to deny the existence of that diabolical power by which they were performed', although, as befitted somebody familiar with Boyle's work, he was sufficiently aware of recent developments to cite John Locke's *Essay on Human Understanding* to support the possibility of the existence of spiritual substance.[19]

Boulton's work provoked a counterblast that is usually regarded as one of the key English witchcraft texts, Francis Hutchinson's *A historical Essay* of 1718. Hutchinson, a Church of England clergyman and a future bishop and religious controversist, wrote what was a scholarly and careful piece of work, gathering together a mass of information, which is still a useful historical source. He was anxious to preserve the possibility of the spirit world, declaring that 'the sober belief' in spirits was 'an essential part of every good Christian's faith', but saw such a belief as something totally separate from 'the fantastick doctrines that support the vulgar opinion of witchcraft'.[20] And, again, we get a sense of the cultural distancing between the learned churchman and those who might hold 'vulgar opinions': 'the credulous multitude,' wrote Hutchinson, 'will ever be ready to try their tricks, and swim the old women, and wonder at and magnify every unaccountable symptom and odd accident.'[21] His arguments, apart from these, were also standard: most of what was attributable to witchcraft was, in fact, explicable by natural causes, the references to witchcraft in Scripture were misunderstood and mistranslated, spectral evidence was a nonsense and so on.

With Hutchinson, then, it appeared that something like a 'modern', 'common-sense' view of witchcraft had finally prevailed. Certainly Wallace Notestein, in his classic pioneering study of English witchcraft history published in 1911, thought so. 'Hutchinson's work was the last chapter in the witch controversy. There was nothing more to say,' declared the American scholar, and demonstrated the extent of his belief in this statement by ending the text of his book with it.[22] If only, one is tempted to say, things were that simple. Certainly Hutchinson himself did not think that the issue was quite so clear-cut; he seemed to consider himself as operating in what was still disputed territory. Referring to works on witchcraft which had been published since the Restoration, he observed: 'These books and narratives are in tradesmen's shops, and farmers' houses, and are read with great eagerness, and are continually leavening the minds of youth, who delight in such subjects; and considering some evils these notions bring where they prevail, I hope no man will think but that they must still be combatted, oppos'd and kept down.'[23] Boulton, in fact, was so concerned that they should not be 'kept down' that in 1722 he published a defence of his earlier book, in which he spent nearly 200 pages restating the need to extirpate witches and the reasons why the reality of witchcraft should be recognized. Holding the line against witchcraft, he argued, was a guarantee against that more general sinfulness to which humankind was prone: 'if the world was let loose to perpetrate and commit all manner of evil as the Devil and their own inclination would suggest,' he wrote, 'it would soon be over-run with the worst of vicious practices, and witchcraft would be rife as ever.'[24]

That Hutchinson felt so worried about the need to combat witchcraft beliefs in 1718, that Boulton still felt able to support them in 1722 and indeed that the statutes making *maleficium* a felony were not repealed until 1736 suggest that witchcraft was not as dead an issue among the nation's élite in the early eighteenth century as has been assumed. Once more, we must admit ruefully that a full investigation of this topic would demand another book as lengthy as this one.[25] Even a preliminary review of the evidence is, however, suggestive. Let us begin with the clergy. Doubtlessly highly placed clerics were able to reject witchcraft beliefs or marginalize them as plebeian vulgar errors. Country parsons were in a more ambivalent position. Consider Humphrey Michel, vicar of the Leicestershire parish of Horninghold. Michel was a staunch Tory, a closet Jacobite, a scourge of the local dissenters and a frequent presenter of moral offenders before the local Church courts. He also seemed to accept the reality of witchcraft. Michel, who died in 1722, kept a diary which contains a number of references to witchcraft. In June 1709, for example, he recorded the swimming of two witches, one of whom, a cripple named Mary Palmer, 'though bound hand and feet, did not sink but swim [*sic*] before the said company' (the other, a man named Joseph Harding, 'sunk immediately like a stone before them all'). Michel also thought that a woman called Goody Ridgway had 'in all probability' been bewitched to death, and noted the behaviour of 'a wench of the widow Barlow, a supposed witch', who 'went out of the church when I had named and read my text, Deut Chap 18, where is the word witch'. One wonders how many other country clergymen there were in the early eighteenth century who had this lively an interest in the witchcraft suspicions of their parishioners.[26]

Further investigation would also probably reveal that many of the provincial gentry had not divested themselves of belief in witchcraft or in that wider supernatural world which, as we have seen in so many contexts, provided the environment within which witchcraft beliefs could flourish. Polite circles in London and the larger provincial centres might have rejected such notions, but in rural and small-town society many gentlemen and their families had not. Demonstration of this point is provided by Nicholas Blundell, of Little Crosby near Liverpool. Blundell was a member of an established family of Catholic gentry who, despite his recusancy, seems to have enjoyed active and broad social and commercial contacts in his area. These contacts and other matters were noted in a 'Diurnall' in which he recorded, on a daily basis, the events of his life, and among those events, at least between 1706 and 1714, was the occasional presence of what seems to have been a poltergeist in his residence. Indeed, on Christmas Day 1717 one of his servants claimed to have heard the voice of one of Blundell's daughters in the chamber they shared, although the girl was absent from home at that point, causing Blundell to note that 'what this means I suppose time will shew, for certainly it was something supernaturall'. And in April 1705 he recorded, in a matter-of-fact way, seeing 'three women that were said to be bewitched'.[27] The gentry's involvement with witchcraft could sometimes be more direct. In 1716 a Hertfordshire justice of the peace, John Goodere alias Dineley, was removed from the commission for, among other things, improper behaviour at the swimming of a witch. He stripped, jumped into the sluice where the witch was being tested, swam naked on his back, exposing himself to the spectators gathered there, and after he had got out exposed himself anew to several women there and made lewd suggestions to them. In this case, the gentleman was clearly deranged, but his presence and that of others like him at swimmings is suggestive of a continuing interest in witchcraft among the gentry, even those of sufficient status to be justices of the peace.[28]

Perhaps the clearest indication that witchcraft was not a dead issue in the early eighteenth century comes, however, from the controversy which surrounded the trial of Jane Wenham in 1712. On the strength of the allegations levelled against her, as we have seen when discussing her case in its legal context, Wenham was a fairly typical witch, an old woman who had gained a bad reputation locally and had irritated her neighbours sufficiently to be indicted. And, it will be recalled, what brought her to court were allegations that she had bewitched a young servant girl called Anne Thorne. The incident is most often remembered as the last known occasion on which a conviction for witchcraft was brought at an English assizes, a verdict whose reversal by a sceptical judge, Sir John Powell, provides evidence of the gap between the attitudes of the witch-hunting public and the more detached, learned approach of the judiciary. What is sometimes forgotten is that the case provoked an active pamphlet debate at the time, involving at least eight publications, in which the reality of witchcraft was debated. Detailed work on the local context of the accusations against Wenham demonstrates how far the élite in her area were also divided on the issue of witchcraft.[29]

What must be grasped is that those supporting court proceedings against Wenham were not just ignorant villagers. Anne Thorne was a servant of the minister of Walkerne, Godfrey Gardiner, and this clergyman's opinions were crucial in the initial focusing of suspicions against Wenham. Another clergyman, Mr Strutt, vicar of the neighbouring parish of Ardley, played a similar role, as indeed did one of Wenham's more respectable relatives, a Mr Archer of Sandon, who at one point joined with the clergymen in urging the woman to confess. Archer is a somewhat obscure figure, but both the clerics were men who had held their livings from the 1680s and might therefore be expected to have some knowledge of their flocks, and of the personalities of such aberrant parishioners as Jane Wenham. Jane was examined by another local authority figure, Sir Henry Chauncy, justice of the peace and local squire, a trained lawyer and antiquarian who was apparently swayed by the opinion of the two clergymen. Chauncy's son, Arthur, was heavily involved in employing various traditional 'proofs' against Wenham. Chauncy's grandson, Francis Bragge, was a friend of Godfrey Gardiner and his wife, was present in their parlour when Anne Thorne first demonstrated those symptoms which were to be diagnosed as witchcraft and was to become the author of two of the pamphlets generated by the case. Thus the minister of Wenham's parish, the minister of an adjacent one and the family of the local squire were all willing to accept the reality of witchcraft and the guilt of Jane Wenham as a witch.

Indeed, it is possible that it was the relatively high status of those supporting the accusations against Wenham which made the jury willing to convict her, and it seems likely that this helped in the generating of a pamphlet controversy. This controversy took on political tones. Hertfordshire was, politically, religiously and economically, a divided county and Walkerne lay on the rough frontier between the county's Whig and Tory zones. Francis Bragge, author of pamphlets against Wenham, believed in the power of witchcraft and the devil, and held that those who did not share his views were atheists, equating, in a nice early-eighteenth-century touch, the rejection of witchcraft beliefs with Whig ideology. Certainly, after the trial Wenham lived out her life in a cottage provided for her on the estate of a local Whig magnate. Francis Hutchinson, who visited her a little after the trial, wrote that 'the whole county is now fully convinced that she was innocent', and that Anne Thorne was thought of as 'an idle hussy, with child at the time, and was well as soon as her sweetheart married her'. He also noted that Wenham was proud of a new-found skill, the utility of which had doubtless been impressed upon her by her experiences as a suspected witch: she could now say the Lord's Prayer without faltering.[30]

Just before the Wenham case occurred, a number of references to witchcraft appeared in the journals of the period, evidence possibly of an undercurrent of interest. Perhaps surprisingly, Daniel Defoe, so often regarded as a prophet of modernity, gave an unequivocal declaration in support of the existence of witchcraft in *The Review* of 20 October 1711. In 'A digression about witches and witchcraft' he argued on the basis of Scripture and 'the records of justice' that witches did exist, and that a witch should be defined as 'one in covenant with the Devil, and uses his help to deceive or hurt others'. It may be significant that *The Review* was, at this point, being subsidized by the Tory government. The pro-Whig *Tatler* had, in May 1709, adopted a dismissive tone about witchcraft when describing some fictional accusations, while another broadly Whig writer, Joseph Addison, had given what was probably very much the general educated person's view a few months before Defoe wrote. For Addison, 'There are some opinions in which a man should stand neuter, without engaging his assent to the one side or the other . . . I believe in general that there is, and has been such a thing as a witchcraft: but at the same time can give no credit to any particular instance of it.' This position was clearly a fudge, but probably one which many relatively progressive people of the period shared: to remain noncommittal was probably seen as a sensible course in the face of a potentially controversial issue. But Addison, it should be noted, went on in this essay to present a tongue-in-cheek treatment of witchcraft in a description of an interview between his fictional hero, Sir Roger de Coverley, and a witch, 'Moll White'. The description of Moll suggests that Addison had a good grasp of current village beliefs about witches, while his portrayal of Sir Roger's reactions was probably not too far removed from the reality of those experienced by many country gentry. He was 'a little puzzled about the old woman, advising her as a justice of peace to avoid all communication with the devil, and never to hurt any of her neighbours' cattle'.[31]

We must repeat a point touched on frequently over the last few chapters, and reinforced by the important analysis carried out by Ian Bostridge: that witchcraft beliefs among the élite in the two generations after 1660 shifted and were redefined, and cannot be interpreted on any simple model of 'decline'. There were a number of competing positions. Some writers, like Henry More, Joseph Glanvill and, perhaps with a somewhat different emphasis, Meric Casaubon attempted to forge a new view of witchcraft which was consistent with a developing Anglican natural theology. Adherents of a thoroughgoing mechanical philosophy, like Thomas Hobbes, could deny malefic witchcraft altogether. Others more attached to social or religious prejudices than new scientific ideas could marginalize witchcraft beliefs on account of their supposed connections with the religious sectarian radicalism of the 1640s and 1650s. Yet others could simply accept the reality of witchcraft in much the same way as people had in the Elizabethan period. What is obvious is that, in the early eighteenth century, witchcraft was becoming a 'political' issue, something which (if only most frequently as a rhetorical device) was, for at least some writers, becoming enmeshed in the current struggle between Whig and Tory. At the very least, the scientific concern over the relationship between the physical and the spiritual world was paralleled by a concern about the relationship between secular civil society and the world of religion.

This would seem, however, to have been a short-term development, a final if significant flicker of serious concern with traditional witchcraft among the educated members of polite society. Certainly, the repeal of the English and Scottish witchcraft laws in 1736 aroused nothing by way of pamphlet controversy in England and little, indeed, by way of comment. House of Commons records suggest a number of alterations in the bill as it progressed through various stages, and examination of the journal literature of that year might well reveal a minor revival in interest in the subject of witchcraft. Yet there seems to have been little by way of sustained parliamentary debate. The act itself was short and to the point. After it entered the statute book, it stated that 'no prosecution, suit, or proceeding' could be launched in a court in Great Britain 'against any person or persons for witchcraft, sorcery, inchantment, or conjuration, or for charging another with any such offence'. The act did, however, attempt to protect 'ignorant persons' from being defrauded by people pretending to use witchcraft, or claiming to tell fortunes or to be able to find stolen or lost goods. With a certain irony, people convicted of attempting such deceptions were to be placed in prison for a year, their incarceration to be punctuated by four spells in the pillory in the market-place of an appropriate market town: the penalty, in fact, laid down for lesser forms of malefic witchcraft by the statute of 1563.[32]

And as the late seventeenth and eighteenth centuries progressed, references to witchcraft in literature and on the stage, although by no means absent, demonstrated a shift. In 1689, Henry Purcell, in his opera *Dido and Aeneas*, used three witches to symbolize evil in much the same way as Shakespeare had in *Macbeth*. But the splintering of any consensual view of witchcraft had been demonstrated earlier, in 1681, with the staging of Thomas Shadwell's play *The Lancashire-Witches, and Tegue o Dively the Irish Priest*. This work took a number of materials, including those relating to the Lancashire trials of 1612 and 1633, but used witches as essentially comic characters in what was an anti-Catholic and pro-Whig satire produced towards the end of the Popish Plot. That the play was staged about fifty times between 1703 and 1729 provides further evidence of how potent the witch image was in early-eighteenth-century politics.[33] But by the early eighteenth century terms like 'bewitch' or 'enchant' were beginning to lose their sinister overtones and to be used in the more modern but less threatening sense of being fooled or sexually attracted. The language of witchcraft was still part of common parlance, but its resonances had altered. The shift is illustrated neatly in the *Oxford English Dictionary*, which notes that 'bewitch' had been used 'formerly often in a bad sense', but that it was since 'more generally said of pleasing influences'. When witchcraft or magic was mentioned, it was usually in a more distanced sense. When, for example, Sir Anthony Absolute in Sheridan's *The Rivals*, a play first staged in 1785, announced, 'Had I a thousand daughters, by heaven! I'd as soon have them taught the black art as their alphabet', the effect intended was clearly a comic one.[34] Few people in the polite audience of the 1780s would have taken the allusion in any other way; two centuries earlier, a more ambivalent response may have been evoked.

As the language of witchcraft altered its emphasis, so the iconography of the witch became standardized. For most people today, witches are easily recognizable, members of that select group of historical figures who can be widely identified. They are normally portrayed as old women, clad in a shawl and a long skirt, wearing a tall, wide-brimmed hat, perhaps riding on a broomstick, living in a cottage with a cat, stirring a cauldron. The re-creation of this image as a stereotype is probably the work of Victorian children's fiction, and the image of the witch current in our own day, and much basic 'knowledge' about witches, is still spread by books for children. Yet the elements of this image were clearly present in the middle of the eighteenth century. In 1762 William Hogarth published his print *Superstition, Credulity and Fanaticism*. Among the subjects treated in this work were Mary Tofts, who earlier in the eighteenth century had achieved brief fame for claiming to have given birth to live rabbits; books on witchcraft by James I and Joseph Glanvill; and a copy of Wesley's sermons. But perhaps the key image is that of the enthusiastic clergyman in the pulpit, holding in one hand a puppet of the devil, in the other a puppet of a witch. And the latter rode a broomstick with a cat perched on it and wore the conical, wide-brimmed hat; the image with which we are familiar was becoming a stereotype even as the reality of witches was becoming untenable for most educated people.

Yet, as we have suggested, this belief had not disappeared quite as totally as has sometimes been claimed. Or, to put it rather differently, just as the language of witchcraft was changing in its emphasis, so, for the educated, aspects of the occult were being redefined: magic and the supernatural were not so much being rejected as recategorized. Perhaps the clearest clue to this process is provided by the cultural history of astrology. As we have noted, by the eighteenth century astrology had ceased to be treated seriously by polite society and was becoming increasingly an intellectual activity patronized by the provincial middling sort or by the common people. But the repackaging of astrological ideas and the relocating of astrological concerns as a part of popular science meant that the subject never quite vanished from the agenda of the educated, and it was to make something of a comeback from the 1790s onwards. The extent of this comeback is perhaps best demonstrated by the reception of the work of Ebenezer Sibly (1751–99), who combined a belief that modern science should be informed by ancient knowledge with what was, in his period, a very fashionable interest in freemasonry and animal magnetism. The ready market for Sibly's publications on astrology, it has been claimed, was evidence of a middlebrow cultural border zone where sets of interests which might once have been satisfied by natural magic were now being catered for by popular science and redefinitions of Christianity.[55]

Another element in the late-eighteenth-century cultural mix which suggests a renewed interest in the occult was the popularity of the Gothic novel, a literary genre generally considered to have been ushered in with the publication of Horace Walpole's *The Castle of Otranto* in 1765. Obviously, a desire to read Gothic novels should not be equated with a belief in witchcraft, but what the taste for this genre does demonstrate is another episode in that repackaging of the occult which seems to have been a feature of European culture since Roman times. Mary Shelley's *Frankenstein*, published in 1818, is an enduring exemplar of the horror story, but the period saw the publication of numerous other works, now forgotten by all but specialist scholars. And these works contained a number of recurring elements: the Gothic castle, the villain who has pledged himself to the devil, a world of ghosts, apparitions, sorcerers and witches, of a mixture of the spirit and the natural world which, as we have seen, was part of the context for witchcraft beliefs among educated writers in the later seventeenth century.[36] Even that less sombre literary movement Romanticism could, in its rejection of Enlightenment intellectual sobriety, be construed as encouraging belief in witches and spirits. Thus in the 1790s the poet Robert Southey could express fears that Wordsworth's poem 'Goody Blake and Harry Gill' might encourage a revival of belief in witchcraft.[37]

And, of course, in the 1790s even 'science' was causing some disruption at the social level of Southey, Wordsworth and the Shelleys. As the history of astrology suggests, popular notions about science never quite divested themselves of an interest in what in earlier centuries would have been categorized as natural magic, and in the late eighteenth century the scientific and medical milieux were very badly shaken up by mesmerism, a phenomenon which, to modern eyes, seems to have much in common with earlier beliefs. Franz Mesmer, born in Swabia in 1734, created and popularized the notion that all natural bodies were penetrated and surrounded by a superfine fluid which acted as a primeval 'agent of nature'. This offered a serious explanation of nature, a nature governed by wonderful, invisible forces, and provided, by analogy, a model for the forces governing society and political life. All of this, of course, sounds very much like the cosmos as imagined by Henry More and Joseph Glanvill, except that by the later eighteenth century Mesmer and his followers could work magnetism, gravity and that recently discovered force electricity into their intellectual frameworks. Perhaps most relevant to our immediate concerns was the application of Mesmer's ideas to medicine. Illnesses, held the mesmerists, were often caused by 'blockages' in the body, and if these were cleared, natural harmony and hence good health would be restored. The way to clear the blockages was through convulsions created by electric shocks and hypnosis, and the accounts of mesmeric healing read very like earlier accounts of exorcisms, with the person undergoing 'treatment' writhing in torment as an 'expert' presided and a large, and often fashionable, audience watched. Mesmer and his adherents regarded what they were doing as 'scientific' and were anxious to distance themselves from earlier occult or magical practices, but the distinction may not have been so clear to many of their contemporaries. Mesmerism enjoyed a massive vogue in pre-Revolutionary France, made some impact in late-eighteenth-century England, but really enjoyed a wide interest there in the early Victorian period.[38]

But by the early Victorian period another of those great refashionings of the occult was already taking place with the advent of spiritualism. It is only in recent years that historians have uncovered the importance of spiritualism in nineteenth-century England. From the 1860s to the end of the century it enjoyed a golden age, with a hard core of several thousand firm believers and a wider public interest which stretched from secularist working men in West Yorkshire through middle-class Christian spiritualists in London to such highly placed dabblers as Queen Victoria and Mr Gladstone. And in nineteenth-century spiritualism, and the debates which its existence engendered, we once again discern, albeit in a different form and surrounded by a different rhetoric, some of those areas of intellectual inquiry which Joseph Glanvill and John Webster regarded as disputed territory. As in the later seventeenth century, for the Victorians 'scientific' proof of the existence of spirits remained elusive. Yet many spiritualists would have regarded the activity in which they were involved as amenable to scientific explanation from a naturalistic position, again illuminating the problems of defining exactly what such terms meant, and were generally happy to incorporate Darwin's ideas on evolution into their conceptual framework. There was also the problem of determining spiritualism's religious status. Many spiritualists considered their activities to be perfectly compatible with Christian belief, in much the same way as Newton had regarded his attempts to understand the nature of the universe two centuries earlier, while spokesmen for the various major Christian faiths were protagonists in the debate about spiritualism. Thus even 'educated' people in the 'scientific' ethos of Victorian Britain were able to envisage contacting the spirit world, that great project of the Renaissance magus, while the fact that the Reverend J. B. Clifford was able in 1873 to publish a book which equated the spiritualism of his day with 'modern witchcraft' demonstrates that at least some Victorian writers were conscious of earlier problems encountered in examining the relationship between the physical and the spiritual worlds.[39]

◗ And so I find myself, on a hot July day in the summer of 1995, taking a break from the toils of authorship by glancing at the products of other writers in the local branch of Waterstone's bookshop. As so often when in such places these days, I gravitate towards the New Age/Occult section and cast an eye over the wares on sale there. And a fine selection meets my eye. I could, if I wished, buy a Merlin Tarot kit ('Images, Insights and Wisdom from the Age of Merlin'), but in preference I turn to the books: that old favourite, Nostradamus, figures prominently, as do instruction books on various aspects of the cabbala, and I could also purchase a handbook on ritual magic or a guide to ghost-hunting

(Joseph Glanvill would have approved), while the onset of middle age is all that deters me from buying a slim volume on aphrodisiacs and love magic. Rubbing shoulders with these books are some larger and more solid works. I am surprised (well, perhaps not really surprised) to discover that Montague Summers's *History of Witchcraft and Demonology* is still in print, but to my joy I come across a large recent edition of Cornelius Agrippa's *Three Books of Occult Philosophy*, and my mind goes back to Justice Holcroft, whose papers I read so assiduously a decade ago, and the books he and his fellow magistrates confiscated from Ann Watts the fortune-teller in 1687.

I reflect, to use again that phrase which occurred to me when writing this conclusion, that the occult is being repackaged yet again. For the occult, including witchcraft, is, it seems, something of a growth area in our post-industrial age. Like the would-be Renaissance adept steeping himself in hermetic knowledge, or the Victorian striving for a deeper understanding of life and the universe through spiritualism, it seems that many of my contemporaries in Europe and North America feel the need for spiritual fulfilment, or for a broadening of their consciousness, and consider that this need is better met through the occult than through conventional religion. For as the established Christian Churches face falling congregations, it would seem, on the evidence of the bookshops at least, that a growing number of people are turning to the occult. Indeed, it appears that even Britain's royal family is taking a keen interest in such matters. A recent, and widely read, biography of Princess Diana reveals that the estranged wife of the heir to the throne of the United Kingdom has regularly consulted astrologers and, among other alternative therapies, has had sessions with Madam Vasso, a spiritualist who attempts to soothe the troubled by placing them beneath a blue plastic pyramid. It also seems that the princess's astrologers have predicted that Prince Andrew will become king, information which apparently delighted the Duke of York. One reflects, with a tinge of nostalgia for defunct practices, that this sort of thing would have led to execution in the sixteenth century.[40]

Moreover, as one is made aware by the bookshops and by the odd sensational story appearing in the press, there are a number of people around who consider themselves to be witches and practise something they describe as witchcraft. This witchcraft seems to me, very much an outside observer, something rather different from the engrained, deep-rooted belief in the power of witches which operated in the centuries with which I am familiar as an historian, and which has been much studied at first hand in modern times by anthropologists working on what we were once pleased to describe as primitive societies. Even in Europe, these older beliefs may still not be dead, or their demise might be much more recent than many city-dwellers would believe. As we have noted at various points in this book, historians working on early modern European witchcraft have occasionally sought succour in the work of anthropologists. It is, therefore, slightly ironic that perhaps the closest parallels to the village witchcraft of the seventeenth century written by an anthropologist come not from a study of the Azande or some other tribal society, but rather from work on the Normandy Bocage in the 1970s.[41] The anthropologist Jeanne Favret-Saada describes a witchcraft which seems in many ways analogous to that which flourished in Tudor and Stuart England. There was not much by way of belief in the devil, but a large amount of what the inhabitants of early modern England would have described as *maleficium*: cattle afflicted, women miscarrying, children falling sick inexplicably and butter refusing to churn. And, given that the French state now provides no legal redress against *maleficium*, and given that the Catholic Church no longer takes as active an interest in such matters as it did three centuries ago, those suffering from witchcraft seek remedies from what are, in effect, cunning folk. These, described as 'unwitchers' in the English translation of Favret-Saada's work, attempt to nullify the 'power', the 'fields of force' generated by the witches.

This world of peasant fears of *maleficium* is, one suspects, rather different from the world of the people who buy handbooks of natural magic from the New Age sections of large bookshops. However, the odd exposé in the tabloid press apart, not much is really known about modern witches, and it is therefore with some gratitude that we turn to the research of another anthropologist, this time from the United States, Tanya Luhrmann.[42] Luhrmann set out to study magic and witchcraft not in some exotic society, but rather in modern London. She claims, probably with some accuracy, that there are several thousand people who currently practise magic as a serious activity in England. Their magic, she writes,

involves a ritual practice based upon ideas about strange forces and the powers of the mind. These are people who don long robes and perform rituals in which they invoke old gods to alter their present reality ... Many of them take this magic as both a religious and a pragmatic result-producing practice, and some of them have practised it regularly, in organized groups, for over a quarter of a century.[43]

Luhrmann stresses the wider context of what might be described as the 'magical culture' within which such people operate. There are now a number of mail-order occult stores and bookshops, the most successful of which in

England when Luhrmann wrote, the Sorcerer's Apprentice, sold between 800 and 1,000 items a week and had 25,000 customers who had placed two or more orders with them in the previous thirteen years.

Luhrmann also confirms the impression formed by browsing in the relevant section of a mainstream bookshop that the sources from which modern magical practitioners derive their ideas are very eclectic: paganism (however that might be defined), astrology, mysticism (again, a fairly broad entity) and, to take something very familiar in the sixteenth century, the cabbalistic tradition. To these might be added, according to individual taste, rites, symbols and paraphernalia or concepts from Celtic, Greek, Egyptian or other religions. This eclecticism operates within an overall framework comprising perhaps three main elements. First, as might be expected, there is an openness about belief: as Luhrmann puts it, 'there is no dogma, and feminist witches, kabbalistic Christians and neo-Nordic shamans socialize together'.[44] Second, there is a genuine seeking for spiritual fulfilment and a sincere quest for ultimate spiritual reality. And third, as the list of influences and sources for ideas suggests, there is a tremendous respect for ancient lore: the values of the modern world are rejected, even though many of these modern practitioners of magic and witchcraft hold responsible jobs in very 'modern' sectors of the economy. It is, in fact, trying to determine what 'magic' means to people living in what sees itself as a technical, 'non-magical' world that provides the biggest challenge to the academic investigator of such people.

Certainly, there seems to be little evidence of Satanism: Luhrmann noted rumours of a cult in California and stories of a cat being sacrificed in Highgate cemetery.[45] There were perhaps a few unstable people attracted to magic, but what struck Luhrmann most about the people she investigated was their normality. Most of them were employed, stable, educated and intelligent. If there was any bias in their sociological profile, it was a tendency to be employed at one level or another in the computer industry.[46] We return, as it were, to John Dee attempting to grasp the understanding of occult cosmic reality through the contemplation and manipulation of numbers. But mention of Dee, of course, reintroduces the role of history in all this. For modern magicians and witches feel that they are operating within a tradition, and most of them would stress the antiquity of magic and witchcraft. The problem is that, for the academic historian, their use of history amounts to little more than the invention of tradition, the creation of a myth. Nowhere is this more true than in modern thinking about witchcraft.

We therefore return to what most educated people in the modern West 'know' about witches: 9 million were burnt at some time in the vague past (except, of course, the total of executions was probably less than 1 per cent of that figure for Europe as a whole, while in England witches were hanged); they met in covens of thirteen (except, of course, over most of peasant Europe in the early modern period they were isolated individual old women); and they were representatives of an ancient fertility religion, or some other antique 'pagan' cult (except, of course, there isn't much by way of evidence to support this from any historical source). It does not particularly worry me that people who consider themselves to be witches meet to attain some sort of spiritual fulfilment through practising what they conceive of as an ancient religion (Satanism, if it exists, is another matter). What worries me is that these modern witches, and the broader public, think that they have some historical basis for what they are doing. The reinvention of witchcraft as an historically based, coherent 'religion' seems to be a recurring feature of the modern occult world. It is interesting to ponder how this notion, so inaccurate and so bereft of any historical foundation, has become so firmly entrenched.

As suggested in the introduction to this book, the origins of the idea are probably attributable to Jules Michelet, while its popularity in educated circles in the English-speaking world probably derives from the writings, now discredited in academic circles, of Margaret Murray. Murray's ideas were reinforced by an influential and much-reprinted book, first published in 1954, Gerald B. Gardner's *Witchcraft Today* (this work, in fact, carried an extremely approbatory introduction from Murray). Gardner reiterated the notion that witchcraft as practised today is essentially the survival of an ancient, pre-Christian religion, and is also essentially a benign force. Gardner, himself a member of a coven, denied the reality of such practices as the Black Mass or blood sacrifice, and also affirmed that he had never known witches to do harm. Conversely, he laid considerable emphasis on the importance of ritual for modern witchcraft, and was particularly emphatic that such rituals should be performed naked. And Gardner contributed to that eclecticism of belief that we have noted as being characteristic of modern witches. In his pages we find jumbled together Celtic beliefs, borrowings from ancient Egyptian religion and African magic, references to cults to ancient goddesses and mention of the ancient wisdom, Wicca, which so many witches today see as one of the major sources of their beliefs, but proves so elusive to the scholarly historical investigator.[47]

The popularizing of Murray's ideas coincided with the achievement of notoriety by another significant figure, Aleister Crowley.[48] Born in 1875, Crowley was the son of Plymouth Brethren, a faith which his father combined with running a successful brewery business. After a troubled early education, Crowley entered Trinity College, Cambridge. He was meant to study chemistry there, but was already attached firmly to other interests, notably mountaineering and the pursuit of 'magick', by which he meant a variety of religious experiences. He was also a poet of considerable talent, although his work was controversial. After 1918, he suffered a reversal in his fortunes. His attitude to the First World War attracted a high degree of what was probably unfair criticism, while his irregular personal life, his apparent advocacy of hedonism and his deepening interest in magic and the occult led to his being increasingly marginalized. He travelled abroad extensively in the inter-war years and died in 1947 at Hastings, as one biographer put it, 'excoriated and ignored'. Yet his writings live on. Whatever criticisms may be made of him, Crowley was a very learned man who wrote a number of large and widely read books on magic, and there are still, as I write nearly a half-century after his death, numerous works by him in print. His career and writings have been very influential in spreading notions about magic into the wider culture.

A further major figure in the 'invention of tradition' about magic and witchcraft was Dennis Wheatley.[49] Born in 1897 in London, Wheatley's early life was troubled. He served in the Royal Artillery during the First World War, but was gassed and invalided out; the wine business he inherited on his father's death in 1927 fell victim to the slump in 1930, while his first marriage also failed. Encouraged to become an author by his second wife, he published his first novel in 1933, and, more relevantly for our immediate purposes, in 1935 published *The Devil Rides Out*, a novel whose major themes were satanic magic and witchcraft. The success of this book meant that it was followed by a number of others along similar lines, and these proved very influential in shaping the twentieth-century view of what witchcraft was about. Wheatley, who evidently researched his books fairly thoroughly, attained something of a reputation as an expert on Satanism and the occult. These themes were not quite so salient in his later novels (he died in 1977), but *The Devil Rides Out* and several other of his 'satanic' novels remain in print.

With the novels of Dennis Wheatley we enter that broadest of topics, the representation of witchcraft and related matters in the entertainment industry and mass media of late-twentieth-century Britain. To narrow the focus, let us restrict ourselves to the cinema, where witchcraft has provided a fairly regular theme for film makers. Few who have seen it will forget *Witchfinder General* of 1968, a film which, apart from inventing a pleasingly robust demise for Matthew Hopkins, did at least get near to historical accuracy. More frequently, however, cinema presentations have preserved the notion of witchcraft as either an aspect of a satanic religion or some form of fertility cult. Wheatley's *The Devil Rides Out* was filmed in 1967, while one of his other novels, *To the Devil a Daughter*, appeared in film form in 1975. Another classic example of this genre is the 1970 production *The Blood on Satan's Claw*, set in a late-seventeenth-century English village. Hollywood has also helped encourage the myth of satanic witchcraft. Such rather different films as *I Married a Witch* (1942), *Bell, Book and Candle* (1958) and *The Witches of Eastwick* (1987) might take a more benign view, but with *Halloween Three: Season of the Witch* (1983) we have a story which would have provided fuel for the authors of the *Malleus Maleficarum*: a satanic toy-maker attempts to corrupt the modern United States through the manufacture of Hallowe'en masks for the nation's children. Another film, *Rosemary's Baby* (1968), is a graphic portrayal of that theme which so occupied demonologists, the possibility of a child being conceived as the outcome of sexual intercourse between a human being and the devil. Cinema-goers in the later twentieth century have obviously had their fair share of exposure to a range of images of witchcraft.

It is, perhaps, with Hallowe'en that we can end our brief survey of how witchcraft stands at present in our culture. Among the things which everybody knows about witches is that they met in their covens on Hallowe'en, the night of 31 October, in order to weave their spells and practise their satanic rites. Thus children (more so, at present, in the United States than elsewhere) dress up in witch costumes on 31 October and go out trick-or-treating, adults have Hallowe'en parties and occasional cases occur of outraged parents complaining to education authorities about the spread of Satanism when schools hold events to mark Hallowe'en. It would be interesting to try to discover at what point Hallowe'en became associated with witchcraft. On the strength of the materials I have read while putting this book together, if witches met together on 31 October, it is something of which everybody writing about witchcraft, trying witches in courts or physically or verbally abusing them in sixteenth- seventeenth- or eighteenth-century England was totally ignorant. John Brand's *Observations of the popular Antiquities of Great Britain*, published in 1795, an important early compendium of popular customs and superstitions, while devoting numerous pages to 31 October, makes no mention of witchcraft, while the later and even more comprehensive *British Calendar Customs* of 1940 mentions only one witchcraft-related custom, which apparently could be dated no further back than 1925, amid the numerous ceremonies and beliefs it associates with the last day of October.[50] The notion of Hallowe'en as a witches' feast seems to owe everything to twentieth-century inventiveness and nothing to historical reality, and its current spread in Britain seems to be just another piece of evidence of the insidious Americanization of British culture.

It would seem, then, that history offers little to those currently interested in witchcraft, whether they are the people who are deeply involved in what they consider to be an ancient religion or the children who come trick-or-treating to my door on Hallowe'en. This does not unduly worry me. As far as I am concerned, one of the historian's main functions is to be critical of his or her surroundings, and to be especially vigilant when the past is inaccurately or meretriciously invoked to support present practices. And witchcraft, something which, as I have suggested, is still part of the cultural baggage even of people who have absolutely no belief in any aspect of the occult, is a subject whose past has constantly been misrepresented.

But why, apart from hoping to set the record straight, should anybody write a book about witchcraft in early modern England? There are a number of answers which could be given to this question, but several of them, I would contend, reside in the deeper question of what is history for. Now the answers to that question are varied, and a full rehearsal of them would not be appropriate at this point. But one of the most important is that history serves to remind us constantly that all human beings have not chosen to order either their social or their political affairs or their belief systems in the same ways as we do, or think we do. Here, perhaps, history runs parallel to anthropology in confronting the denizen of the modern, rational, technological, capitalist, industrial or post-industrial state with a view of 'the other'. And in so doing, it reminds us of the diversity of human arrangements and thus, it is to be hoped, broadens us in our humanity. Arguably, few subjects do this more effectively than witchcraft. The fundamental question, perhaps, is how could our forebears believe in witchcraft? I hope to have provided at least some answers to this question, and in so doing I hope to have demonstrated at least something of the complexity of the past, of the way in which good history ought to mean a questioning of the assumption that there are always easy answers.

And in so doing, I hope to have achieved a cognate goal, that of demonstrating that the people who held such different views from my own, and those of most of my compatriots, were neither particularly stupid nor particularly wicked. As for stupidity, I am very unconvinced that the men and women I have met through the variety of source materials I have consulted when following through the history of witchcraft were any more stupid than I or the generality of people I encounter on a daily basis. They were bound by a different set of intellectual assumptions, but, as I have suggested at a variety of points, simply to write those assumptions off as 'ignorance' or 'superstition' does not seem helpful. And, if we return to the early modern debates, I would find it difficult to argue that Reginald Scot was more intelligent, or at least more intellectually complex, than William Perkins, or John Webster than Joseph Glanvill. As for wickedness, there were, doubtlessly, some people who brought witchcraft accusations maliciously, and some others in the legal system who enjoyed the power they had over the old women who were sucked into the legal process as witches. But such people, I would contend, were a minority. Far more common was a fear of witchcraft, a sense of dread as the suspicion crystallized that particular sets of misfortunes were caused by a witch, and a sense of duty that suspected witches should be tried as fairly as current practices allowed, and punished according to the law if found guilty.

Yet the gulf remains: most people in Britain around 1600 believed in witches; most today do not. Yet explaining why we moderns do not entertain such beliefs is difficult. Perhaps part of the answer does lie in technology. We now have ways of explaining natural phenomena and personal misfortune which do not involve witchcraft, while we are more confident than our early modern forebears of being able to understand and control our cosmos. Part of the answer probably lies in the fact that most of us do not live in the same sort of 'face to face' environment as did an Elizabethan villager. And if we accept the once fashionable view that witch-hunting was a form of social scapegoating, it could be argued that later societies have developed other scapegoats and that, to take the two most-quoted examples, Jews in Nazi Germany and Communists in Senator McCarthy's United States fulfilled much the same function as did witches in Europe between the fifteenth and eighteenth centuries. Yet none of these explanations seems to me fully satisfying. The answer, perhaps, lies in some combination of a lack of belief that harm can be done between humans invisibly at a distance, a different set of 'explanations' for unusual diseases and the lack of any real notion of cosmic evil.

But whatever the reasons, and despite any other inadequacies, absurdities and injustices which do exist, most modern developed states, Britain among them, do not encourage either belief in malefic witchcraft or criminal action against people as witches. We have, at least, left that behind. And this knowledge should encourage us to be critical of any intolerances and persecutory urges which still flourish, and to be vigilant in protecting that fragile and imperfect, yet still precious, rationality and tolerance which we have achieved. New Thomas Colleys, Kramers and Sprengers are already inside the gates, awaiting their opportunity.

Notes

Introduction

1. The main sources for the Colley case are two pamphlets, *The Tryal of Thomas Colley at the Assizes at Hertford on Tuesday the 30th of July 1751, before the Right Hon. Sir William Lee, Knight, Lord Chief Justice of the Court of King's Bench* (London, 1751) and *The remarkable Confession and last dying Words of Thomas Colley, executed on Saturday, August the 24th, 1751, at Gubblecot Cross, near Marlston (vulgarly called Wilston) Green* (London, 1751); all quotations used here are taken from these pamphlets. The case also attracted widespread notice in the provincial press: for extracts from the *Northampton Mercury*, for example, see Clifford Morsley, *News from the English Countryside 1750–1850* (London, 1979), pp. 15–20. The incident also forms the basis of W. B. Carnochan, 'Witch-Hunting and Belief in 1751: The Case of Thomas Colley and Ruth Osborne', *Journal of Social History*, 4 (1970–71), pp. 389–404, where a number of other relevant references, notably those found in contemporary issues of the *Gentleman's Magazine*, are noted.

2. The literature on the history of witchcraft in Europe is massive, and even a brief summary of recent publications would fill several pages. Those coming new to the subject would perhaps be best advised to turn to one of the number of recent works of synthesis which have been published. Of these, perhaps the best-rounded is Brian P. Levack, *The Witch-Hunt in Early Modern Europe* (London and New York, 1987). Other general works are listed in the Bibliographical Essay.

3. Lord Morley (ed.), *The Works of Voltaire: A Contemporary Version* (22 volumes, New York, 1927), Vol. 7, Part 1, p. 191; Vol. 12, Part 1, p. 34; Vol. 3, Part 2, pp. 236–7.

4. For a discussion of Summers, see Norman Cohn, *Europe's Inner Demons* (London, 1976), pp. 120–21.

5. I have used the translation of *La Sorcière* published as Jules Michelet, *Satanism and Witchcraft: A Study in Medieval Superstition* (London, 1958). Michelet's view of witchcraft is discussed in Cohn, *Europe's Inner Demons*, pp. 105–7.

6. Margaret Murray, *The Witch-Cult in Western Europe* (Oxford, 1921; many subsequent reprintings). For the major critique of Murray's work, see Cohn, *Europe's Inner Demons*, pp. 107–15. Cf. C. L'Estrange Ewen, *Some Witchcraft Criticisms: A Plea for the Blue Pencil* (np, 1938). Details of her life are taken from *DNB*.

7. Feminist thinking on the connections between women and witchcraft will be returned to in Chapter 7. For an accessible introduction to the subject, drawing together most of the relevant references, see two articles by Rachel Hasted, 'The New Myth of the Witch', *Trouble and Strife*, 2 (Spring 1982), pp. 9–17, and 'Mothers of Invention', *Trouble and Strife*, 7 (Winter 1985), pp. 17–25.

8. The connections between witchcraft prosecutions and modern scapegoating theory were popularized by H. R. Trevor-Roper, *The European Witch-Craze of the Sixteenth and Seventeenth Centuries* (Harmondsworth, 1969). The work which has done most in the English-speaking world to make the connection between 'witch-hunting' and modern political persecution is Arthur Miller's *The Crucible*, a powerful dramatic evocation of the 1692 Salem trials, written in the aftermath of the McCarthy era in the United States.

9. A number of works on mental health touch on witchcraft, although the pioneering study in this respect was Sigmund Freud, 'A Seventeenth-century Demonological Neurosis' (Standard Edition of the Complete Psychological Works of Sigmund Freud, London, 1961), Vol. 4. The most recent work to revive this approach to the subject is Lyndal Roper, *Oedipus and the Devil: Witchcraft, Sexuality and Religion in Early Modern Europe* (London, 1994). For the Freudian interpretation of the Salem outbreak, see Marion L. Starkey, *The Devil in Massachusetts: A Modern Enquiry into the Salem Witch Trials* (New York, 1950).

10. A point made in Levack, *The Witch-Hunt in Early Modern Europe*, pp. 44–5. For a more optimistic discussion of the connections between drugs and witchcraft accusations, see G. R. Quaife, *Godly Zeal and Furious Rage: The Witch in Early Modern Europe* (London and Sydney, 1987), pp. 201–4, and Michael J. Harner, 'The Role of Hallucinogenic Plants in European Witchcraft', in M. J. Harner (ed.), *Hallucinogens and Shamanism* (New York, 1973).

11. Macfarlane, *A Regional and Comparative Study*; Thomas, *Religion and the Decline of Magic*.

12. Christina Larner, *Enemies of God: The Witch-Hunt in Scotland* (London, 1981). This should be read in conjunction with the pieces collected in Larner's *Witchcraft and Religion: The Politics of Popular Belief* (Oxford, 1984). Unfortunately, Larner's early death from cancer prevented her from developing her ideas on witchcraft and related beliefs.

13. E. E. Evans-Pritchard, *Witchcraft, Oracles and Magic among the Azande* (Oxford, 1937), p. 21.

14. Ibid.

15. I have leant very heavily in the pages which follow on what is possibly the clearest guide to the formation of the witch-hunting mentality, Cohn, *Europe's Inner Demons*. Another lively introduction to the subject, which takes the story further chronologically, is Trevor-Roper, *The European Witch-Craze*. Although being too solid to be readily accessible, and despite being in many ways dated in its interpretations, H. C. Lea, *Materials*

toward a History of Witchcraft (3 volumes, Philadelphia, 1939; reprinted New York, 1957), still has much to offer the determined reader.

16. These and similar law codes are discussed in Cohn, *Europe's Inner Demons*, pp. 149–50; Trevor-Roper, *The European Witch-Craze*, pp. 13–14.

17. These developments are discussed in R. I. Moore, *The Formation of a Persecuting Society: Power and Deviance in Western Europe, 950–1250* (Oxford, 1987).

18. A process discussed in an excellent short guide, Richard Kieckhefer, *Magic in the Middle Ages* (Cambridge, 1990), which should be read with the more detailed if more chronologically narrow Valerie J. Flint, *The Rise of Magic in Early Medieval Europe* (Oxford, 1991). Both these books contain excellent bibliographies. For an example of how magic interacted with other areas of creativity in the early modern period, see Gary Tomlinson, *Music in Renaissance Magic: Toward a Historiography of Others* (Chicago and London, 1993).

19. For the Templars, see Cohn, *Europe's Inner Demons*, Chapter 5, 'The Crushing of the Knights Templars', and the more detailed account in Malcolm Barber, *The Trial of the Templars* (Cambridge, 1978). Materials relating to the Kyteler case are gathered in Thomas Wright (ed.), *A contemporary Account of the Proceedings against Dame Alice Kyteler, prosecuted for Sorcery in 1324 by Richard Ledrede, Bishop of Ossory* (Camden Society, London, 1843).

20. For a brief recent discussion of the contribution of Augustine's work to late medieval and early modern demonological theory, see Marcel Gielis, 'The Netherlandic Theologians' Views of Witchcraft and the Devil's Pact', in Marijke Gijswijt-Hofstra and Willem Frijhoff (eds.), *Witchcraft in the Netherlands from the Fourteenth to the Twentieth Century* (Rotterdam, 1991), pp. 38–9.Gielis provides a number of references here, but the most important relevant discussions by Augustine probably appear in Chapters 9 and 10 of *De Civitate Dei*, and Book 2, Chapters 20–27 of *De Doctrina Christiana*.

21. Similarly, Aquinas's contribution to later demonology is discussed, and references cited, in Gielis, 'Netherlandic Theologians', pp. 40–41. Cf. Cohn, *Europe's Inner Demons*, pp. 175–7.

22. Cohn, *Europe's Inner Demons*, pp. 196–7, 203–5.

23. Perhaps the surest guide to this process is Richard Kieckhefer, *European Witch-trials: Their Foundations in Learned and Popular Culture, 1300–1500* (London and Henley, 1976).

24. This evidence is discussed in Carlo Ginzburg, *The Night Battles: Witchcraft and Agrarian Cults in the Sixteenth and Seventeenth Centuries* (London, 1983).

25. As I write, Montague Summers's 1928 translation of the *Malleus Maleficarum* is still in print. Given the attribution of so much significance to the book, the lack of a good modern edition of the *Malleus* is a matter of regret; but for some useful comments, see Sydney Anglo, 'Evident Authority and Authoritative Evidence: The *Malleus Maleficarum*', in Sydney Anglo (ed.), *The Damned Art: Essays in the Literature of Witchcraft* (London, 1977). The Innsbruck trials are referred to in Richard Kieckhefer, *The Repression of Heresy in Medieval Germany* (Liverpool, 1979), pp. 105–7, while the Spanish Inquisition's misgivings about the *Malleus* are noted in Gustav Henningsen, *The Witches' Advocate:*

Basque Witchcraft and the Spanish Inquisition (Reno, Nevada, 1980), p. 347. Attempts to reassess the *Malleus*, along with its authors, would probably still have to begin with the source materials gathered in Joseph Hansen's classic work of scholarship *Quellen und Untersuchungen des Hexenwahns und der Hexenvervolgung im Mittelalter* (Bonn, 1901; reprinted Hildesheim, 1963).

26. For Scotland, see Larner, *Enemies of God*, pp. 61–2; for Lorraine, Robin Briggs, *Communities of Belief: Cultural and Social Tensions in Early Modern France* (Oxford, 1987), p. 67; for Bavaria, Wolfgang Behringer, *Hexenverfolgung in Bayern: Volksmagie, Glaubenseifer und Staatsräson in der Frühen Neuzeit: Studiensausgaber* (Munich, 1988), p. 55; for Catholic areas of Germany, H. C. Erik Midelfort, *Witch Hunting in Southwestern Germany, 1562–1684: The Social and Intellectual Foundations* (Stanford, California, 1972), pp. 180–82.

27. Detailed analysis of medieval witchcraft beliefs in England has yet to be carried out, and would involve exhaustive study of chronicles, theological and pastoral texts, and a wide range of court records, including those of numerous local manorial, ecclesiastical and borough jurisdictions. In the absence of a more modern attempt at a comprehensive overview, the reader might still profitably begin with the relevant sections of a pioneering study, Kittredge, *Witchcraft in Old and New England*, Chapter 2, 'English Witchcraft before 1558'.

28. For the Anglo-Saxon period, see Jane Crawford, 'Evidences for Witchcraft in Anglo-Saxon England', *Medium Aevum*, 32 (1963), pp. 99–116; references from later writers are found in Kittredge, *Witchcraft in Old and New England*, p. 51.

29. This account is based on H. A. Kelly, 'English Kings and the Fear of Sorcery', *Medieval Studies*, 39 (1977), pp. 206–38.

30. Ibid., p. 221.

31. These and other early cases are listed in Ewen, *Witchcraft and Demonianism*, pp. 28–9.

32. Paul Hair, *Before the Bawdy Court: Selections from Church Court and Other Records Relating to the Correction of Moral Offences in England, Scotland and New England, 1300–1800* (London, 1972), pp. 182, 80, 128, 176, 194.

33. There is an extensive literature on the Lollards, although, regrettably for our purposes, little discussion of the propaganda levelled against them by their adversaries. Standard works include A. G. Dickens, *Lollards and Protestants in the Diocese of York, 1509–1558* (Oxford, 1959); John A. F. Thomson, *The Later Lollards, 1414–1520* (Oxford, 1965); Margaret Aston, *Lollards and Reformers: Images and Literacy in Late Medieval Religion* (London, 1984); Anne Hudson, *Lollards and Their Books* (London, 1985). Much of interest is to be found in Charles Kightly, 'The Early Lollards, 1382–1482' (University of York D.Phil. thesis, 1975). The official recognition of the Lollards as a subversive group is charted in M. E. Aston, 'Lollardy and Sedition, 1381–1431', *Past and Present*, 17 (1960), pp. 1–44.

34. For Wyclif's views, see Ewen, *Witch Hunting and Witch Trials*, p. 8. For later Lollard connections with sorcery, see Thompson, *Later Lollards*, p. 241.

35. Bale is mentioned by Kittredge, *Witchcraft in Old and New England*, pp. 34–5; for the portrayal of Idolatry, John Bale, *Comedy concerninge thre Lawes, of Nature, Moses & Christ*

(London, 1538), sigs. B3–B4v; details of Bale's life are given in *DNB* and in the 'Biographical Notice' which is found in Henry Christmas (ed.), *Select Works of John Bale D.D. Bishop of Ossory* (Parker Society, Cambridge, 1849).

36. Walter Howard Frere (ed.), *Visitation Articles and Injunctions of the Period of the Reformation* (3 volumes, Alcuin Club Collection, London, 1910), Vol. 2, pp. 58, 111, 353, 372. This concern was carried into Queen Elizabeth I's Articles of 1559, which asked priests 'whether you know of any that do use charms, sorcery, enchantments, invocations, circles, witchcrafts, soothsaying, or any like crafts or imaginations invented by the devil, and specially in the time of woman's travail': ibid., Vol. 3, p. 5.

37. Kelly, 'English Kings and the Fear of Sorcery', p. 236.

38. Francis Coxe, *A short Treatise declaringe the detestable wickednesse of magicall Sciences, as Necromancie, Conjuration of Spirites, curiouse Astrologie and suche lyke* (London, 1561), pp. 2, 5.

39. For a recent discussion of this legislation, see Stanford E. Lehmberg, *The Later Parliaments of Henry VIII* (Cambridge, 1977), pp. 156–7. For the 1510 Yorkshire treasure-hunt, see Ewen, *Witchcraft and Demonianism*, pp. 142–4.

40. 33 Henry VIII, cap. 8. The text of the act is given in Ewen, *Witch Hunting and Witch Trials*, pp. 13–15.

41. These and other West Country cases are gathered in Janet A. Thompson, *Wives, Widows, Witches and Bitches: Women in Seventeenth-century Devon* (New York, etc., 1993), pp. 185–234.

42. For Scotland, see Larner, *Enemies of God*. For Ireland, nothing has yet replaced the classic account by St John D. Seymour, *Irish Witchcraft and Demonology* (Dublin and London, 1913). A possible direction for research into Welsh witchcraft is suggested by the comment that as late as 1800 Methodist leaders 'were still having to urge their brethren from dabbling in magic and witchcraft': Geraint H. Jenkins, *The Foundations of Modern Wales: Wales 1642–1780* (Oxford, 1987), p. 368. Channel Island witchcraft is described in another work from the Victorian era, John L. Pitts, *Witchcraft and Devil Lore in the Channel Islands* (Guernsey, 1886). Manx witchcraft is the subject of work in progress by Mr Stephen Miller.

1. Witchcraft and Élite Mentalities

1. For an up-to-date and judicious account of Renaissance Platonism, see B. P. Copenhaver and C. B. Schmitt, *Renaissance Philosophy* (Oxford, 1992), pp. 14–16 and Chapter 3, 'Platonism'. This work has an exhaustive bibliography. Like many people, I was first alerted to the wider importance of occult themes in the intellectual life of Elizabethan and Jacobean England by reading the work of F. A. Yates. This work, although criticized by more recent scholarship, is still well worth reading, and her *The Occult Tradition in the Elizabethan Age* (London, 1979) is especially useful for readers coming fresh to this subject area. A more recent perspective on some of the issues is provided by Vaughan Hart, *Art and Magic in the Court of the Stuarts* (London, 1994).

2. For a recent discussion of Dee's thought, see Nicholas H. Clulee, *John Dee's Natural*

Philosophy: Between Science and Religion (London and New York, 1988). A more general introduction is provided by Peter J. French, *John Dee: The World of an Elizabethan Magus* (London, 1972).

3. A clear introduction to astrology is provided by Eugenio Garin, *Astrology in the Renaissance: The Zodiac of Life* (London, 1983), which should be read in conjunction with B. P. Copenhaver, Chapter 10, 'Astrology and Magic', in C. B. Schmitt and Q. Skinner (eds.), *The Cambridge History of Renaissance Philosophy* (Cambridge, 1988). For a more general account, see S. J. Tester, *A History of Western Astrology* (Woodbridge, 1987). Patrick Curry, *Prophecy and Power: Astrology in Early Modern England* (Oxford, 1989), provides an excellent overview of the phenomenon in England. For the medieval background to alchemy, see R. Halleux's article in Joseph R. Strayer (ed.), *Dictionary of the Middle Ages* (13 volumes, New York, 1982), Vol. 1, pp. 134–40, and R. Kieckhefer, *Magic in the Middle Ages* (Cambridge, 1989), pp. 133–9. For the Renaissance period, see W. Shumaker, *The Occult Sciences in the Renaissance* (Berkeley, Los Angeles and London, 1972), pp. 160–99, and the work of Allen G. Debus, in particular his *The Chemical Philosophy* (2 volumes, New York, 1977), Vol. 1. pp. 1–61, and *Man and Nature in the Renaissance* (Cambridge, 1978), pp. 16–33. For a short guide to the contribution of alchemic studies to 'science', see Allen G. Debus and R. P. Multhauf, *Alchemy and Chemistry in the Seventeenth Century* (William Andrews Clark Memorial Library, Los Angeles, 1966).

4. Forman's thought, career and sex life are discussed in A. L. Rowse, *The Case Books of Simon Forman: Sex and Society in Shakespeare's Age* (London, 1974). Deeper insights into the connection between astrology and medicine in Forman's thought will be provided by work in progress by Lauren Kassell.

5. Napier's career and case books form the basis of Michael MacDonald, *Mystical Bedlam: Madness, Anxiety and Healing in Seventeenth-century England* (Cambridge, 1981).

6. Witchcraft in the drama of this period is discussed in Anthony Harris, *Night's Black Agents: Witchcraft and Magic in Seventeenth-century English Drama* (Manchester, 1980). Three key texts are gathered together, with a useful introduction, in Peter Corbin and Douglas Sedge (eds.), *Three Jacobean Witchcraft Plays: The Tragedy of Sophonisba; The Witch; The Witch of Edmonton* (Manchester, 1986).

7. This litigation is discussed in C. L'Estrange Ewen, *Witchcraft in the Star Chamber* (np, 1938), pp. 57–63.

8. The circumstances of the death of Lambe are described in a contemporary tract, *A briefe Description of the notorious Life of John Lambe, otherwise called Doctor Lambe, together with his ignominious Death* (London, 1628). For references to witchcraft elements in the Essex divorce and the investigation of Sir Thomas Overbury's murder, see Beatrice White, *Cast of Ravens: The Strange Case of Sir Thomas Overbury* (London, 1965), pp. 41–3, 122–4.

9. This case is reported in *The wonderful Discoverie of the Witchcrafts of Margaret and Phillip Flower, Daughters of Ioan Flower neere Bever Castle, executed at Lincolne, March 11, 1618* (London, 1618). Details of Manners's life are taken from *DNB*.

10. The incident is described and relevant references assembled in Kittredge, *Witchcraft in Old and New England*, pp. 87–8.

11. *APC, 1550–1552*, p. 279; *APC, 1552–1554*, pp. 13, 131, 69, 156; cf. pp. 165, 170, 287, 287.

12. *CSPD, 1581–1590*, p. 220.

13. *HMC, Vol. 9, Calendar of the Manuscripts of the Most Hon. The Marquis of Salisbury, KG*, Part 5 (HMSO, London, 1894), p. 25.

14. *APC, 1578–1580*, pp. 22, 36; *APC, 1580–1581*, p. 25. For the Windsor case, see *A Rehearsall both straung and true, of hainous and horrible Actes committed by Elizabeth Stile, alias Rockingham, Mother Dutten, Mother Devell, Mother Margaret, fower notorious Witches, apprehended at Winsore in the Countie of Barks, and at Abington arraigned, condemned, and executed the 28 Daye of Februarie last Anno 1579* (London, 1579).

15. *APC, 1578–1580*, p. 427; *APC, 1580–1581*, pp. 29–30.

16. *APC, 1581–1582*, p. 228.

17. These references are collected in Kittredge, *Witchcraft in Old and New England*, pp. 276–7.

18. James VI's work on witchcraft is discussed in Stuart Clark, 'King James's Daemonologie: Witchcraft and Kingship', in Sydney Anglo (ed.), *The Damned Art: Essays in the Literature of Witchcraft* (London, 1977), which should be read in conjunction with Christina Larner, *Witchcraft and Religion: The Politics of Popular Belief* (Oxford, 1984), Chapter 1, 'James VI and I and Witchcraft'. The printing of the *Daemonologie* consulted in connection with this book is that included in *The Workes of the most high and mighty Prince, James, by the Grace of God Kinge of Great Brittaine, France, Ireland, Defender of ye faith, &c* (London, 1616).

19. 'Daemonologie', in James VI and I, *Workes*, p. 91. The key biblical text for those linking witchcraft to attacks on monarchical authority was, of course, I Samuel 15: 23, 'rebellion is as the sin of witchcraft'.

20. These cases are discussed in Kittredge, *Witchcraft in Old and New England*, p. 321.

21. *CSPD, 1619–1623*, p. 125; G. B. Harrison, *A Jacobean Journal: Being a Record of Those Things Most Talked of during the Years 1603–1606* (London, 1941), p. 185.

22. Scot's significance is discussed in Sydney Anglo, 'Reginald Scot's *Discoverie of Witchcraft*: Scepticism and Saduceeism', in Anglo (ed.), *The Damned Art*, and Robert H. West, *Reginald Scot and Renaissance Writings on Witchcraft* (Twayne's English Authors Series, Boston, 1984). Some of the complexities of his opinions on witchcraft are discussed in Leland L. Estes, 'Reginald Scot and his *Discoverie of Witchcraft*: Religion and Science in Opposition to the European Witch Craze', *Church History*, 52 (1983), pp. 444–56. Scot's impact on Continental Europe awaits investigation, although it is perhaps significant that the *Discoverie* was translated into Dutch in 1609, with a second Dutch edition in 1638: Herman Belien, 'Judicial Views on the Crime of Witchcraft', in Marijke Gijswijt-Hofstra and Willem Frijhoff (eds.), *Witchcraft in the Netherlands from the Fourteenth to the Twentieth Century* (Rotterdam, 1991), pp. 60–61. The Dover Publications Inc. edition of Montague Summers's edition of the *Discoverie* (New York, 1972) is the one referred to here.

23. Scot, *Discoverie*, p. 29.

24. Ibid., p. 274.
25. Ibid., p. 273.
26. Ibid., p. 10.
27. Ibid., pp. 25–6.
28. Ibid., pp. 52, 24.
29. Ibid., pp. 41–5.
30. Ibid., p. 4.
31. Ibid., p. 5.
32. Ibid., p. 278.
33. Ibid., p. 280.
34. Ibid., p. 63.
35. Ibid., p. 252.
36. Ibid., pp. 1–2. For Scot's religious position in 1584, see Peter Clark, *English Provincial Society from the Reformation to the Revolution: Religion, Politics and Society in Kent, 1500–1640* (Hassocks, Sussex, 1977), pp. 169–70, 180, Clark describing Scot as a renegade Puritan at the latter point. For the religious situation in Kent at the time when Scot published his *Discoverie*, see ibid., pp. 170–73. It is hoped that work in progress by Peter Elmer will further contextualize Scot's book.
37. Cited by Anglo, 'Scepticism and Saduceeism', p. 129. This section of the *Discoverie* is not, unfortunately, reproduced in the Dover Publications Inc. edition.
38. Anglo, 'Scepticism and Saduceeism', p. 134.
39. Scot, *Discoverie*, p. 19.
40. 'Daemonologie', in James VI and I, *Workes*, pp. 91–2; Henry Holland, *A Treatise against Witchcraft: or, a Dialogue, wherein the greatest Doubts concerning that Sinne, are briefly answered* (Cambridge, 1590), sig. B2; William Perkins, *A Discourse of the damned Art of Witchcraft. So farre forth as it is revealed in the Scriptures, and manifest by true Experience* (Cambridge, 1608), sig. A5; John Darrell, *A Survey of certaine dialogical Discourses, written by John Deacon and John Walker concerning the Doctrine of Possession and Dispossession of Divels* (London, 1602), p. 30; Richard Bernard, *A Guide to Grand Iury Men: divided into two Bookes* (London, 1627), sig. A4.
41. Anglo, 'Scepticism and Saduceeism', p. 139, dates this tradition to a Dutch work of 1659.
42. Dorothy Gardiner (ed.), *The Oxinden Letters, 1607–1642: Being the Correspondence of Henry Oxinden of Barham and His Circle* (London, 1933), pp. 200–202. The Oxindens were one of the thirty or so leading 'county families' in mid-seventeenth-century Kent, and figured prominently in the county's affairs at that time: Alan Everitt, *The Community of Kent and the Great Rebellion, 1640–1660* (Leicester, 1966), *passim*.

2. Witchcraft in Popular Culture

1. Most of Aubrey's relevant writings are gathered in John Buchanan-Brown (ed.), *John Aubrey: Three Prose Works* (Pontwell, Sussex, 1972). For another significant primitive

folklorist, almost exactly contemporary with Aubrey, see C. H. Josten (ed.), *Elias Ash-mole (1617–1692): His Autobiographical and Historical Notes, His Correspondence, and Other Contemporary Sources Relating to His Life and Work* (5 volumes, Oxford, 1966).

2. Thomas, *Religion and the Decline of Magic*, is an important initial guide to these beliefs. A useful general guide to the problem of popular culture in this period is Peter Burke, *Popular Culture in Early Modern Europe* (London, 1978).

3. *Witches apprehended, examined and executed, for notable Villanies by them committed both by Land and Water. With a strange and most true Triall how to know whether a Woman be a Witch or not* (London, 1613), sig. A3v.

4. Macfarlane, *A Regional and Comparative Study*, especially pp. 147–210; Thomas, *Religion and the Decline of Magic*.

5. PRO, Northern Circuit Assize Depositions, ASSI 45/1/5/38–39.

6. John Denison, *The most wonderfull and true storie of a certaine Witch named Alse Gooderidge of Stapenhill, who was arraigned and convicted at Darbie at the Assises there* (London, 1597), p. 4.

7. PRO, Star Chamber Records, STAC 8 4/10, ff. 160, 162.

8. Todd Gray, 'Witchcraft in the Diocese of Exeter: Dartmouth 1601–2', *Devon and Cornwall Notes and Queries*, 36, Part 7 (1990), pp. 230–38, reprinting original MS held by Harvard University, Houghton Library, MS 84–0745.

9. Richard Bernard, *A Guide to Grand Iury Men: divided into two Bookes* (London 1627), pp. 22–3, 11; George Gifford, *A Dialogue concerning Witches and Witchcrafts, in which it is layed open how craftily the Divell deceiveth not onely the Witches but many other, and so leadeth them awrie into manie great Errours* (London, 1593; second edition of 1603 reprinted by Percy Society, 8, 1843), p. 67. Gifford is one of the few English writers on witchcraft whose thoughts on that subject have been set into the context of his other writings: see James Hitchcock, 'George Gifford and Puritan Witch Beliefs', *Archiv für Reformationgeschichte*, 58 (1967), pp. 90–99; Dewey D. Wallace Jr, 'George Gifford, Puritan Propaganda and Popular Religion in Elizabethan England', *Sixteenth-century Journal*, 9 (1978), pp. 27–49; and Alan Macfarlane, 'A Tudor Anthropologist: George Gifford's *Discourse* and *Dia-logue*', in Sydney Anglo (ed.), *The Damned Art: Essays in the Literature of Witchcraft* (London, 1977).

10. Bernard, *A Guide to Grand Iury Men*, pp. 80–81.

11. Henry Holland, *A Treatise against Witchcraft: or, a Dialogue, wherein the greatest Doubts concerning that Sinne, are briefly answered* (Cambridge, 1590), sig. F4; William Perkins, *A Discourse of the damned Art of Witchcraft. So farre forth as it is revealed in the Scriptures, and manifest by true Experience* (Cambridge, 1608), sig. A3v, p. 257.

12. Gifford, *A Dialogue concerning Witches and Witchcrafts*, p. 116; Bernard, *A Guide to Grand Iury Men*, pp. 146–54.

13. Lancashire Record Office, Quarter Sessions Records, QSB 1/139(81).

14. Bodleian Library, Oxford, MS Add B. 1 (Western 30208), f. 25; Lancashire Record Office, QSB 1/255(38); Devonshire Record Office, Exeter Records, C1 64, Sessions Minute Book 1642–60, f. 27v; Essex Record Office, Archdeaconry of Colchester Act Books, D/ACA/18, f. 80.

15. Thomas Ady, *A Candle in the Dark: or, a Treatise concerning the Nature of Witches and Witchcraft: being Advice to Judges, Sheriffes, Justices of the Peace, and Grand Jury Men, what to do, before they passe sentence on such as are arraigned for their Lives, as Witches* (London, 1656), p. 40; Essex Record Office, Quarter Sessions Rolls, Q/SR 67/2, 44–6. This and related Essex cases are discussed in Macfarlane, *A Regional and Comparative Study*, pp. 122–3.

16. PRO, ASSI 45/3/2/97.

17. P. Tyler, 'The Church Courts at York and Witchcraft Prosecutions, 1567–1640', *Northern History*, 4 (1969), pp. 84–109; Essex Record Office, D/ACA/13, f. 35v.

18. Bernard, *A Guide to Grand Jury Men*, p. 137; *The wonderful Discoverie of the Witchcrafts of Margaret and Phillip Flower, Daughters of Ioan Flower neere Bever Castle, executed at Lincolne, March 11, 1618* (London, 1618), sig. B2; Lancashire Record Office, QSB 1/78/(49); 1/139(81); PRO, ASSI 45/4/2/70.

19. *The Examination and Confession of certaine Wytches at Chensforde in the Countie of Essex, before the Quenes Maiesties Judges, the xxvi day of July Anno 1566* (London, 1566); *The Examination of John Walsh, before Maister Thomas Williams, Commissary to the Reverend Father in God William, Bishop of Excester, upon certayne Interrogatories touchyng Wytchcrafte and Sorcerye* (London, 1566).

20. For example, Devon Record Office, C1 64, ff. 200v, 260v; C1 65, f. 1v. See also C1 64, f. 182, where a woman was allegedly defamed in 1651 as 'witch and toade'.

21. G. R. Quaife, *Godly Zeal and Furious Rage: The Witch in Early Modern Europe* (London and Sydney, 1987), p. 46. Future research into witchcraft beliefs in other areas may reveal wider evidence of the importance of beliefs in the familiar. For a preliminary survey, see Jacqueline Susan Bell, 'The Familiar Spirit in Early Modern English Witchcraft' (University of York M.A. thesis, 1995).

22. *The Examination and Confession of certaine Wytches at Chensforde, passim.* John Walsh, examined in the South-West in 1566, also knew about familiars: *The Examination of John Walsh*, sig. A4v.

23. *A true and just Recorde, of the Information, Examination, and Confession of all the Witches taken at S. Oses in the Countie of Essex, whereof some were executed, and some entreated according to the Determination of the Lawe* (London, 1582), sig. A3v–A4v, C7; *The Apprehension and Confession of three notorious Witches. Arraigned and by Justice condemnede and executed at Chelmesforde in the Countye of Essex, the 5 Day of July last past 1589* (London, 1589), sig. A3v.

24. Ewen, *Witchcraft and Demonianism*, p. 73; *The Examination and Confession of certaine Wytches at Chensforde*, Part 1, sig. A7, B1; *The Disclosing of a late counterfeyted Possession of the Devyl in two Maydens within the Citie of London* (London, 1574), sig. A6v; Barbara Rosen, *Witchcraft* (London, 1969), p. 85; *The Apprehension and Confession of three notorious Witches*, sig. A4; *The most strange and admirable Discoverie of the three Witches at Warboys arraigned, convicted and executed at the last Assizes at Huntingdon* (London, 1593), sig. G1v.

25. Ewen, *Witchcraft and Demonianism*, p. 63; Michael Dalton, *The Countrey Justice, containing the Practice of the Justices of the Peace out of their Sessions* (London, 1630 edn), p. 338.

26. *The Examination and Confession of certaine Wytches at Chensforde*, Part 3, sig. A7v–A8.

27. John Cotta, *The infallible, true and assured Witch: or, the second Edition of the Tryall of*

Witch-Craft: shewing the right and true Method of the Discoverie London, 1625), p. 84; Henry Goodcole, *The wonderfull Discoverie of Elizabeth Sawyer a Witch, late of Edmonton, her Conviction and Condemnation and Death* (London, 1621), sig. C3.

28. *The Disclosing of a late counterfeyted possession*, sig. B1v–B2.

29. *The most strange and admirable Discoverie of the three Witches at Warboys*, sig. H2v, M1, P3v.

30. PRO, STAC 8 4/10, f. 222; Cheshire Record Office, Consistory Court Papers, EDC 5(1608)11.

31. Thomas Potts, *The Trial of the Lancaster Witches, A.D. MDCXII*, G. B. Harrison (ed.) (London, 1929; reprinted 1971), p. 22; Alexander Roberts, *A Treatise of Witchcraft: wherein sundry Propositions are laid downe, plainely discovering the Wickednesse of that damnable Art* (London, 1616), pp. 46–7; Bodleian Library, Oxford, MS Dodsw. 61 (Western 5003[1]), f. 47.

32. *A Booke declaringe the fearfull Vexasion of one Alexander Nyndge: being most horriblye tormented wyth an evyll Spirit, the xx daie of Ianuarie in the yere of our Lord 1573 at Lyeringswell in Suffolke* (np, 1573), p. 7.

33. Bodleian Library, Oxford, MS Ashmole 207, f. 59v. For Napier's involvement with those who thought themselves to be troubled by the devil or bewitched, see Michael MacDonald, *Mystical Bedlam: Madness, Anxiety and Healing in Seventeenth-century England* (Cambridge, 1981), pp. 107–10, 200–204, 208–10.

34. Ewen, *Witchcraft and Demonianism*, p. 57; Quaife, *Godly Zeal and Furious Rage*, p. 59.

35. Rosen,*Witchcraft*, p. 86; PRO, STAC 8 4/10, f. 203v.

36. Potts, *The Trial of the Lancaster Witches*, pp. 27, 83–107.

37. William Grainge (ed.), *Daemonologia: A Discourse on Witchcraft, as it was acted in the Family of Mr Edward Fairfax, of Fuyston, in the County of York, in the Year 1621: along with the only two Eclogues of the same Author known to be in Existence* (Harrogate, 1882), pp. 107–8.

38. Devon Record Office, Quarter Sessions Rolls, Box 41, Bapt 1638/57. I am grateful to Mary Wolffe for providing me with this reference.

39. There are several versions of Robinson's and Johnson's depositions, in both print and manuscript. The one used here is Bodleian Library, Oxford, MS Dodsw. 61 (Western 5003[1]), ff. 45–7.

3. The Theological and Legal Bases for Witch-hunting

1. William Perkins, *A Discourse of the damned Art of Witchcraft. So farre forth as it is revealed in the Scriptures, and manifest by true Experience* (Cambridge, 1608). There is no good modern biography of Perkins and the details given here are taken from the *DNB*.

2. Henry Holland, *A Treatise against Witchcraft: or, a Dialogue, wherein the greatest Doubts concerning that Sinne, are briefly answered* (Cambridge, 1590); John Cotta, *The Triall of Witchcraft, shewing the True and right Method of the Discovery* (London, 1616; this was reprinted in London in 1625 as *The infallible, true and assured Witch: or, the second Edition of the Tryall of Witch-Craft: shewing the right and true Method of the Discoverie*, and it is this edition which is cited here); Alexander Roberts, *A Treatise of Witchcraft: wherein sundry Propositions are laid*

downe, plainely discovering the Wickednesse of that damnable Art (London, 1616); Thomas Cooper, *The Mystery of Witch-Craft: discovering the Truth, Nature, Occasions, Growth and Power thereof: together with the Detection and Punishment of the same* (London, 1617); Richard Bernard, *A Guide to Grand Iury Men: divided into two Bookes* (London 1627). Mention should also be made of the English translation of a work by a French Protestant writer cited by a number of English writers, notably Henry Holland, Lambert Daneau's *A Dialogue of Witches in Foretime named Lot-Tellers and now commonly called Sorcerers* (London, 1575). John L. Teall, 'Witchcraft and Calvinism in Elizabethan England: Divine Power and Human Agency', *Journal of the History of Ideas*, 23 (1962), pp. 21–36, is an important reminder that there were a variety of positions to which the theology of the period could lead, while Stuart Clark, 'Protestant Demonology: Sin, Superstition and Society (*c.* 1520–*c.* 1630)', in B. Ankarloo and G. Henningsen (eds.), *Early Modern European Witchcraft: Centres and Peripheries* (Oxford, 1990), provides the broader context for English Protestant demonological thinking.

3. Perkins, *A Discourse of the damned Art*, sig. A2v, pp. 3–4; Roberts, *A Treatise of Witch-craft*, p. 24.

4. Cooper, *The Mystery of Witch-Craft*, pp. 131, 227.

5. Cotta, *The infallible, true and assured Witch*, p. 36.

6. Perkins, *A Discourse of the damned Art*, p. 19.

7. Holland, *A Treatise against Witchcraft*, sig. C2.

8. Perkins, *A Discourse of the damned Art*, pp. 25, 31; Cooper, *The Mystery of Witch-Craft*, p. 56.

9. Perkins, *A Discourse of the damned Art*, p. 253; Cooper, *The Mystery of Witch-Craft*, pp. 31, 32; Perkins, *A Discourse of the damned Art*, p. 49; Cooper, *The Mystery of Witch-Craft*, pp. 49, 11.

10. Perkins, *A Discourse of the damned Art*, pp. 41–2, 48; Cooper, *The Mystery of Witch-Craft*, p. 30; Cotta, *The infallible, true and assured Witch*, p. 59.

11. Perkins, *A Discourse of the damned Art*, p. 78; Holland, *A Treatise against Witchcraft*, sig. D1.

12. Perkins, *A Discourse of the damned Art*, pp. 151–2; Cooper, *The Mystery of Witch-Craft*, p. 15; Bernard, *A Guide to Grand Iury Men*, p. 99.

13. Perkins, *A Discourse of the damned Art*, p. 229; Bernard, *A Guide to Grand Iury Men*, p. 73.

14. Perkins, *A Discourse of the damned Art*, pp. 206, 5, 152.

15. Perkins, *A Discourse of the damned Art*, pp. 154–6; Holland, *A Treatise against Witchcraft*, sig. F4; Cooper, *The Mystery of Witch-Craft*, p. 4; Perkins, *A Discourse of the damned Art*, p. 257.

16. Perkins, *A Discourse of the damned Art*, pp. 35, 230; Cooper, *The Mystery of Witch-Craft*, p. 295, sig. A5–A5v; Holland, *A Treatise against Witchcraft*, sig. K3–K4; Roberts, *A Treatise of Witchcraft*, p. 16.

17. Cooper, *The Mystery of Witch-Craft*, p. 199.

18. Holland, *A Treatise against Witchcraft*, sig. A2.

19. John Ayre (ed.), *The Works of John Jewel, Bishop of Salisbury. The Second Portion* (Parker Society, Cambridge, 1847), pp. 1,027–8. Jewel's letter to Peter Martyr, in which, interestingly, he seems to regard witchcraft as an aspect or consequence of popish superstition, is printed in Rev. Hastings Robinson (ed.), *The Zurich Letters (Second Series) comprising the Correspondence of several English Bishops and Others, with some of the Helvetian Reformers during the early Part of the Reign of Queen Elizabeth* (Parker Society, Cambridge, 1842), pp. 44–5.

20. Ewen, *Witchcraft and Demonianism*, pp. 45–6.

21. What can be reconstructed of the background to this legislation, 5 Eliz I, cap. 16, is discussed in G. R. Elton, *The Parliament of England 1559–1581* (Cambridge, 1986), pp. 110–11. The deliberations of the 1563 Convocation are discussed in William P. Haugaard, *Elizabeth and the English Reformation: The Struggle for a Stable Settlement of Religion* (Cambridge, 1968). For an attack on the traditional view that this legislation owed much to the influence of returned Marian exiles, see Kittredge, *Witchcraft in Old and New England*, pp. 253–65.

22. Notestein, *A History of Witchcraft*, p. 104. Our description of the background to this statute, 1 James I, cap. 12, has depended heavily on Notestein's account, and on the fuller analysis provided by Kittredge, *Witchcraft in Old and New England*, pp. 307–13, which is especially valuable in giving the membership of the relevant committees.

23. Elton, *The Parliament of England*, p. 190.

24. Macfarlane, *A Regional and Comparative Study*, pp. 271–7.

25. Norfolk Record Office, Norwich City Records, Case 20a, Minute Book of Quarter Sessions 1581–1591, ff. 174, 184v, 225, 228.

26. Macfarlane, *A Regional and Comparative Study*, p. 297.

27. Rev. William Nicholson (ed.), *The Remains of Archbishop Grindal, D.D., successively Bishop of London, and Archbishop of York and Canterbury* (Parker Society, Cambridge, 1843), p. 174.

28. Michael Dalton, *The Countrey Justice, containing the Practice of the Justices of the Peace out of their Sessions* (London, 1630 edn), pp. 338–9. This passage should be compared with the much briefer description given in the original 1618 edition, pp. 242–3.

29. A comprehensive listing is provided in Montague Summers, *The History of Witchcraft and Demonology* (London, 1926: reprinted, 1965), pp. 329–38. Notestein, *A History of Witchcraft*, pp. 345–83, provides a critical discussion of this literature. A number of the Elizabethan tracts are reprinted, although with some parts omitted and with modernized spelling, in Barbara Rosen, *Witchcraft* (London, 1969).

30. *The Examination and Confession of certaine Wytches at Chensforde in the Countie of Essex, before the Quenes Maiesties Judges, the xxvi day of July Anno 1566* (London, 1566). The relevant indictments against these witches survive in the Home Circuit assize indictments: PRO, ASSI 35/8/4/4, 6, 21–2.

31. *A Rehearsall both straung and true, of hainous and horrible Actes committed by Elizabeth Stile, alias Rockingham, Mother Dutten, Mother Devell, Mother Margaret, fower notorious Witches, apprehended at Winsore in the Countie of Barks, and at Abington arraigned, condemned, and executed the 28 Daye of Februarie last Anno 1579* (Lor don, 1579).

32. *A Detection of damnable Driftes, practized by three Witches arraigned at Chelmisforde in Essex, at the late Assizese holden, which were executed in Aprill 1579* (London, 1579).

33. These are listed in Summers, *The History of Witchcraft and Demonology*, p. 329.

34. John Denison, *The most wonderfull and true storie of a certaine Witch named Alse Gooderidge of Stapenhill, who was arraigned and convicted at Darbie at the Assises there* (London, 1597).

35. *The most strange and admirable Discoverie of the three Witches at Warboys arraigned, convicted and executed at the last Assizes at Huntingdon* (London, 1593). The contemporary ballad is listed in earlier works but is now apparently lost: Summers, *The History of Witchcraft and Demonology*, p. 330.

36. The literature generated by Darrell's activities is discussed in Corinne Holt Rickert, *The Case of John Darrell: Minister and Exorcist* (University of Florida Monographs, Humanities, 9, Gainsville, Florida, Winter 1962).

37. *A true and just Recorde, of the Information, Examination, and Confession of all the Witches taken at S. Oses in the Countie of Essex, whereof some were executed, and some entreated according to the Determination of the Lawe* (London, 1582).

38. A number of editions of Potts's work survive, the most recent being Thomas Potts, *The Trial of the Lancaster Witches A.D. MDCXII*, G. B. Harrison (ed.) (London, 1929; reprinted 1971: originally published in 1613 in London as *The Wonderfull Discoverie of Witches in the Countie of Lancaster. With the arraignment and Triall of nineteene notorious Witches, at the Assizes and generall Gaole Deliverie, holden at the Castle of Lancaster, upon Munday, the seventeenth of August last, 1612*).

39. *The Witches of Northamptonshire, Agnes Browne, Arthur Bill, Joane Vaughan, Hellen Jenkenson, Mary Barber, Witches, who were all executed at Northampton the 22 July last 1612* (London, 1612).

40. *Witches apprehended, examined and executed, for notable Villanies by them committed both by Land and water. With a strange and most true Triall how to know whether a Woman be a Witch or not* (London, 1613).

41. *The wonderful Discoverie of the Witchcrafts of Margaret and Phillip Flower, Daughters of Ioan Flower neere Bever Castle, executed at Lincolne, March 11, 1618* (London, 1618), sig. C1.

42. Henry Goodcole, *The wonderfull Discoverie of Elizabeth Sawyer a Witch, late of Edmonton, her Conviction and Condemnation and Death* (London, 1621).

43. *The Examination and Confession of certaine Wytches at Chensforde*, sig. A2v.

44. Ibid., sig. A4.

45. Potts, *The Trial of the Lancaster Witches*, p. 16.

4. Patterns of Prosecution and Punishment

1. Ewen, *Witch Hunting and Witch Trials*. More recent work on criminal archives includes Joel Samaha, *Law and Order in Historical Perspective: The Case of Elizabethan Essex* (New York and London, 1974); J. S. Cockburn, 'The Nature and Incidence of Crime in England 1559–1625: A Preliminary Survey', in J. S. Cockburn (ed.), *Crime in England 1550–1800* (London, 1977); J. A. Sharpe, *Crime in Seventeenth-century England: A County Study* (Cambridge, 1983); C. B. Herrup, *The Common Peace: Participation and the Criminal Law in*

Seventeenth-century England (Cambridge, 1987); and John Beattie, *Crime and the Courts in England 1660–1800* (Oxford, 1986). The standard introduction to work on the history of crime in this period remains J. A. Sharpe, *Crime in Early Modern England 1550–1750* (London 1984).

2. Ewen, *Witch Hunting and Witch Trials*, gives abstracts of Home Circuit assize indictments throughout our period. For the background to the assizes and its records more generally, see J. S. Cockburn, *A History of English Assizes 1558–1714* (Cambridge, 1972). Professor Cockburn has also edited *A Calendar of Assize Indictments* (11 volumes, London, 1975–85), which gives a complete list of indictments surviving from the Elizabethan and Jacobean periods, sometimes amplifying or correcting the information given by Ewen. The introductory volume to this series is an excellent guide to the technicalities of these sources and the practices of the court which produced them.

3. This figure is different from the total of 790 given by Ewen, *Witch Hunting and Witch Trials*, p. 81. For reasons of consistency, I have not followed Ewen's practice of including a number of passing references to witches (for example, those awaiting trial) contained in the documentation, but restricted myself to cases for which an indictment survives, or for which fairly full details, at least equivalent to those given on indictments, can be reconstructed. To the total thus gained I have added a few cases missed by Ewen, or not in the documentation available to him when he wrote, given in Cockburn, *A Calendar*, or Macfarlane, *A Regional and Comparative Study*. These adjustments neither detract from the value of Ewen's original work nor create serious modifications to the patterns he uncovered. Home Circuit assize indictments are classified as PRO, ASSI 35.

4. PRO, ASSI 35/2/5/7–8, 16. The fact that these cases were tried, presumably as normal homicides, in the absence of a statutory provision against witchcraft may be evidence of the type of pressure from below which helped to encourage the 1563 witchcraft statute. The last two of these cases concerned an Essex man called John Smyth, alias Salmond, and it is a possible indication of the legal confusion surrounding his alleged offences that the second charge against him was first investigated at Essex quarter sessions and then sent to the Queen's Bench before being referred back to the assizes.

5. For France, see the various essays in Alfred Soman, *Sorcellerie et justice criminelle (16e–18e siècles)* (Croft Road, Hampshire, and Brookfield, Vermont, 1992); for Germany, Wolfgang Behringer, *Hexenverfolgung in Bayern: Volksmagie, Glaubenseifer und Staatsräson in der Frühen Neuzeit: Studiensausgaber* (Munich, 1988); for the Dutch Republic, Marijke Gijswijt-Hofstra and Willem Frijhoff (eds.), *Nederland betoverd: Toverij en Hekserij van de veertiende tot in de twintigste Eeuw* (Amsterdam, 1987); for Spain, Gustav Henningsen, *The Witches' Advocate: Basque Witchcraft and the Spanish Inquisition, 1609–1614* (Reno, Nevada, 1980).

6. These figures are taken from Brian P. Levack, *The Witch-Hunt in Early Modern Europe* (London and New York, 1987), Table 1, p. 20.

7. Sharpe, *A County Study*, Table 6, p. 108; Table 4, p. 95; Table 12, p. 124; p. 63.

8. PRO, ASSI 35/19/4/33; 20/2/43, 106; 30/1/68; 15/4/11; 40/1/53.

9. Ibid., 10/3/35.

10. Ibid., 26/1/40–41; 26/1/18–20.

11. Macfarlane, *A Regional and Comparative Study*, Table 14, p. 154.

12. Ewen, *Witch Hunting and Witch Trials*, Case 668, p. 235.

13. PRO, ASSI 35/30/1/36.

14. Ibid., 24/2/13; 31/2/58; 33/9/24.

15. Ibid., 26/2/43; Ewen, *Witch Hunting and Witch Trials*, p. 250. The accused in this latter case, a widow named Judeth Sawkens, was also indicted for causing two deaths by witchcraft and was hanged in 1658.

16. PRO, ASSI 35/7/5/14, 25.

17. Ibid., 26/1/21; 58/2/31–4, 30.

18. Ewen, *Witch Hunting and Witch Trials*, Cases 786–7, p. 263.

19. PRO, ASSI 35/24/4/20–23.

20. Ewen, *Witch Hunting and Witch Trials*, Cases 750–51, pp. 254–5; Case 755, p. 256; Case 781, p. 262; Case 765, p. 258; Case 779, p. 261.

21. These figures are derived from cases listed by Macfarlane, *A Regional and Comparative Study*, pp. 278–93; for his comments on Essex ecclesiastical court cases, see pp. 66–75.

22. M. J. Ingram, *Church Courts, Sex and Marriage in England 1570–1640* (Cambridge, 1987), pp. 97, 113–14, comments on the paucity of witchcraft accusations at the Wiltshire ecclesiastical courts; for Yorkshire, P. Tyler, 'The Church Courts at York and Witchcraft Prosecutions, 1567–1640', *Northern History*, 4 (1970), pp. 84–109.

23. These cases are listed, and references given, in Ewen, *Witchcraft and Demonianism*, pp. 439–46. The relevant document reference is PRO, ASSI 23/1–4. For a more recent and more comprehensive listing of witchcraft prosecutions in the South-West, see Janet A. Thompson, *Wives, Widows, Witches and Bitches: Women in Seventeenth-century Devon* (New York, etc., 1993).

24. PRO, ASSI 23/2, Gaol Delivery at Exeter 14 August 34 Charles II; Gaol Delivery at Exeter 20 March 1 James II. For the Lloyd, Edwards and Trembles case see *The Tryal, Condemnation, and Execution of three Witches, viz Temperance Floyd, Mary Floyd and Susanna Edwards, who were all arraigned at Exeter on the 18th of August 1682* (London, 1682).

25. Cheshire cases are listed in Ewen, *Witchcraft and Demonianism*, pp. 413–22, where detailed references to the Cheshire cases mentioned in the text here are provided. These are drawn from the gaol books of the Court of Great Sessions (PRO, CHES 21/1–5), indictments (PRO, CHES 24/95–144), and Plea Rolls (PRO, CHES 29). For an initial survey of the Great Sessions general criminal business in the period 1580–1709, based on an analysis of PRO, CHES 21/1–5, see Sharpe, *Crime in Early Modern England*, pp. 57–63.

26. See the list in Ewen, *Witchcraft and Demonianism*, pp. 430–35, these cases being largely gleaned from J. C. Jeaffreson (ed.), *Middlesex County Records* (4 volumes, London, 1886–92). As suggested in the text, the information given in these sources has been revised by Barbara Singleton 'Witchcraft in Middlesex, 1563–1738 (unpublished University of Reading M.Phil. thesis, 1997).

27. Sharpe, *Crime in Early Modern England*, Table 1, p. 55. The remainder of cases in this sample included seventy sexual offences and eleven miscellaneous felonies.

28. Ewen, *Witchcraft and Demonianism*, p. 407.

29. Ibid., pp. 436–8, lists references to witchcraft contained in the Oxford Circuit gaol books, PRO, ASSI 2/1–2.

30. Ewen, *Witch Hunting and Witch Trials*, p. 112; Christina Larner, *Witchcraft and Religion: The Politics of Popular Belief* (Oxford, 1984), pp. 71–2.

31. Robin Briggs, *Communities of Belief: Cultural and Social Tensions in Early Modern France* (Oxford, 1989), p. 22.

32. Materials relating to this episode are scattered, but most of them are listed in Ewen, *Witchcraft and Demonianism*, pp. 244–51.

5. England's Mass Witch-hunt: East Anglia, 1645–7

1. The most important manuscript sources are indictments and gaol delivery rolls relating to prosecution of witches at Chelmsford, July 1645, PRO, ASSI 35/86/1/7–13, 19, 32–3, 41–3, 46, 51–6, 58–64, 66–73, 78–80, 82–91, 98; a large body of what appear to be notes taken from depositions relating to the investigation of witchcraft in 1645 in Suffolk, written in a mid-seventeenth-century hand, British Library Additional MSS 27402, ff. 104–21; and sets of depositions relating to the examination of seventeen witches held in the Isle of Ely's gaol delivery records, Michaelmas 1647, Cambridge University Library, EDR E. 12. Printed sources include *A true and exact Relation of the severall Informations, Examinations and Confessions of the late Witches arraigned and executed at the late Sessions holden before the Right Honorable Robert, Earle of Warwicke, and severall of his Majesties Justices of Peace, the 29 of July 1645* (London, 1645); *A true Relation of the Arraignment of eighteene Witches that were tried, convicted and condemned, at a Sessions holden at St Edmonds-bury, in Suffolk . . . the 27 Day of August 1645* (London, 1645); John Davenport, *The Witches of Huntingdon, their Examinations and Confessions, exactly taken by his Majesties Justices of the Peace for that County* (London, 1645). Both the main protagonists in the trials wrote works defending their witch-hunting activities: Matthew Hopkins, *The Discovery of Witches* (London, 1647), and John Stearne, *A Confirmation and Discovery of Witchcraft* (London, 1648). The 1645–7 trials have not been the subject of a full-scale scholarly study, although references to many of the relevant sources can be found in Richard Deacon, *Matthew Hopkins: Witch Finder General* (London, 1976), while Essex's contribution is discussed in Macfarlane, *A Regional and Comparative Study*, Chapter 9, 'The Witchfinding Movement of 1645 in Essex'.

2. *Signs and Wonders from Heaven. With a true Relation of a Monster borne in Ratcliffe Highway* (London, 1645), p. 4.

3. For Norwich: Norfolk Record Office, Norwich City Records, Case 20a, Quarter Sessions Minute Book 1639–52, f. 80v. Two further witches were sentenced to be hanged at Norwich in December 1648, ibid., f. 110. For Great Yarmouth: J. G. Nall, *Great Yarmouth and Lowestoft* (London, 1867), p. 92, n. 2, and Notestein, *A History of Witchcraft*, p. 181, n. 50. For Aldeburgh: Suffolk Record Office, EE1/12/2 (Aldeburgh

Borough Records, Chamberlain's Account Book Michaelmas 1624 to Christmas 1649), ff. 248, 249–50, 258, 273v; Deacon, *Matthew Hopkins*, p. 171, records that Hopkins received payments of £23 at Stowmarket and £15 at King's Lynn.

4. Francis Hutchinson, *A historical Essay concerning Witchcraft. With Observations of Matters of Fact, tending to clear the Texts of the sacred Scriptures, and confute the vulgar Errors about that Point* (London, 1718), p. 37.

5. Samuel Butler, *Hudibras*, John Wilders (ed.) (Oxford, 1967), Second Part, Canto III, line 144.

6. Stearne, *A Confirmation and Discovery*, sig. A2v. In another contemporary estimate, the royalist historian James Howell, writing early in 1647, referred to 'multitudes of witches among us, in Essex and Suffolk there were above two hundred indicted within these two years, and above one half of them executed', figures which are more in line with those I have suggested: Joseph Jacobs (ed.), *Epistolae Ho-Elianae: the familiar Letters of James Howell, Historiographer Royal to Charles II* (2 volumes, London, 1890), Vol. 1, p. 506.

7. Suffolk Record Office, B 105/2/1 (Quarter Sessions Order Book), f. 79. Needless to say, the attempt to shift the costs of keeping suspected witches led to a number of disputes between the county authorities and various parishes: for example, ibid., ff. 81–81v, 84.

8. Ewen, *Witchcraft and Demonianism*, p. 52; Macfarlane, *A Regional and Comparative Study*, p. 139.

9. Keith Thomas, 'The Relevance of Social Anthropology to the Historical Study of English Witchcraft', in Mary Douglas (ed.), *Witchcraft Confessions and Accusations* (London, 1970), p. 50.

10. Records from the unusually well-documented Suffolk parish of Framlingham, for example, which was the home of possibly as many as sixteen suspected witches in 1645, demonstrate that suspects were drawn from the local poor, while their accusers and witnesses against them were usually persons of at least some substance: Suffolk Record Office, FC 101/E2/26 (Framlingham Churchwarden's Accounts, 1642–6); FC 101/G7/1–2 (Framlingham Overseers of the Poor Accounts, 1640, 1646).

11. Notestein, *A History of Witchcraft*, p. 174, citing *A Diary or an exact Journall* (July 24–31, 1645); *A true Relation of the Arraignment of eighteene Witches . . . at St Edmonds-bury*, p. 9; Stearne, *A Confirmation and Discovery*, p. 25; *The Lawes against Witches and Coniuration. And some brief Notes and Observations for the Discovery of Witches . . . Also the Confession of Mother Lakeland, who was arraigned and condemned for a Witch at Ipswich in Suffolke* (London, 1645), pp. 7–8.

12. Relevant details are given in Deacon, *Matthew Hopkins*, Chapter 9, 'The Extraordinary Case of John Lowes', while the background to the case is discussed in C. L'Estrange Ewen, *The Trials of John Lowes, Clerk* (London, 1937). A note on the case, apparently dating from the early eighteenth century but incorporating the memories of persons present in 1645, survives in the parish register for Brandeston: Suffolk Record Office, FC 105/D1/1.

13. BL Add. MSS 27402, f. 114v; *A true and exact Relation*, p. 5; Cambridge UL, EDR 12/19; BL Add. MSS 27402, f. 118; Cambridge UL, EDR 12/11, 12/2.

14. BL Add. MSS 27402, ff. 110, 117v.

15. Ibid., f. 121v; *A true and exact Relation*, pp. 21–2; Davenport, *The Witches of Huntingdon*, pp. 8, 5; *A true and exact Relation*, p. 25; Cambridge UL, EDR 12/1.

16. BL Add. MSS 27402, f. 110; Cambridge UL, EDR 12/2, 12/10, 12/1, 12/15.

17. Stearne, *A Confirmation and Discovery*, p. 32.

18. BL Add. MSS 27402, ff. 110v, 111v, 114, 121, 117v.

19. Ibid., ff. 114, 108, 107, 117v; Stearne, *A Confirmation and Discovery*, p. 31.

20. BL Add. MSS 27402, f. 116; Stearne, *A Confirmation and Discovery*, p. 29; BL Add. MSS 27402, f. 121v.

21. BL Add. MSS 27402, ff. 110v, 117v; *A true and exact Relation*, p. 2; Stearne, *A Confirmation and Discovery*, p. 30; BL Add. MSS 27402, f. 116; Davenport, *The Witches of Huntingdon*, p. 12; Cambridge UL, EDR 12/20, 12/16; BL Add. MSS 27402, ff. 111, 116v.

22. Ibid., f. 117v.

23. Ibid., f. 115v.

24. Ibid., f. 121v.

25. Ibid., ff. 110, 115.

26. Ibid., f. 120v.

27. Ibid., f. 117v.

28. Hutchinson, *A historical Essay*, p. 69.

29. Hopkins, *The Discovery of Witches*, p. 6.

30. Ibid., p. 1.

31. Stearne, *A Confirmation and Discovery*, pp. 11, 26.

32. Kittredge, *Witchcraft in Old and New England*, pp. 273, 564, n. 146.

33. A point discussed in Clive Holmes, 'Popular Culture? Witches, Magistrates and Divines in Early Modern England', in Steven L. Kaplan (ed.), *Understanding Popular Culture: Europe from the Middle Ages to the Nineteenth Century* (Berlin, etc., 1984).

34. Notestein, *A History of Witchcraft*, p. 201.

35. Philip Morant, *The History and Antiquities of the County of Essex* (2 volumes, London, 1768), Vol. 1, p. 462; Essex Record Office, T/P 51 (W. K. S. King's Notes on Mistley and Manningtree).

36. Hutchinson, *A historical Essay*, p. 63.

37. Macfarlane, *A Regional and Comparative Study*, p. 137.

38. For example, BL Add. MSS 27402, ff. 111, 115v.

39. Notestein, *A History of Witchcraft*, pp. 177–8. I am grateful to Sir Keith Thomas for informing me of Fairclough's involvement in the Suffolk trials. It should be noted, however, that of the two sermons he preached before the Commission's sitting, one confirmed the existence of witchcraft, but the second stressed 'the hainousness of the sins of those, who would violently prosecute, or unduly endeavour to convict any person, except plain convincing evidence could be brought', which suggests a

somewhat guarded attitude: Samuel Clark, *The Lives of sundry eminent Persons in this later Age* (London, 1683), p. 172. In any case, Fairclough's sermons in Suffolk in late August cannot have affected earlier investigations in that county or in Essex. Fairclough was, indeed, almost certainly the 'Master Fairecloth ... an able orthodox divine' whom Stearne records as being invoked by a suspected witch from Haverhill apparently in hopes of clearing her name: Stearne, *A Confirmation and Discovery*, p. 54.

40. Hutchinson, *A historical Essay*, p. 61.

41. John Gaule, *Select Cases of Conscience touching Witches and Witchcrafts* (London, 1646). For a note on Gaule's career, see *DNB*.

42. Clive Holmes (ed.), *The Suffolk Committees for Scandalous Ministers 1644–6* (Suffolk Record Society, 13, 1970); J. A. Sharpe, 'Scandalous and Malignant Priests in Essex: The Impact of Grass-roots Puritanism', in Colin Jones, Malyn Newitt and Stephen Roberts (eds.), *Politics and People in Revolutionary England: Essays in Honour of Ivan Roots* (Oxford, 1986).

43. Dowsing's activities await reassessment by a modern scholar; for an initial guide to his activities, see C. H. Evelyn White (ed.), *The Journal of William Dowsing of Stratford* (Ipswich, 1885). For an incisive recent discussion of Dowsing, see: John Morril, 'William Dowsing, the Bureaucratic Puritan', in John Morrill, Paul Slack and Daniel Woolf (eds.), *Public Duty and Private Conscience in Seventeenth-century England: Essays presented to G. E. Aylmer* (Oxford, 1993).

44. Notestein, *A History of Witchcraft*, p. 198.

45. Most of the evidence and myths relating to him are discussed in Deacon, *Matthew Hopkins*, Chapter 1, 'In Search of Matthew Hopkins'.

46. Hutchinson, *A historical Essay*, p. 63.

47. *A true Relation of the Arraignment of eighteene Witches ... at St Edmonds-bury*, p. 4; Stearne, *A Confirmation and Discovery*, p. 48; Hopkins, *The Discovery of Witches*, p. 3.

48. Macfarlane, *A Regional and Comparative Study*, pp. 135–40.

49. Stearne, *A Confirmation and Discovery*, p. 61; Hopkins, *The Discovery of Witches*, p. 10; Gaule, *Select Cases of Conscience*, p. 93.

50. Suffolk Record Office, EE1/12/2, ff. 248, 249–50, 258, 273v.

51. Stearne, *A Confirmation and Discovery*, p. 58.

52. Wilson's comments are cited in Deacon, *Matthew Hopkins*, pp. 104–5.

53. *The Moderate Intelligencer*, 4–11 September 1645.

6. Accusations, Counter-measures and the Local Community

1. Barbara Rosen, *Witchcraft* (London, 1969), p. 87; PRO, ASSI 45/3/1/242–3; 45/4/1/111; 45/5/2/30–31.

2. Reginald Scot, *The Discoverie of Witchcraft* (London, 1584; reprinted New York, 1972), p. 4; George Gifford, *A Dialogue concerning Witches and Witchcrafts, in which it is layed open how craftily the Divell deceiveth not onely the Witches but many other, and so leadeth them awrie into manie great Errours* (London, 1593; second edition of 1603 printed by Percy Society, 8, 1843), p.

9; William Grainge (ed.), *Daemonologia: A Discourse on Witchcraft, as it was acted in the Family of Mr Edward Fairfax, of Fuyston, in the County of York, in the Year 1621: along with the only two Eclogues of the same Author known to be in Existence* (Harrogate, 1882), p. 34; J. Horsfall Turner (ed.), *The Rev. Oliver Heywood, B.A., 1630–1712. His Autobiography, Diaries, Anecdote and Event Books* (4 volumes, Brighouse, 1882–5), Vol. 3, p. 111; Devonshire Record Office, Exeter City Records, Quarter Sessions Minute Books, C1 65, f. 11.

3. Thomas Potts, *The Trial of the Lancaster Witches, A.D. MDCXII*, G. B. Harrison (ed.) (London, 1929; reprinted 1971), p. 75; PRO, ASSI 45/11/1/90; Joseph Brogen Baker, *The History of Scarborough from the earliest Date* (London, 1882), p. 482; Horsfall Turner (ed.), *The Rev. Oliver Heywood*, Vol. 3, p. 111; PRO, ASSI 45/10/2/83.

4. William Perkins, *A Discourse of the damned Art of Witchcraft. So farre forth as it is revealed in the Scriptures, and manifest by true Experience* (Cambridge, 1608), p. 193; Potts, *The Trial of the Lancaster Witches*, pp. 16–17; *The Apprehension and Confession of three notorious Witches. Arraigned and by Justice condemnede and executed at Chelmesforde in the Countye of Essex, the 5 Day of July last past 1589* (London, 1589), sig. B1.

5. Cambridge University Library, Isle of Ely Gaol Delivery Records, Michaelmas 1647, EDR 12/12; Devonshire Record Office, Quarter Sessions Rolls, Box 41, Bapt 1638/52, 56–7.

6. Perkins, *A Discourse of the damned Art*, p. 140; Thomas Cooper, *The Mystery of Witch-Craft: discovering the Truth, Nature, Occasions, Growth and Power thereof: together with the Detection and Punishment of the same* (London, 1617), p. 163; J. C. Cox, *Three Centuries of Derbyshire Annals as illustrated by the Records of the Quarter Sessions of the County of Derby from Queen Elizabeth to Queen Victoria* (2 volumes, London, 1890), Vol. 1, p. 89; Borthwick Institute of Historical Research, York, Cause Papers, CP. H 1961.

7. Rosen, *Witchcraft*, p. 94; Samuel Harsnett, *A Discovery of the fraudulent Practices of John Darrell Bachelor of Artes* (London, 1599), p. 37; Devonshire Record Office, Okehampton Borough Records, Quarter Sessions Minute Book, 1648–1658, 3248A/3/5, unfoliated, 7 June 1658; PRO, ASSI 45/4/1/131; 45/3/1/242.

8. Perkins, *A Discourse of the damned Art*, p. 149; Rosen, *Witchcraft*, p. 87; Potts, *The Trial of the Lancaster Witches*, p. 20; *The wonderful Discoverie of the Witchcrafts of Margaret and Phillip Flower, Daughters of Ioan Flower neere Bever Castle, executed at Lincolne, March 11, 1618* (London, 1618), sig. E1v; Cooper, *The Mystery of Witch-Craft*, p. 167.

9. For scolding, see David Underdown, 'The Taming of the Scold: The Enforcement of Patriarchal Authority in Early Modern England', in Anthony Fletcher and John Stevenson (eds.), *Order and Disorder in Early Modern England* (Cambridge, 1985), and Martin Ingram, '"Scolding Women Cucked or Washed": A Crisis in Gender Relations in Early Modern England?', in Jenny Kermode and Garthine Walker (eds.), *Women, Crime and the Courts in Early Modern England* (London, 1994); for defamation, J. A. Sharpe, *Defamation and Sexual Slander in Early Modern England: The Church Courts at York* (Borthwick Papers, 58, 1980), and Peter Rushton, 'Women, Witchcraft and Slander in Early Modern England: Cases from the Church Courts of Durham, 1560–1675', *Northern History* 18 (1982), pp. 116–32; for images of male and female violence, J. A. Sharpe, 'Plebeian

Marriage in Stuart England: Some Evidence from Popular Literature', *Transactions of the Royal Historical Society*, 5th series, 36 (1986), pp. 69–90.

10. Bodleian Library, Oxford, Western MSS, Herne Diaries 158–9 ('Analecta Ro. Plot'), f. 146; Perkins, *A Discourse of the damned Art*, p. 135.

11. Cooper, *The Mystery of Witch-Craft*, pp. 208–9; Borthwick Institute, CP. H 758; Cheshire Record Office, Cause Papers, EDC 5(1593)5; 5(1690)8.

12. Cooper, *The Mystery of Witch-Craft*, p. 275; Cambridge UL, EDR 12/1; Henry Goodcole, *The wonderfull Discoverie of Elizabeth Sawyer a Witch, late of Edmonton, her Conviction and Condemnation and Death* (London, 1621), sig. A4v.

13. Essex Record Office, Colchester Examination and Recognizance Books T/A 465/17, unfoliated, 26 May 1599; Lancashire Record Office, Quarter Sessions Records, QSB 1/170/55; PRO, ASSI 45/5/5/1.

14. Cooper, *The Mystery of Witch-Craft*, p. 246; PRO, ASSI 45/5/3/133; Matthew Hale, *A Collection of modern Matter of Fact concerning Witches and Witchcraft upon the Persons of People* (Part 1, London, 1693), pp. 54, 57; Goodcole, *The wonderfull Discoverie of Elizabeth Sawyer*, sig. D1.

15. Alexander Roberts, *A Treatise of Witchcraft: wherein sundry Propositions are laid downe, plainely discovering the Wickednesse of that damnable Art* (London, 1616), p. 16; PRO, ASSI 45/4/2/13; 45/9/3/97; 45/6/1/88.

16. PRO, ASSI 45/5/3/133; Grainge (ed.), *Daemonologia*, p. 89.

17. Horsfall Turner (ed.), *The Rev. Oliver Heywood*, Vol. 4, pp. 53–4. Thomas, *Religion and the Decline of Magic*, pp. 543–4, notes the widespread use of this type of counter-magic. For a recipe for a witch cake, see Bodleian Library, Oxford, MS Ashmole 1442, section 4, f. 27.

18. Devonshire Record Office, C1 64, f. 200v.

19. Grainge (ed.), *Daemonologia*, p. 42.

20. PRO, Star Chamber Records, STAC 8 4/10, f. 97v.

21. Grainge (ed.), *Daemonologia*, p. 80; Cambridge UL, EDR12/2.

22. Horsfall Turner (ed.), *The Rev. Oliver Heywood*, Vol. 3, p. 100; PRO, ASSI 45/1/5/38; Gifford, *A Dialogue*, p. 11.

23. PRO, ASSI 45/16/3/56; Perkins, *A Discourse of the damned Art*, pp. 54–5, 152, 206, 207; *The most strange and admirable Discoverie of the three Witches at Warboys arraigned, convicted and executed at the last Assizes at Huntingdon* (London, 1593), sig. B3–3v, P3.

24. H. R. McIlwaine (ed.), *Minutes of the Council and General Court of Colonial Virginia, 1622–1632* (Richmond, Virginia, 1924), p. 111. I am grateful to Dr James Horn for bringing this reference to my attention.

25. John Denison, *The most wonderfull and true storie of a certaine Witch named Alse Gooderidge of Stapenhill, who was arraigned and convicted at Darbie at the Assises there* (London, 1597), p. 5; Potts, *The Trial of the Lancaster Witches*, p. 146; PRO, ASSI 45/4/1/131; 45/1/5/38.

26. PRO, STAC 8 4/10, f. 101v; Goodcole, *The wonderfull Discoverie of Elizabeth Sawyer*, sig. A4v; PRO, STAC 8 4/10, f. 193; *The most strange and admirable Discoverie of the three Witches at Warboys*, sig. E3; *The triall of Maist Dorrell, or a Collection of Offences against Allegations not yet suffered to receive convenient Answere* (London, 1599), p. 100.

27. Grainge (ed.) *Daemonologia*, p. 35; *The most strange and admirable Discoverie of the three Witches at Warboys*, sig. P3; Lancashire Record Office, QSB 1/64(22); Essex Record Office, Archdeaconry of Essex Act Books, D/AEA/34, f. 79v.

28. For a typical contemporary listing of such remedies see John Gaule, *Select Cases of Conscience touching Witches and Witchcrafts* (London, 1646), p. 76.

29. *Witches apprehended, examined and executed, for notable Villanies by them committed both by Land and Water. With a strange and most true Triall how to know whether a Woman be a Witch or not* (London, 1613), sig. B4v; George More, *A true Discourse concerning the certaine Possession and Dispossession of 7 Persons in one Familie in Lancashire* (London, 1600), p. 59; *The most strange and admirable Discoverie of the three Witches at Warboys*, sig. H3; *A true and just Recorde, of the Information, Examination, and Confession of all the Witches taken at S. Oses in the Countie of Essex, whereof some were executed, and some entreated according to the Determination of the Lawe* (London, 1582), sig. D5.

30. Devonshire Record Office, Quarter Sessions Rolls, Box 41, Bapt 1638/52, 56–7; Grainge (ed.), *Daemonologia*, pp. 35, 93, 98; *CPSD, 1634–35*, p. 141; Lancashire Record Office, QSB 1/33(16).

31. Harsnett, *A Discovery of the fraudulent Practices of John Darrell*, p. 8.

32. Lawrence Stone, *The Family, Sex and Marriage in England 1500–1800* (London 1977), pp. 98–9; Thomas, *Religion and the Decline of Magic*, p. 526.

33. Borthwick Institute of Historical Research, CP. H 1504; Denison, *The most wonderfull and true storie of a certaine Witch named Alse Gooderidge*, p. 15; Potts, *The Trial of the Lancaster Witches*, p. 113; Borthwick Institute of Historical Research, York, CP. H 3601.

34. Oxfordshire Archives, MS OXF DIOC papers d. 16, f. 179; Cheshire Record Office, Consistory Court Papers, EDC 5(1661)38; Grainge (ed.), *Daemonologia*, p. 127; PRO, Northern Circuit, Prisoners' Petitions, ASSI 47/20/512–13.

35. Annabel Gregory, 'Witchcraft, Politics and "Good Neighbourhood" in Early Seventeenth-century Rye', *Past and Present*, 133 (1991), pp. 31–66. For the history of Rye in this period, see Graham Mayhew, *Tudor Rye* (Falmer, Sussex, 1987).

36. PRO, ASSI 45/11/1/93; Horsfall Turner (ed.), *The Rev. Oliver Heywood*, Vol. 1, p. 362.

7. Women and Witchcraft

1. Barbara Ehrenreich and Deirdre English, *Witches, Midwives and Healers: A History of Women Healers* (London, 1974), pp. 6, 8; Mary Daly, *Gyn/Ecology: the Metaethics of Radical Feminism* (London, 1979), pp. 179, 197, 190; Marianne Hester, *Lewd Women and Wicked Witches: A Study of the Dynamics of Male Domination* (London and New York, 1992); Silvia Bovenschen, 'The Contemporary Witch, the Historical Witch, and the Witch Myth: The Witch, Subject of the Appropriation of Nature and the Object of the Domination of Nature', *New German Critique*, 15 (1979), p. 83. For other relevant works, see the Bibliographical Essay.

2. The *Malleus* figures prominently in Trevor-Roper's *The European Witch-Craze of the Sixteenth and Seventeenth Centuries* (Harmondsworth, 1969).

3. Daly, *Gyn/Ecology*, p. 188. For two works written from the same perspective which rely heavily and uncritically on the *Malleus*, see Jean L. Bullough, *The Subordinate Sex: A History of Attitudes towards Women* (Urbana, 1973), p. 223, and Ann Oakley, *Subject Women* (London, 1982), pp. 325–6.

4. We have already suggested in the Introduction to this book that the importance of the *Malleus* has been overrated by modern scholars. Its lack of influence on English witchcraft writers is illustrated by the first English demonological tract, that written by Henry Holland. Holland appears only to have been aware of Kramer and Sprenger indirectly via Reginald Scot, and makes no reference to the *Malleus* in his tract, although he refers frequently to works by Jean Bodin and Lambert Daneau, and, less frequently, to works by the Danish theologian Neils Hemmingsen: *A Treatise against Witchcraft: or, a Dialogue, wherein the greatest Doubts concerning that Sinne, are briefly answered* (Cambridge, 1590), *passim*.

5. William Perkins, *A Discourse of the damned Art of Witchcraft. So farre forth as it is revealed in the Scriptures, and manifest by true Experience* (Cambridge, 1608), pp. 168–9; Alexander Roberts, *A Treatise of Witchcraft: wherein sundry Propositions are laid downe, plainely discovering the Wickednesse of that damnable Art* (London, 1616), pp. 40–47. Stuart Clark's perceptive comments on the treatment of this issue make an interesting comparison, while he, too, criticizes the weight which modern writers have afforded to the *Malleus*: 'The "Gendering" of Witchcraft in French Demonology: Misogyny or Polarity?', *French History*, 5 (1991), pp. 426–37.

6. Christina Larner, *Witchcraft and Religion: the Politics of Popular Belief* (Oxford, 1984), pp. 62, 87. This collection reprints Larner's earlier 'Was Witch Hunting Woman Hunting?', *New Society*, 58 (1981), pp. 11–12.

7. Lyndal Roper, *Oedipus and the Devil: Witchcraft, Sexuality and Religion in Early Modern Europe* (London, 1994). This book draws together a number of Dr Roper's essays and articles, of which perhaps the most immediately relevant is her 'Witchcraft and Fantasy in Early Modern Germany', *History Workshop Journal*, 32 (Autumn 1991), pp. 19–43.

8. Roper, *Oedipus and the Devil*, p. 228.

9. John Gaule, *Select Cases of Conscience touching Witches and Witchcrafts* (London, 1646), pp. 4–5.

10. This is one of the major themes of Carol F. Karlsen, *The Devil in the Shape of a Woman: Witchcraft in Colonial New England* (New York and London, 1987).

11. Scolding is discussed in David Underdown, 'The Taming of the Scold: The Enforcement of Patriarchal Authority in Early Modern England', in Anthony Fletcher and John Stevenson (eds.), *Order and Disorder in Early Modern England* (Cambridge, 1985), and Martin Ingram, '"Scolding Women Cucked or Washed": A Crisis in Gender Relations in Early Modern England?', in Jenny Kermode and Garthine Walker (eds.), *Women, Crime and the Courts in Early Modern England* (London, 1994). Problems of threats to the gender hierarchy as part of a wider discussion of a problem of order in this period can be found in Susan Amussen, *An Ordered Society: Gender and Class in Early Modern England* (Oxford, 1988).

12. The depositions are found in PRO, ASSI 45. For the borough cases, see 'Alleged

Witchcraft at Rossington, near Doncaster, 1605', *Gentleman's Magazine* (1857), part 1, pp. 592–5; Joseph Brogden Baker, *The History of Scarborough from the earliest Date* (London, 1882), pp. 481–3.

13. PRO, ASSI 45/1/5/38; 4/1/110; 5/3/133; 7/1/109.

14. Ehrenreich and English, *Witches, Midwives and Nurses*, p. 4. It should be noted that one of the sub-themes of this interpretation, that midwives tended to be disproportionately liable to be accused of being witches, has been exploded by David Harley, 'Historians as Demonologists: The Myth of the Midwife-Witch', *The Journal for the Social History of Medicine*, 3 (1990), pp. 1–26.

15. PRO, ASSI 45/3/1/244; Borthwick Institute of Historical Research, Cause Papers, CP. H 1475; 'Alleged Witchcraft at Rossington', *passim*.

16. Borthwick Institute, CP. H 1504, 2177.

17. *A full and impartial Account of the Discovery of Sorcery and Witchcraft practis'd by Jane Wenham of Walkerne in Hertfordshire, upon the Bodies of Anne Thorne, Anne Street, &c* (London, 1712), p. 13.

18. Cambridge University Library, Isle of Ely Gaol Delivery Records, Michaelmas 1647, EDR 12/15.

19. PRO, ASSI 45/10/3/124.

20. Baker, *The History of Scarborough*, pp. 481–3.

21. 'Alleged Witchcraft at Rossington', *passim*.

22. These figures are based on an analysis of abstracts of assize cases given in C. L'Estrange Ewen, *Witch Hunting and Witch Trials*, pp. 187–264, and J. S. Cockburn (ed.), *A Calendar of Assize Records: Hertfordshire Indictments James I* (London, 1975), pp. 70–223. Cf. the comments of Clive Holmes, 'Women: Witnesses and Witches', *Past and Present*, 140 (1993), pp. 45–78.

23. Ewen, *Witchcraft and Demonianism*, p. 63.

24. *The Examination and Confession of certaine Wytches at Chensforde in the Countie of Essex, before the Quenes Maiesties Judges, the xxvi day of July Anno 1566* (London, 1566).

25. F. J. C. Hearnshaw and D. M. Hearnshaw (eds.), *Court Leet Records, Vol. 1, part 2, A.D. 1578–1602* (Southampton Record Society, Southampton, 1906), p. 187; *A true and just Recorde, of the Information, Examination, and Confession of all the Witches taken at S. Oses in the Countie of Essex, whereof some were executed, and some entreated according to the Determination of the Lawe* (London, 1582), sig. D4; R. G. Usher (ed.), *The Presbyterian Movement in the Reign of Queen Elizabeth* (Camden Society, 3rd series, 8, 1905), p. 70.

26. William Grainge (ed.), *Daemonologia: A Discourse on Witchcraft, as it was acted in the Family of Mr Edward Fairfax, of Fuyston, in the County of York, in the Year 1621: along with the only two Eclogues of the same Author known to be in Existence* (Harrogate, 1882), p. 78; PRO, ASSI 45/3/2/129; 5/2/30; 4/1/131; *A true and exact Relation of the severall Informations, Examinations and Confessions of the late Witches arraigned and executed at the late Sessions holden before the Right Honorable Robert, Earle of Warwicke, and Severall of his Majesties Justices of Peace, the 29 of July 1645* (London, 1645), p. 22.

27. Henry Goodcole, *The wonderfull Discoverie of Elizabeth Sawyer a Witch, late of Edmonton, her Conviction and Condemnation and Death* (London, 1621), sig. B2v–B3v.

28. *A true and exact Relation*, p. 26; Cambridge UL, Isle of Ely Gaol Delivery Records, Michaelmas 1647, EDR 12/20.

29. J. Boys, *The Case of Witchcraft at Coggeshall, Essex, in the Year 1699* (London, 1909), pp. 21–2.

30. Oxfordshire Archives, Quarter Sessions Records, Q3/1687 Mi/14.

31. PRO, ASSI 45/4/1/131.

32. Quoted in Shulamith Shahar, *The Fourth Estate: A History of Women in the Middle Ages* (London and New York, 1983), p. 275.

33. PRO, STAC 8 4/10, f. 196v.

34. Peter Rushton, 'Women, Witchcraft and Slander in Early Modern England: Cases from the Church Courts of Durham, 1560–1675', *Northern History*, 18 (1982), p. 131.

35. Jill Dubisch (ed.), *Gender and Power in Rural Greece* (Princeton, 1986), pp. 13, 25.

36. Larner, *Witchcraft and Religion*, pp. 86, 87.

37. Cheshire Record Office, Chester Consistory Court Papers, EDC 5(1662)63. Dr Garthine Walker, who has completed a Ph.D. thesis based on Cheshire court records, informs me that Mary Briscoe was accused of harming a Richard Wright by witchcraft at the Cheshire Court of Great Sessions in 1664, and although acquitted was bound over for about two years subsequently: PRO, CHES 21/5, ff. 33v, 39v, 52v.

38. *The Parliament's Post*, 13, 29 July–4 August 1645, pp. 1–3: I am grateful to Joad Raymond for reminding me of this reference.

39. John Stearne, *A Confirmation and Discovery of Witchcraft* (London, 1648), pp. 21–2; Cambridge UL, EDR 12/12. For a broader discussion of this case, see Malcolm Gaskill, 'Witchcraft and Power in Early Modern England: The Case of Margaret Moore', in Kermode and Walker (eds.), *Women, Crime and the Courts*.

40. *The Tryal, Condemnation, and Execution of three Witches, viz Temperance Floyd, Mary Floyd and Susanna Edwards, who were all arraigned at Exeter on the 18th of August 1682* (London, 1682), pp. 4–6. The depositions taken at Bideford are reproduced in *A true and impartial Relation of the Informations against three Witches viz Temperance Lloyd, Mary Trembles, and Susanna Edwards* (London, 1682).

41. Roper, *Oedipus and the Devil*, p. 20.

42. PRO, ASSI 35/2/5/8; 35/14/4/19, 20; 35/29/1/15; 35/29/2/45, 46; Ewen, *Witch Hunting and Witch Trials*, pp. 117, 158.

43. Macfarlane, *A Regional and Comparative Study*, p. 160; Stearne, *A Confirmation and Discovery of Witchcraft*, pp. 7, 11.

8. Possession

1. For a very dated but wide-ranging survey of the subject, see Montague Summers, *The History of Witchcraft and Demonology* (London, 1926; reprinted 1965), Chapter 6, 'Diabolic Possession and Modern Spiritism'. D. P. Walker, *Unclean Spirits: Possession and Exorcism in France and England in the Late Sixteenth and Early Seventeenth Centuries* (Philadelphia, 1981), is a good short guide to the phenomenon in the period it covers. For a brief, recent

discussion of the subject which explores some of its less obvious aspects, see Stephen Greenblatt, 'Loudon and London', *Critical Inquiry*, 12 (1985–6), pp. 326–46.

2. Such cases figured prominently, for example, in the case books of the 'astrological physician' Richard Napier, who treated over 2,000 patients between 1597 and 1634: Michael MacDonald, *Mystical Bedlam: Madness, Anxiety and Healing in Seventeenth-century England* (Cambridge, 1981), pp. 198–217.

3. *The most strange and admirable Discoverie of the three Witches at Warboys arraigned, convicted and executed at the last Assizes at Huntingdon* (London, 1593).

4. Samuel Harsnett, *A Discovery of the fraudulent Practices of John Darrell Bachelor of Artes* (London, 1599), pp. 297–315, provides an account of the Katherine Wright case; the Darling case forms the subject matter of John Denison, *The most wonderfull and true storie of a certaine Witch named Alse Gooderidge of Stapenhill, who was arraigned and convicted at Darbie at the Assises there* (London, 1597); the sufferings of the Starkie household are described in John Darrell, *A true Narration of the strange and grevous Vexation by the Devil, of 7 Persons in Lancashire, and William Somers of Nottingham* (London, 1600). The Somers case provoked a lively literary debate, which included the works by Harsnett and Darrell already referred to. These and the other relevant publications are listed in Corinne Holt Rickert, *The Case of John Darrell: Minister and Exorcist* (University of Florida Monographs, Humanities, 9, Gainsville, Florida, Winter 1962).

5. Materials relating to the Mary Glover case are gathered with a useful introduction in Michael MacDonald, *Witchcraft and Hysteria in Elizabethan London: Edward Jorden and the Mary Glover Case* (London, 1990).

6. PRO, STAC 8, 4/10. This case is discussed in C. L'Estrange Ewen, *Witchcraft in the Star Chamber* (np, 1938), Chapter 6, 'A Berkshire Demoniac', while other references relevant to it are given in Henry N. Paul, *The Royal Play of Macbeth: When, Why, and How It was Written by Shakespeare* (New York, 1971), pp. 119–27.

7. BL, Add. MSS, 32496, f. 42v; William Grainge (ed.), *Daemonologia: A Discourse on Witchcraft, as it was acted in the Family of Mr Edward Fairfax, of Fuyston, in the County of York, in the Year 1621: along with the only two Eclogues of the same Author known to be in Existence* (Harrogate, 1882); PRO, ASSI 45/5/3/132–3; Matthew Hale, *A Collection of modern Matter of Fact concerning Witches and Witchcraft upon the Persons of People* (Part I, London, 1693), pp. 52–9.

8. *The Disclosing of a late counterfeyted Possession of the Devyl in two Maydens within the Citie of London* (London, 1574).

9. PRO, STAC 8, 32/12.

10. The Dugdale case was another which provoked a lively debate. Summers, *The History of Witchcraft and Demonology*, pp. 335–6, lists eight works published about it between 1697 and 1699. Aspects of these episode are currently the subject of work in progress by Mr Jonathan Westaway and Mr Richard Harrison.

11. Walker, *Unclean Spirits*, pp. 43–9. These exorcisms were eventually to prompt the publication of Samuel Harsnett, *A Declaration of egregious popish Impostures, to with-draw the Harts of her Maiesties Subiects from their Allegeance and from the Truth of the Christian Religion as professed in England, under the Pretence of Casting out Devils* (London, 1603).

12. Thomas Potts, *The Trial of the Lancaster Witches A.D. MDCXII*, G. B. Harrison (ed.) (London, 1929; reprinted 1971), pp. 83–107.

13. *The Boy of Bilson: or a true Discovery of the late notorious Impostures of certaine Romish Priests in their pretended Exorcisme, or Expulsion of the Divell out of a young Boy, named William Perry* (London, 1622). For an initial exploration of the possible input of seminary priests into English witchcraft beliefs, see Warren J. Karle, 'The Devil in the Vineyard: the Role of Seminary Priests in the Introduction of Continental Witchlore into England' (University of York M.A. thesis, 1992).

14. Walker, *Unclean Spirits*, pp. 61–73; Notestein, *A History of Witchcraft*, pp. 84–92.

15. Quoted in *The Cheshire Sheaf* (August, 1902), p. 85. I am grateful to Paul Booth for bringing this case to my attention.

16. Grainge (ed.), *Daemonologia*, p. 37.

17. Denison, *The most wonderfull and true storie of a certaine Witch named Alse Gooderidge*, p. 2.

18. *The most strange and admirable Discoverie of the three Witches at Warboys*, sig. B1–B2.

19. Hale, *A Collection of modern Matter of Fact*, pp. 52–9, *passim*.

20. Harsnett, *A Discovery of the fraudulent Practices of John Darrell*, p. 36.

21. *A Booke declaringe the fearfull Vexasion of one Alexander Nyndge: being most horriblye tormented wyth an evyll Spirit, the xx daie of Ianuarie in the yere of our Lord 1573 at Lyeringswell in Suffolke* (np, 1573).

22. *The most strange and admirable Discoverie of the three Witches at Warboys, passim*.

23. Denison, *The most wonderfull and true storie of a certaine Witch named Alse Gooderidge*, p. 33.

24. MacDonald, *Witchcraft and Hysteria*, p. xiv.

25. Denison, *The most wonderfull and true storie of a certaine Witch named Alse Gooderidge*, pp. 2, 12, 31.

26. Grainge (ed.), *Daemonologia*, p. 38.

27. Ibid., pp. 51, 56, 62, 63.

28. For an account of Cooke's life and a list of his anti-Roman Catholic tracts, see *DNB*. Anthony Wood, cited there, described him as 'a good and learned man, a man abounding in charity and exemplary in his life and conversation, yet hated by the R. Catholics who lived near Leeds and in Yorkshire, and indeed by all elsewhere who had read his works'.

29. Grainge (ed.), *Daemonologia*, pp. 58, 68, 107–8, 122.

30. Ibid., pp. 88, 97–8.

31. Ibid., p. 35.

32. Ibid., p. 42.

33. Ibid., p. 93.

34. Ibid., p. 98. The strength of witch traditions might be gauged from the fact that the supposed place of her execution, near Ledston, was known as Mary Pannell Hill into the twentieth century: Ewen, *Witchcraft and Demonianism*, p. 393.

35. Grainge (ed.), *Daemonologia*, pp. 43, 71.

36. Perhaps the most exciting work on youth in early modern England is that of Paul

Griffiths, author of an important dissertation, 'Some Aspects of the Social History of Youth in Early Modern England' (University of Cambridge Ph.D. thesis, 1992), which is currently being prepared for publication.

37. Marion Starkey, *The Devil in Massachusetts* (New York, 1950); John Demos, *Entertaining Satan: Witchcraft and the Culture of Early New England* (New York, 1982); Lyndal Roper, *Oedipus and the Devil: Witchcraft, Sexuality and Religion in Early Modern Europe* (London, 1994), especially Chapter 8, 'Exorcism and the Theology of the Body'.

38. Joseph Klaits, *Servants of Satan: The Age of the Witch Hunts* (Bloomington, Indiana, 1985), p. 125.

39. Thomas, *Religion and the Decline of Magic*, p. 481.

40. MacDonald, *Witchcraft and Hysteria*, p. 67; *The Hartford-Shire Wonder: or, Strange News from Ware* (London, 1669), p. 6; Harsnett, *A Discovery of the fraudulent Practices of John Darrell*, p. 34; John Darrell, *The Replie of John Darrell, to the Answer of John Deacon and John Walker, concerning the Doctrine of the Possession and Dispossession of Demoniakes* (London, 1602), p. 21. The theatricality of possession cases is discussed in Stephen Greenblatt, *Shakespearian Negotiations: The Circulation of Social Energy in Renaissance England* (Oxford, 1988), Chapter 4, 'Shakespeare and the Exorcists'.

41. MacDonald, *Witchcraft and Hysteria*, p. 30; John Swan, *A true and briefe Report, of Mary Glover's Vexation, and of her Deliverance by the Meanes of Fastinge and Prayer* (London, 1603), pp. 8, 18.

42. PRO, ASSI 45/5/3/132–3.

43. Harsnett, *A Discovery of the fraudulent Practices of John Darrell*, pp. 68–9.

44. Darrell, *A true Narration . . . of 7 Persons in Lancashire*, p. 9; *The Lord's arm stretched out in Answer of Prayer: or, a true Relation of the wonderful Deliverance of James Barrow, the son of John Barrow of Olaves Southwark, who was posessed with Evil Spirits near two Years* (London, 1663), p. 7; Swan, *A true and briefe Report, of Mary Glover's Vexation*, p. 43; *A true Relation of the wonderful Deliverance of Hannah Crump. Daughter of John Crump of Warwick, who was sore afflicted by Witchcraft, for the space of nine Months, with the several Means used, and Way in which she was relieved* (London, 1663), pp. 19–20.

45. *The most strange and admirable Discoverie of the three Witches at Warboys*, sig. C2v.

46. Ibid., sig. G3–G3v, L4v–M1.

47. Hale, *A Collection of modern Matter of Fact*, p. 56.

48. PRO, STAC 8 4/10, f. 15v.

49. Mary Moore, *Wonderfull News from the North: or, a true Relation of the sad and grievous Torments, inflicted upon the Bodies of three Children of Mr George Muschamp, late of the County of Northumberland, by Witchcraft* (London, 1650), p. 16.

50. PRO, STAC 8 4/10, f. 94.

51. Grainge (ed.), *Daemonologia*, p. 124.

52. Hale, *A Collection of modern Matter of Fact*, p. 55.

53. PRO, ASSI 45/5/5/1.

54. Harsnett, *A Discovery of the fraudulent Practices of John Darrell*, pp. 16–17.

55. PRO, STAC 8 4/10, ff. 123A, 9.

9. The Growth of Judicial Scepticism

1. For a succinct introduction to this aspect of the period of the witch persecutions, see Brian P. Levack, *The Witch-Hunt in Early Modern Europe* (London, 1987), Chapter 3, 'The Legal Foundations'. For a brief and scholarly discussion of the use of torture in the legal process, a subject upon which many historians of witchcraft have commented, see John H. Langbein, *Torture and the Law of Proof: Europe and England in the Ancien Régime* (Chicago and London, 1977). Sixteenth-century legal changes are discussed in Professor Langbein's *Prosecuting Crime in the Renaissance: England, Germany and France* (Cambridge, Mass., 1974). For a more specific analysis, see C. R Unsworth, 'Witchcraft Beliefs and Criminal Procedure in Early Modern England', in Thomas G. Watkins (ed.), *Legal Record and Historical Reality: Proceedings of the Eighth British Legal History Conference, Cardiff, 1987* (London and Ronceverte, 1989).

2. *CSPD, 1634–35*, p. 79: Ewen, *Witchcraft and Demonianism*, p. 125.

3. Quoted in Barbara Rosen, *Witchcraft* (London, 1969), pp. 314–15.

4. The background to this important trial remains elusive. For some important initial comments, see Rachel A. C. Halsted, *The Pendle Witch-Trial 1612* (Preston, 1993), pp. 5–10; J. T. Swain, 'The Lancashire Witch Trials of 1612 and 1634 and the Economics of Witchcraft', *Northern History*, 30 (1994), pp. 64–85.

5. *A true and just Recorde, of the Information, Examination, and Confession of all the Witches taken at S. Oses in the Countie of Essex, whereof some were executed, and some entreated according to the Determination of the Lawe* (London, 1582), sig. A7v, B1v, C3v. Indictments generated by these investigations survive: PRO, ASSI 35/24/1/18, 21–9, 33, 36. For listings of the Essex witches tried in 1582, see Ewen, *Witch Hunting and Witch Trials*, pp. 143–6; Macfarlane, *A Regional and Comparative Study*, p. 173, where brief summaries of the harm they allegedly caused are given. This outbreak deserves to be better known and, like the celebrated Lancashire trials of 1612, would repay deeper investigation.

6. Reginald Scot, *The Discoverie of Witchcraft* (London, 1584: reprinted New York, 1972), p. 4.

7. George Gifford, *A Dialogue concerning Witches and Witchcrafts, in which it is layed open how craftily the Divell deceiveth not onely the Witches but many other, and so leadeth them awrie into manie great Errours* (London, 1593: second edition of 1603 reprinted by Percy Society, 8, 1843), p. 106.

8. For Faversham, Rosen, *Witchcraft*, pp. 163–7; for Newcastle, Roger Howell, *Newcastle upon Tyne and the Puritan Revolution: A Study of the Civil War in North England* (Oxford, 1967), pp. 232–3.

9. Sir Robert Filmer, *An Advertisement to the Jurymen of England, touching Witches. Together with a Difference between an English and an Hebrew Witch* (London, 1653), p. 11; James VI and I, 'Daemonologie', in *The Workes of the most high and mighty Prince, James, by the Grace of God Kinge of Great Brittaine, France, Ireland, Defender of ye faith &c* (London, 1616), p. 136; *The Witches of Northamptonshire, Agnes Browne, Arthur Bill, Joane Vaughan, Hellen Jenkenson, Mary Barber, Witches, who were all executed at Northampton the 22 July last 1612* (London, 1612);

Witches apprehended, examined and executed, for notable Villanies by them committed both by Land and water. With a strange and most true Triall how to know whether a Woman be a Witch or not (London, 1613). For French evidence, see Alfred Soman, *Sorcellerie et justice criminelle (16e–18e siècles)* (Croft Road, Hampshire, and Brookfield, Vermont, 1992), Section VI, pp. 24–5.

10. Matthew Hopkins, *The Discovery of Witches* (London, 1647), p. 6. Hopkins, answering the suggestion that the water test was 'a tryall not allowable by law or conscience', claimed that some of those who were swum under his supervision had offered themselves voluntarily in hopes of clearing themselves. It should be remembered that Hopkins wrote this tract in response to criticism from the judges who presided over the Norfolk assizes.

11. J. Horsfall Turner (ed.), *The Rev. Oliver Heywood, B.A., 1630–1712. His Autobiography, Diaries, Anecdote and Event Books* (4 volumes, Brighouse, 1882–5), Vol. 3, p. 100.

12. *The most strange and admirable Discoverie of the three Witches at Warboys arraigned, convicted and executed at the last Assizes in Huntingdon* (London, 1593), sig. B3v, E3, H2v, H3.

13. Ibid., sig. H4, O4.

14. Henry Goodcole, *The wonderfull Discoverie of Elizabeth Sawyer a Witch, late of Edmonton, her Conviction and Condemnation and Death* (London, 1621), sig. B2v.

15. Filmer, *An Advertisement to the Jurymen of England*. Biographical details of Filmer are given in *DNB* and in the introduction to Peter Laslett (ed.), *Patriarcha and Other Political Works of Sir Robert Filmer* (Oxford, 1949).

16. Filmer, *An Advertisement to the Jurymen of England*, p. 2.

17. Ibid., p. 7.

18. Ibid., p. 13.

19. Ibid., sig. A3.

20. Thomas Potts, *The Trial of the Lancaster Witches A.D. MDCXII*, G. B. Harrison (ed.) (London, 1929; reprinted 1971), pp. 50–51, where the evidence of nine-year-old Jennet Device was crucial in obtaining the conviction of her mother.

21. Ibid., pp. 179, 185.

22. *The most strange and admirable Discoverie of the three Witches at Warboys*, sig. P4: John Denison, *The most wonderfull and true storie of a certaine Witch named Alse Gooderidge of Stapenhill, who was arraigned and convicted at Darbie at the Assises there* (London, 1597), p. 9.

23. Ewen, *Witchcraft and Demonianism*, p. 197.

24. John Stearne, *A Confirmation and Discovery of Witchcraft* (London, 1648), p. 39.

25. William Grainge (ed.), *Daemonologia: A Discourse on Witchcraft, as it was acted in the Family of Mr Edward Fairfax, of Fuyston, in the County of York, in the Year 1621: along with the only two Eclogues of the same Author known to be in Existence* (Harrogate, 1882), pp. 68–83; PRO, ASSI 45/3/2/129; Devon Record Office, Minute Books of the Sessions of the Peace, Exeter City, C1/65 (1660–1672), f. 3v; PRO, ASSI 45/6/1/69.

26. Details of Hale's life are taken from *DNB*. For a good recent introduction to Hale, see Alan Cromartie, *Sir Matthew Hale 1609–1676: Law, Religion and Natural Philosophy* (Cambridge, 1995). This contains only a brief discussion of Hale's handling of the 1662 witch

trial, and adds little to the account given here, although it does note a later tradition that Hale's experiences in 1662 made him a sceptic about witchcraft later in life.

27. *A Tryal of Witches at the Assizes held at Bury St Edmunds for the County of Suffolk on the tenth day of March 1664 before Sir Matthew Hale Kt then Lord Chief Baron of his Majesties Court of Exchequer. Taken by a Person then attending the Court* (London, 1682). This pamphlet attributes an incorrect date to the trial, which was in fact held in 1662.

28. Ibid., pp. 41–2.

29. Ibid., pp. 43–5.

30. Ibid., p. 2.

31. Ibid., p. 57.

32. Ibid., p. 40.

33. Ibid., pp. 55–6.

34. Abstracts of references to these cases in the Gaol Books of the Western Circuit of the assizes are given in Ewen, *Witchcraft and Demonianism*, p. 444. For the 1682 trials, see *The Life and Conversation of Temperance Floyd, Mary Lloyd, and Susanna Edwards, three eminent Witches lately condemned at Exeter Assizes* (London, 1682); *A true and impartial Relation of the Informations against three Witches, viz Temperance Lloyd, Mary Trembles, and Susanna Edwards* (London, 1682); *The Tryal, Condemnation, and Execution of three Witches, viz Temperance Floyd, Mary Floyd and Susanna Edwards, who were all arraigned at Exeter on the 18th of August 1682* (London, 1682); 'Witches discovered and punished: or, the trials and Condemnation of three notorious Witches, who were tryed at the last Assizes, holden at the Castle of Exeter, in the County of Devon: where they received Sentence of Death, for bewitching several Persons, destroying Ships at Sea, and Cattel by Land, etc', in J. Woodfall Ebsworth (ed.), *Roxburgh Ballads* (7 volumes, London, 1869–93), Vol. 6, pp. 706–8.

35. *An Account of the Tryal and Examination of Joan Buts, for being a common Witch and Inchantress* (London, 1682: single-sheet broadside). For the opinions of the Surrey justice of the peace, see Kitteridge, *Witchcraft in Old and New England*, p. 596.

36. *The Tryal of Richard Hathaway upon an Information for being a Cheat and Imposter, for endeavouring to take away the Life of Sarah Morduck, for being a Witch* (London, 1702). Indictments survive in the Home Circuit Assize Files for both Hathaway's original accusation against Moordike, and his subsequent trial for false accusation, and are noted in Ewen, *Witch Hunting and Witch Trials*, pp. 264–5.

37. *The Tryal of Richard Hathaway*, pp. 3, 5.

38. Ibid., p. 5.

39. Ibid., p. 19.

40. Ibid., p. 23.

41. Ibid., pp. 25–6.

42. The Wenham case is discussed in Phyllis J. Guskin, 'The Context of English Witchcraft: The Case of Joan Wenham (1712)', *Eighteenth-century Studies*, 15 (1981–2), pp. 48–71. The pamphlet giving the fullest account of the trial, our main concern here, is *A full and impartial Account of the Discovery of Sorcery and Witchcraft practis'd by Jane Wenham of Walkerne in Hertfordshire, upon the Bodies of Anne Thorne, Anne Street, &c* (London, 1712).

43. *A full and impartial Account*, p. 1.

44. Ibid., p. 3.

45. Ibid.

46. Ibid., p. 7.

47. Ibid., pp. 21–8.

48. Ibid., p. 28.

49. Ibid., p. 10.

50. Ibid., p. 12.

51. Roger North, *The Lives of the Right Hon. Francis North, Baron Guilford, The Hon. Sir Dudley North, and the Hon. and Rev. Dr John North, together with the Autobiography of the Author*, Augustus Jessop (ed.) (3 volumes, London, 1890). Further details of Roger North's life are given in *DNB*.

52. North, *Lives*, Vol. 3, pp. 130–31, Vol. 1, pp. 168–9.

53. Ibid., Vol. 1. p. 169.

54. For a discussion of this aspect of witchcraft history in the context of a 'withdrawal of the upper classes' from popular culture, see Peter Burke, *Popular Culture in Early Modern Europe* (London, 1978), pp. 273–5. This theme appears in a much more developed form in many of the essays in Soman, *Sorcellerie et justice criminelle*.

55. North, *Lives*, Vol. 3, p. 131.

56. Scot, *The Discoverie of Witchcraft*, p. 5.

57. North, *Lives*, Vol. 3, p. 131.

10. A Changing Religious Context

1. Douglas G. Greene (ed.), *The Meditations of Lady Elizabeth Delaval, written between 1662 and 1671* (Surtees Society, 190, 1975), pp. 77–8. The details of Elizabeth's life are taken from the introduction to this text.

2. Christina Larner, *Enemies of God: The Witch-Hunt in Scotland* (London, 1981).

3. E. William Monter, *Witchcraft in France and Switzerland: The Borderlands during the Reformation* (Ithaca, New York, 1976); H. C. Erik Midelfort, *Witch Hunting in Southwestern Germany, 1562–1684: The Social and Intellectual Foundations* (Stanford, California, 1972). More recent findings by Wolfgang Behringer do, however, suggest a clearer pattern of severe witch-hunting in German Catholic territories after 1600: 'Allemagne, Mère de tant de sorcières', in Robert Muchembled (ed.), *Magie et sorcellerie en Europe: du Moyen Age à nos jours* (Paris, 1994), p. 75.

4. Midelfort, *Witch Hunting in Southwestern Germany*, Chapter 3, 'Witchcraft Theories in the German Southwest'.

5. Samuel Harsnett, *A Declaration of egregious popish Impostures, to with-draw the Harts of her Maiesties Subiects from their Allegeance, and from the Truth of the Christian Religion as professed in England, under the Pretence of Casting out Devils* (London, 1603); *The Boy of Bilson: or a true Discovery of the late notorious Impostures of certaine Romish Priests in their pretended Exorcisme, or Expulsion of the Divell out of a young Boy, named William Perry* (London, 1622); Thomas

Potts, *The Trial of the Lancaster Witches, A.D. MDCXII*, G. B. Harrison (ed.) (London, 1929), pp. 96–107.

6. Thomas, *Religion and the Decline of Magic*, pp. 25–173.

7. G. L. Burr, *Selections from his Writings*, L. O. Gibbons (ed.) (Ithaca, New York, 1943), pp. 360–62; R. Trevor Davies, *Four Centuries of Witch Beliefs* (London, 1947).

8. Gabriel Towerson, *An Explication of the Decalogue or the Commandments, with Reference to the Catechisme of the Church of England* (London, 1676), pp. 96, 97; James Durham, *A practical Exposition of the X Commandments with a Resolution of several momentous Questions and Cases of Conscience* (London, 1675); Zachary Bogan, *A View of the Threats and Punishments recorded in the Scriptures alphabetically composed with some brief Observations upon severall Texts* (Oxford, 1653), p. 42.

9. *The most strange and admirable Discoverie of the three Witches at Warboys arraigned, convicted and executed at the last Assizes at Huntingdon* (London, 1593); Alexander Roberts, *A Treatise of Witchcraft: wherein sundry Propositions are laid downe, plainely discovering the Wickednesse of that damnable Art* (London, 1616); Henry Goodcole, *The wonderfull Discoverie of Elizabeth Sawyer a Witch, late of Edmonton, her Conviction and Condemnation and Death* (London, 1621).

10. John Darrell, *A true Narration of the strange and grevous Vexation by the Devil, of 7 Persons in Lancashire, and William Somers of Nottingham* (London, 1600), p. 2.

11. Macfarlane, *A Regional and Comparative Study*, p. 187.

12. Alan Macfarlane (ed.), *The Diary of Ralph Josselin 1616–1683* (British Academy Records of Social and Economic History, New Series, 3, 1976), pp. 379, 404.

13. John Gaule, *Select Cases of Conscience touching Witches and Witchcrafts* (London, 1646), pp. 9, 6. Gaule's career and other publications are described, and the adverse comment about him given, in *DNB*.

14. William Monter, *Ritual, Myth and Magic in Early Modern Europe* (Brighton,1983), p. 115.

15. For recent reappraisals of Latitudinarianism, see John Spurr, '"Latitudinarianism" and the Restoration Church', *Historical Journal*, 31 (1988), pp. 61–82; Richard Ashcraft, 'Latitudinarianism and Toleration: Historical Myth versus Political History' and Michael Hunter, 'Latitudinarianism and the "Ideology" of the Early Royal Society: Thomas Spratt's History of the Royal Society (1667) Reconsidered', both in Richard Kroll, Richard Ashcraft and Perez Zagorin (eds.), *Philosophy, Science and Religion in England 1640–1700* (Cambridge, 1992).

16. Basic details on Glanvill's life are given in *DNB*. For an assessment of his thought, see J. I. Cope, *Joseph Glanvill, Anglican Apologist* (St Louis, Miss., 1956), and M. E. Prior, 'Joseph Glanvill, Witchcraft and Seventeenth-century Science', *Modern Philology*, 30 (1932), pp. 167–93.

17. More has been the subject of recent scholarly works, unlike Glanvill. See A. Rupert Hall, *Henry More, Magic, Religion and Experiment* (Oxford, 1990); S. Hutton (ed.), *Henry More (1614–1687): Tercentenary Studies* (Dordrecht, Boston and London, 1990).

18. Joseph Glanvill, *Saducismus Triumphatus: or full and plain Evidence concerning Witches and Apparitions* (London, 1681), Part 1, p. 2; Part 2, pp. 1, 89 ff. Glanvill's book was one of

the most influential defences of the belief in witchcraft in the late seventeenth century and continued to be read well into the eighteenth. It began its publishing history in 1668 as *A Blow at modern Sadducism, or some philosophical Considerations about Witchcraft*, and was then expanded and reprinted as *Saducismus Triumphatus* in 1681. It was reprinted with some additions in 1689, an extended third edition was published in 1700 and a fourth edition in 1726.

19. Henry More, *An Antidote against Atheisme: or an Appeal to the natural Faculties of the Minde of Man, whether there be not a God* (London, 1653), pp. 110–29. Historians are undecided on how important atheism actually was in the seventeenth century: for a good recent discussion of the point, see Michael Hunter, 'The Problem of "Atheism" in Early Modern England', *Transactions of the Royal Historical Society*, Fifth Series, 35 (1985), pp. 135–58.

20. *Strange News from Arpington near Bexly in Kent: being a true Narrative of a young Maid who was possest with several Devils or evil Spirits* (London, 1679), p. 1.

21. A useful recent guide to this subject is provided by R. M. Burns, *The Great Debate on Miracles: From Joseph Glanvill to David Hume* (London and Toronto, 1981).

22. Ibid., p. 10.

23. Edward Stillingfleet, *Origines Sacrae: or, a rational Account of the Grounds of the Christian Faith, as to the Truth and divine Authority of the Scriptures and the Matters therein contained* (London, 1662), p. 142.

24. Burns, *The Great Debate*, p. 17.

25. This account is based on Eamon Duffy, 'Valentine Greatrakes, the Irish Stroker: Miracles, Science and Orthodoxy in Restoration England', *Studies in Church History*, 17 (1981), pp. 251–74. Greatrakes has been the subject of attention by a number of modern scholars and it is hoped in particular that work in progress by Peter Elmer will throw light on his significance.

26. Cited ibid., p. 272.

27. Cited ibid., pp. 264–5.

28. Conyers Middleton, *A free Enquiry into the miraculous Powers which are supposed to have subsisted in the Christian Church from the earliest Ages through several successive Centuries* (London, 1749), p. 221.

29. The significance of genre during the 1640s and 1650s is discussed in Jerome Friedman, *Miracles and the Pulp Press during the English Revolution* (London, 1993).

30. These are the titles of some of the ballads drawn together in a collection by an important pioneering scholar of this type of literature: H. E. Rollins, *The Pack of Autolycus: Or Strange and Terrible News of Ghosts, Apparitions, Monstrous Births, Showers of Wheat, Judgements of God, and Other Prodigious and Fearful Happenings as Told in Broadside Ballads of the Years 1624–1693* (Cambridge, Mass., 1927).

31. Ibid., p. 150.

32. *CSPD, 1682*, p. 347.

33. For a discussion of the French Prophets which places them in the contemporary context, see Hillel Schwartz, *Knaves, Fools, Madmen, and that Subtile Effluvium: A Study of the*

Opposition to the French Prophets in England, 1706–17 (University of Florida Social Science Monographs, 62, Gainsville, Florida, 1978).

34. John Telford (ed.), *The Letters of the Rev. John Wesley* (8 volumes, London, 1931), Vol. 7, p. 300; Nehemiah Curnock (ed.), *The Journal of the Rev. John Wesley* (8 volumes, London, 1909–16), Vol. 6, p. 109; Telford (ed.), *The Letters*, Vol. 6, p. 82.

35. Curnock (ed.), *The Journal*, Vol. 2, pp. 298, 301–2.

36. Ibid., Vol. 5, pp. 374–5.

37. Robert Halsband (ed.), *The Complete Letters of Lady Mary Wortley Montagu* (3 volumes, Oxford, 1965), Vol. 3, p. 26; Curnock (ed.), *The Journal*, Vol. 2, p. 299, n. 1.

11. Science and the Decline of Witchcraft

1. Quoted in David C. Lindberg, 'Conceptions of the Scientific Revolution from Bacon to Butterfield: A Preliminary Sketch', in David C. Lindberg and Robert S. Westman (eds.), *Reappraisals of the Scientific Revolution* (Cambridge, 1990), pp. 8–9.

2. The history of science in the early modern period is currently an expanding and contentious field where previous assumptions are constantly being actively challenged. The literature on the subject is correspondingly vast. An invaluable introduction to this literature is provided by H. Floris Cohen, *The Scientific Revolution: A Historiographical Enquiry* (Chicago and London, 1994). Two collections demonstrating the directions of new thinking are Lindberg and Westman (eds.), *Reappraisals*, and M. L. Righini Bonelli and W. R. Shea (eds.), *Reason, Experiment and Mysticism in the Scientific Revolution* (London, 1975). Those wishing to examine the more traditional paradigm might read Herbert Butterfield, *The Origins of Modern Science 1300–1800* (London, 1947), while both pleasure and profit can be derived from Roy Porter, 'The Scientific Revolution: A Spoke in the Wheel', in Roy Porter and Miklaus Teich (eds.), *Revolution in History* (Cambridge, 1986).

3. A. Rupert Hall, *Isaac Newton: Adventurer in Thought* (Oxford, 1992), p. 217.

4. Stuart Clark, 'The Rational Witchfinder: Conscience, Demonological Naturalism and Popular Superstitions', in Stephen Pumfrey, Paolo L. Rossi and Maurice Slawinski (eds.), *Science, Culture and Popular Belief in Renaissance Europe* (Manchester, 1991).

5. Current scholarship is emphasizing the vitality and continuing influence of Aristotelianism: see in particular C. B. Schmitt, *Aristotle and the Renaissance* (Cambridge, Mass., and London, 1983), and B. P. Copenhaver and C. B. Schmitt, *Renaissance Philosophy* (Oxford, 1992), pp. 60–126.

6. Joseph Glanvill, *Plus Ultra: or, the Progress and Advancement of Knowledge since the Days of Aristotle: In an Account of some of the most remarkable late Improvements of practical, useful, Learning* (London, 1668), pp. 6–7.

7. O. L. Dick (ed.), *Aubrey's Brief Lives* (Harmondsworth, 1972), p. 287. For the story of Harvey and the witch's toad familiar, see Ewen, *Witchcraft and Demonianism*, pp. 134–5.

8. For a short and judicious introduction to this subject see Copenhaver and Schmitt, *Renaissance Philosophy*, pp. 127–95.

9. Perhaps the best introduction to the mechanical philosophy of this period is to read a

recent biography of one of its most celebrated practitioners: Stephen Gaukroger, *Descartes: An Intellectual Biography* (Oxford, 1995).

10. On this point, see the illuminating study by J. E. McGuire, 'Neoplatonism and Active Principles: Newton and the Corpus Hermeticum', in R. Westman and J. F. McGuire (eds.), *Hermeticism and the Scientific Revolution* (Los Angeles, 1977).

11. William H. Huffman, *Robert Fludd and the End of the Renaissance* (London and New York, 1988), p. 74.

12. There is an extensive literature on Newton and alchemy, offering varying interpretations of its significance in the totality of his intellectual endeavours. Perhaps the best way into this subject, and other aspects of Newton's thought, is via two recent biographies: Richard S. Westfall, *Never at Rest: A Biography of Isaac Newton* (Cambridge, 1980), which is a more reliable guide than the more recent Hall, *Isaac Newton*. Those with no or little knowledge of Newton or the science of his period should consult Derek Gjertsen, *The Newton Handbook* (London and New York, 1986), a delightful and edifying work.

13. Perhaps the best introduction to the Royal Society, and the more general context of scientific thought in the period, is provided by Michael Hunter, *Science and Society in Restoration England* (Cambridge, 1981). The standard contemporary account of the early years of the Society is Thomas Sprat, *History of the Royal Society* (London, 1669). For the Baconian spirit, so important to the English science of the period, see Charles Webster, *The Great Instauration: Science, Medicine and Reform 1621–1660* (London, 1975).

14. Charles Webster, *From Paracelsus to Newton: Magic and the Making of Modern Science* (Cambridge, 1982), p. 75. Chapter 4 of this book, 'Demonic Magic', is an excellent introduction to some of the problems with connecting new scientific ideas to the decline of witchcraft beliefs.

15. Steven Shapin and Simon Schaffer, *Leviathan and the Air-Pump: Hobbes, Boyle, and the Experimental Life* (Princeton, 1985).

16. For some contemporary comments on this matter, see Brian Easlea, *Witch-Hunting, Magic and the New Philosophy: An Introduction to the Debates of the Scientific Revolution* (Brighton, 1980), pp. 143–5. Easlea's book is interesting in suggesting the value of a gendered approach to the scientific revolution, as does Carolyn Merchant, *The Death of Nature: Women, Ecology and the Scientific Revolution* (New York, 1980).

17. Thomas Hobbes, *Leviathan: or, the Matter, Forme and Power of a Commonwealth ecclesiasticall and civil*, Michael Oakeshott (ed.) (Oxford, 1960). For the contemporary reception of Hobbes's ideas, see Samuel I. Mintz, *The Hunting of Leviathan: Seventeenth-century Reactions to the Materialism and Moral Philosophy of Thomas Hobbes* (Cambridge, 1962).

18. A. Rupert Hall and Marie Boas Hall (eds.), *The Correspondence of Henry Oldenburg* (3 volumes, Madison, Milwaukee, and London, 1965–6). The sketch of Oldenburg's life is based on the account in *DNB*.

19. Hartlib Papers, University of Sheffield: 4/2/19A; 11/1/20A; 18/1/43A; 25/15/17B; 51/22B, 25/5/25A.

20. Meric Casaubon, *Of Credulity and Incredulity in Things natural, civil and divine* (London, 1668).

21. Richard Bovet, *Pandaemonium, or the Devil's Cloyster. Being a further Blow to modern Sadduceism, proving the Existence of Witches and Spirits* (London, 1684), pp. 31, 54, 75.

22. Notestein, *A History of Witchcraft*, p. 285.

23. Casaubon, *Of Credulity and Incredulity*, p. 49; Henry Hallywell, *Melampronoea: or a Discourse of the Polity and Kingdom of Darkness, together with a Solution of the chiefest Objections brought against the Being of Witches* (London, 1681), p. 3; Michael Hunter, 'The Witchcraft Controversy and the Nature of Free Thought in Restoration England: John Wagstaffe's *The Question of Witchcraft debated* (1669)', to appear in Michael Hunter, *Science and the Shape of Orthodoxy: Intellectual Change in Late Seventeenth-century England*. I am grateful to Professor Hunter for sending me a typescript of this chapter.

24. Details of Webster's life are taken from *DNB* and from Peter Elmer, *The Library of Dr John Webster: The Making of a seventeenth-century Radical* (London, 1986). It is interesting to note that the author of one of the standard introductions to the history of early modern witchcraft should describe Webster as a 'crotchety Yorkshire surgeon-parson': H. R. Trevor-Roper, *The European Witch-Craze of the Sixteenth and Seventeenth Centuries* (Harmondsworth, 1969), p. 97.

25. For an introduction to this debate, see Thomas Harmon Jobe, 'The Devil in Restoration Science: The Glanvill–Webster Witchcraft Debate', *Isis*, 72 (1981), pp. 343–56.

26. John Webster, *The Displaying of supposed Witchcraft* (London, 1677), p. 49.

27. Ibid., p. 4.

28. Ibid., pp. 124–5.

29. Henry More, *Enthusiasmus Triumphatus: or, a Discourse of the Nature of Causes, Kinds and Cure of Enthusiasme* (London, 1656), p. 50.

30. These comments are based on Thomas Shadwell, *The Virtuoso*, David Stuart Rodes (ed.) (London, Regents Restoration Drama Series, 1966).

31. This section owes much to Patrick Curry, *Prophecy and Power: Astrology in Early Modern England* (Oxford, 1989). For a recent biography of Lilly, see Derek Parker, *Familiar to All: William Lilly and Astrology in the Seventeenth Century* (London, 1975). Another astrological adept's mental world is explored in Michael Hunter and Annabel Gregory (eds.), *An Astrological Diary of the Seventeenth Century: Samuel Jeake of Rye, 1652–99* (Oxford, 1988), while the astrological culture of the Interregnum is explored in Patrick Curry, 'The Astrologers' Feasts', *History Today*, 38 (April 1988), pp. 17–22. The decline of another of the 'pseudo-sciences' is traced in J. Andrew Mendelsohn, 'Alchemy and Politics in England 1649–1655', *Past and Present*, 135 (1992), pp. 30–78.

32. Richard Mead, *Medica Sacra: or, a Commentary on the most remarkable Diseases mentioned in the Holy Scriptures* (London, 1755), pp. xi–xiii. For Mead's contemporary reputation, see the 'Memoir of the Life and Writings of the Author' which prefaces the book and *DNB*.

33. Mead, *Medica Sacra*, pp. xiii, xv.

34. This account owes much to David Harley, 'Mental Illness, Magical Medicine and the

Devil in Northern England, 1650–1700', in Roger French and Andrew Wear (eds.), *The Medical Revolution of the Seventeenth Century* (Cambridge, 1989). For a broader perspective, see Michael MacDonald, 'Religion, Social Change and Psychological Healing in England 1600–1800', *Studies in Church History*, 19 (1982), pp. 101–25.

35. Webster, *The Displaying of supposed Witchcraft*, p. 323.

36. Ibid., pp. 323–4.

37. For a useful initial discussion of this issue, including some comments on witchcraft, see Barbara J. Shapiro, *Probability and Certainty in Seventeenth-century England: A Study of the Relationships between Natural Science, Religion, History, Law and Literature* (Princeton, New Jersey, 1983).

38. Quoted in Keith Thomas, *Man and the Natural World: Changing Attitudes in England 1500–1800* (London, 1983), p. 67.

39. Francis Hutchinson, *A historical Essay concerning Witchcraft. With Observations of Matters of Fact, tending to clear the Texts of the sacred Scriptures, and confute the vulgar Errors about that Point* (London, 1718), pp. 33–5.

40. *A full Confutation of Witchcraft: more particularly of the Depositions against Joan Wenham, lately condemned for a Witch, at Hertford* (London, 1712); *The Case of the Hertfordshire Witchcraft consider'd: being an Examination of a Book, entitl'd, a full and impartial Account of the Discovery of Sorcery & Witchcraft practis'd by Jane Wenham of Walkerne, upon the Bodies of Anne Thorne, Anne Street, &c* (London, 1712); *The Impossibility of Witchcraft, plainly proving, from Scripture and Reason, that there never was a Witch, and that it is both irrational and impious to believe there ever was* (London, 1712).

41. *A full Confutation of Witchcraft*, p. 5.

42. Joseph Juxon, *A Sermon upon Witchcraft: occasion'd by a late illegal Attempt to discover Witches by Swimming. Preach'd at Twyford in the County of Leicester, July 11, 1736* (London, 1736).

43. Ibid., p. 24.

44. Ibid., p. 25.

45. Ibid., pp. 20–22.

Conclusion

1. J. C. Atkinson, *Forty Years in a moorland Parish: Reminiscences and Researches in Danby in Cleveland* (London, 1892), pp. 72–3. Details of his life are taken from *DNB*.

2. Harriet Martineau, *The History of England during the Thirty Years Peace* (2 volumes, London, 1849), Vol. 2, pp. 707–13.

3. Judith Devlin, *The Superstitious Mind: French Peasants and the Supernatural in the Nineteenth Century* (New Haven, 1987).

4. PRO, ASSI 45/10/3/34, 36, 40, 43–54. The Armstrong case is the subject of a detailed study being conducted by Miranda Chaytor.

5. A transcript of the relevant documentation and a commentary are provided by Sheila Gates, 'Documentary: An Accusation of Witchcraft: 1736', *Old West Riding*, New Series, 10 (1990), pp. 17–19. I am grateful to Jane Whittaker for bringing this reference to my

attention. For the earlier case involving the Hartleys, see PRO, ASSI 45/5/5/1.

6. Essex Record Office, Notebook of Sir William Holcroft, JP, 1661–89, D/DCvi, f. 24.

7. The relevant shifts are discussed in Patrick Curry, *Prophecy and Power: Astrology in Early Modern England* (Oxford, 1989). For a briefer introduction to Curry's arguments on this point, see his essay 'Astrology in Early Modern England: The Making of a Vulgar Knowledge', in Stephen Pumfrey, Paolo L. Rossi and Maurice Slawinski (eds.), *Science, Culture and Popular Belief in Renaissance Europe* (Manchester, 1991). Considerable relevant information is gathered in an important work by Bernard Capp, *Astrology and the Popular Press: English Almanacs 1500–1800* (London and Boston, 1979).

8. Essex Record Office, D/P/36/1/3 (Coggeshall Parish Register); Thomas, *Religion and the Decline of Magic*, p. 221.

9. These incidents are listed in Kittredge, *Witchcraft in Old and New England*, p. 236.

10. These references to later Essex witchcraft cases are taken from three articles by Eric Maple: 'The Witches of Canewdon', *Folklore*, 71 (December 1960), pp. 241–50; 'The Witches of Dengie', *Folklore*, 73 (Autumn 1962), pp. 178–84; and 'Witchcraft and Magic in the Rochford Hundred', *Folklore*, 76 (Autumn 1965), pp. 213–24.

11. Atkinson, *Forty Years in a moorland Parish*, pp. 72–115, *passim*.

12. Ibid., p. 59, n. 1.

13. Mary Nattrass, 'Witch Posts and early Dwellings in Cleveland', *Yorkshire Archaeological Journal*, 39 (1956–8), pp. 136–46.

14. Wendy Boase, *The Folklore of Hampshire and the Isle of Wight* (London, 1976), pp. 109, 114, 118; Doris Jones Baker, *The Folklore of Hertfordshire* (London, 1977), pp. 63–4, 95, 110–20, 128, 153; Kingsley Palmer, *The Folklore of Somerset* (London, 1976), p. 45; Ralph Whitlock, *The Folklore of Wiltshire* (London, 1976), pp. 153, 163, 164; Marjorie Rowling, *The Folklore of the Lake District* (London, 1976), pp. 24, 26, 94, 95, 96, 123, 124.

15. Flora Thompson, *Lark Rise to Candleford* (Harmondsworth, 1973), pp. 266–7.

16. Ibid., pp. 68–9.

17. Richard Boulton, *A compleat History of Magick, Sorcery and Witchcraft* (2 volumes, London, 1715), Vol. 1, p. 7. The titles of Boulton's works, as listed in *DNB*, suggest that he is a figure who would merit further research.

18. Ibid., Vol. 1, Chapters 3, 4, 9; Vol. 2, Chapter 1.

19. Ibid., Vol. 1, pp. 2, 1.

20. Francis Hutchinson, *A historical Essay concerning Witchcraft. With Observations of Matters of Fact, tending to clear the Texts of the sacred Scriptures, and confute the vulgar Errors about that Point* (London, 1718), p. vi.

21. Ibid., p. viii.

22. Notestein, *A History of Witchcraft*, p. 343.

23. Hutchinson, *A historical Essay*, p. xiv.

24. Richard Boulton, *The Possibility and Reality of Magick, Sorcery and Witchcraft demonstrated. Or, a Vindication of a compleat History of Magick, Sorcery and Witchcraft* (London, 1722), p. 12.

25. Some of the possible lines of inquiry have been sketched in an important doctoral thesis: Ian Bostridge, 'Debates about Witchcraft in England 1650–1736' (unpublished Oxford University D. Phil. thesis, 1990).

26. John H. Pruett, 'A Late Stuart Leicestershire Parson: The Reverend Humphrey Michel', *Transactions of the Leicestershire Archaeological and Historical Society*, 54 (1978–9), pp. 26–38. The quotations about witchcraft are on p. 36. I owe this reference to Dr Peter Elmer.

27. Frank Tyrer (ed.), *The Great Diurnall of Nicholas Blundell of Little Crosby, Lancs* (3 volumes, Record Society of Lancashire and Cheshire, 110, 112, 114, 1968, 1970, 1972), Vol. 110, pp. 83, 121, 130, 142, 154; Vol. 112, pp. 38, 116, 218.

28. This incident is noted and references to the original documentation are given in Norma Landau, *The Justices of the Peace 1679–1760* (Berkeley, Los Angeles and London, 1984), p. 91.

29. Phyllis J. Guskin, 'The Context of English Witchcraft: The Case of Jane Wenham (1712)', *Eighteenth-century Studies*, 15 (1981–2), pp. 48–71. The main contemporary publications dealing with the Wenham Case are *A full and impartial Account of the Discovery of Sorcery and Witchcraft practis'd by Jane Wenham of Walkerne in Hertfordshire, upon the Bodies of Anne Thorne, Anne Street, &c* (London, 1712); *The Case of the Hertfordshire Witchcraft consider'd: being an Examination of a Book, entitl'd, a full and impartial Account of the Discovery of Sorcery & Witchcraft practis'd by Jane Wenham of Walkerne, upon the Bodies of Anne Thorne, Anne Street, &c* (London, 1712); *The Belief of Witchcraft vindicated: proving, from Scripture, there have been Witches: and from Reason, that there may be such still* (London, 1712); *The Impossibility of Witchcraft, plainly proving, from Scripture and Reason, that there never was a Witch, and that it is both irrational and impious to believe there ever was* (London, 1712); *Witchcraft further display'd* (London, 1712); *A full Confutation of Witchcraft: more particularly of the Depositions against Joan Wenham, lately condemned for a Witch, at Hertford* (London, 1712).

30. Hutchinson, *A historical Essay*, p. 130.

31. *The Tatler*, 16 May 1709; *The Spectator*, 117, 14 July 1711.

32. 9 Geo II, cap. 5: the background to this statute is discussed by Bostridge, 'Disputes about Witchcraft', Chapter 7, 'The Repeal of the Witchcraft Act 1736', which indicates some of the possible areas of contention. For the Bill's passage, see *House of Commons Journals*, Vol. 22, pp. 510, 533, 544, 554, 556, 558, 608, 610–11, 625, 651; *House of Lords Journals*, Vol. 24, pp. 589, 591, 596–600, 602–3, 623–4.

33. For a recent edition of this work with a useful introduction, see Thomas Shadwell, *The Lancashire-Witches, and Tegue o Divelly the Irish Priest*, Judith Bailey Slagle (ed.) (New York and London, 1991).

34. Act I, scene ii.

35. Curry, *Prophecy and Power* (Oxford, 1989), pp. 121 ff.

36. The literature on the Gothic novel is massive. For some recent commentaries on the subject, however, which discuss many of the relevant issues, see Coral Ann Howells, *Love, Mystery and Misery: Feeling in Gothic Fiction* (London, 1978); Victor Sage (ed.), *The Gothick Novel: a Casebook* (London, 1990); and Anne Williams, *Art of Darkness: A Poetics*

of Gothic (Chicago and London, 1995). Those with a taste for original texts should read Peter Fairclough (ed.), *Three Gothic Novels* (Harmondsworth, 1968).

37. P. A. Spacks, *The Insistence of Horror: Aspects of the Supernatural in Eighteenth-century Poetry* (Cambridge, Mass., 1962), p. 117.

38. For a brief introduction to the impact of mesmerism in late-eighteenth-century England, see Roy Porter, 'Under the Influence: Mesmerism in England', *History Today*, 35 (September 1985), pp. 22–9. Mesmerism in France receives a fuller treatment in Robert Darnton, *Mesmerism and the End of the Enlightenment in France* (Cambridge, Mass., 1968).

39. There is a growing literature on Victorian spiritualism, although an excellent introduction is provided by Alex Owen, *The Darkened Room: Women, Power and Spiritualism in Late Victorian England* (Philadelphia, 1990). The full citation for the Reverend Clifford's book, which originated as a sermon, is J. B. Clifford, *Modern Witchcraft, or Spiritualism: a Sign of the Times* (London, 1873). Two other works which deserve mention in this context are Miles Grant, *Spiritualism unveiled, and shown to be the Work of Demons: an Examination of its Origins, Doctrines and Politics* (London, nd), and H. A. H., *The satanic Origins and Character of Spiritualism* (London, 1876). For a wider recent discussion of the range of beliefs present in Victorian England, see Patrick Curry, *A Confusion of Prophets* (London, 1992).

40. Andrew Morton, *Diana: Her True Story* (2nd paperback edn, London, 1993), pp. 87, 104–6, 139–40.

41. Jeanne Favret-Saada, *Deadly Words: Witchcraft in the Bocage* (Cambridge and Paris, 1980).

42. Tanya Luhrmann, *Persuasions of the Witch's Craft: Ritual Magic and Witchcraft in Present-day England* (Oxford, 1989).

43. Ibid., pp. 4–5.

44. Ibid., p. 7.

45. Ibid., p. 81.

46. Ibid., pp. 106–7.

47. Gerald B. Gardner, *Witchcraft Today* (London, 1954). For an informed discussion of the strength of Gardner's influence, see Luhrmann, *Persuasions*, pp. 42–9.

48. Many of Crowley's works, some of them to an extent autobiographical, are still in print, while a number of books have been written about him. One of the more recent of these is Gerald Suster, *The Legacy of the Beast: The Life, Work and Influence of Aleister Crowley* (London, 1988).

49. Much of interest about Dennis Wheatley's life can be gleaned from his *The Time Has Come: The Autobiography of Dennis Wheatley* (3 volumes, London, 1979).

50. John Brand, *Observations of the Popular Antiquities of Great Britain* (2 volumes, New York, 1970; reprint of the London 1848–9 edition), Vol. 1, pp. 377–96; A. R. Wright, *British Calendar Customs*, T. E. Jones (ed.) (3 volumes, London, 1940), Vol. 3, pp. 107–20.

Bibliography

I have decided, rather than add a large and unwieldy bibliography, to provide a list of early modern works on witchcraft published in England cited in the text. To this I have added a Bibliographical Essay, aimed at providing an initial guide to recent publications on the history of witchcraft, particularly those dealing with England.

Early modern works on English witchcraft cited in the text

Francis Coxe, *A short Treatise declaringe the detestable wickednesse of magicall Sciences, as Necromancie, Conjuration of Spirites, curiouse Astrologie and suche lyke* (London, 1561)

The Examination and Confession of certaine Wytches at Chensforde in the Countie of Essex, before the Quenes Maiesties Judges, the xxvi day of July Anno 1566 (London, 1566)

The Examination of John Walsh, before Maister Thomas Williams, Commissary to the Reverend Father in God William, Bishop of Excester, upon certayne Interrogatories touchyng Wytchcrafte and Sorcerye (London, 1566)

A Booke declaringe the fearfull Vexasion of one Alexander Nyndge: being most horriblye tormented wyth an evyll Spirit, the xx daie of Ianuarie in the yere of our Lord 1573 at Lyeringswell in Suffolke (np, 1573)

The Disclosing of a late counterfeyted Possession of the Devyl in two Maydens within the Citie of London (London, 1574)

A Rehearsall both straung and true, of hainous and horrible Actes committed by Elizabeth Stile, alias Rockingham, Mother Dutten, Mother Devell, Mother Margaret, fower notorious Witches, apprehended at Winsore in the Countie of Barks, and at Abington arraigned, condemned, and executed the 28 Daye of Februarie last Anno 1579 (London, 1579)

A Detection of damnable Driftes, practized by three Witches arraigned at Chelmisforde in Essex, at the late Assizese holden, which were executed in Aprill 1579 (London, 1579)

A true and just Recorde, of the Information, Examination, and Confession of all the Witches taken at S. Oses in the Countie of Essex, whereof some were executed, and some entreated according to the Determination of the Lawe (London, 1582)

Reginald Scot, The Discoverie of Witchcraft (London, 1584; reprinted New York, 1972)

The Apprehension and Confession of three notorious Witches. Arraigned and by Justice condemnede and executed at Chelmesforde in the Countye of Essex, the 5 Day of July last past 1589 (London, 1589)

Henry Holland, A Treatise against Witchcraft: or, a Dialogue, wherein the greatest Doubts concerning that Sinne, are briefly answered (Cambridge, 1590)

George Gifford, A Dialogue concerning Witches and Witchcrafts, in which it is layed open how craftily the Divell deceiveth not onely the Witches but many other, and so leadeth them awrie into manie great Errours (London, 1593; second edition of 1603 reprinted in Percy Society, 8, 1843)

The most strange and admirable Discoverie of the three Witches at Warboys arraigned, convicted and executed at the last Assizes at Huntingdon (London, 1593)

John Denison, The most wonderfull and true storie of a certaine Witch named Alse Gooderidge of Stapenhill, who was arraigned and convicted at Darbie at the Assises there (London, 1597)

Samuel Harsnett, A Discovery of the fraudulent Practices of John Darrell Bachelor of Artes (London, 1599)

The triall of Maist Dorrell, or a Collection of Offences against Allegations not yet suffered to receive convenient Answere (London, 1599)

George More, A true Discourse concerning the certaine Possession and Dispossession of 7 Persons in one Familie in Lancashire (London, 1600)

John Darrell, A true Narration of the strange and grevous Vexation by the Devil, of 7 Persons in Lancashire, and William Somers of Nottingham (London, 1600)

John Darrell, The Replie of John Darrell, to the Answer of John Deacon and John Walker, concerning the Doctrine of the Possession and Dispossession of Demoniakes (London, 1602)

John Darrell, A Survey of certaine dialogical Discourses, written by John Deacon and John Walker concerning the Doctrine of Possession and Dispossession of Divels (London, 1602)

John Swan, A true and briefe Report, of Mary Glover's Vexation, and of her Deliverance by the Meanes of Fastinge and Prayer (London, 1603)

Samuel Harsnett, A Declaration of egregious popish Impostures, to with-draw the Harts of her Maiesties Subiects from their Allegeance and from the Truth of the Christian Religion as professed in England, under the Pretence of Casting out Devils (London, 1603)

William Perkins, A Discourse of the damned Art of Witchcraft. So farre forth as it is revealed in the Scriptures, and manifest by true Experience (Cambridge, 1608)

Thomas Potts, The Trial of the Lancaster Witches A.D. MDCXII, G. B. Harrison (ed.) (London, 1929; reprinted 1971: first published London, 1613, as The Wonderfull Discoverie of Witches in the Countie of Lancaster. With the arraignment and Triall of nineteene notorious Witches, at the Assizes and generall Gaole Deliverie, holden at the Castle of Lancaster, upon Munday, the seventeenth of August last, 1612)

The Witches of Northamptonshire, Agnes Browne, Arthur Bill, Joane Vaughan, Hellen Jenkenson, Mary Barber, Witches, who were all executed at Northampton the 22 July last 1612 (London, 1612)

Witches apprehended, examined and executed, for notable Villanies by them committed both by Land and Water. With a strange and most true Triall how to know whether a Woman be a Witch or not (London, 1613)

Alexander Roberts, *A Treatise of Witchcraft: wherein sundry Propositions are laid downe, plainely discovering the Wickednesse of that damnable Art* (London, 1616)

James VI and I, 'Daemonologie', in *The Workes of the most high and mighty Prince, James, by the Grace of God Kinge of Great Brittaine, France, Ireland, Defender of ye faith, &c* (London, 1616: first published as separate work Edinburgh, 1597)

Thomas Cooper, *The Mystery of Witch-Craft: discovering the Truth, Nature, Occasions, Growth and Power thereof: together with the Detection and Punishment of the same* (London, 1617)

The wonderful Discoverie of the Witchcrafts of Margaret and Phillip Flower, Daughters of Ioan Flower neere Bever Castle, executed at Lincolne, March 11, 1618 (London, 1618)

Henry Goodcole, *The wonderfull Discoverie of Elizabeth Sawyer a Witch, late of Edmonton, her Conviction and Condemnation and Death* (London, 1621)

Daemonologia: A Discourse on Witchcraft, as it was acted in the Family of Mr Edward Fairfax, of Fuyston, in the County of York, in the Year 1621: along with the only two Eclogues of the same Author known to be in Existence, William Grainge (ed.) (Harrogate, 1882)

The Boy of Bilson: or a true Discovery of the late notorious Impostures of certaine Romish Priests in their pretended Exorcisme, or Expulsion of the Divell out of a young Boy, named William Perry (London, 1622)

John Cotta, *The infallible, true and assured Witch: or, the second Edition of the Tryall of Witch-Craft: shewing the right and true Method of the Discoverie* (London, 1625)

Richard Bernard, *A Guide to Grand Iury Men: divided into two Bookes* (London, 1627)

A briefe Description of the notorious Life of John Lambe, otherwise called Doctor Lambe, together with his ignominious Death (London, 1628)

A true and exact Relation of the severall Informations, Examinations and Confessions of the late Witches arraigned and executed at the late Sessions holden before the Right Honorable Robert, Earle of Warwicke, and severall of his Majesties Justices of Peace, the 29 of July 1645 (London, 1645)

A true Relation of the Arraignment of eighteene Witches that were tried, convicted and condemned, at a Sessions holden at St Edmonds-bury, in Suffolk ... the 27 Day of August 1645 (London, 1645)

The Lawes against Witches and Coniuration. And some brief Notes and Observations for the Discovery of Witches ... Also the Confession of Mother Lakeland, who was arraigned and condemned for a Witch at Ipswich in Suffolke (London, 1645)

John Davenport, *The Witches of Huntingdon, their Examinations and Confessions, exactly taken by his Majesties Justices of the Peace for that County* (London, 1645)

John Gaule, *Select Cases of Conscience touching Witches and Witchcrafts* (London, 1646)

Matthew Hopkins, *The Discovery of Witches* (London, 1647)

John Stearne, *A Confirmation and Discovery of Witchcraft* (London, 1648)

Mary Moore, *Wonderfull News from the North: or, a true Relation of the sad and grievous*

Torments, inflicted upon the Bodies of three Children of Mr George Muschamp, late of the County of Northumberland, by Witchcraft (London, 1650)

Sir Robert Filmer, *An Advertisement to the Jurymen of England, touching Witches. Together with a Difference between an English and an Hebrew Witch* (London, 1653)

Henry More, *An Antidote against Atheisme: or an Appeal to the natural Faculties of the Minde of Man, whether there be not a God* (London, 1653)

Thomas Ady, *A Candle in the Dark: or, a Treatise concerning the Nature of Witches and Witchcraft: being Advice to Judges, Sheriffes, Justices of the Peace, and Grand Jury Men, what to do, before they passe sentence on such as are arraigned for their Lives, as Witches* (London, 1656)

The Lord's arm stretched out in Answer of Prayer: or, a true Relation of the wonderful Deliverance of James Barrow, the son of John Barrow of Olaves Southwark, who was posessed with evil Spirits near two Years (London, 1663)

A true Relation of the wonderful Deliverance of Hannah Crump. Daughter of John Crump of Warwick, who was sore afflicted by Witchcraft, for the space of nine Months, with the several Means used, and Way in which she was relieved (London, 1663)

Meric Casaubon, *Of Credulity and Incredulity in Things natural, civil and divine* (London, 1668)

The Hartford-Shire Wonder: or, Strange News from Ware (London, 1669)

John Wagstaffe, *The Question of Witchcraft debated* (London, 1669)

John Webster, *The Displaying of supposed Witchcraft* (London, 1677)

Strange News from Arpington near Bexly in Kent: being a true Narrative of a young Maid who was possest with several Devils or evil Spirits (London, 1679)

Joseph Glanvill, *Saducismus Triumphatus: or full and plain Evidence concerning Witches and Apparitions* (London, 1681)

Henry Hallywell, *Melampronoea: or a Discourse of the Polity and Kingdom of Darkness: together with a Solution of the chiefest Objections brought against the Being of Witches* (London, 1681)

Strange and wonderfull News from Yowell in Surry . . . Giving a true and just Account of one Elizabeth Burgess, who was most strangely bewitched and tortured at a sad Rate (London, 1681)

A Tryal of Witches at the Assizes held at Bury St Edmunds for the County of Suffolk on the tenth day of March 1664 before Sir Matthew Hale Kt then Lord Chief Baron of his Majesties Court of Exchequer. Taken by a Person then attending the Court (London, 1682)

The Life and Conversation of Temperance Floyd, Mary Lloyd, and Susanna Edwards, three eminent Witches lately condemned at Exeter Assizes (London, 1682)

A true and impartial Relation of the Informations against three Witches, viz Temperance Lloyd, Mary Trembles, and Susanna Edwards (London, 1682)

The Tryal, Condemnation, and Execution of three Witches, viz Temperance Floyd, Mary Floyd and Susanna Edwards, who were all arraigned at Exeter on the 18th of August 1682 (London, 1682)

An Account of the Tryal and Examination of Joan Buts, for being a common Witch and Inchantress (London, 1682)

Richard Bovet, *Pandaemonium, or the Devil's Cloyster. Being a further Blow to modern Sadduceism, proving the Existence of Witches and Spirits* (London, 1684)

Matthew Hale, *A Collection of modern Matter of Fact concerning Witches and Witchcraft upon the Persons of People* (Part 1, London, 1693)

The Tryal of Richard Hathaway upon an Information for being a Cheat and Imposter, for endeavouring to take away the Life of Sarah Morduck, for being a Witch (London, 1702)

The Case of the Hertfordshire Witchcraft consider'd: being an Examination of a Book, entitl'd, a full and impartial Account of the Discovery of Sorcery & Witchcraft practis'd by Jane Wenham of Walkerne, upon the Bodies of Anne Thorne, Anne Street, &c (London, 1712)

A full and impartial Account of the Discovery of Sorcery and Witchcraft practis'd by Jane Wenham of Walkerne in Hertfordshire, upon the Bodies of Anne Thorne, Anne Street, &c (London, 1712)

The Belief of Witchcraft vindicated: proving, from Scripture, there have been Witches: and from Reason, that there may be such still (London, 1712)

The Impossibility of Witchcraft, plainly proving, from Scripture and Reason, that there never was a Witch, and that it is both irrational and impious to believe there ever was (London, 1712)

Witchcraft further display'd (London, 1712)

A full Confutation of Witchcraft: more particularly of the Depositions against Joan Wenham, lately condemned for a Witch, at Hertford (London, 1712)

Richard Boulton, *A compleat History of Magick, Sorcery and Witchcraft* (2 volumes, London, 1715)

Francis Hutchinson, *A historical Essay concerning Witchcraft. With Observations of Matters of Fact, tending to clear the Texts of the sacred Scriptures, and confute the vulgar Errors about that Point* (London, 1718)

Richard Boulton, *The Possibility and Reality of Magick, Sorcery and Witchcraft demonstrated. Or, a Vindication of a compleat History of Magick, Sorcery and Witchcraft* (London, 1722)

Joseph Juxon, *A Sermon upon Witchcraft: occasion'd by a late illegal Attempt to discover Witches by Swimming. Preach'd at Twyford in the County of Leicester, July 11, 1736* (London, 1736)

The Tryal of Thomas Colley at the Assizes at Hertford on Tuesday the 30th of July 1751, before the Right Hon. Sir William Lee, Knight, Lord Chief Justice of the Court of King's Bench (London, 1751)

The remarkable Confession and last dying Words of Thomas Colley, executed on Saturday, August the 24th, 1751, at Gubblecot Cross, near Marlston (vulgarly called Wilston) Green (London, 1751)

Bibliographical Essay

As stated in the notes to the introduction, the literature on the history of witchcraft, even if we restrict ourselves to serious and scholarly works, is immense. All that can be offered here is a brief guide to what is available, this in turn being limited almost exclusively to publications in English.

There are a number of recent works of synthesis on the history of early modern witchcraft, of which Brian P. Levack, *The Witch-Hunt in Early Modern Europe* (London and New York, 1987; 2nd edn, 1993) is probably the best, although others which deserve mention are Joseph Klaits, *Servants of Satan: The Age of the Witch Hunts* (Bloomington, Indiana, 1985); G. R. Quaife, *Godly Zeal and Furious Rage: The Witch in Early Modern*

Europe (London and Sydney, 1987); and Geoffrey Scarre, *Witchcraft and Magic in Sixteenth- and Seventeenth-century Europe* (London, 1987). On the origins of the craze, nothing has yet replaced Norman Cohn, *Europe's Inner Demons* (London, 1976), while H. R. Trevor-Roper, *The European Witch-Craze of the Sixteenth and Seventeenth Centuries* (Harmondsworth, 1969), remains a stimulating introduction to what might be termed the 'intellectual history' aspects of the subject. On a more technical level, Bength Ankarloo and Gustav Henningsen (eds.), *Early Modern European Witchcraft: Centres and Peripheries* (Oxford, 1990), is an important collection of essays which demonstrates the sheer variety of beliefs about witchcraft present in various European territories, while Stuart Clark, 'Inversion, Misrule and the Meaning of Witchcraft', *Past and Present*, 87 (1980), pp. 98–127, offers a characteristically stimulating interpretation. Readers of French will find much of value, not least a superb collection of illustrations, in Robert Muchembled (ed.), *Magie et sorcellerie en Europe: du Moyen Age à nos jours* (Paris, 1994). Although it appeared in print too late to have its findings assessed in the present book, Robin Briggs, *Witches and Neighbours: The Social and Cultural Context of European Witchcraft* (London, 1996), is clearly a work of major importance which deepens our understanding of many aspects of the subject.

There are a number of regional or national studies of early modern witchcraft, of which perhaps the most valuable are Christina Larner, *Enemies of God: The Witch-Hunt in Scotland* (London, 1981); H. C. Erik Midelfort, *Witch Hunting in Southwestern Germany, 1562–1684: The Social and Intellectual Foundations* (Stanford, California, 1972); Wolfgang Behringer, *Hexenverfolgung in Bayern:Volksmagie, Glaubenseifer und Staatsräson in der Frühen Neuzeit: Studiensausgaber* (Munich, 1988); Robin Briggs, *Communities of Belief: Cultural and Social Tensions in Early Modern France* (Oxford, 1987); John Demos, *Entertaining Satan: Witchcraft and the Culture of Early New England* (New York, 1982); and Richard Godbeer, *The Devil's Dominion: Magic and Religion in Early New England* (Cambridge, 1992).

Turning to England, one rapidly realizes (in fact, this realization was the major reason for my deciding to write this book) that no modern overview of witchcraft exists. There are, however, four important works by pioneering scholars which, however dated their interpretations might sometimes now seem, are still invaluable guides to the relevant published and documentary materials: Wallace Notestein, *A History of Witchcraft in England from 1558 to 1718* (Washington, DC, 1911; reprinted New York, 1965); George L. Kittredge, *Witchcraft in Old and New England* (Cambridge, Mass., 1929); C. L'Estrange Ewen, *Witch Hunting and Witch Trials: The Indictments for Witchcraft from the Records of 1373 Assizes held for the Home Circuit A.D. 1559–1736* (London, 1929); and C. L'Estrange Ewen, *Witchcraft and Demonianism: A Concise Account Derived from Sworn Depositions and Confessions Obtained in the Courts of England and Wales* (London, 1933).

Although little of value has been produced more recently by way of general surveys, our current view of English witchcraft has been dominated from the early 1970s by two important works of interpretation: Alan Macfarlane, *Witchcraft in Tudor and Stuart England: A Regional and Comparative Study* (London, 1970), based on archives relating to Essex, unfortunately the only English county with sufficiently good records to make such a study possible; and Keith Thomas's magisterial *Religion and the Decline of Magic: Studies in Popular Beliefs in Sixteenth- and Seventeenth-century England* (London, 1971), a work which, although more broadly based than Macfarlane's, showed a similar interest in witchcraft beliefs at village level and sought to use anthropological models to help interpret these beliefs and locate them in their cultural context.

The sheer impact of these books meant that little scholarly work was done on English witchcraft for some time; there was a sense that a new standard interpretation had been established and there was little else to be said. Even so, a trickle of articles and essays appeared in learned publications, and the fact that this trickle has now become something rather more substantial is the surest sign of a new wave of interest in the subject among historians of early modern England. Noteworthy contributions include John L. Teall, 'Witchcraft and Calvinism in Elizabethan England: Divine Power and Human Agency', *Journal of the History of Ideas*, 23 (1962), pp. 21–36; P. Tyler, 'The Church Courts at York and Witchcraft Prosecutions, 1567–1640', *Northern History*, 4 (1970), pp. 84–109; Phyllis J. Guskin, 'The Context of English Witchcraft: The Case of Jane Wenham (1712)', *Eighteenth-century Studies*, 15 (1981–2), pp. 48–71; Peter Rushton, 'Women, Witchcraft and Slander in Early Modern England: Cases from the Church Courts of Durham, 1560–1675', *Northern History*, 18 (1982), pp. 116–32; Clive Holmes, 'Popular Culture? Witches, Magistrates and Divines in Early Modern England', in Steven L. Kaplan (ed.), *Understanding Popular Culture: Europe from the Middle Ages to the Nineteenth Century* (Berlin, etc., 1984); C. R. Unsworth, 'Witchcraft Beliefs and Criminal Procedure in Early Modern England', in Thomas G. Watkins (ed.), *Legal Record and Historical Reality: Proceedings of the Eighth British Legal History Conference, Cardiff, 1987* (London and Ronceverte, 1989); Ronald C. Sawyer, '"Strangely handled in all her Lyms": Witchcraft and Healing in Jacobean England', *Journal of Social History* 22 (1988–9), pp. 461–86; David Harley, 'Historians as Demonologists: The Myth of the Midwife-Witch', *The Journal for the Social History of Medicine*, 3 (1990), pp. 1–26; Annabel Gregory, 'Witchcraft, Politics and "Good Neighbourhood" in early Seventeenth-century Rye', *Past and Present*, 133 (1991), pp. 31–66; J. A. Sharpe, 'Witchcraft and Women in Seventeenth-century England: Some Northern Evidence', *Continuity and Change*, 6 (1991), pp. 179–99; J. A. Sharpe, *Witchcraft in Seventeenth-century Yorkshire: Accusations and Counter-measures* (Borthwick Papers, 81, York, 1992); Clive Holmes, 'Women: Witnesses and Witches', *Past and Present*, 140 (1993), pp. 45–78; J. T. Swain, 'The Lancashire Witch Trials of 1612 and 1634 and the Economics of Witchcraft', *Northern History*, 30 (1994), pp. 64–86; and Malcolm Gaskill, 'Witchcraft and Power in Early Modern England: The Case of Margaret Moore', in Jenny Kermode and Garthine Walker (eds.), *Women, Crime and the Courts in Early Modern England* (London, 1994).

The ideas of English demonological writers have not received much attention, but some interesting insights are opened up by Sydney Anglo, 'Reginald Scot and His *Discoverie of Witchcraft*: Scepticism and Saduceeism', and Alan Macfarlane, 'A Tudor Anthropologist: George Gifford's *Discourse* and *Dialogue*', both in Anglo (ed.), *The Damned Art: Essays in the Literature of Witchcraft* (London, 1977). A number of contemporary works have been republished, and the modern reader might find the texts gathered in Michael MacDonald, *Witchcraft and Hysteria in Elizbethan London: Edward Jorden and the Mary Glover Case* (London, 1990) of especial interest, not least because of the guidance provided by MacDonald's introduction.

One aspect of English witchcraft which has attracted considerable attention is the connection between women and witchcraft. For a variety of interpretations of the nature of this connection, see Marianne Hester, *Lewd Women and Wicked Witches: A Study of the Dynamics of Male Domination* (London and New York, 1992); Janet A. Thompson, *Wives, Widows, Witches, and Bitches: Women in Seventeenth-century Devon* (New York, etc., 1993); and Francis E. Dolan, *Dangerous Familiars: Representations of Domestic Crime in England 1550–1700* (Ithaca, New York and London, 1995). For involvement of women in the legal process, see the 1991 article by Sharpe and the 1993 article by Holmes cited above, and J. A. Sharpe, 'Women, Witchcraft and the Legal Process', in Kermode and Walker (eds.), *Women, Crime and the Courts*. A very useful and balanced short guide to the European context is provided by Merry E. Wiesner, *Women and Gender in Early Modern Europe* (Cambridge, 1993), Chapter 7, 'Witchcraft', while a new approach to the whole subject is provided by a work based on German materials, Lyndal Roper, *Oedipus and the Devil: Witchcraft, Sexuality and Religion in Early Modern Europe* (London, 1994). Deborah Willis, *Malevolent Nurture: Witch-Hunting and Maternal Power in Early Modern England* (Ithaca, New York and London, 1995), which also appeared too late to be discussed in this book, develops another interpretation of the connection between witchcraft and women, while another very recent work, Diane Purkiss, *The Witch in History: Early Modern and Twentieth-Century Interpretations* (London and New York, 1996), provides a refreshingly individualistic analysis of the issue.

As has been emphasized at various points in this book, witchcraft beliefs cannot be separated from the wider intellectual context of the period in which they flourished. There is no single work which explores this context, although Thomas, *Religion and the Decline of Magic*, is a tremendously useful guide which, despite its subtitle, does not restrict itself to popular beliefs. Those wishing to explore this context can do so through a number of accessible and stimulating works, among which might be included Peter J. French, *John Dee: The World of an Elizabethan Magus* (London, 1972); Derek Parker, *Familiar to All: William Lilly and Astrology in the Seventeenth Century* (London, 1975); F. A. Yates, *The Occult Tradition in the Elizabethan Age* (London, 1979); Michael MacDonald, *Mystical Bedlam: Madness, Anxiety and Healing in Seventeenth-century England* (Cambridge, 1981); William H. Huffmann, *Robert Fludd and the End of the Renaissance* (London, 1988); Patrick Curry, *Prophecy and Power: Astrology in Early Modern England* (Oxford, 1989); and Vaughan Hart, *Art and Magic in the Court of the Stuarts* (London and New York, 1994).

Index